America and the Germans

America
and the Germans

AN ASSESSMENT OF
A THREE-HUNDRED-YEAR HISTORY

Frank Trommler
and Joseph McVeigh, EDITORS

VOLUME TWO
The Relationship
in the Twentieth Century

University of Pennsylvania Press
PHILADELPHIA

Library of Congress Cataloging in Publication Data

Main entry under title:

America and the Germans.

   Rev. versions of papers presented at the Tricentennial
Conference of German-American History, Politics,
and Culture, held at the University of Pennsylvania,
Philadelphia, Oct. 3–6, 1983.
   Includes indexes.
   Contents: v. 1. Immigration, language, ethnicity—
v. 2. The relationship in the twentieth century.
      1. German Americans—History—Congresses.
2. United States—Foreign relations—Germany—Congresses.
3. Germany—Foreign relations—United States—Congresses.
I. Trommler, Frank, 1939–   . II. McVeigh, Joseph.
III. Tricentennial of German-American History, Politics,
and Culture (1983 : University of Pennsylvania,
Philadelphia)
E184.G3A39   1985   973'.0431   85-1063
ISBN 0-8122-7979-4 (v. 1)
ISBN 0-8122-7980-8 (v. 2)
ISBN 0-8122-7996-4 (set)

Printed in the United States of America

Contents

Förster, "Nachgetragen: Der organisierte Einsatz sudetendeutscher Kommunisten in der SBZ 1945/46," *Vierteljahrshefte für Zeitgeschichte* 31 (April 1983): 308–54.

17. Hans Woller, "Zur Demokratiebereitschaft in der Provinz des amerikanischen Besatzungsgebietes," *Vierteljahrshefte für Zeitgeschichte* 31 (April 1983): 543.

18. I discussed this issue in "The Defeat of Germany in 1918 and the European Balance of Power," *Central European History* 2 (September 1969): 248–60.

Preface

THE ESSAYS IN THIS BOOK, together with those of the first volume, *Immigration, Language, Ethnicity*, are the revised versions of papers delivered at the Tricentennial Conference of German-American History, Politics and Culture at the University of Pennsylvania, Philadelphia, on October 3–6, 1983. The conference, part of the German-American Tricentennial celebrations in Philadelphia, was made possible through generous grants from institutions in the United States and the Federal Republic of Germany. The contributions of the William Penn Foundation, Philadelphia, the Fritz Thyssen Stiftung, Cologne, the United States Information Agency, Washington, D.C., the German Marshall Fund of the United States, Washington, D.C., and the Ford Foundation, New York, are gratefully acknowledged. The editors would like to express their special appreciation to the Max Kade Foundation, New York, the William Penn Foundation, Philadelphia, and the American Association of Teachers of German for making this publication possible.

Many friends and colleagues helped in preparing the conference and provided valuable advice concerning its composition and program. We would particularly like to thank Erich Angermann, James Bergquist, Thomas Childers, Ernst-Otto Czempiel, Horst Daemmrich, Peter Demetz, Reinhard Doerries, Richard Dunn, Hans Gatzke, Ira Glazier, Wolfram Hanrieder, Theodore Hershberg, Walter Hinderer, Peter Uwe Hohendahl, Carl-Ludwig Holtfrerich, Martin Jay, John Jentz, Walter Kamphoefner, Hartmut Keil, Anna Kuhn, Bruce Kuklick, Vernon Lidtke, Albert Lloyd, John McCarthy, Günter Moltmann, William Parsons, Eric Rentschler, George Romoser, Scott Swank, Hans Trefousse, Hermann Wellenreuther, and Don Yoder.

Introduction

COMMENTATORS HAVE STRESSED the turbulence of American-German relations in the twentieth century. Symbolic reminders that the nature of these relations has been erratic since World War I would be superfluous. Current political uncertainties are reminder enough, even though the friendship between the United States and Germany has appeared to rest upon solid foundations for some years now.

Symbolic celebrations generally conceal problem areas. The three-hundredth anniversary of the landing of thirteen families from Krefeld, Germany, was commemorated in Philadelphia in 1983 with considerable celebratory rhetoric. The Tricentennial of the founding of Germantown as the first German settlement in North America became an ornate affair, and the weight of history was duly recognized in the many speeches marking the occasion. As the first of these two volumes documents, however, the events of 1983 were more than an invocation of the brighter side of American-German relations. Rather, the Tricentennial also served as a focal point of current trends and emotions. While American Vice-President George Bush and German President Karl Carstens were celebrating with eighteen hundred representatives of German-American organizations from across the country at a glittering banquet in Center City Philadelphia on October 6, 1983, some fifteen thousand Americans and Germans gathered in front of the Philadelphia Art Museum in a peace rally opposing the official American-German policy of stationing new medium-range missiles in West Germany. There were more demonstrators than had been expected, and both sides claimed to represent the "true" tradition of the "invented anniversary date" of October 6, 1983. The contrast of these events confirms all the more the extent to which the ethnic revival in America has enlivened not only old legends but current discussions as well.

Like numerous other academic events around the country, the Tricentennial Conference of German-American History, Politics and Culture can be counted among the more critical ventures of October 1983, although it also had its share of official representation when a delegation of thirty members of the German Bundestag, led by Vice-President Annemarie Renger, attended its concluding session. The German parliamentarians witnessed an address by the President of the Federal Republic, Karl Carstens, who used the historical focus of the conference—the story of German immigration to America—for an elaborate statement of German gratitude toward the United States and the assurance of a solid alliance in the future. Carstens summed up much of German-American history with a quote by Benjamin Franklin: "America cultivates best what Germany brought forth." He then turned to Plato for his assessment of America's current status in the world: "One of life's odd things is that so many people are disturbed by the shortcomings in what is good rather than what is truly bad. It seems that evil is being accepted while the shortcomings of what is essentially good arouse incessant criticism. If I may be allowed to make the following observation as a European: the Americans can stand up to this criticism. When America could have achieved world domination after the Second World War, it did not want it. America has seldom abused its political power. But the fact remains: America is the strongest nation. And anyone who has power wears the mantle of responsibility, be it willingly or unwillingly. Plato once said that he who refuses to rule must reckon with being ruled by somebody worse than himself. This sentence also applies to world responsibility. And many nations and individuals in the world hope that the United States will not shirk this responsibility."

President Carstens's address was imbued with the festive and confident atmosphere of the Tricentennial and was similar in most respects to the other forty speeches he gave on his state visit from October 4 to 13, 1983. He received a friendly welcome on his travels throughout the country, but critics of the trip were not long in making themselves heard. The most outspoken of these were the peace groups, aiming at what they perceived to be Carstens's attempt to pave the way for public acceptance of the deployment of new missiles in West Germany. But there were also grumblings in the West German press at what was viewed as a missed opportunity to present the American ally with a more intensive and critical assessment of the relations between the two countries. Theo Sommer, editor-in-chief of the West German weekly *Die Zeit*, presented his criticism on the front page under the headline "Falsches Pathos beim Familienfest. Dreihundertjahrfeier in Philadelphia: eine vertane Chance" (Misplaced Emotion at the Family Reunion. The Tricentennial in Philadelphia: A Wasted Opportunity).

Sommer's article, in turn, drew considerable criticism from German-Americans. They asserted that the German journalist had missed the point of the festivities, which were above all a celebration of ethnic pluralism in the United States and of which the criticized message of harmonious relations, the mutual embracing, and the ceremonious events were an integral part. That was the case, they noted, at all such ethnic celebrations. For German-Americans this occasion was a rare opportunity, and in light of their difficult history in the twentieth century, this opportunity would have to be celebrated in such a fashion before the interests of German foreign policy could be taken into account. Similar differences of opinion surfaced regarding the activities of the peace groups, which pointed out that the famous first settlers in Germantown were Mennonites and Quakers, who rejected war and armed conflict. These differences clearly indicate how uncertain the marriage of an ethnic anniversary and a political celebration was in October of 1983.

It is interesting, however, to note how much common ground Theo Sommer found with his American counterpart, Fritz Stern, when they assessed the current state of affairs between Washington and Bonn at the conference. The titles of their chapters are indicative of this commonality: "German-American Relations: Learning to Live with Our Differences" (Sommer) and "U.S.-German Relations: An Alliance Turned Normal" (Stern). Both presentations are contained in this volume as part of the section "The State of the Alliance: An Assessment in 1983." Wolfram Hanrieder opens this section with a critical review of political developments since 1945 and leads into Kurt Sontheimer's assessment of anti-Americanism in Germany, an especially timely topic in the fall of 1983 when protests against increasing the number of American missiles in Europe reached their peak. In view of a new wave of anti-Americanism in Europe, Sontheimer's thesis drew much attention: he argued that there is no significant anti-Americanism in West Germany, yet negative reactions to specific American policies have increased considerably.

Of course, the various forms of anti-Americanism cannot be critically ascertained without a comprehensive analysis of a particular political and economic situation as well as cultural factors, which include the media and, above all, television and the press. There is still little solid information in this area; the planned conference panel on the role of the media in American-German relations did not materialize. By the same token, the various trends of pro-American thinking in the twentieth century need more scrutiny to reach a more precise notion of what has been praised or condemned as Americanization or Americanism. This theme is illustrated by two contributions to this volume: Anton Kaes demonstrates through film how the infatuation with America changed the traditional German attitude toward culture, and Frank Trommler shows the precarious role "Americanism" played in the German conception of modernization.

The political and diplomatic relations between the United States and Germany, however, are more familiar terrain. This volume offers some cross-sections of the considerable material already amassed in these areas. Reinhard Doerries's contribution spans the period from 1848 to the German-American confrontation of World War I. Klaus Schwabe examines the consequences of the war in conjunction with the question of whether a special relationship existed between the United States and the Weimar Republic. The contributions of Detlef Junker and Gerhard Weinberg represent two differing viewpoints in assessing the relations between Hitler's Germany and Roosevelt's America; both scholars engaged in a lively discussion on this point at the conference. Charles Maier traces this development up to West Germany's reemergence as a dominant industrial power after 1945 on the basis of America's policy of reconciliation. Jost Hermand scrutinizes this reemergence in light of the Cold-War confrontations between East and West.

A critical examination of the extensive body of research on political relations is presented in this volume by both an American and a German contributor. Arnold Offner and Hans-Jürgen Schröder outline areas of dispute as well as questions that still remain to be analyzed. To this we can also add American relations with East Germany, which were officially established in 1974. At the conference, too, the term *Germany* primarily referred to the Federal Republic when applied to contemporary politics. A contribution on contemporary American–East German relations was planned but did not materialize.

Although strongly tied to American-German political relations, the history of the German-Americans in the twentieth century has attracted only scattered scholarly attention. The papers on this theme that were presented at the conference led to considerable discussion. The general assessments of Christine Totten and Victor Lange as well as the studies by Henry Schmidt and La Vern Rippley on the drastically altered relations before and after World War I also offer some suggestions for a more detailed investigation of this area. The discussion made clear that the history of German-Americans is beginning to play a certain role in the current self-reflection of many German departments at colleges and universities across the country. The new interest in the social and ethnic roots of American culture can benefit the area of German studies as long as scholars maintain a critical distance in their investigations. One conference participant noted that German studies in the United States should not entirely neglect the study of Germans in America. Such a broader conception of German studies has been represented for some time by the German Studies Association (formerly the Western Association of German Studies) with its yearly conference and its periodical *German Studies Review*. The yearbook of the Society for German-American Studies in particular offers much material for further investigation of the history and culture of German-Americans. And long-established periodicals such as the *German Quarterly* and *Monatshefte* have integrated these themes into their discussions of the future of German in the United States, as has also been done by the many local chapters of the American Association of Teachers of German. Similarly, the establishment of the Max Kade Institute for German-American Studies at the University of Wisconsin in Madison attracted considerable attention in 1983.

The study of German at colleges and universities in America naturally focuses heavily on current cultural relations between the United States and Germany, and the conference likewise offered contributions on modern literature and film (including the film series "German Directors Look at America," which was supported by the Goethe Institute). Considerations of the length of this volume as well as the existence of several books devoted to this theme preclude the inclusion of these papers here.

Another very important focus for the discussion of German-American relations in the twentieth century lies in the history of the emigration from Nazi Germany after 1933. Thanks in large part to Herbert Strauss, the study of this primarily Jewish emigration to the United States has made tremendous progress in recent years. Strauss's contribution is at the same time an impressive personal document from the perspective of the older generation of émigrés. Anthony Heilbut and Paul Breines, both of the younger generation, approach the question of Jewish-German integration or nonintegration into American society differently than does Strauss. John Spalek, on the other hand, shows how much material on German artistic and academic immigration to the United States remains to be evaluated. He points out in particular how many disciplines have profited from the flood of German émigrés. The special case of the Frankfurt School and

its influence in the United States up to the present is more closely analyzed by Andrew Arato. Peter Gay reminds us, however, that there existed a strong intellectual exchange between central Europe and
America before 1933. Gay deals with America's first contacts with psychoanalysis and attempts to reconstruct and explain by means of fascinating argumentation Freud's overly critical image of America.

Many Americans have bitterly complained about imports such as
Marxism and psychoanalysis having made their way beyond Ellis Is-
land. Their cumbersome vocabulary seemed to many a subtle revenge
on the New World for draining so much intellectual substance from
central Europe. There might indeed be some truth to these sentiments.
Many disciplines seem to have visibly changed under the impact of the
tremendous influx of talent and German academic complexities. This
development is no longer an unwritten chapter of American-German
relations. But the migration from Nazi Germany did not just contribute to the recovery of the United States from isolationism and the
Great Depression. Although the majority of the new immigrants turned
their backs on Germany once and for all, many were instrumental in
helping the Germans rebuild their connections with America after
World War II. Without their help and expertise in economic, political,
and intellectual matters, the return of Germany as a respected though
closely observed country and its ascendancy from a defeated nation to
an ally could not have happened with such swiftness.

The period in which this wave of immigrants provided close links
between the two countries is coming to an end. In the 1970s, immigration from Germany fell off considerably. There are many signs that
with the disappearance of the older generation of intermediators a gap
is developing in the understanding of political, economic, and intellectual affairs on both sides of the Atlantic. The younger generation has a
different orientation. The recognition of this fact and the creation of
alternative modes of understanding has been a slow and often painful
process in both the United States and Germany.

The symbolism of the Tricentennial celebration provided a useful
setting for appealing declarations. The German side has shown—
among other things—a new commitment to closer cultural exchanges
with the expansion of the Goethe Institutes in the United States, and
the American side initiated new exchange programs as well. An American Institute for Contemporary German Studies was founded in Washington by the Johns Hopkins University. There was considerable
publicity concerning the President's Youth Initiative and the concept
of a United States–German teenage exchange sponsored by members

of the U.S. Congress and the West German Bundestag. Its announcement constituted part of the Senate resolution on the official observance of the Tricentennial in 1983. Whether such initiatives are
substantial enough to provide the necessary new channels of communication between the United States and the Federal Republic of Germany still remains to be seen.

Frank Trommler and Joseph McVeigh

PART I:

American-German Relations, 1900 – 1950

actually larger than Economic Cooperation Administration (ECA) commitments, than Marshall Plan payments, and finally an EPU transfusion. In return, they provided the assurance that they would not remain a drain on the British and Americans forever and, more important, the security that they would not turn to the East. Doubtless, too, German recovery contributed to every European nation's prosperity, for a depression-ridden Germany would have inhibited growth elsewhere. In this sense, the failure of economic recovery that might have accompanied German isolation would have been far more costly to her partners than the subsidies they had to provide. The situation was not unlike that of the 1920s, when Germany absorbed more funds from abroad, especially American investments, than she paid in reparations. Nonetheless, then, too, the West had been far better off subsidizing German economic health than fretting about the balance of direct flows.

In effect, West Germany resumed in 1950 the orientation that Stresemann had worked to secure in the 1920s. Perhaps it was easier for Adenauer than for Stresemann to impose this course, for there were fewer alternatives. Under Stresemann a powerful nationalist alternative course did exist, whereas under Adenauer the nationalist alternative would mean a feeble effort to tack between East and West. Both statesmen understood the importance of reconciliation with France and of forging a connection with the United States. Reconciliation with Paris meant overcoming the political vetoes to German participation in a Western concert. Forging a connection with Washington brought Germany the economic support needed to fulfill the obligations to the other European countries, including France. Over the long run, American aid to Adenauer's Germany was more predictable and steady than the private investment assistance that was mobilized between 1924 and 1929. The United States proved more willing to act as a responsible great power, with continuing obligations toward Western Europe, after the second war than after the first.

In both cases acting as a responsible great power meant investing in the future prosperity of Germany. Examining the German-American relationship of the 1950s reveals both the German role and the American architecture of leadership. Washington's primacy in a Western international system rested upon American economic resources and not just military power. If the Soviet Union exploited its military preponderance in part to transfer resources from its bloc to its own society, the United States secured its allies' loyalties by providing the capital for their economic reconstruction. More specifically, the United States

1.
Empire and Republic: German-American Relations Before 1917

REINHARD R. DOERRIES

THE YEAR 1983 has produced a veritable flood of public statements and printed matter commemorating three hundred years of German immigration to America and more than two centuries of German-American relations. Future graduate students may well be impressed by the apparent overwhelming agreement publicly voiced on both sides of the Atlantic in our time. The celebrations of common interest have tended to emphasize the seven million German immigrants and their numerous contributions to all phases of American life, as well as the positive sociopolitical impact of American democratic thought and practice upon German life, particularly during the post–World War II period.[1] Undoubtedly, the statements of 1983 reflect the increasing political, economic, and social interdependence of the transatlantic community, and it is difficult to overlook the specific economic and political concerns shared by the Federal Republic of Germany and the United States of America. To recall that in the course of history German and American interests have not always been harmonious is not an effort to dampen the elation of the festive occasion but rather the recognition that today's relations are but the result of a historical process characterized also by misunderstandings, conflict, confrontation, and indeed two wars in three generations.

Looking back at the nineteenth century, we realize that other nations such as France and England were culturally and politically of much greater importance to the young United States than was Germany. It is true that a great number of immigrants came from the German regions and that they were generally welcomed in the New World. But the Germans, driven from their homes by severe economic hardship, political illiberalism, and religious intolerance, did not become a significant political force in the United States; rather, their efforts were directed toward achieving a degree of economic security for themselves and above all for their descendants.[2] Only few of them, such as the Forty-eighters[3] and a number of socialists,[4] both somewhat atypical because as political refugees they often hoped to return to a new Germany, maintained significant political contacts with the Old World. Nor did the German government undertake any efforts before World War I to maintain a German culture among the emigrants. Otto von Bismarck, for example, left little doubt as to what he thought of those who left the country: "I am strongly against supporting emigration; a German who throws off his fatherland like an old coat is for me no longer a German; I am no longer interested in him as a fellow countryman."[5]

In 1785, as part of what Felix Gilbert has termed its "idealistic and internationalist" foreign policy, the United States concluded a Treaty of Amity and Commerce with Prussia that, in the words of George Washington, was "the most liberal treaty ever concluded between independent powers."[6] The German Chargé d'Affaires Ludwig Niederstetter renegotiated the treaty and in 1828 signed the new instrument. A treaty with the German Customs Union drawn up in 1844 was not ratified, but in the first half of the nineteenth century a series of separate agreements were made with Hamburg and Bremen, as well as with a number of German states not belonging to the Zollverein. Economic concerns, manifested by trade barriers and the attempts to overcome them through treaties, however, do not appear to have been of sufficient importance to create a climate of serious mutual interest between the relatively impotent German principalities and the rapidly growing United States.[7]

Indeed, it was not until 1848, when the tremors of revolution briefly shook the crusted political structures in the Old World, that events in Germany became a matter of interest in the United States. The failure of the Frankfurt parliament and the apparent inability of the Germans to create a democratic state were received with disappointment by informed sectors of the U.S. public.[8] Reactionary postrevolutionary Prussia again was not of great import to most Americans, and the spectacle of German immigrant revolutionaries, liberals, socialists, and freethinkers fiercely battling one another in the New World was ill-suited to bring Germany and its culture closer to the heart of the American "man on the street."

During the turbulent years of the Civil War, Germany was still among the backbenchers of international diplomacy, and, aside from certain trade interests and credit arrangements of German bankers, was not, in contrast to France and England, in a position to meddle in American developments. It was the Franco-Prussian War which, except for the events in 1848, for the first time caused Americans to follow German developments with some curiosity. The Germans were aware of this interest and on July 12, 1870, asked for U.S. naval assistance. Although American textbooks of diplomatic history barely mention U.S. reaction to Bismarck's campaign against France, other sources clearly indicate that a good measure of American sympathy initially went out to the Germans, because, among other things, France by pursuing its imperialist policy in Mexico had seriously interfered in the Western Hemisphere. The American minister in Berlin at the time was the historian George Bancroft, who cultivated friendships with many influential Germans and was able to establish good connections to the court. Harboring little sympathy for Catholic France, Bancroft suggested that German interests paralleled those of the United States, and he advised Washington against mediating in the conflict. Much of American so-called public opinion also took the side of the Germans, and in spite of Ulysses S. Grant's adherence to strict neutrality, all seemed well until the French government fell. Then Washington, at least officially, and many Americans welcomed the new French Republic and openly expressed disapproval of German plans for the annexation of Alsace-Lorraine.[9] When in January 1871 the Germans affronted the vanquished France by proclaiming their Kaiser and Reich in the hall of mirrors at Versailles, German-Americans of nearly every regional, economic, political, and religious faction joined in the exuberant festivals, and the uninformed onlooker might well have arrived at false conclusions from this unusual display of German-American unity.[10] As it was, when the festivities ended, the German-American community returned to its divisive infighting. The patriotism of the spring of 1871 gave way to renewed criticism of Germany: "The German Empire has come to bring our people not peace but the sword."[11] Relations between the German Empire and the American republic, however, entered a decidedly new era.

Clearly, Germany had gained access to the arena of international competition among the greater powers. In spite of its wish to have no part in the historical quarrels of Europe, the United States could hardly avoid recognizing the new Germany as an ambitious economic and political entity. The ensuing conflicts and near-confrontations with the empire over Venezuela and Samoa or in the Philippines persuaded a number of leading Americans that Berlin's foreign policy presented a potential threat to American interests. German-American relations lacked the sometimes feeble but never entirely vanished flavor of latent good feeling that since the days of the Marquis de Lafayette and the Comte de Rochambeau had characterized French-American relations.[12] In contrast also to the British, who following the Civil War exercised sagacious circumspection in dealing with the descendants of their former colonial subjects, the Germans evidently found it very difficult to accommodate the Americans and at the same time pursue their own power politics in the Western Hemisphere and the Pacific.

Although no serious differences marred the relations between the two countries in the period before 1914, there is little evidence to suggest that the goodwill between Washington and Berlin was sufficiently based on common interests to withstand the foreseeable difficulties arising from a larger conflict or war. Certainly, the documents indicate that a German-American treaty of alliance, in spite of suggestions to the contrary, was not a likely possibility.[13] Economic competition, as expressed for instance in a silly confrontation over the importation of American pork to Germany, the intensive search for markets, and especially the rapidly changing political climate arising from this competition led to mutual suspicion and the recognition among leading statesmen on both sides that a future conflict was not impossible.[14] The combination of the German emperor's inability to construct a modus vivendi with the British and the shrewd British policy of accommodation to America contributed to the threat of a German-American confrontation. Boisterous voices from leading Germans and, in fact, from the impetuous emperor himself reinforced American suspicion. On one occasion in 1908, to avoid embarrassment, Theodore Roosevelt had to intervene personally to prevent American papers from publishing the unwise pronouncements of the emperor.[15] Moments of relief, such as the occasion when Wilhelm II gave a friendly hand to Theodore Roosevelt in the latter's attempts to arrange at Portsmouth an end to the Russian-Japanese War, did not have the impact needed to check this trend.[16] The myth of a special relationship between Theodore Roosevelt and Wilhelm II, in spite of all claims to the contrary,[17] was never more than just that. Although both men were swept along on the great currents of their time, the documentary evidence shows clearly that Roosevelt kept a watchful eye on his contemporary across the sea. Even the tactful maneuvers of the two German ambassadors in Washington during the prewar years, Hermann Baron Speck von Sternburg and Johann-Heinrich Count von Bernstorff, could not appreciably change the ominous direction of events. In spite of their

 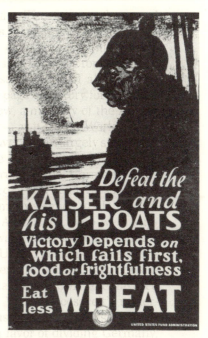

Kaiser Wilhelm II as the focus of the American image of the Germans—both positive and negative. Left: the title page of a march composed in 1913 by the popular American composer E. T. Paull in honor of the emperor's 25th anniversary on the German throne. Here, an American army officer pays tribute to the Kaiser. Right: an American war poster of 1918 in which the Kaiser appears with "his" U-boats as the symbol of a threatening enemy. The poster encourages Americans to "Eat Less Wheat" in order to stretch food supplies for the war effort. (Roughwood Collection; The Balch Institute, Philadelphia)

urgent advice, Berlin could not bring itself to sign an arbitration treaty with the United States, and the Germans rejected respective American offers with formal and legalistic tactics.[18] Indeed Germany would not even conclude an arbitration treaty with the United States in the fall of 1914, when France and Britain rushed to complete such an instrument of goodwill.[19]

As hostilities in Europe began, the differences between the German Empire, with its traditional social structures, powerful military, and limited democratic experience, and the American republic, with its more mobile multiethnic society and established democratic tradition, became all the more apparent. The unbridgeable gulf between the insecure and yet overly confident and aggressive Wilhelm II and the pensive and reserved Woodrow Wilson at times seemed almost symbolic of the divided interests of the two nations. During the ensuing three years of official U.S. neutrality from 1914 to 1917, Berlin and Washington were to clash on three major issues: the conduct of German submarine warfare, the question of Wilsonian peace mediation, and the attempts of the German government to influence conditions inside the United States by a far-flung campaign of propaganda and sabotage.

The submarine was a relatively new weapon, which because of its specific qualities could not be deployed effectively if the generally accepted principles of conduct on the high seas were to be respected. That is, the submarine could not be used in surface naval warfare. With the employment of the new weapon against commerce, confrontation with the United States was almost inevitable. The German government and military leaders knew well that the submarine conflict eventually would bring Washington into the war on the side of the Entente. The small number of vessels available and the short operational range of most boats were insufficient to blackmail the United States into acquiescence. Yet gross overestimation of Germany's resources and capabilities combined with a stunning lack of appreciation of the potential U.S. economic and military clout led the emperor and his military leaders, particularly following the realization that the war could not be won on the land, to seek a military victory through unrestricted deployment of the submarine. They came to this decision in spite of numerous warnings from the German ambassador in Washington that unlimited submarine warfare would certainly lead to American entry into the war. Ironically, it was, therefore, the issue of the freedom of the seas, agreed upon in the Treaty of Amity and Commerce between the United States and Frederick the Great's Prussia in 1785, that became one of the major reasons for America's declaration of war against Germany.[20]

The second area of conflict, Wilsonian mediation between the warring powers, has received less publicity, possibly because the complicated negotiations, often on a private and quasi-unauthorized level between the German ambassador Count Bernstorff and Wilson's adviser Colonel Edward M. House, lend themselves less to dramatic treatment than, for instance, the torpedoing of large passenger liners such as the *Lusitania* or the *Ancona* by German submarines.[21] Actually, Berlin's continuous rejection of Wilson's mediation efforts and the less than candid procedure chosen by the German government to stall the American president probably did as much as the bloody statistics of the submarine war to persuade Wilson that he would have to join the Entente. The height of imperial German duplicity came on December 12, 1916, little more than two months before the final rupture of diplomatic relations, when the Wilhelmstrasse published a so-called peace offer, which, as the documents clearly show, had the explicit purpose of taking the wind out of the imminently expected mediation offer from the American president.[22] Even taking into account a legitimate German fear of the American president's pro-Entente disposition at future peace negotiations, in view of the implications of the submarine war decision and considering Germany's overall military position, any negotiated peace clearly promised a more advantageous outcome for Germany than full-scale American participation on the side of the Entente. Only a few German leaders appear to have comprehended these facts, and fewer, one of them the ambassador in Washington, cared to expose themselves by taking a stand against the powerful military.[23]

George Washington as an ally of the Germans against England: "He fought the same foe then that Germany fights today." Title page of *The Fatherland*, the most prominent pro-German magazine, which was financed with German support and which called for "fair play" for Germany and Austria-Hungary from the outset of the war. The weekly was published by George Sylvester Viereck, a German-American whose loud propaganda was generally counterproductive to his goal of drawing American public opinion over to the German side and keeping America neutral in the European conflict. (Kings Court Collection)

Price 5 Cents   No. 21—Dec. 30th, 1914

THE

Fatherland
A Weekly

GEORGE WASHINGTON
VALLEY FORGE ••• CHRISTMAS 1777
HE FOUGHT THE SAME FOE THEN THAT GERMANY FIGHTS TODAY

The third area of conflict between the United States and Germany during the period of American neutrality has received only very limited treatment by historians, even though all evidence suggests that the German campaign of propaganda and sabotage inside the United States had no small part in turning the American public against Germany and thus preparing the ground for U.S. entry into the war. Fully in line with their prewar policy of accommodation, the British organized a shrewd, low-key propaganda campaign, infiltrating American public opinion on many levels but carefully avoiding aggressive statements or brash public appearances. The German government entrusted the difficult task to a group of men who either lacked a thorough knowledge of the American political and social mentality or who were already well known in the United States for their partiality toward Germany and therefore were inept and unable to establish significant contacts with influential professional and social groups. In charge of the German campaign was Bernhard Dernburg, former colonial secretary in Berlin, whose contentious tenor was ill-suited to convince Americans that the German Empire had been forced into the war and that Great Britain was to be blamed for the turn of events.[24] The rape of Belgium, a harsh German military regime in the occupied territories, the deportation of forced labor from Belgium, and the sinking of passenger liners and commercial ships carrying civilians would have been troublesome matters to explain away even by highly qualified public relations experts. When the chief of the German propaganda organization in America told an enraged public that the submarine had been fully justified in torpedoing the *Lusitania* and thereby sending more than a thousand civilians to their death, his usefulness had come to an end.[25] A factor contributing to the failure of the public relations effort was the Germans' surprising lack of information or false information about the United States. Reading press comments and academic opinions of the time, one senses at least a latent current of anti-Americanism. Very conceivably some of the German propaganda errors had their origin in such animosities.[26]

If imperial propaganda made few inroads with the American public, the results of the German sabotage campaign in the United States were even more dubious, especially when one assumes that the primary motivation behind these operations was to keep U.S. war material shipments from reaching the Allies and, furthermore, to prevent America from joining the war against Germany. Standard texts emphasize the escapades of Heinrich Albert, falsely declared as commerical attaché in Washington,[27] and Captain Franz von Papen, the military attaché, who incorrectly is still thought of as the chief engineer of German underground activities in the United States.[28] The record of these men and their colleague, the naval attaché Captain Karl Boy-Ed, was sufficiently bleak to satisfy most historians.[29] In reality, however, the German army and navy maintained their own intelligence networks in North America. Their operatives received their orders directly from military headquarters in Germany and were not subordinate to the Imperial German Embassy in Washington. Among their best-known sabotage acts are the destruction in July 1916 of the Black Tom Terminal, a large freight station in the harbor of New York, and the demolition in January 1917 of the Canadian Car and Foundry Company in Kingsland, New Jersey. These events shocked the American public and, in fact, carried the European war into the United States already during the period of American neutrality.[30] A sordid campaign of bacteriological warfare, ordered by the military intelligence in Germany, was not executed, apparently largely because the cultures brought to the United States did not survive the long clandestine journey.[31]

Although the documents show that the still young U.S. intelligence services enjoyed the cooperation of British agents,[32] it is certain that the American government was not informed about the details and scope of these German operations. Yet we know that President Wilson became aware of a number of German covert operations in the country relatively early in the war, and it is not surprising that these developments did not enhance his sympathy for the German viewpoint in other matters.[33]

The final hiatus was brought about, however, not by covert operations but by the official German declaration of the opening of unrestricted submarine warfare on February 1, 1917, and the incredible offer of an alliance to the Mexican government in return for the reacquisition by Mexico of Texas, Arizona, and New Mexico. As if to underline that American neutrality was no longer of any concern to Berlin, the German Foreign Office attached its offer to Mexico, Telegram No. 158, to the note declaring unlimited submarine warfare, Telegram No. 157.[34] In fact, the Wilhelmstrasse did not hesitate to dispatch one version of this message to Count Bernstorff through the American State Department, which promptly passed the coded text on to the German Embassy. It was with some glee that the British government, whose intelligence service, known as Room 40 and directed by the "Blinker," Admiral Reginald Hall, had intercepted all three versions of the message, presented to a startled American government the text of the Ger-

Anti-German posters of the First World War, 1917/18. The characterization of Germans as the Huns was common to much of the American war propaganda and had a devastating effect on German-Americans. This image grew out of Germany's attack on neutral Belgium in 1914 and especially out of British propaganda reports of German atrocities. The perception is expressed in the image of the German soldier threatening innocent women and children who are defended by the American soldier. The posters usually encouraged the purchase of war bonds or the enlistment of volunteers in the armed services. (The Balch Institute, Philadelphia)

man offer to Mexico. The curtain was now to close on the final act of the tragicomedy in which the German Reich, already beleaguered by serious economic difficulties, had openly defied the American president and challenged him to lead the United States into war.

On April 2, 1917, after the emperor had rejected additional feelers from Washington, Woodrow Wilson went before Congress and asked it to accept the state of war "thrust upon it" by the German Empire. Congress applauded when the president called out: "We are glad . . . to fight thus for the ultimate peace of the world and for the liberation of its peoples, the German peoples included: for the rights of nations great and small and the privilege of men everywhere to choose their way of life and of obedience. The world must be made safe for democracy."[35] The fate of Wilhelminian Germany was sealed. It would be only a question of time before the United States would throw its full economic and military weight behind the Allies and thereby bring about the certain defeat of the German Empire. An army of three million men was raised, many of them Americans of German descent, and at the end of 1917, 176,000 American soldiers were deployed in Europe. By September 1918 their numbers had swelled to one and a half million. But the Americans paid a price for their first participation in a war on the European continent: more than 50,000 men died in battle, and some 200,000 were wounded. On November 11, 1918, the representatives of the two-day-old German republic signed the terms of surrender dictated by Marshal Ferdinand Foch, the commander in chief of the Allied forces. Ironic as it may seem, at the moment of their defeat, the German leaders clung to President Wilson's Fourteen Points and hoped for reasonable terms from the Allies. Less than two years after the imperial Foreign Office had bluntly declined Wilson's offer to serve as a "clearinghouse" for the warring nations on their way to the conference table, the program of the American president was seen as a protective shield against the vengeful designs of England and France. Surely, A.J.P. Taylor strains the evidence when he suggests that Germany became a republic "as a further gesture to placate Wilson," but he is not far off the mark when he concludes that "the ideals championed by the revolutionaries of 1848 thus triumphed in Germany by American order."[36]

Notes

1. See Hans Dietrich Genscher, "Die geistigen Grundlagen der deutsch-amerikanischen Freundschaft," speech in Würzburg, January 13, 1983, in *Bulletin* (Bonn), no. 5 (January 15, 1983): 41–44; Genscher, speech in Worms, June 12, 1983, in *Bulletin*, no. 66 (June 22, 1983): 617–18; Helmut Kohl, speech in Krefeld, June 25, 1983, in *Bulletin*, no. 70 (June 29, 1983): 646–48; Arthur F. Burns, speech in Hamburg, March 14, 1983, printed as "The Human Side of German-American Relations," *Current Policy*, no. 469 (March 14, 1983). "Amerika ist eben auch ein Stück von uns," interview with Berndt von Staden (German Foreign Office), *Die Welt*, no. 145 (June 25, 1983): 8.

2. See J. Turner, "German Immigration in the Colonial Period," *Chicago Record-Herald*, August 28, 1901, p. 7; Alfred Vagts, *Deutschland und die Vereinigten Staaten in der Weltpolitik*, 2 vols. (New York: Macmillan, 1935), 1:570: "Der Deutsche war ökonomisch regsam, aber nicht politisch." See also Theodor von Holleben (German ambas-

sador in Washington) to the German Foreign Office, June 19, 1900, ibid., 571; H. L. Mencken, "Die Deutschamerikaner," *Die Neue Rundschau*, no. 10 (October 1928): 188–89.

3. Carl Wittke, *Refugees of Revolution* (Philadelphia: University of Pennsylvania Press, 1952), remains the standard study of this group of German-Americans.

4. Philip S. Foner and Brewster Chamberlin, eds., *Friedrich A. Sorge's Labor Movement in the United States* (Westport, Conn.: Greenwood Press, 1977); Karl Marx and Frederick Engels, *Letters to Americans, 1848–1895*, ed. Alexander Trachtenberg (New York: International Publishers, 1953); A. Sartorius Frhr. von Waltershausen, *Der moderne Socialismus in den Vereinigten Staaten von Amerika* (Berlin: Hermann Bahr, 1890).

5. Bismarck in the Reichstag on June 26, 1884, quoted in *Die Reden des Reichskanzlers Fürsten von Bismarck im Deutschen Reichstage, 1884–1885* (Stuttgart: J. G. Cotta, 1894), 203. Vagts, *Deutschland und die Vereinigten Staaten in der Weltpolitik*, 1:570. The German ambassador, Speck von Sternburg, warned against an official request of this nature from Berlin.

6. Felix Gilbert, *To the Farewell Address* (1961; rpt. Princeton: Princeton University Press, 1970), 72; German, French, and American texts of the treaty and comments in Karl J. R. Arndt, ed., *Der Freundschafts- und Handelsvertrag von 1785 zwischen Seiner Majestät dem König von Preussen und den Vereinigten Staaten von Amerika* (Munich: Heinz Moos, 1977); George Washington to Count Rochambeau, 1786, in Frank Lambach, *Our Men in Washington* (Cologne: Rudolf Müller, 1976), 10.

7. About the various treaty negotiations see Otto Graf zu Stolberg-Wernigerode, *Deutschland und die Vereinigten Staaten von Amerika* (Berlin: Walter de Gruyter, 1933), 26–30.

8. See Hans W. Gatzke, *Germany and the United States: A "Special Relationship?"* (Cambridge, Mass.: Harvard University Press, 1980), 30. For a background analysis of the German failure see Erich Angermann, "Early German Constitutionalism and the American Model," paper presented at the Fourteenth International Congress of Historical Sciences, San Francisco, 1975. Published as CISH-AHA brochure.

9. Henry Blumenthal, *A Reappraisal of Franco-American Relations, 1830–1871* (Chapel Hill: University of North Carolina Press, 1959) 185–97; Blumenthal, *France and the United States: Their Diplomatic Relations, 1789–1914* (Chapel Hill: University of North Carolina Press, 1970), 91–92, 117, 127; Henry Adams, *Prussian-American Relations, 1775–1871* (Cleveland: Press of Western Reserve University, 1960), 101–3. For historical reasons, a great number of Irish-Americans had sided with the French. See excerpts from John Mitchel's address at the St. Patrick's Day Banquet of the Knights of St. Patrick in New York, *Irish Citizen*, March 25, 1871, p. 192; editorial, "German 'Peace' Jubilees," ibid., April 8, 1871, p. 205.

10. *Die Deutschen in Amerika und die deutsch-amerikanischen Friedensfeste im Jahr 1871* (New York: Verlags-Expedition des deutsch-amerikanischen Conversations' Lexicons, 1871); Heinz Kloss, *Um die Einigung des Deutschamerikanertums* (Berlin: Volk und Reich Verlag, 1937), 231–32; see also F. A. Sorge to Wilhelm Liebknecht, Hoboken, September 25, 1870, in Georg Eckert, ed., *Wilhelm Liebknecht. Briefwechsel mit deutschen Sozialdemokraten*, vol. I: *1862–78* (Assen: Van Gorcum, 1973–), 342.

11. Cincinnati *Courier*, November 7, 1871, quoted in G. A. Dobbert, "German-Americans between New and Old Fatherland, 1870–1914," *American Quarterly* 19 (Winter 1967): 666.

12. Just before the German-American festivities held in Philadelphia, French and

Americans celebrated the Treaty of Paris, which in 1783 had ended the revolutionary war and recognized the de facto existence of the United States. See Dominique Dhombres, "La naissance des États-Unis d'Amérique," *Le Monde*, September 5, 1983, p. 5; "Un défilé historique: Quand l'armée de Rochambeau investit Vendôme . . . ," *Le Monde*, September 1, 1983, p. 8.

13. Cf. notes of Anton Count Monts de Mazin, Rome, June 1907, and comments in margin by Bernhard Prince von Bülow, Political Archive, Foreign Office, Bonn, Vereinigte Staaten von Amerika No. 16, Geheim, vol. 2; Ernst Graf zu Reventlow, *Deutschlands auswärtige Politik, 1888–1914* (Berlin: Mittler, 1917), 217.

14. Andrew D. White, U.S. ambassador to Germany from 1897 to 1903, recalled in his memoirs that the sensational press on both sides had contributed to an ill feeling between the two countries. Only "two newspapers of real importance" in Germany were friendly disposed toward the United States. White was especially concerned to find a strong anti-American disposition among the highly educated, and he feared that war was a likely consequence. *Autobiography of Andrew Dickson White*, 2 vols. (London: Macmillan, 1905), 2:144–47. Concerning German-American trade and tariff problems see Glenn C. Altschuler, *Andrew D. White—Educator, Historian, Diplomat* (Ithaca: Cornell University Press, 1979), 237–38.

15. Among other things the German emperor was reported to have said in an interview granted to the American journalist William Bayard Hald: "The future . . . belongs to the white race; never fear. . . . It belongs to the Anglo-Teuton, the man who came from northern Europe—where you to whom America belongs came from—the home of the Germans. It does not belong—the future—to the yellow or to the black or the olive-colored; it belongs to the fair-skinned man, and it belongs to Christianity and to Protestantism. We are the only race who can save it. There is no power in any other civilization or any other religion that can save humanity; and the future—belongs—to—us." For further detail and respective documentary background see Reinhard R. Doerries, *Washington-Berlin 1908/1917* (Düsseldorf: Schwann, 1975), 32–33.

16. Eugene P. Trani, *The Treaty of Portsmouth* (Lexington: University of Kentucky Press, 1969), 58–60; Justus Hashagen, "Zur Geschichte der amerikanisch-deutschen Beziehungen 1897–1907," *Zeitschrift für Politik* 16 (1927): 122–29, places too much weight on common interests.

17. Cf. Howard Beale, "Theodore Roosevelt, Wilhelm II. und die deutsch-amerikanischen Beziehungen," *Die Welt als Geschichte* 15 (1955): 155–87. Hashagen (see n. 16) also overestimates the influence of Speck von Sternburg on Theodore Roosevelt.

18. See especially documents in Akten betreffend deutsch-amerikanischen Schiedsgerichtsvertrag, Political Archive, Foreign Office, Bonn.

19. Britain and France signed arbitration treaties with the United States on September 15, 1914. Both treaties were ratified in 1915. See U.S. State Department, *Foreign Relations of the United States* (Washington, D.C.: Government Printing Office, 1914), 304–7.

20. For different views on the submarine conflict see Thomas G. Frothingham, *The Naval History of the World War*, 3 vols. (Cambridge, Mass.: Harvard University Press, 1924–26); R. H. Gibson and Maurice Pendergast, *The German Submarine War, 1914–1918* (London: Constable, 1931); Arno Spindler, *Der Handelskrieg mit U-Booten* (Berlin: Mittler, 1932–41).

21. The *Lusitania*, a British passenger liner, was torpedoed by *U-20* on May 7, 1915. Among the 1,198 victims were 124 U.S. citizens. See Thomas A. Bailey's (with

Paul B. Ryan) competent study *The Lusitania Disaster* (New York: Free Press, 1975). The *Ancona*, an Italian liner, was sunk on November 7, 1915, by a German submarine showing the Austrian flag.

22. For details and documentary background see Doerries, *Washington-Berlin 1908/1917*, 232–33.

23. Cf. Johann-Heinrich Graf von Bernstorff, *Deutschland und Amerika* (Berlin: Ullstein, 1920), 389–91; "Graf Bernstorff wird 70," *Frankfurter Zeitung*, November 13, 1932; William L. Langer, "An Honest German Diplomat," *New York Herald Tribune Books*, October 25, 1936, sec. 10, p. 2.

24. Among the people working with the German Information Office were the American journalist William Bayard Hale, the Harvard professor Hugo Muensterberg, the German economist Moritz Julius Bonn, George Sylvester Viereck of the *Fatherland*, M. B. Claussen from the Hamburg-Amerika Line, the Celtic studies specialist Kuno Meyer, the journalist Edward Lyell Fox, and several men from the German diplomatic service.

25. Bailey and Ryan, *Lusitania Disaster*, 237; Arthur S. Link, *Wilson: The Struggle for Neutrality, 1914–1915* (Princeton: Princeton University Press, 1960), 377–79.

26. Hans-Ulrich Wehler, in his noteworthy analysis of present-day problems in "Zum dritten Mal: Deutscher Anti-Amerikanismus," *Der Monat*, no. 281 (October–December 1981), may have dated the onset of what he identifies as the first wave of anti-Americanism in Germany too late (1917, Versailles).

27. Secretary of the Foreign Office Jagow to Secretary of the Interior, October 25, 1915, Personnel File, Heinrich Albert, Bundesarchiv, Koblenz.

28. Colin Simpson, *Lusitania* (Harmondsworth: Penguin, 1983), 64.

29. Both von Papen and Boy-Ed eventually were declared persona non grata and had to leave the United States. Papen's memoirs *Der Wahrheit eine Gasse* (Munich: Paul List, 1952), contain no reliable information on these activities. Boy-Ed's publications *Die Vereinigten Staaten von Amerika und der U-Boot-Krieg* (Berlin: Karl Sigismund, 1918) and *Verschwörer?* (Berlin: August Scherl, 1920) do not contain much useful information for the historian.

30. These and other projects of German intelligence have never been fully investigated by scholars. I have collected material from various sources for a more complete treatment of German intelligence work in the United States during World War I.

31. Richmond Levering to Bruce Bielaski (BI), March 28, 1918, Record Group 165, No. 10546, National Archives, Washington, D.C. (hereafter RG, NA).

32. The British work was largely directed by Captain Guy R. A. Gaunt, who was appointed military attaché in Washington on April 22, 1914, and by William Wiseman, who came to the United States in late 1916. On their activities see M. L. Sanders and Philip M. Taylor, *British Propaganda during the First World War, 1914–1918* (London: Macmillan, 1982), 178–207.

33. The German ambassador, Count Bernstorff, inadvertently became linked with a number of German intelligence and propaganda activities, causing Wilson and House to question Bernstorff's reliability in the negotiations concerning potential U.S. mediation. Several times Bernstorff tried to persuade the German government of the necessity to restrain or withdraw representatives of the intelligence services. The records indicate that Berlin did not heed his requests (Bernstorff to Foreign Office, June 2, 1916, and August 19, 1916, RG 59, Box 244, NA).

34. Since the *Lusitania* negotiations in the summer of 1915, Washington had permitted Count Bernstorff to send and receive coded messages through the facilities of the

State Department, which offered quicker communication than the regular German dispatches going from Berlin via Stockholm and Buenos Aires to Washington.

35. Address to a Joint Session of Congress, April 2, 1917, in Arthur S. Link, ed., *The Papers of Woodrow Wilson*, at present 47 vols. (Princeton: Princeton University Press, 1966–), 41:519–27.

36. A. J. P. Taylor, *From Sarajewo to Potsdam* (London: Thames and Hudson, 1966), 51.

2.

The United States and the Weimar Republic: A "Special Relationship" That Failed

KLAUS SCHWABE

ONE OF THE MOST DAMAGING denunciations hurled against the Weimar Republic by its right-wing foes was the assertion that, as a form of government, the republic was un-German, that it was a political system forced upon Germany by its enemies, especially the United States. Unintentionally and indirectly, the American ambassador to Germany, Jacob Gould Schurman, confirmed that there was at least a grain of truth in this allegation, when he told a Steuben Day audience in New York in 1927: "Never in our history have the political institutions and international ideas of Germany and the United States been as much in agreement as they are today. Both nations believe in government of the people, by the people, and for the people. Both are instinctively and unalterably opposed to dictators, no matter whether the dictator is an individual or a class." [1]

Whether cursed or welcomed, strong ties apparently existed between the United States and the first German Republic. What was the nature of these ties? Was there a special relationship between the two countries? Why was this relationship short-lived and followed by another period of bitter enmity between Germany and America? This essay is an attempt to elucidate this problem by addressing five specific issues. The first question is whether the introduction of a republican form of government in Germany was one of the major aims of the American government, after the United States had entered World War I. Second, I will examine the extent of and the reasons for U.S. support of the Weimar Republic. Third, one must ask what means America employed to uphold and strengthen Weimar Germany. A fourth issue is to determine the German perspective of contemporary German-American relations so as to show how German foreign policy made use of America's support in pursuing its own objectives. Fifth and finally, an answer will have to be found to the question as to why America's policy to assure the existence of the Weimar Republic ultimately failed.

The Weimar Republic originated following World War I. Was its origin of a purely domestic nature or were there foreign influences?[2] Specifically, was America in some way involved with the prehistory of the Weimar Republic? There are some indications that tend to confirm this suggestion. Was it by accident that the proclamation of the German Republic on November 9, 1918, and the conclusion of the armistice of Compiègne nearly coincided? Many contemporaries thought not. They claimed that the "November Revolution," the armistice, Germany's abandoning the monarchical order, and her military defeat were closely interrelated. They believed that the German people had parted with the monarchy and laid down their arms because America had promised that Germany would fare better as a republic at the coming peace conference. But was this allegation true? Had the American government made such a promise, thereby in effect imposing a republican system of government on the Germans?

America's war propaganda and the distinction President Woodrow Wilson had made between Germany's military masters and autocrats and the German people had created the impression that the elimination of the ruling caste in Germany (including the Kaiser) was one of America's major war aims. But the attitude Wilson displayed during the last weeks of World War I tells a different story. As is well known, the German government, in a note dated October 4, 1918, and addressed to the American president, sued for peace on the basis of Wilson's Fourteen Points program for peace. To be sure, the American government chose strong language in answering the German request and pressed for liberalizing changes in the political structure of the German Empire. Much to the dismay of his European associates, however, Wilson did not immediately reject the German request. Instead he basically endorsed it and passed it on to the Allies. Ultimately, after the terms of the armistice to be granted to Germany had been agreed upon by the Allies and the United States, the American government through the Lansing Note of November 5, 1918, accepted the German request for an armistice and peace negotiations on the basis of the American peace program (with two reservations) in the name of its associates. America thus indirectly recognized the still existing, albeit reformed, monarchical government of Germany as the legitimate representative of the German people. The establishment of a republican form of government was not among the conditions the victorious powers set up as a prerequisite to peace negotiations on the basis of the Fourteen Points. In Washington, some advisers to Wilson feared a revolution in Germany, and all evidence available today suggests that the president would have been satisfied to have a truly parliamentary government in Germany as a partner to negotiate peace, even if a monarchy reduced to more decorous functions were preserved.[3]

Wilson had good reasons for being cautious. He did not want Germany to collapse totally but hoped instead to see a certain measure of power—even military power—left to Germany as a counterweight to the western European powers so as to discourage imperialist ambitions on the part of the Allies. In addition, Wilson feared that the fall of the monarchy in Germany would soon result in a triumph of Bolshevism in that country and would thus lead not only to the destruction of civilized society in the heart of Europe but also to a combination of power which would extend from the Rhine River to the Pacific. This was a specter that was to create nightmares in Washington in years to come.

The establishment of a republican form of government, not to mention a revolution, thus was not an essential war aim of the United States. The Weimar Republic, in other words, was to America an unwanted or, at best, a half-wanted child.

After the armistice American policy makers, including Herbert Hoover and General Tasker H. Bliss as well as Wilson, did seek to assure the political survival of the Weimar Republic. But they adopted this attitude—and this leads to the second point of this chapter—not so much because they were convinced of the democratic virtue of the new Germany but because they did not perceive any alternative to a German republic that could assure orderly political development and ultimately carry out the terms of the peace treaty.

Wilson, more successfully than many of his contemporaries were willing to admit, insisted on fair treatment of Germany's claims at the peace table. He did so, however, not because he considered the early Weimar Republic fundamentally democratic but because he generally strove for a fair peace, acceptable to both victors and vanquished and not open to moral criticism by Bolshevist spokesmen. In fact, the more the peace terms were criticized in Germany, the more convinced he became that Germany was not reconstructed but was still under the influence of the traditional and reactionary forces.[4]

Relations between the United States and the new German republic began inauspiciously but were to see a change for the better within a few years. America under the Republican administrations that followed Wilson gradually came more and more to make common cause with the Weimar Republic.

Seen from the perspective of the early 1920s, this cooperation was not a foregone conclusion. After the American Senate had rejected the Versailles Treaty the United States government maintained a position of decided aloofness from European disputes. In the separate peace treaty that was concluded between Germany and America in August 1921, Washington disclaimed all responsibility for the political and military provisions of the Versailles peace settlement and their execution. It was understandable that the U.S. government kept in the background when in 1923 tensions in Germany reached a new high and led to the French occupation of the Ruhr. America's only reaction was to withdraw the last American troops of occupation that had remained in the Rhineland. Secretary of State Charles Evans Hughes thought that a "bit of chaos" would not hurt the Europeans but might bring them to their senses.[5] When total French control of Germany's western industries seemed imminent and chaos threatened in Germany, however, America became less aloof. An economic diplomacy, which was typical of the following years, was initiated. First, the United States participated unofficially but decisively in the preliminary solution of the reparation problem, which affected it more than any other issue in postwar Europe because the United States had become the largest creditor of its former associates, who had reparation claims against Germany. The Dawes Plan for German payment of reparations was based on an American conception. It was more or less forced on a reluctant but financially weakened France. Adopted in 1924, it considered Germany's capacity to pay, precluded future military sanctions on the part of the French, and led to the evacuation of the Ruhr district by French troops. It was, as a recent monograph called it, the "end of French predominance in Europe," and had a significance perhaps even greater than that.[6]

Once the stumbling block of the reparation question had been removed, American businessmen systematically invested in the German economy. American credits poured into Germany; American companies were fused with their German counterparts. The Weimar Republic knew relative prosperity for a few golden years.

America's growing involvement in the German economy not only contributed to the domestic stability of the Weimar Republic; it also extended U.S. influence in diplomatic relations. The American government increasingly supported Germany's demands for a peaceful revision of the Versailles Treaty. The United States felt that the German-Polish frontier should be modified in Germany's favor, cautiously supported the idea of Austria's joining the German republic, and met German wishes at least halfway in decisions to disarm the victors of World War I.[7]

American financial leverage also helped Germany get more favorable terms for the payment of its reparation obligations. This was the meaning of the Young Plan, which was agreed on in 1929 and led to the withdrawal of the last French occupation troops from the Rhineland. Finally, the moratorium proclaimed by President Hoover in 1931 suspending reparation and international debt payments for one year proved to be the first step on the road toward a final waiver by the Western powers of their reparation claims. Indeed, in 1932 the Lausanne Conference virtually canceled these claims. All these foreign policy successes of the Weimar Republic would have been unthinkable without the backing of the United States.[8]

Why was America increasingly determined to support the aims of German foreign policy? An economic motivation seems to have been prevalent in a threefold sense. Until 1925 Germany was subjected to various forms of commercial discrimination imposed by the Versailles Treaty. This discrimination conflicted with the Open Door principle for which the United States stood. Thus a natural community of interest was created between the two countries. The German-American commercial treaty of 1924 bore witness to the desire of both countries to restore the Open Door in Europe as soon as possible. Furthermore, America had always been convinced that—to quote Secretary of State Hughes—there could be no "economic recuperation in Europe, unless Germany recuperates."[9] A major objective of American foreign policy was to remove all obstacles in the way of Germany's economic recovery, including the occupation of German territory by foreign troops and the reparations. Germany's demand that these obstacles be eliminated thus had to be supported. A third reason why America tended to side with Germany in its disputes in Europe, especially with France, was that American credits and investments in Germany since the adoption of the Dawes Plan had resulted in a heavy stake in the German economy. Secretary of State Henry Stimson was referring to this investment when he told Hoover in 1931 that "we are tied up with Germany's situation."[10]

Yet it would be one-sided to reduce American policy toward Weimar Germany strictly to economic motives. The overriding objective of all American administrations from Wilson to Hoover was to create conditions in Europe that would assure social and political stability in Germany and contribute to its speedy reintegration into the family of peaceful nations. Ultimately, America hoped that peace in Europe would be safe and a repetition of a senseless tragedy (as World War I increasingly appeared to have been) would be prevented. One precondition for the success of this policy seemed to be preservation of political regimes in central Europe and the support of political personalities such as Walther Rathenau, Gustav Stresemann, and even Heinrich Brüning, whose outlook was liberal progressive.[11] Again, the idea that liberal systems of government such as the Weimar Republic were by nature peaceful was shared by all American administrations after Wilson. Such governments likewise appeared to be the best barrier against the spread of Bolshevik ideas. American policy makers were fully aware of the necessity to assure a certain measure of foreign policy successes to the liberal forces, which stood behind the Weimar Republic, because only visible diplomatic achievements promised to provide these German liberals with the popularity at home which they needed to stay in power.[12]

Another political motive explains why American foreign policy increasingly favored the Weimar Republic, particularly against France. Although continuously disclaimed, the balance of both political and economic power remained one of the guiding principles of America's diplomacy. Up to the Ruhr crisis and beyond, France seemed to violate this principle in the pursuance of hegemonial aspirations.[13] Voluntary Franco-German agreements, especially in the economic field, were seen as a "ganging-up" of the Europeans, and America consistently objected to them. Whether subject to French pressure or as a voluntary economic satellite of France, Germany was encouraged by America to take an independent stand against French designs.[14]

Discussion of our third issue—the means American administrations employed to put their increased support of Weimar Germany into practice—can be brief because the answer to this question is fairly simple. America primarily relied on the economic influence it had acquired as the result of the war. Wilson had expected that America, as the major world creditor, would need to resort to financial pressure to realize its foreign policy objectives.[15] The Republican administrations shared the conviction that the exclusive use of economic leverage would assure peace and stability in Europe. And most of the time during the 1920s it indeed did so. The diplomatic means America employed at that time—mediation—proved most effective when American eco-

nomic power was thrown into the balance. The Dawes Plan, the Locarno Treaty, and the Young Plan are examples of the effectiveness
of this economic diplomacy. Actually, it seemed so effective that policy makers in Washington and members of Congress became increasingly convinced that economic means made the use of military means
dispensable.[16]

Thus the prevalent belief that America should never again enter
into military commitments in Europe seemed to be substantiated by
the course of events. A general reduction in armaments seemed to be
the primary military need. America participated in the respective negotiations and largely shared the German view that France was the
country that should reduce its armaments. A military comeback by
Germany seemed unthinkable—not the least because American military representatives since the armistice had established fairly close,
even cordial relations with the German Reichswehr, which seemed to
be unreservedly pro-American.[17]

What was the Weimar Republic's attitude toward the United
States? What role did Germany assign to America in framing its foreign policy conception? This fourth question introduces the German
perspective.

A few weeks after the armistice the former German ambassador
to Washington, Johann Heinrich Graf von Bernstorff, recommended
that because America had decided the outcome of the war and had
thereby gained a crucial position, Germany should follow the American lead at the peace conference and later rebuild its political and economic structure with American support and assistance.[18] At Versailles
the German representatives realized that they had overestimated America's ideological solidarity vis-à-vis the Weimar Republic, as well as the
weight America's diplomacy would generally have at the peace table.

But even this disappointment only briefly affected the basically
pro-American orientation of the foreign policy of the Weimar Republic.
This orientation, however, was somewhat ambivalent. On the one
hand, Berlin welcomed the rejection of the Versailles Treaty by the
American Senate, hoping that America would make common cause
with Germany in the revision of that peace. On the other hand, it did
not want to acknowledge that the rejection of the Versailles Treaty actually meant that America wished to disentangle itself from European
affairs and had cut back its influence on European affairs, an influence that might have helped Germany in the financial crisis of the
coming years. Much to the disappointment of the German governments
from Joseph Wirth to Wilhelm Cuno, it took nearly three years after

the signing of the American-German peace before America was ready to mediate in the reparation dispute, which at the time of the Ruhr occupation in 1923 had nearly disrupted the national unity of the Weimar Republic.[19]

Even though Germany had to wait unexpectedly long for America to intervene in the reparation dispute, its leading political figures always hoped that, in the words of Gustav Stresemann in 1920, "The common sense of the leading economic circles in America will recognize that America will have to decide to seek not isolation, but the initiative in rebuilding the world economy. This problem, however, can only be solved with German cooperation *on equal terms.*"[20]

When Stresemann took over the reins of German foreign policy in September 1923, he based his diplomatic calculation on the assumption that America, the strongest world power, soon would throw its weight into the balance to reintegrate Germany into the world economy and the "club" of the bigger powers.[21] To achieve this goal, America was expected to support Germany's claims for a revision of the Versailles Treaty.[22] The Dawes settlement of the reparation issue appeared to Berlin as the first step on a road leading to Germany's reinstatement as one of the major world powers. American support for the German demand that France start to reduce its armaments seemed particularly important in this respect. To be sure, Stresemann's only goal was a peaceful revision of the Versailles Treaty; but could one be certain that this was also the view of the military leaders?[23] In any event, the German foreign policy elite had no doubts about the effectiveness of economic pressure exercised by the United States against a France that was reluctant to accept a revision of the Versailles Treaty. German diplomacy, therefore, made every effort to avoid friction with America and carefully abstained from diplomatic steps that could be interpreted as a "ganging-up" with the western European powers against the United States.[24]

Brüning continued this basic orientation; he exploited the American stake in Germany's economy to win American support for cancellation of reparation claims. His deflationary policies were partly designed to create a good impression in Washington—which they did. Brüning thus increased German demands for a revision of the Versailles Treaty. In fact, he wanted to abandon it altogether, as far as reparations were concerned, and again he hoped for American backing. Brüning echoed an increasingly impatient public opinion in Germany, which had become aware of the nation's growing economic strength, which was largely attributable to American support. Thus the Young Plan came under attack from the Right even before the depression had set in.[25] When Adolf Hitler came to power and the extreme Right gained the upper hand, an anti-Americanism, which had always lingered on in extreme rightist circles, supplanted the previous pro-American attitude of all the governments of the Weimar Republic.[26] Hitler's ascent to power meant that America's policy of stabilization in Germany had utterly failed. American observers had already gained this impression when Franz von Papen, of bad repute in America since his covert activities in World War I, became the German chancellor.[27]

What had gone wrong? Why had that special relationship, characterized by the unprecedented influence of one foreign country on Germany, turned out to be no more than an episode? Could its failure have been, at least partly, the fault of the policy of stabilization America pursued in the 1920s? This is the last issue to be taken up in this essay. The preceding account suggests that what was faulty in the American policy of stabilization and appeasement was not the conception but its implementation. It was reasonable to reintegrate the new Germany into the postwar world, but mistakes were made in the selection of means, both in the economic and the political spheres.

Economically, America's stabilization policy was ambiguous. Since the end of the Ruhr crisis America tried to ease the burden of Germany's reparation obligations, but it was not prepared to admit that Germany's reparation payments to some extent conditioned the Allies' capacity to repay their war debts to America. By 1931—and by then it was too late—all American administrations, including Wilson's, had refused to consider an overall financial settlement that addressed the issue of German reparations as well as Allied war debts. Only such an agreement would have disposed of the reparation problem as early as necessary and thereby stabilized Germany's economic position.[28]

For understandable reasons, America was not willing to abandon the favored financial position it had gained during the war. This was the overriding consideration behind U.S. economic policy in the 1920s.

The much touted Open Door played only a secondary role, although it also affected Germany's position in Europe. As has been shown, in the name of an Open Door in Europe America had on various occasions (for example, after the Thoiry negotiations in 1926) objected to attempts to merge French and German industries and instead insisted on the principle of bilateralism. This attitude, well understood in Berlin, ran counter to the American aim to improve Franco-German relations.[29]

But the supreme American diplomatic error in the 1920s was the illusion that economic means could solve any political problem in Europe. The hope of American policy makers that political issues could be reduced to their underlying economic dimensions was the real motivation behind America's interventions in the reparation conflict in 1923 and again in 1928–29. The reparation problem, it was hoped, could be depoliticized. Contemporary American opinion overlooked the political consequences of this policy in destroying the means by which France could enforce the Versailles Treaty.[30]

Germany, of course, was aware of this fact. America's support for Germany's foreign policy aims and the successes of this assistance led the German people to overestimate the nation's diplomatic strength, thereby providing grist for the mills of the Right and rendering a moderate foreign policy politically difficult. Even the Foreign Office believed that it could always count on American backing against France as long as Germany strove for a peaceful revision of the Versailles Treaty.

Failing to realize the political and psychological consequences of its economic foreign policy, contemporary American diplomacy was likewise unable to perceive that the generous reconstruction of Germany was bound to shift the balance of power in Europe to the detriment of France. Concessions to the German view regarding reparations were never accompanied by American guarantees, even of the most indirect sort, for the security of France. American diplomacy was blind to the military consequences of its stance in Europe. Its article of faith remained that America should never again be committed militarily in Europe. In this respect Republican foreign policy differed sharply from Wilson's. In helping Germany to stabilize its economy, America increased Germany's military potential; and yet it was not prepared to counterbalance these effects of its policy by assisting France in strengthening its own security. This American attitude, in turn, made it more difficult for France to accept a revision of the Versailles Treaty, which the Americans demanded in unison with the Germans.[31]

There are many good explanations for America's European and German foreign policy, and I have mentioned some of them. This foreign policy fully reflected the views of the American Congress. It was designed to have a maximum effect at a minimum of costs. In due time the American people discovered that it had been based on a costly miscalculation.

Notes

1. Hans W. Gatzke, *Germany and the United States: A "Special Relationship?"* (Cambridge, Mass.: Harvard University Press, 1980), 1.

2. Klaus Schwabe, "Äussere und innere Bedingungen der deutschen November-revolution," in Michael Salewski, ed., *Die Deutschen und die Revolution* (Göttingen: Musterschmidt, 1985), 320–45.

3. Klaus Schwabe, *Woodrow Wilson, Revolutionary Germany, and Peacemaking 1918–1919* (Chapel Hill: University of North Carolina Press, 1985), 58–81, 93, 118–23. I disagree with Gatzke's view of this situation expressed in *Germany and the United States*, 73.

4. Arthur S. Link, *Woodrow Wilson: Revolution, War, and Peace* (Arlington Heights, Ill.: AHM Publishing Corp., 1979), 99–103; Schwabe, *Woodrow Wilson*, 354–56.

5. Hughes, memorandum, February 23, 1923, in U.S. Department of State, *Papers Relating to the Foreign Relations of the United States, 1923*, vol. 2 (Washington, D.C.: Government Printing Office, 1938), 56.

6. Stephen A. Schuker, *The End of French Predominance in Europe: The Financial Crisis of 1924 and the Adoption of the Dawes Plan* (Chapel Hill: University of North Carolina Press, 1976); Werner Link, *Die amerikanische Stabilisierungspolitik in Deutschland 1921–32* (Düsseldorf: Droste, 1970), 241–92; Marc Trachtenberg, *Reparation in World Politics: France and European Economic Diplomacy, 1916–1923* (New York: Columbia University Press, 1980), 291–335.

7. Melvyn P. Leffler, *The Elusive Quest: America's Pursuit of European Stability and French Security, 1919–1933* (Chapel Hill: University of North Carolina Press, 1979).

8. Ibid., 116; Werner Link, "Die Beziehungen zwischen der Weimarer Republik und den USA," in Manfred Knapp et al., *USA und Deutschland 1918–1975* (Munich: C. H. Beck, 1978), 98–102.

9. Link, "Die Beziehungen," 72.

10. Ibid., 100.

11. Leffler, *Elusive Quest*, 251, 285; Link, "Die Beziehungen," 102.

12. Leffler, *Elusive Quest*, 234.

13. Ibid., 85.

14. Link, *Die amerikanische Stabilisierungspolitik*, 350–52.

15. Schwabe, *Woodrow Wilson*, 18.

16. Link, *Die amerikanische Stabilisierungspolitik*, 263–72; Leffler, *Elusive Quest*, 40–43, 79–81, 228–30.

17. Link, *Die amerikanische Stabilisierungspolitik*, 517; Edward W. Bennett, *German Rearmament and the West, 1932–1933* (Princeton: Princeton University Press, 1979), 20–22; Michael Geyer, *Aufrüstung oder Sicherheit. Die Reichswehr in der Krise der Machtpolitik 1924–36* (Wiesbaden: Steiner, 1980), 160–64. For the early period see Lloyd E. Ambrosius, "Secret German-American Negotiations during the Paris Peace Conference," *Amerikastudien/American Studies* 24 (1979): 288–309; Schwabe, *Woodrow Wilson*, 155–60, 221–24, 309–12, 324–29, 348–51.

18. Quoted by Hagen Schulze, *Die Deutschen und ihre Nation*. 6 vols., Vol. 4: *Weimar. Deutschland 1917–1933* (Berlin: Severin and Siedler, 1982), 191.

19. Link, "Die Beziehungen," 65–74.

20. Michael Olaf Maxelon, *Stresemann und Frankreich, 1914–1929. Deutsche Politik der Ost-West Balance* (Düsseldorf: Droste, 1972), 92.

21. Ibid., 287.

22. Link, "Die Beziehungen," 65, 79, 104.

23. Ibid., 79.

24. Ibid., 80.

25. Schulze, *Die Deutschen und ihre Nation*, 310–12.

26. Klaus Schwabe, "Anti-Americanism within the German Right, 1917–1933," *Amerikastudien/American Studies* 21 (1976): 89–108.

27. Link, *Die amerikanische Stabilisierungspolitik*, 529–34.

28. Denise Artaud, *La question des dettes interalliées et la reconstruction de l'Europe, 1917–1929*, 2 vols. (Paris: Champion, 1978).

29. Leffler, *Elusive Quest*, 151–54.

30. Ibid., 364–66.

31. Link, *Die amerikanische Stabilisierungspolitik*, 509–11.

3.
Roosevelt and the National Socialist Threat to the United States

DETLEF JUNKER

THE UNITED STATES OF AMERICA, blessed among the nations of the world, was the only major power to enjoy the privilege of being able to discuss over a period of a few years whether its vital interests were threatened by the Axis powers and Japan. The United States owed this privilege to its location in the Western Hemisphere, which made it strategically unassailable. The Atlantic and Pacific oceans guaranteed a free discussion of alternatives and a decision-making process that was not predetermined by the will of the aggressor nations alone. A comparison with France, England, the Soviet Union, and China clearly shows the uniqueness of the American situation.

The historian in searching for the circumstances and causes of the American entry into World War II is therefore well advised to reconstruct the internal American struggle between the isolationists on the one hand and President Franklin D. Roosevelt on the other. The reason for the American entry into the war did not lie in the challenge by Nazi Germany, fascist Italy, and imperial Japan as such, but rather in the way in which the internationalists—with Roosevelt in the forefront—interpreted this danger. It is no coincidence, therefore, that this internal conflict should claim a prominent role in the literature concerning the period leading up to the U.S. entry into the war. Recently, Wayne S. Cole has summarized the results of his lifelong research in this field in a major work.[1]

When reconstructing the situation surrounding this momentous decision, the historian should remember that if he is honored at all, it is for his capacity for hindsight rather than for his moralistic and prophetic talents. In this I agree with Lord Acton: "The morality of historians consists of those things which affect veracity."[2]

The historian thus esteemed must make the greatest possible use of his ability to know more about a given period than the contemporaries themselves did—provided the sources are as plentiful as in this case. He knows the context of actions and their effects, which were obscure to contemporaries. He knows the long-term consequences of political decisions and is in a position to compare the intentions of those acting at the time with the results of their actions. This knowledge gives him not only the opportunity but the obligation to examine in the cold light of academic research the factual validity of assertions and accusations made in the course of a hot political debate.

Only findings arrived at in such a way deserve to be called historical judgments. In reaching their verdicts historians should neither content themselves with merely reproducing the positions of the contemporaries nor find pleasure in taking sides, thus assuming the role of a retrospective prophet. This unfortunate outcome has happened all too often in the historiography on the American entry into the war. On the one hand, there are revisionists who adopt the position of the isolationists and Roosevelt critics of the time; and on the other hand, there are traditionalists whose conclusions are little more than a repetition of Roosevelt's internationalist outlook.

Let me begin, however, with the historical criticism—not the moralistic political valuation—of the isolationist positions and accusations against Roosevelt and the internationalists which I consider to be valid on the basis of all we know today.

The isolationists' assertion that Roosevelt's treatment of the American people in the all-important issue of war and peace was governed by tactical considerations and that he withheld considerable parts of the truth from them is correct. Indeed, Roosevelt avoided confronting the American people openly with the one alternative that had been the nation's only foreign policy issue ever since 1939: the question whether the United States should enter the wars in Asia and Europe. On the contrary, Roosevelt "sold" the gradual surrender of a neutral position, the American help "short of war" for countries threatened by the aggressors, and the development of a global system of forward defense by claiming that these steps would make U.S. entry into the war unnecessary. He did this knowing full well that all American help short of war could at best prevent the collapse of England and China but could never force a victory over Germany, Italy, and Japan. And he did it even though he feared nothing more than the probable consequences of such a policy—a peace by negotiation which would sanction the conquest of the European continent by Nazi Germany and would lead to a "Super Munich."

This strategy was indeed, as claimed by the isolationists, bound to create false hopes. It led Roosevelt again and again to misleading, sometimes even absurd, public statements and to misrepresentations. Three examples will suffice to illustrate.

First, on January 31, 1939, he announced to members of the Senate Military Affairs Committee in a meeting behind closed doors at the White House that he had received definite information three years earlier that Germany, Italy, and Japan were preparing a policy of global conquest. This challenge, Roosevelt contended, could be met in one of two ways. One was to hope someone would kill Hitler or Germany would break apart from inside. The second was the attempt to prevent that world conquest by peaceful means. Second, after the outbreak of the war in Europe, Roosevelt refused to declare publicly that his intention behind lifting the arms embargo clause in the Neutrality Act was to help the Western democracies. Finally, both the name of the Lend-Lease Act and Roosevelt's famous analogy of the garden hose one lends one's neighbor when his house is aflame concealed the true meaning of the act: it was indeed, as the isolationists declared repeatedly, a milestone on America's path into the war. The isolationists' ironic criticism of the act's misleading name hit the nail on its head: "Lending war equipment is much like lending chewing gum. We certainly do not want the same gum back."[3]

The isolationists' allegation that the president was trying to smear them as disloyal Americans was justified. Roosevelt did not treat prominent isolationists as loyal American citizens who had a legitimate right to differ fundamentally on the reach of the vital foreign policy interests of their country and of its position in the world. Instead, the president and other members of his administration tried to associate these Americans with enemies of the democratic system, with Nazi sympathizers, with Nazi agents, even with traitors. Roosevelt said he was "absolutely convinced" that his most influential opponent, Charles A. Lindbergh, was a Nazi. He denied the pilot of world renown entry into the U.S. military service after Pearl Harbor.

Roosevelt did not hesitate to use J. Edgar Hoover's Federal Bureau of Investigation, the Department of Justice, and other administration agencies in his fight against the isolationists—though to no great avail. No prominent isolationist could be proven to have committed any disloyal acts against the United States. With Roosevelt's consent, telephones of isolationists were tapped. Wayne Cole described the situation of prominent isolationists as follows: "Leading isolationists were scared for life. Many suffered the destruction of their careers. Their reputations were irreparably damaged because they chose to risk all in battling against the President's foreign policies."[4]

The central argument of the isolationists that the security of the continental United States of America was not endangered by a Nazi invasion was correct. At no time before Pearl Harbor—the historian might add, before the invention of strategic missiles—was the continental United States threatened militarily. Nevertheless, ever since his Quarantine Speech in October 1937 Roosevelt had been warning against the illusion that the United States and the Western Hemisphere would not be attacked. His own public statements in 1940–41 as well as those of cabinet members such as Cordell Hull, Frank Knox, and Henry Stimson were strewn with warnings of the danger of a Nazi attack. A typical instance is reflected in the words with which Roosevelt justified the proclamation of an unlimited national state of emergency on March 27, 1941:

The first and fundamental fact is that what started as a European war has developed, as the Nazis always intended it should develop, into a world war for world domination.

Adolf Hitler never considered the domination of Europe as an end in itself. European conquest was but a step toward ultimate goals in all the other continents. It is unmistakably apparent to all of us that, unless the advance of Hitlerism is forcibly checked now, the Western Hemisphere will be within range of the Nazi weapons of destruction.[5]

A totally different conclusion was reached in a report by the Senate Committee on Naval Affairs published on April 24, 1940, based on the testimonies of the most prominent naval and military experts of the United States. I have yet to find an argument that invalidates the findings of this report:

From the military point of view the United States must be considered as an insular nation. We are separated from potential enemies on the east and west by broad and deep oceans. On our northern and southern borders are nations which have been friendly heretofore. Across these land frontiers could come no armies of sufficient strength to menace our security. Our situation is not similar to that of the British at the present time. Prior to the advent of air power the British Isles were insular countries. This complete insularity is now compromised in the military sense in that they are subject to damaging attack by aircraft based on the continent. The armies of Europe and Asia do not menace us. To be a menace they must be transported across the sea in ships. Airplanes based on the continents of Europe and Asia do not menace us. To threaten seriously our continental security they must be conveyed across the sea and operated from bases in or near this hemisphere.

The armed forces of no foreign nation or group of nations can seriously threaten our continental security if we make sure that we command the seas which separate us from all potential enemies. . . . The United States today is the only great power in the world situated in this fortunate position, as we are the only great nation out of reach of direct attack by any means whatsoever save those with which the Navy and air forces can deal adequately.[6]

So much for the four central claims made by the isolationists, which I maintain to have been correct in the light of what we know today.

The isolationists, however, did misjudge Roosevelt's motives and the underlying causes for his policy. Roosevelt did not intend to make himself dictator of America—an accusation leveled repeatedly against him by the isolationists—nor was he a warmonger eager to engage the United States in the wars of Europe and Asia out of sheer lust of aggression.

When the isolationist Senator Burton K. Wheeler from Montana polemically characterized the Lend-Lease Act as "the New Deal's triple 'A' foreign policy—it will plow under every fourth American boy"— Roosevelt was deeply hurt and with some justification.

Both Roosevelt's attempts at smearing his American opponents as disloyal citizens and the isolationists' misrepresentation of his motives obscured for the majority of Americans what the debate was really about. The crux of the internal American struggle was not the moral or democratic problem of whether Roosevelt was lying to the American people, but rather the irreconcilable conflict between the two camps over the future position of the United States in the world. In the period between 1937 and 1941, a major debate took place over the foreign policy issue of whether the United States was to be a world power in the literal sense of the term or whether it should content itself with the role of a great power confined to the Western Hemisphere—the fourth such debate after those of 1898, 1914 to 1917, and 1920. In this controversy the assessment of the National Socialist threat to America was of crucial importance.

I will next attempt to reduce the positions and arguments of both camps to their essence. Let me begin with the isolationists.

The four principles proclaimed by the isolationist America First

Committee limited the vital interests of the United States—that is, the interests that were to be defended by force of arms if necessary—to the Western Hemisphere, the eastern Pacific, and the western Atlantic Ocean, geographically just under one-half of the globe. These four principles were worded as follows:

1. The United States must build an impregnable defense for America.
2. No foreign power, nor group of powers, can successfully attack a *prepared* America.
3. American democracy can be preserved only by keeping out of the European war.
4. "Aid short of war" weakens national defense at home and threatens to involve America in war abroad.[7]

As long as the United States itself was not attacked, the isolationists argued, American entry into war could not be justified—no matter what was happening in Europe and Asia. The dangers to the United States from participation in foreign wars were greater than the consequences of an Axis victory.

For many isolationists World War I and its aftermath were a perfect example of the senselessness of attempting to have a voice in the fate of the Old World, morally rotten and perpetually shaken by wars as it was. Had not, they asked rhetorically, the developments since 1919 proved convincingly how right the traditional American "splendid isolation" of the nineteenth century had been? Had not the committee chaired by Senator Gerald P. Nye only recently demonstrated to the public that it was the international bankers and the armaments industry, the so-called "merchants of death," who had drawn the American nation into World War I for the sake of their own profits? Instead of once more assuming the role of a world policeman, instead of once more being made Britain's cat's paw, the United States would do well to remember the wisdom of George Washington's Farewell Address with its warning against entanglements in European wars.

The security of the United States, the isolationists insisted, was not threatened by Hitler; moreover, an America armed to its teeth for defensive purposes, an impregnable "Fortress America" with a two-ocean navy, was impossible for any attacker to conquer. Furthermore, the United States could cope economically with losing the Eurasian markets. Even after a complete victory in Europe, Hitler would not be in a position to dictate the terms of trade: trade was never a one-way street. According to isolationist calculations, a domestic trade increase

Fritz Kuhn, the self-appointed "Führer" of the German-American Volksbund, speaking at the opening of Camp Nordland, New Jersey, 1938. The Bund, founded in 1936, made such aggressive use of anti-Semitic Nazi slogans and paramilitary bravado that it quickly alienated the American public. Even the leaders of the Third Reich distanced themselves from the organization. Members were recruited primarily from among recent immigrants (between 1919 and 1932 some 500,000 Germans emigrated to America), rather than from native German-Americans. The actual membership was well under the figure of 25,000 often cited by Kuhn. (UPI, Bettmann Newsphotos)

of only 5 percent yielded more profit than a 100 percent growth in the export trade.

The isolationists concluded that there was no "clear and present danger" for the survival of the United States. On the other hand, the internationalists led by President Franklin D. Roosevelt refused to limit the national interests of the United States to the Western Hemisphere. On the contrary, they defined these interests globally in the economic, military, and idealistic sense, although until Pearl Harbor they shrank

Counterdemonstrators cause a premature end to the "Victory Celebration" of the Bund in Union City, New Jersey, on October 2, 1938. They prevented Bund leader Fritz Kuhn from speaking before 400 members of the German-American Business League on the occasion of Germany's annexation of the Sudetenland. The placards read "Fritz Kuhn fights the Bill of Rights" and "Freedom, not Concentration Camps." The effigy of Hitler was burned in front of the building housing the German-American Business League which was also stoned by the crowd. The Bund provoked such demonstrations. (UPI, Bettmann Newsphotos)

from telling the isolationist majority in the country that an American entry into the war was the inevitable consequence of such a definition of the national interests. To the internationalists it was of crucial importance for the economic well-being of the United States that the world's markets be kept open, that the world economy continue to function according to the principles of liberalism, and that the development of exclusive economic regions in Europe and Asia, aiming at autarky, be prevented. What was more, such a development would undermine the economic position of the United States in Latin America.

The future security of the United States could be safeguarded only by defeating the Axis powers and thus preventing the establishment of armed and aggressive empires in Europe and Asia. And the liberal democratic American system could survive only if the world outside the Western Hemisphere was not governed by Nazi and fascist principles. For the internationalists a famous phrase by Abraham Lincoln now took on a global meaning: The world could not be half free and half slave.

The national interests of the United States were seen by Roosevelt and the internationalists to be indivisible in four respects: they depended worldwide on an indivisible market, indivisible security, indivisible justice, and indivisible freedom. These national interests, it is important to remember, were postulated in the face of the challenge by the Axis powers and Japan, and they followed from an anticipation of the future. The anticipation of the consequences a possible victory by these powers would have for the economic, military, and idealistic position of the United States in the world was the decisive, true motive behind the internationalists' policy before United States entry into World War II.

The isolationist historian Charles Beard attacked President Roosevelt and the internationalists in the course of the dramatic hearing on the Lend-Lease Bill by declaring that their childish messianic complex was identical with that of the Bolshevists: both were preaching the gospel of one model for the whole world.[8] Even if we dismiss Beard's evaluation for what it was—a judgment based on personal ideological preferences rather than the result of empirical research—it cannot be denied that he did grasp the essence of the matter: the internationalists were indeed globalists.

This threefold anticipation of the future can now be examined more closely, beginning with the economic side. The military and the idealistic aspects will follow in due course.

Ever since about 1934, when the United States proclaimed its new foreign trade program, an antagonism over trade issues had developed between the United States and the aggressor nations. The latter's military victories gave this conflict a new quality which contributed to the American decision to enter the war.

With every military success by Germany, Italy, and Japan a possible economic future seemed to draw nearer that, once reality, would have meant disaster for the American economy. From the time of

Munich this negative vision entertained by Roosevelt and the internationalists began to appear in confidential memorandums regarding the isolationist temper of the time, in reports from American ambassadors abroad, and in private correspondence. After the crisis in the summer of 1940, however, such warnings were to play an ever more prominent role in public speeches, in congressional hearings, and in programmatic statements by internationally-minded associations and pressure groups. Basically, the scenario was always the same. A victory by Germany and Italy in Europe and by Japan in the Far East would force both regions under a system of planned economies close to complete autarky. The United States would lose its investments, its trade volume would decrease drastically, and foreign trade would be possible only under the conditions laid down by the Axis powers, if at all. South America, the Old World's natural supplier, would fall more and more under the influence of Hitler-dominated Europe. Because of the reduction of the American import-export industries and the secondary effects on the national economy, the unemployment problem which the New Deal had not been able to solve would come to a head, resulting in social tensions that could not be dealt with within the framework of the existing system.

In other words, the internationalists regarded the open, undivided world market as one of the basic requirements for the survival of the American system. This conclusion was only a different version of a famous statement made by President Calvin Coolidge in 1928: American investments and trade relations were such that it was almost impossible to imagine a conflict anywhere in the world that would not be harmful to American interests.

Until the beginning of Roosevelt's presidency, the American security zone consisted of the Western Hemisphere and half the Pacific Ocean—one-third of the globe. Ever since Munich and the proclamation of a "New Order" in East Asia by Japan, Roosevelt had extended the boundaries of this American security zone farther and farther until by the time of the Lend-Lease program they had taken on global dimensions. This extension was to a certain degree founded on Roosevelt's conviction that world conquest was the ultimate aim of the Axis powers, especially of Hitler, and that these plans included the United States. In April 1941, the majority of Americans shared this internationalist opinion. According to a survey, 70 percent of the population thought that Hitler wanted to control the United States, and 53 percent believed that Hitler would be able to stage a successful invasion of the United States once England had fallen and the British navy had been eliminated. The result of this assessment of the enemy's war aims was a security concept that can be characterized as "global forward defense."

Shortly after Munich, Roosevelt interpreted the situation in analogy to 1818, when the United States had been threatened by the Holy Alliance. According to notes taken by his secretary of the treasury, Henry Morgenthau, on November 14, 1938, at a cabinet meeting, "The President then pointed out that the recrudescence of German Power at Munich had completely reoriented our own international relations; that for the first time since the Holy Alliance in 1818 the United States now faced the possibility of an attack on the Atlantic side in both the Northern and Southern Hemisphere."[9]

One of the bedrocks of this reorientation was the new definition of the limits of the national security zone. For the United States to confine itself to the defense of the Western Hemisphere was regarded as suicidal; without U.S. control over the high seas, Roosevelt repeatedly pointed out, these resembled highways which the Axis powers could use at any time for an attack on the United States. The United States Navy, however, could not control the oceans on its own if the Axis powers and Japan dominated Europe and Asia and had the shipbuilding capacities of two continents at their disposal. Therefore, France, England, and China—and from mid-1941 onward the Soviet Union as well—had to be supported because they were contributing to the defense of the United States. So for military reasons, too, the United States had a vital interest in the restoration of the balance of power in Europe.

The third global factor in the determination of American national interests before Pearl Harbor was the question of idealism. With almost tiresome monotony the internationalists declared again and again that the right of all peoples to self-determination in freedom and the obligation of all states to submit to the rules of international law in their foreign policy were indivisible. These principles had to apply equally to all states all over the world without qualification. It was illegitimate to use force and aggression, or the threat thereof, to change the status quo. The Roosevelt administration had adopted without reservation the Stimson Doctrine of 1932, which stated that the United States would not recognize territorial changes brought about by force.

To Roosevelt, the oncoming conflict with the Axis powers was never simply a struggle between the "haves" among the nations of the world and the "have nots." He interpreted it as an epoch-making fight for the future shape of the world between aggressive and peaceful na-

German-Americans at a garden party in Philadelphia, 1940. The onset of the Second World War did not halt the organized social events and beer-drinking for which the Germans had always been known. While Japanese-Americans were interned shortly after the beginning of hostilities in the Pacific, German-Americans were generally spared such hardships, despite being the objects of persistent suspicion. (Historical Society of Pennsylvania)

Social club and social life, 1940. German-American women pose in updated traditional costumes with beer glass in hand in front of the "Fruit Column" constructed each year by the Cannstatter Volksfestverein in Philadelphia for the club's celebration on Labor Day weekend. (Historical Society of Pennsylvania)

tions, between liberal democracy and fascism, between Western, Christian, and humanistic civilization and barbarism, between law-abiding citizens and outlaws, between good and evil.

In conclusion, I will formulate five brief points regarding the years between 1937 and 1941 in an attempt to place this period in the long-term continuity of American foreign policy and the history of German-American relations.

First, in the period between the two world wars the United States was economically present in Europe and Asia but in military influence or alliance politics it was absent from both continents. The challenge by the Axis powers and Japan forced the United States to face the alternative either of abandoning the international system of the postwar era and retreating to "Fortress America" or entering the oncoming world war both to prevent the establishment of new orders in Europe and Asia and to secure its own position as a world power.

Second, faced with this challenge, the idealistic and economic globalism of freedom—Wilson's liberal globalism enshrined in his Fourteen Points—was supplemented in Roosevelt's thinking by a new military globalism resulting from advances in arms technology and Hitler's alleged plans for world domination. The peculiar dialectic in American world power politics—the global definition of one's own national interests in connection with the enemy's claimed bid for world domination—is not a phenomenon of the post-1945 era but can clearly be discerned in the period between 1937 and 1941.

Third, from 1938 to 1943–44 National Socialist Germany was America's world problem and enemy number one. During this period German-American relations reached their greatest intensity in the negative sense.

Fourth, from the point in the history of World War II at which the ultimate defeat of National Socialism became a certainty, Germany played an ever less prominent role in the president's and the American nation's planning for the future. To a crucial degree Germany became a function only of American policy toward the Soviet Union—at first of Roosevelt's attempts to establish a European peace order with Stalin and the Soviet Union, then, from 1946–47 onward, of the global policy of containment directed at the Soviet Union and international communism.

Finally, the dialectic of American globalism first formulated by Roosevelt in the years from 1937 to 1941 did not change in the post–World War II period. Hitler and National Socialism were merely replaced by Stalin and communism as America's world enemy number one.

Max Weber's famous verdict about the illegitimacy of value judgments in history and in the social sciences did not mean for him—nor does it mean for me—that a historian committed to such a position is personally devoid of any moral values or ethical standards. If I had been an adult and an American citizen before the United States's entry into World War II, I most probably would have agreed with the theologian Reinhold Niebuhr, who, on January 30, 1941, said when testifying before the Senate Committee on Foreign Relations:

Beyond the problem of our national interest is the larger problem of the very quality of our civilization, with its historic liberties and standards of justice, which the Nazis are sworn to destroy. No nation can be unmindful of its obligations to a civilization of which it is a part, even though no nation is able to think of these obligations in terms disassociated from its national interest. If we should define the present struggle in Europe as merely a clash between rival imperialisms, it would merely mean that a strange combination of cynicism and abstract idealism had so corrupted the common sense moral insights of a people that we could no longer distinguish between right and wrong. History never presents us with choices of pure good against pure evil. But the Nazis have achieved something which is so close to the very negation of justice that if we cannot recognize it and react to it with a decent sense of moral indignation, we would prove ourselves incapable of preserving the heritage of western culture.[10]

Notes

This essay is based on the findings of my research, published in my Habilitationsschrift *Der unteilbare Weltmarkt. Das ökonomische Interesse in der Aussenpolitik der USA 1933–1941* (Stuttgart: Klett, 1975). This book is an interpretative synthesis of unpublished primary sources, published documents, and the corpus of European and American historiography. See also Detlef Junker, "Nationalstaat und Weltmacht. Die globale Bestimmung des nationalen Interesses der USA durch die Internationalisten 1938–1941," in Oswald Hauser, ed., *Weltpolitik II, 1939–1945*, 14 lectures (Göttingen: Musterschmidt, 1975), 17–36; Detlef Junker, *Franklin D. Roosevelt. Macht und Vision. Präsident in Krisenzeiten* (Göttingen: Musterschmidt, 1979).

1. Wayne S. Cole, *Roosevelt and the Isolationists, 1932–1945* (Lincoln: University of Nebraska Press, 1983). Robert Dallek, *Franklin D. Roosevelt and American Foreign Policy, 1932–1945* (New York: Oxford University Press, 1979), also focuses on the domestic dimensions of Roosevelt's foreign policy.

2. Quoted in Geoffrey Barraclough, "History, Morals and Politics," *International Affairs* 34 (1958): 15.

3. *Congressional Record*, 77th Cong. 1st sess. February 22, 1941, 1277.

4. Cole, *Roosevelt*, 457–58.

5. *The Public Papers and Addresses of Franklin Delano Roosevelt*, comp. Samuel I. Rosenman, 13 vols., vol. 10: *The Call to Battle Stations, 1941* (New York: Random House, 1950), 181.

6. U.S. Congress, Senate, 76th Cong., 3d sess., Report 1615 (to Accompany H.R. 8026), pp. 2–3. The report was introduced with the following remarks: "The views on national defense recorded in this report which the committee considered in arriving at its conclusions and recommendations do not represent the views of any one person or group of persons. They represent composite opinions derived from one or more of the following sources: Statements made by our best informed citizens who have studied this problem, prior reports made by the committee to the Senate and data represented to the committees during the past 5 or 6 years by the most responsible naval officers and naval experts in America, including such prominent officers as Admirals Stark and Leahy, Chief and former Chief of Naval Operations; Admirals King and Cook, former Chiefs of the Bureau of Aeronautics; Admiral Laning, former president of the Naval War College; Admiral Taussig; and an outstanding national defense expert, Maj. George Fielding Eliot."

7. Cole, *Roosevelt*, 381.

8. U.S. Congress, Senate, *To Promote the Defense of the United States . . . Hearings before the Committee on Foreign Relations*, January 27–February 11, 1941, 77th Cong., 1st sess., Report 45, p. 311.

9. Morgenthau Diary, 150:340, Roosevelt Library, Hyde Park, New York.

10. U.S. Congress, Senate, *To Promote the Defense of the United States*, 170.

4.

From Confrontation to Cooperation: Germany and the United States, 1933–1949

GERHARD L. WEINBERG

OVER THE YEARS FROM 1933 TO 1949 German-American relations fluctuated more violently than before or since. The inheritance of those fluctuations is still with us today. In tracing the dramatic events of those years, I shall combine two approaches: broad interpretive generalization and specific details of recent scholarship.

From a low point in World War I, as well as at and after the peace conference, German-American relations improved steadily in the 1920s. At the beginning of the 1930s, it could safely be said that no two major powers had fewer difficulties and worked better with each other than the United States and Germany. In the United States, reaction against participation in the war, doubts about the peace settlement, hopes for the success of Germany's experiment in democracy, growing economic ties, and interest in some circles in the cultural experimentation identified with Weimar Germany made for a generally pro-German view of European affairs. In Germany, appreciation of past support for revisions of the peace settlement, hope for more of the same, and less friction than in Germany's relations with most other countries made the United States appear as a benevolent if distant associate in world affairs. This situation would change rapidly after Hitler came to power in Germany.[1]

The economic crisis in the United States kept most Americans from following the details of the last years of the Weimar Republic, a neglect that contributed to the shock produced by the widely reported, extraordinary events surrounding the advent of the new regime in Germany. The American public reacted with astonishment and indignation to the end of democratic institutions and rights in Germany, the interference with the universities, the burning of books, the attacks on the churches, and the discrimination against Jews. Although in America practice—as most knew—often fell short of ideals, the public proclamation in Germany of ideals diametrically opposed to the American ones aroused disgust and distrust. This reaction was accentuated by the conduct of Nazi organizations in the United States, the Friends of the New Germany and the German-American Volksbund, and in a way unrelated to the small size of those formations.[2] The repercussions of a movement looking to foreign political models on a country of immigrants would be hard to exaggerate.

It is, of course, true that various groups of immigrants into the United States have maintained and cherished an ethnic identity, but their motives have always been a combination of the desire to preserve their cultural heritage in a new land and continuing interest in the fate of the former homeland. No Polish-Americans, Irish-Americans, or Italian-Americans ever suggested that the political institutions of their prior home should be brought to the United States and substituted for those established in the formative years of the republic. The overwhelming majority of German-Americans fit into this well-established, practically universal pattern. The apparently excessive alarm of the American public at the antics of the Nazi Bund should, I believe, be seen as an understandable reaction to a unique development that was intuitively and correctly perceived as being novel and dangerous. And if this new movement was described in a term that came to have other connotations—"un-American"—there was in fact a muddled accuracy in that label.[3]

Two additional characteristics of the new Germany contributed to its estrangement from the United States. In both, the policies of Germany and America were moving in opposite directions. While the 1930s saw pacifism reach its greatest strength in this country in the twentieth century, Germany was in the midst of a vast rearmament program. Contrary to the German propaganda fables of the 1920s about a highly armed world, the United States like the other victors of World War I had disarmed extensively and had reduced its army voluntarily to approximately the one-hundred-thousand-man level specified for Germany. It would be years before the United States began to rearm—a point I shall return to later—but in the meantime, the rearmament of Germany—still today numbered among the alleged successes of the Third Reich—made a fatal impression on the American public. And the German propagandistic boasting about rearmament only reinforced the impression that any danger of a new war in Europe stemmed primarily from Germany.

A second alienating issue was to be found in economic policy. Those who were brought to power in this country by the election of 1932 were identified with the policy of tariff reduction in American politics, and they had fought for years against the protectionist policies of Republican opponents and their supporters in trade, industry, and finance. Among those who had long believed in the importance of freeing world trade from barriers both to preserve peace and to promote prosperity was a man whose position in the new administration would give special weight to such views: Cordell Hull, the secretary of state from 1933 to the end of 1944. Hull's role in the years when President Roosevelt was necessarily preoccupied with domestic affairs made his devotion to the cause of freeing the channels of world trade especially significant for American policy at the same time that Germany's trade policies were moving in an opposite direction. The German attempt in 1934 to pressure the United States into a new treaty by terminating the German-American Friendship and Trade Treaty of 1923 proved to be a total failure. In spite of the desperate situation during the depression, the State Department could resist all efforts at new forms of trade with Germany urged by some inside and outside the administration; the American public's view of Germany had changed too drastically. Hjalmar Schacht had made his own contribution to this process by his procedures, happily cheered on by Hitler, for defrauding American holders of German bonds in order to subsidize German foreign trade. The man who could pick out of a country with 125 million inhabitants precisely those whose funds had helped Germany so that they might be turned against the Third Reich surely deserved his reputation as a wizard.

The German government hardly reacted to the deterioration in German-American relations. Hitler had long anticipated a war against the United States as a necessary part of Germany's future, and as we now know, he initiated important preparations for such a war in the 1930s.[4] The negative reaction of the American public to the new developments in Germany—developments of which he was exceedingly proud—only showed what dolts they were. His racial views made the United States out to be a country incapable of serious effort on the international scene.[5] And his belief, shared by most of those around him, in the truth of the stab-in-the-back legend made the military role of the United States in World War I appear unimportant, a point to which I shall also return. The use of Germany's last reserves in World War II in the Ardennes offensive, the Battle of the Bulge, shows that until the end of his career, America would remain in Hitler's eyes the land of unlimited incompetence.

In Washington, on the other hand, the obvious dangers posed by Germany caused increasing alarm, even if the isolationist preferences of the population meant that no active steps were taken in the international arena. President Roosevelt was a tireless collector of information and impressions, and the materials and details he received increasingly pointed toward a new war initiated by Germany. As this danger appeared to grow in the years 1936–38, the president considered a number of nebulous projects designed to awaken the American public to the problems and to alleviate the danger through new forms of international negotiations. All of these fell by the wayside, which gave greater impetus to the one aspect of international policy that appeared capable of implementation: the efforts at revival of world trade through multilateral trade concessions and arrangements. It is in this context that one should, in my judgment, see the Tripartite Stabilization Agreement with France and England of September 25, 1936, and the Trade Agreement with England of November 17, 1938. Roosevelt sympathized in general with the attempts of the British and French governments to reconcile the new Germany by concessions in Europe and Africa to a world order unchanged in its essential nature, but he also gave what support he could to their rearmament projects against the possibility of a new war. He hoped to avert war in 1939 by altering America's neutrality legislation and by advising Stalin to align himself with the Western powers against the dangers that would be posed for all by Germany if she triumphed in the West. The American Congress, however, left the neutrality laws unamended, and Stalin—as he himself expressed it—preferred to demolish the old equilibrium in Europe with Hitler rather than maintain it against him.[6]

When the war was begun by Germany in September 1939, the American government wanted to remain neutral and hoped that assistance to the Allies would make it possible to stay out of hostilities. The minute size of the American army—in May 1940 less than a third the size of Belgium's—the almost total absence of an air force, and the fact that the navy was smaller than twenty years earlier both reflected and reinforced a strong preference for continued neutrality. The German victories in Scandinavia and in the West in the spring of 1940 brought about something like a political revolution in the United States, which has too often been overlooked by subsequent observers and scholars. Roosevelt decided to run for a third term, and Hull's predecessor as Republican secretary of state, Henry Stimson, as well as Frank Knox, the most recent Republican candidate for vice-president (in view of the refusal of the Republican candidate for President Al Landon), joined the Roosevelt cabinet—events without precedent in the history of the United States. A massive rearmament program was inaugurated, the most dramatic steps being the bill for the two-ocean navy and the country's first peacetime draft. The direct alliance with Canada created by the Ogdensburg Agreement and the sale, however reluctant, of some of the World War I equipment in American storage to Britain may be seen as the external portions of this reaction to the German triumphs of April, May, and June 1940.

How did Roosevelt see German-American relations in this world turned upside down? There has been endless argument over the issue, and I would like to suggest an interpretation strongly supported by the most recent evidence to come to light. Roosevelt hoped that aid to Britain would enable that power to survive and fight on. Convinced of the German danger to all—as he had warned Stalin—he wanted to rearm the United States, as he had once tried to help France build up its air force, against the possibility that it would be involved in war against its wishes; but he retained a strong preference for avoiding involvement in the war. Britain's success in holding out, and in the following year Russia's ability after initial disasters also to hold out, suggested the possibility that Germany could be defeated by others. Too many in this country and elsewhere have imagined that countries can only be either at peace or at war with each other. A knowledgeable Roosevelt, however, was aware that in the past, the American navy had taken its main origins from the Undeclared War with France, a limited struggle of naval engagements without general hostilities between the two former allies; and he was equally aware that Japan and the Soviet Union had in 1938 and 1939 engaged in bloody but limited hostilities at flashpoints in East Asia without becoming involved in general conflict with each other. The "shoot-on-sight" order and the incidents attendant on the flow of American supplies first to England and later to Russia have been interpreted by some as indicating a search for pretexts for war, but they can also be seen as a return to a prior American naval policy. This view is reinforced by what we now know about the way American knowledge of German naval signals in 1941, derived from the British breaking German naval codes, was put to use. Far from using this signal intelligence to arrange for a maximum number of incidents in the Atlantic, as would have been possible, the knowledge was used to minimize incidents and as far as possible avoid them altogether.[7]

This picture of Roosevelt trying to keep the United States from becoming embroiled in general war with Germany was dramatically reinforced by the recent discovery of recordings of his comments in the fall of 1940 when a recording machine was not turned off after the end of the press conference it was supposed to record.[8] Roosevelt explained to the Democratic leaders of the House that if Germany, Italy, or Japan threatened to declare war on the United States if it did not cease aiding Britain, he would reply that that was their problem; the United States would not declare war on them. They could consider themselves belligerents if they wished, but the Americans would defend themselves only if others attacked them. This view of Roosevelt's coincides with extraordinary precision with events when Hungary, Bulgaria, and Romania declared war on the United States in December of 1941: for half a year the American government, in accordance with Roosevelt's personal directives, tried unsuccessfully to persuade those countries that perhaps their people could manage without a war with the United States before finally declaring war in return on June 5, 1942.[9] A similar policy was followed—with almost the precise words used by Roosevelt on October 4, 1940—when Thailand declared war on the United States in January 1942.[10] But all such hopes would be shattered by German policy.

The German navy had been pushing for war with the United States since the fall of 1939, but at first Hitler wanted to postpone hostilities until he had been able to build the blue-water navy Germany lacked and to provide it with bases to operate against the Western Hemisphere. Work on such a navy had been started in the mid-1930s but had been interrupted by the outbreak of war in 1939. When the war seemed to be over in the summer of 1940, the work on that program was resumed, but then again had to be postponed in favor of the buildup for the attack on Russia. When that appeared to be going well in the summer of 1941, the battleship and aircraft carrier projects were again reactivated, only to have to be postponed once more because of the bitter fighting in the East. But by that time, Hitler had found a ready substitute for his own navy in that of Japan.

The German government had been trying to secure the support of Japan against the Western powers since 1938; in the summer of 1940 it became increasingly insistent that Japan join in the war against England and attack toward Singapore. When the Japanese hesitated, Hitler tried to spur them on. Recognizing that in the view of Tokyo, a move south would have to come either after the Americans had left the Philippines in 1946 or would require a war with the United States,

Hitler pressured the Japanese to move more quickly; and in early April 1941 he promised to join in war against the United States if required by Tokyo as a necessary part of an attack on Britain. If Japan joined in, there would be a blue-water navy on the Axis side right away, and the German navy was straining at the leash. Unlike all previous steps to expand the war, German moves toward war with the United States found practically no opposition within the German government. It may be unpopular to recount today, but blind ignorance, devout belief in the truth of the stab-in-the-back legend, and enthusiasm at the prospect of an open season on Americans combined to make the German official declaration of war on the United States, preceded by several days by the orders to open hostilities, the one occasion in the history of the Third Reich when the cheering of the Reichstag reflected unanimity within the government. For the second time Germany entered war with the United States so as to win more quickly an ongoing war with Britain.[11]

The tremendous victories of Japan in East Asia and of the German U-boats off the North American coast in the Atlantic in the first half of 1942 appeared to substantiate the calculations of those in Tokyo, Berlin, and Rome who had gambled on war. But contrary to the expectations of the Germans and the Japanese, the American government was not only determined to conclude the war into which the country had been forced with a total victory, but it was backed by a united public and the necessary human and material resources, even if several years might be required to mobilize them for battle. The American leadership was well aware that such a long delay carried with it the danger of a breakup in the Allied coalition and knew from bitter personal experience the discussion inside and outside the United States concerning the armistice of 1918 and the legends subsequently spread about it in Germany and therefore was firmly convinced that this time the enemies should be forced to capitulate.[12] What Germany had required of Belgium on May 27, 1940—unconditional surrender[13]—would be Germany's fate. Whatever the difficulties at the front, at home, or with the Allies, there were no substantial divergences within the United States on this issue. The picture which the Third Reich presented to the world by its hopes and ambitions left the Americans no alternatives, and what became known about German-dominated Europe in the later years of the war could only reinforce that view within the American government and public.

Expectations for the postwar world within the American government were imprecise on many points until very late in the war and

Anti-German posters of the Second World War. The importance of such posters declined with the expanded role of radio and film during the Second World War. While
the primary role of posters during the First World War was that of mobilization, their
function in the Second World War was directed more toward ideological confrontation and the encouragement of a particular kind of behavior. (Historical Society of
Pennsylvania)

fluctuated considerably. Conscious of the experience of the "secret
treaties" of World War I and of the slow unfolding of American military
power, President Roosevelt preferred to postpone decisions about such
matters as long as possible. He resisted British preference for recognizing and accepting Soviet aspirations in Eastern Europe; knowing
this reluctance, the British government without prior consultation
with the United States proposed its scheme for the zones of occupation
in Germany and joined the Russians in urging this solution on the
Americans. On only one point was Roosevelt, like Winston Churchill,
ready to commit the United States in advance to a specific position at
the forthcoming peace conference, which all then anticipated would
take place soon after the end of the war: East Prussia would never be
returned to Germany. On this point the German propaganda about the
alleged deficiencies of the peace settlement of 1919 could record one
delayed, if unanticipated, final "success."[14]

Anti-German war poster of 1942 which uses humor to sell war bonds by alluding to the activities of the Nazi Bund in America. Hitler confuses "Bond" with "Bund" and falsely concludes that Americans are supporting the latter with 10 percent of their wages. Goebbels attempts to get Goering to enlighten Hitler about the difference between the two words. (Historical Society of Pennsylvania)

American strategy in the final phase of the war in Europe was subordinated to the requirements of the war in the Pacific, which was then expected to last an additional eighteen months and which, in the months that the fighting in Europe was ending, was in its bloodiest phase. When the first important American headquarters was pulled out of the European front on May 1, 1945, for shipment to the Pacific, the Third Reich already lay in ruins. At the last minute, the British government tried to get the Americans to revise the occupation zone arrangement which they had persuaded a reluctant Roosevelt to accept a few months before, but Roosevelt's successor, Harry S. Truman, was not to be persuaded. I suspect that the internal American comments on this proposal were considerably less polite than Truman's firm refusal. The American troops withdrew or entered into the areas assigned to them by Allied agreement, and an entirely new period of German-American relations began.

The situation in which Americans and Germans faced each other at the end of the European portion of World War II was new for both. There had been an American occupation of parts of Germany after World War I, but it had differed not only geographically but, more important, in purpose and political nature. The American occupation

forces of 1918–23 were to demonstrate within their zone the contribution of the United States to the victory over Germany; they were also to
make certain that the peace treaty was accepted by Germany and then
not broken by a new war. But the United States then not only had to
deal with other occupying powers but with a German central government and an administrative apparatus more or less subordinated to it.
The situation in occupied Germany in July 1945 was entirely different.

The developments following 1945 cannot be reviewed in detail
here, but I would like to set forth some theses concerning events up to
1949. In answering the questions how Germany came to be divided for
the foreseeable future between East and West, how the three Western
zones came to be joined into one unit—a far less likely event than is
now often assumed—and how German-American relations came to
turn around once more as symbolized by the airlift, I emphasize four
aspects of the situation in those years as being decisive.

In the first place, the conceptions of Germany's future held by the
Soviets and by the Americans were diametrically opposed from the
start in one most important area. Whatever a new Germany might look
like, and whatever its borders might be, Stalin wanted to start the new
German system from the top, whereas the Americans wanted to start
from the bottom. The Soviet government flew the Ulbricht group to
Berlin before the German surrender of May 1945 and attempted to
erect a building under this roof during the following years. The major
steps and the main difficulties of this process can be understood only if
seen from such a perspective.[15] In the years between 1945 and 1948
that meant primarily the creation of the SED, the Socialist Unity Party.
Recognizing that the new roof could never be supported by the thin
walls of the German Communist party, the Soviet leadership quickly
concluded that only a forced union of the Communist and Socialist
parties combined with a ban on the formation of any other workers'
party could sustain the new construction.[16] During the period under
discussion here, this process produced the party that still today dominates the German Democratic Republic, and it also had major repercussions on the other zones of occupation. After 1949, and into the
present and indefinite future, this birthmark of the system would leave
it permanently in search of internal and external supports to hold up a
roof constantly in danger of falling in.

The Americans, operating on their political and ideological perspectives, did the exact opposite. They began at the bottom. Not always very carefully or consistently, and with much confusion and
many errors, they built, or encouraged or kicked the Germans into

building, from the local to the regional and wider levels. Those Germans who believed this policy was mistaken and complained, for example, about the delays in the licensing of political parties, would get their chance eventually. Seen from a subsequent perspective, "later" is indeed very different from "never." It has recently become fashionable, especially in West Germany, to pontificate on the alleged interference of the American occupation forces with a real reorganization of German society; what all such speculations overlook is that the extreme Right was far stronger and had a far greater support potential in post-1945 Germany and that the American occupation forces hindered the unreconstructed nationalists and Nazis far more than any other elements in the population from affecting developments in a country where great privation was much more a postwar than a wartime phenomenon as compared with World War I.[17] The development of the American zone of occupation was not only entirely different from that in the Soviet zone, but it was to be far more influential than might have been expected. This brings me to the second and third aspects of the postwar situation.

The British government had insisted that England get the northwest zone. Until late in the fall of 1944 President Roosevelt had opposed this allocation and had insisted for reasons intertwining political and transportation factors that the northwest should go to the United States. Only the united advice of his associates had finally persuaded him to accept a division according to which the Russians got the agriculture, the British the industry, and the Americans the scenery, as the allocation was described at the time. It would quickly become evident that the London government had miscalculated very badly. At a time when, as we now know, American occupation policy was greatly affected by the pressure to reduce the extent to which costs weighed on the American taxpayer, the influence of the obvious and rapid decline of British power in the postwar years was decisive for England's policy in Germany. London simply could not afford a policy of its own: the poorest of the great victors had selected for itself the zone of occupation which under the circumstances of the time was by far the most expensive. New decisions would certainly be needed.

The government of France had been the most consistent of the occupying powers in opposing any larger units or central governmental apparatus in Germany. Under the influence of the national idea—which was itself largely of French origin—and of the perceived impossibility of occupying all of Germany, the French government of 1919 had accepted the continued existence of a Germany then less than fifty years old.[18] The French would strive to avoid such a settlement in the future. It is difficult to describe with precision what future the French visualized for Germany, but it was definitely not to include any larger units or centralized institutions. In this regard the combination of French colonial wars and the real or presumed threat from Russia would lead to new decisions. The first—the colonial wars—undermined the position of France in Europe; the second pushed the French government in new directions in its German policy.

The fourth element was pressure from the East. Whether understood correctly or not, the policies of Stalin in the second half of the 1940s led to new choices in the West; and each time difficulties arose among the Western powers, Soviet action pushed them aside. The blockade of Berlin played a special role in this process. I want to emphasize that this was universally seen and understood as a highly dramatic event. On the German side—including both the people of Berlin and the simultaneously convening founders of the Federal Republic— the time had arrived when Germans themselves for the first time since 1945 played a major role in deciding significant aspects of their own fate. And at this time the daily deliveries of the airlift were not only conspicuous at three-minute intervals over Berlin but were everywhere on the radio, in the newspapers, in the newsreels, at the center of both sight and thought. Suddenly one looked on the swarms of large American and British planes in the sky with hope rather than fear. More was turning than the new radar equipment at the Berlin airports.

It was a new beginning for the American public as well. Whatever people might think about the details of American occupation policy— if they thought about the subject at all—they saw the Germans as the recently defeated enemy. This attitude changed in the year of the airlift, and we should recall that it lasted for practically a full year. A new chapter began, and not only for pilots who had perhaps once carried bombs to Berlin and now learned in Montana how to land at Tempelhof in the winter. The point which I consider decisive is that this was a development which took place in full view of the public. It would be difficult to imagine anything more likely to attract attention and influence the average American. The challenge to the technical competence of a proud people combined with the possibility of starvation and enslavement for many who had chosen the American side—no one could have dreamed up a scenario more shrewdly designed for an American audience. Who would consider it a credible plot for a movie or a novel? Only the Soviet government could conceive of such an effective way of forcing masses of people to rethink their own perceptions and preconceptions. A new state was founded in Germany, and this state would have a new relationship with the United States. Whether or not this chapter in German-American relations is now moving toward an end, I have no doubt whatever that it began over Berlin in 1948–49.

Notes

1. The subject is reviewed in detail in Gerhard L. Weinberg, *The Foreign Policy of Hitler's Germany*, 2 vols. (Chicago: University of Chicago Press, 1970, 1980), esp. vol. 1, chap. 6, and vol. 2, chap. 8.

2. A good description can be found in Sander A. Diamond, *The Nazi Movement in the United States, 1924–1941* (Ithaca: Cornell University Press, 1974).

3. What came to be known as the House Committee on Un-American Activities was originally established in March 1934 to investigate Germany's activities in the United States. See Walter Goodman, *The Committee: The Extraordinary Career of the House Committee on Un-American Activities* (New York: Farrar, Straus and Giroux, 1968).

4. A preliminary summary can be found in Jochen Thies, *Architekt der Weltherrschaft: Die "Endziele" Hitlers* (Düsseldorf: Droste, 1976), 136–48.

5. See Gerhard L. Weinberg, *World in the Balance: Behind the Scenes of World War II* (Hanover, N.H.: University Press of New England, 1981), 53–95.

6. Ibid., 7.

7. See Jürgen Rohwer, "Die USA und die Schlacht im Atlantik" in: Jürgen Rohwer and Eberhard Jäckel, eds., *Kriegswende Dezember 1941: Referate und Diskussionsbeiträge des internationalen historischen Symposiums in Stuttgart vom 17. bis 19. September 1981* (Koblenz: Bernard & Graefe, 1984), 81–103, esp. 97, 99, 101.

8. Robert J. C. Butow, "The FDR Tapes," *American Heritage* 33 (February–March 1982): 16–17.

9. U.S. State Department, *Foreign Relations of the United States, 1942*, 2: 833–42.

10. Ibid., 1:916.

11. These events are discussed in detail in my "Die Deutsche Politik gegenüber den Vereinigten Staaten im Jahr 1941," in *Kriegswende Dezember 1941*, 73–79.

12. Raymond G. O'Connor, *Diplomacy for Victory: FDR and Unconditional Surrender* (New York: Norton, 1971).

13. Franz Halder, *Kriegstagebuch*, 3 vols., ed. Hans-Adolf Jacobsen, vol. 1 (Stuttgart: Kohlhammer, 1962), 322.

14. The formal approval for turning over part of East Prussia to the Soviet Union was given by Truman at Potsdam, but Roosevelt had earlier agreed that East Prussia would not remain a part of Germany.

15. Alexander Fischer, *Sowjetische Deutschlandpolitik im Zweiten Weltkrieg, 1941–1945* (Stuttgart: Deutsche Verlags-Anstalt, 1975), 156–58, reaches the same conclusion.

16. A useful account is in Henry Krisch, *German Politics under Soviet Occupation* (New York: Columbia University Press, 1974). It must now be supplemented by Jan

Foitzik, "Kadertransfer: Der organisierte Einsatz sudetendeutscher Kommunisten in der SBZ 1945/46," *Vierteljahrshefte für Zeitgeschichte* 31 (April 1983): 308–34.

17. Hans Woller, "Zur Demokratiebereitschaft in der Provinz des amerikanischen Besatzungsgebiets," *Vierteljahrshefte für Zeitgeschichte* 31 (April 1983): 343.

18. I discussed this issue in "The Defeat of Germany in 1918 and the European Balance of Power," *Central European History* 2 (September 1969): 248–60.

5.

Production and Rehabilitation: The Economic Bases for American Sponsorship of West Germany in the Postwar Atlantic Community

CHARLES S. MAIER

WHEN INSTITUTIONS AND RELATIONSHIPS last for a generation or more, it is easy to forget that at the outset their stability may have seemed questionable. Few people viewing the ruins of Hitler's Reich in 1945 would have ventured that West Germany would become an economic superpower and the implicit keystone of the United States's alliance system in Europe. Indeed, no one could have safely wagered that the United States would commit itself to an enduring Atlantic framework. How to keep Germany from beginning another war remained the starting point for political thinking about the future—not only for the advocates of a basic transformation such as the Morgenthau Plan but also for those who approached the German problem without wishing to reorient her industrial economy. Deep into the 1950s, authoritative American spokesmen had to address continued doubts that Germany's democratic revisal was too fragile to survive the long haul. James Bryant Conant returned to Harvard to assure his listeners in the late 1950s that Germany would most likely remain stable and democratic.[1] The fact that he perceived the need to emphasize this positive outlook remains most notable for the historian.

How did a country that had been the problematic national state since the late nineteenth century—so problematic that it dragged Americans into European rivalries more deeply than any country had previously, including revolutionary France—become (at least until the last two or three years) the most unproblematic of partners? The answer that first springs to mind is the obvious one. Germany was divided by the force of circumstances, that is, by the growing antagonism between the great powers that had defeated Nazism, and had no alternative. The rump political entity in the West had to stay on good behavior and develop under the benevolent guidance of the United States. Only a united Germany might reassemble the resources to become a great power. Hence dividing Germany solved all the problems and transformed the lion, if not into a lamb, at least into a beaver.

This initial response is not wrong. Indeed, so many consequences have flowed from the division of Germany that it must be granted priority. Nonetheless, there was no guarantee that Western Germany might not turn out to be, if not a rival for power, at least a sullen and separatist unit. Nor can the vulnerability arising from division explain the key variables: democratic commitment, Atlantic cooperation, and economic success. After all, even though her unity was never placed in doubt, Japan also recovered as an economically powerful and democratic nation. We need to look at other factors as well.

I will suggest here that it was precisely the attractiveness and rewards of an American-based international system—a comity of states organized both as economies and as defense partners—that facilitated the German reorientation. If we recall the worried diagnoses of the German problem in 1950, commentators usually argued that even though institutions appeared to be developing in a healthy way, the German citizen had not been inwardly converted. Democracy was only skin deep. Part of this worry reflected the American belief in education and the need for inner convictions of citizenship, which had proved key concepts for seeking to integrate the American polity through the nineteenth century. But without joining the argument as to whether the average adult German of 1950 had been inwardly converted to democracy, I would suggest that we asked too much and what was not really necessary. As historians and witnesses alike have stressed, the American approach to denazification was an ambiguous success at best.[2] It seemed willful, harsher on the little man than on more well-connected perpetrators (without even touching on such disgraceful cases as Klaus Barbie), and ill-designed to secure genuine democratization. But did this really matter in the long run? What was important was that the United States constructed an international network in which West Germany found a rewarding role and that West German participation in this network foreclosed nondemocratic or hostile internal development. International inducements made it rational for West Germans to become democratic, just as when Spain chose to join Europe in the late 1970s that option buttressed democratic development at home. Individual democratic commitment may not, after all, be the key to a society's democratic stability. An international structure that rewards democratic compliance may be more critical, at least for a generation or so. This is not to claim that Germans today are not democratic but that their civic convictions followed more slowly than their institutional adaptation. (The *Spiegel* affair of 1962 and the passage of power to the modernized Sozialdemokratische Partei Deutschlands (SPD) in 1969 seem to provide surer indicators of the more active democratic commitment that the United States had sought to inculcate earlier. The former revealed a sense of public rejection of the government's high-handed procedure; the latter demonstrated that the all-important transition from a ruling party to an opposition could be undertaken without endangering basic institutions.)

Part of the international structure that helped to anchor democracy within West Germany was a political and defense network. Gerhard Weinberg's chapter in this volume suggests that the Berlin airlift was decisive in making that structure credible and visible. But the other component of the international framework was economic, and that is the specific theme of this essay. The overarching economic system that the Americans erected and that included a major role for the West Germans—even before their own postwar takeoff had occurred—was also crucial to the political anchoring of the new society. Nor do I mean only to suggest that it is easier to be democratic on a full stomach. Rather, economic institutions in effect served as political ones for postwar Germany; her economic recovery and production within the emerging Atlantic economy proved a surrogate for citizenship. In his post-1945 reflections, Friedrich Meinecke deplored that *Homo Faber* (Man the Producer) had displaced the man of cultured civic participation.[3] But in fact under postwar conditions *Homo Faber* was man the citizen. Even if the role lacked dimensions of cosmopolitan culture, it still served to organize a democratic state. Production and integration within a transnational network of production and exchange were the paths to democratic rehabilitation.

This result should not be surprising. If Germany were to become democratic, if it were to cast aside the models that had been thrust upon it during the previous dozen years and look to how the Americans and British ran their commonwealths, it was natural that economic productivity should seem a major component of the civic package. After all, Germans and Americans shared, perhaps more than any other two nations, an economic vigor and fascination with technology. Americans had attended German universities to absorb mathematics and science and the seminar or institute model for organizing higher learning. (Indeed, American historians today have just begun to emphasize the derivation of the Progressive-era gospel of national efficiency and civic management from the models of local German government at the turn of the century. In the very years that the Japanese were borrowing, alas, the national constitutional institutions of the Second Reich, reformist American economists and political leaders were bringing back local government institutions, bureaucratic welfarism, and the evangelical social concern of the Verein für Sozialpolitik. Academic rigor was part of the overall doctrine of expertise that Americans brought back. This expertise might serve elitist politics and the battle against the urban Irish-dominated machines; it could also serve Progressives who wanted to ameliorate the social consequences of unbridled plutocratic capitalism.)

In return Germans brought back American lessons in how to spread the fruits of technology. Physics and mathematics might emanate from Göttingen and Berlin (and the Cavendish Laboratories in Cambridge), but electric lighting and the assembly line started on the other shore. Businessmen, engineers, social scientists, and trade unions reported on these developments and often recommended their application within Germany. Thus there was a shared fascination with applying science and technology, with pushing ahead industrial development quickly, with getting things done. Mutual enthusiasm for engineering subsisted underneath the divergent political courses of the two countries. It could be reinvoked after World War II, as it was, for instance, in the productivity missions of the 1950s.

A further reason lay behind the political efficacy of economic arrangements. Germans had to rebuild their state from the economy up, so to speak, during the occupation period. The Federal Republic originated in the institutions of the Bizone in which Germans gained democratic experience by debating the merits of a planned or market economy in the Economic Council, which served as a proto-parliament. Although this assembly faced strict limits on what it might discuss and even stricter ones on what it might decide, it was not the first time that Germans had tested the waters for politics by wading first into forums for economic policy making. The Zollverein had served as a forerunner of Prussian-German alignment, and between 1867 and 1870 Bismarck had attempted to exploit the Zollparlament as an institutional path toward unifying the South German states with the North German Confederation. Economic deliberation was then to be an opening wedge for political institution-building, as it was to be after the defeat of 1945 left Germany without a sovereign state. Obviously the Allies reserved veto rights over the initiatives of the Wirtschaftsrat des Vereinigten Wirtschaftsgebietes. Nonetheless, debates were spirited, and although the key issue of rearmament was left to the future Bonn Republic and the issues of federalism and parliamentary reconstruction were left to the constituent bodies, the major choices of political economy were vigorously debated in the Wirtschaftsrat.[4]

A further reason why economic councils might serve as proto-political legislatures was that much of modern German political life had not transcended economic debate. Politics was often political economy. In Bismarck's empire "rye and iron" and the tariff issue had been major points of political orientation. In the Weimar Republic, the reduction of politics to political economy seemed even more pervasive, and the Reichstag was criticized for becoming an arena for contending special interests, especially those of heavy industry and big labor. Both the socialist Left and the authoritarian Right criticized the eclipse of a genuine state standing above economic society. In part the success of the Nazis might be seen as a search for a political master that desperate individuals could turn to over and against the organized interests. For most domestic issues, economic choices summed up political ones.

The United States also shared some of this primacy of economics. To resort to an imperfect cliché, Americans did not have a state in the sense that Germans or Frenchmen understood the state. The United States periodically saw its politics crystallize around a crusade against economic monopoly. Every generation a reformist coalition would emerge to halt the political encroachment of the banks, the trusts, or the "malefactors of great wealth." These crusades won some partial reforms but tended to dissipate and endorse a compromise concept of enhanced production that could reconcile the adversaries. Fighting for power, the antibusiness Left in America usually settled for efficiency, as had happened during World War II, when Roosevelt switched from Dr. New Deal to Dr. Win-the-War and business leaders recently castigated as economic royalists came back as dollar-a-year men to coordinate the massive production effort. In a nation, where as President Coolidge once said, the business of America was business, the concept of the political sphere was limited. To be sure, just as the Germans had developed a powerful tradition of public bureaucracy, so the United States had made political parties a major instrument of governance. Nonetheless, in the public importance given to economic issues and capitalist organization, Germany and the United States remained akin.

The experience of both countries allowed economic development to serve as the surrogate for, and eventually the opening wedge of, political reconstruction.

Americans entered defeated Germany with some basic ideas about the relationship of German economic organization to German politics. None of the other occupying powers put so much effort into individual rehabilitation and educational formation. Nonetheless, only the proper economic organization might reinforce on a societal level the democracy that would, it was hoped, be inculcated on the individual level. Three or four strands of thinking about the proper reconstruction of the German economy can be distinguished among American policy makers. The first, of course, was that incorporated in the Morgenthau Plan, which, because of the personal closeness of the treasury secretary to the president, became enshrined briefly as public policy in 1944. Morgenthau envisaged the reduction of Germany as an industrial power; when skeptics asked not only how the country would feed itself but how the previous economic interchanges of Europe might be reconstructed without Germany's industrial output, Morgenthau's Treasury Department argued that the Ruhr and other centers of German industrial potential were not essential for the wider European economy. They denied any interdependence.[5] Roosevelt himself, always susceptible to the last emphatic recommendation he encountered, was already backing away from this draconian vision after he saw the force of Churchill's opposition at the Second Quebec Conference. The president, however, died without asserting a clear alternative, and the pastiche method of putting together American position papers assured that some of Morgenthau's objectives would remain in JCS 1067, the major guideline for occupation policy.[6]

A second mode of thinking was essentially German-derived: that of the social-democratic exiles, whose analysis influenced the Office of Strategic Services and preparations for civil administration. Franz Neumann's influential book *Behemoth*, published first in 1942, familiarized knowledgeable Americans with a quasi-Marxian analysis of Weimar's defects and the socioeconomic sources of Nazi power. It fit in well with the American Left's preoccupation with concentrated economic power. (At the height of Roosevelt's antimonopoly concerns in 1938, the president had stated that fascism rested on concentrated private economic power; the analysis also appeared in such scholarly interpretations as Robert Brady's *Spirit and Structure of German Fascism.*[7]) These studies provided a rationale for emphasizing the importance of socialist and trade-union leaders in German postwar reconstruction. The analysis of private industrial power allowed sophisticated commentators and officials to switch their focus from a simplistic condemnation of Prussian militarism as the source of Nazi brutality. It suggested that a reconstructed republic might function satisfactorily if the social bases of right-wing politics were removed by land reform, some socialization or public control of heavy industry as in the Ruhr, and the restoration of powerful trade unions. Naturally, this view also motivated the concepts of the Labour party for reconstruction of the British zone with its concentrations of coal and steel production, even if British occupation authorities on the scene were more conservative.

These concepts of structural socioeconomic reform related to the third American strand of thinking—that of the vigorous antitrusters—much as the First New Deal related to the Second New Deal. By the antitrusters, I refer to those who from the Antitrust Division of the Justice Department, which was reinvigorated by Thurman Arnold in 1938, migrated to the Deconcentration and Decartelization Element of the American and later the Bipartite Economic Division of the occupation authorities. In effect Germany provided these officials with an arena for continuing the trust-busting policy revived in 1938 by the Temporary National Economic Committee but then quashed by the priorities of wartime production and coordination in the United States. Suppressed in Washington, the antitrust offensive might continue in Frankfurt, where the Nazi government, so the analysis went, had rested on concentrated economic power. But for a mixture of personal and bureaucratic reasons, this crusade quickly ended. Its acerbic advocates—whether Bernard Bernstein, a major advocate of Morgenthau's ideas, or the lawyers such as Alexander Sachs and others dismissed in 1948–49, or James Stuart Martin, who left a polemical defense of their approach—were eased out of Germany after 1947 once Lucius Clay's deputy, William Draper, took effective control of economic policy.[8]

Draper, who came from the investment house of Dillon-Reed, represented the fourth strand. He and Clay and the secretary of the army, Kenneth Royall, did not disavow the analysis that connected cartels with Nazism. They sincerely believed it. Indeed, they tended to see decartelization as a remedy that might preclude socialism, which they saw as somewhat akin to Nazism. Their interpretation of what constituted monopoly, however, reflected the antitrust controversies at home. If the committed antitrusters (the third strand) viewed a firm's domination of the market as justifying decartelization and deconcentration, the post-1947 occupation officials—reflecting in turn the

Truman administration's more conservative consensus on economic policy—defined monopoly in terms of abusive results. Bigness alone was not an offense, according to the "rule of reason" that American courts had come to apply in limiting domestic antitrust proceedings. The result in Germany was that although officials continued to voice theoretical approval of vigorous deconcentration, the agency entrusted with carrying it out ended up focusing primarily on the linoleum trust—hardly a strategic industry for Germany's war machine and one that in 1949 was producing only at 3 percent of its prewar output. To be sure, deconcentration was the watchword in three key sectors: I. G. Farben was broken up, to be succeeded by the four major chemical firms of today; banks were reconstructed; and the steel industry was reorganized. Nonetheless, the new units formed in these sectors retained substantial continuity with the older ones.

In retrospect these limited results should not have been surprising. The antimonopoly crusade in the United States had usually yielded similar insubstantial results, for trust-busting had prevailingly served as an ideological alternative to public ownership. Why should it have provided a radical transformation of capitalism in Germany when its impact had been limited at home? Moreover, given the test of time, Draper, Royall, and others seem to have been correct when they suggested that large-scale industry in itself was not a sufficient cause of fascism. To safeguard German democracy it was probably more fruitful to pursue what John Kenneth Galbraith a decade later would term "countervailing power": in effect, the safeguarding of pluralist rivalry.

Looking back at these disputes within the spectrum of American occupation concepts, it seems that what was at stake was as much the end of the New Deal as the future of Germany. The losers of 1947–48 were the homeless Left of the Democratic party: on the one hand, the sympathizers of the Popular Front who still yearned for cooperation with the heroic Soviet Union and now campaigned feebly in the *Nation* or the Committee against World War III; on the other hand, the more southern- and western-oriented populist antitrust Left that had lost its battles first within the Justice Department and then in the military government. What succeeded was that fusion of partial reform and restored faith in business and production which the war had revived and Truman's Fair Deal attempted to balance with reformist social advances at home.[9] The West German political economy, in effect, would emerge as one of the triumphs of the Truman compromise.

The struggles over German economic organization and the defeat of socialist alternatives helped encourage a positive assessment of Germany's productive capacity. So too did the rush of events toward the Cold War. By the end of 1947 a revived level-of-industry ceiling on German economic revival (allowing for 1936 levels of production rather than those of 1932) suggested that the United States and Britain badly wanted the Germans to produce as much as they could.[10] The controversies within the military government led to the ouster of those who feared that industrial concentration was likely to revive fascism. The American announcement of the Marshall Plan and the response to the multiple economic and political crises of 1947–48 established that German economic recovery would count in American eyes as a positive step toward national rehabilitation. Germany was entrusted with a positive mission of production. In its wake would come the country's recovery of sovereignty and its rehabilitation.

Announcement of the Marshall Plan was triggered, in the short run, by the European economic setbacks of late 1946 and early 1947 and by the failure of the Moscow Conference to restore four-power cooperation in administration of Germany. The Marshall Plan was innovative in its idea of taking Western Europe as a unit and assigning Western Germany a role within that unit. Once German economic potential was envisaged as a contribution to a broader region, the restrictions on the country's capacity to produce seemed self-defeating. Of course, such criticism of occupation policy as Herbert Hoover's report of spring 1947 may have spurred such a change in policy faster than otherwise. But the logic of the change was clear in any case. Germany's coal mines and her highly skilled, industrious workers could labor on behalf of the West as a whole. Coal was the critical material of 1947, the basis for industrial recovery. If German miners could be adequately fed and housed, provided with pit props and calories, they could produce for their own economic recovery and that of their neighbors. When Secretary of Commerce Averell Harriman traveled to Germany in the summer of 1947, he listened to mine workers and managers, heard older trade unionists reaffirm their commitment to the idea of production, and cautioned that strikes, no matter how desperate the condition of the miners, would create a bad impression in the United States. As Secretary George C. Marshall, chairman of the Senate Foreign Relations Committee, Thomas Connally, and other influential Americans insisted, the German economy was at the heart of Europe and hence central to the Continent's recovery. The requisites of production could legitimately overrule French concerns about German recovery or British desires for a socialist reorganization of the coal and steel industries. Like victory in wartime, economic recovery in a period of scarcity appeared to Americans as a self-evident priority that displaced lesser political considerations.

It was clear to all observers that monetary reform was the prerequisite for establishing recovery on firm ground. Once the German population anticipated monetary reform, moreover, it was all the more necessary because in the waiting period, goods were withdrawn from the market. But monetary reform was also the ticket of admission to the American-sponsored international economy. The administration of the European Recovery Program demanded the maximum satisfaction of European economic needs first within a European system of exchange: Germans could hardly participate in that revived network on the basis of cigarettes as a reserve currency. At the same time currency reform was the most tangible act of West German reunification. It proceeded apace with the early 1948 London Conference that in turn led to talks on establishing a West German government, and it helped provoke the Soviets' blockade of Berlin after June.

Once the Germans understood that production was now a Western priority, they lost no time in appealing to the rationale of a common effort to reverse remaining Allied plans for the dismantling of factories or the deconcentration of industry. Workers, managers, and local officials led a chorus for years demanding that such decisions be suspended or reversed. By 1950 the Thyssen works were justifying expansion of their rolling facilities at Hamborn as the contribution of good Europeans.[11] At the same time, Konrad Adenauer understood that the issue of production must lead to political concessions and rehabilitation. Once the Schuman Plan was broached in May 1950, he insisted that the particularist fears of German firms about French competition must not stand in the way of negotiating agreement on the Coal-Steel Community. For steel industry managers new political concepts justified demands for economic modernization and expansion. For Adenauer economic potential allowed Germany to pursue its quest for sovereignty.

American officials were enthusiastic about Jean Monnet and Robert Schuman's initiative to merge the coal and steel industries of the two countries under a common regulatory agency. Harmonious relations between Monnet and John J. McCloy, the American high commissioner, helped nurture the concept. Conversely, Washington was disappointed in British reluctance to approve the idea and in London's dog-in-the-manger efforts to offer less far-reaching alternatives. Nonetheless, London's embarrassment at the French initiative ultimately accelerated the process of German national rehabilitation. For if British policy makers were reluctant to accept the Schuman Plan, they proposed in compensation quicker political recovery of rights and quicker relaxation of political controls, that is, quick inclusion in NATO and less insistence on democratic orientation than even Washington thought proper.[12]

If productivity was the watchword of 1947–48, integration was that of 1950. But integration—whether military or economic by means of the Schuman Plan and the emerging European Payments Union— depended on Germany's economic capacity. As Dean Acheson frankly stated, "No useful distinction can be drawn between controls over internal affairs and those over external affairs and trade. What we want Germany to do is to entangle herself and integrate herself with [the] West."[13] But if France was willing after May 1950 to let the Germans revive their industry it still remained leery about a German army. Britain was willing to revive an army but was anxious about German industry. The United States urged steps toward both. The upshot was the multiple-track negotiations of late 1950, 1951, and 1952 that yielded the Coal-Steel Community and the European Defense Community. The economic agreement became the foundation of today's European Common Market. The military agreement proved too ambitious to survive. But as a counterpart Germany secured an end to the state of war by virtue of the Contractual Agreements of 1951–52. These settled the overhanging foreign debt issues and permitted the young Bonn republic to establish a Foreign Office and, in effect, recover limited sovereignty.

In effect the Western Allies were buying more of an insurance policy for the future than a powerful partner at the moment. Only by the fall of 1950 did German steel capacity finally begin to press against the level-of-industry constraints. Germany continued to absorb more goods from other countries than she exported; indeed, the first major episode in the life of the European Payments Union (EPU) was a crisis that required German imports to be funded through emergency loans. As of 1950 German production remained more one of potential than of actuality. This does not mean that Western policy was not prescient, but it leads us to ask who gained what in the exchange.

The Germans won political valorization of their economic potential. Holding out the promise of great productive capacity, they could trade their potential for piecemeal political rehabilitation after they appeared utterly disgraced and defeated. And they got more than political accreditation. They won continuing economic subsidies and investments deep into 1950: first relief and GARIOA funds, which were actually larger than Economic Cooperation Administration (ECA) commitments, than Marshall Plan payments, and finally an EPU transfusion. In return, they provided the assurance that they would not remain a drain on the British and Americans forever and, more important, the security that they would not turn to the East. Doubtless, too, German recovery contributed to every European nation's prosperity, for a depression-ridden Germany would have inhibited growth elsewhere. In this sense, the failure of economic recovery that might have accompanied German isolation would have been far more costly to her partners than the subsidies they had to provide. The situation was not unlike that of the 1920s, when Germany absorbed more funds from abroad, especially American investments, than she paid in reparations. Nonetheless, then, too, the West had been far better off subsidizing German economic health than fretting about the balance of direct flows.

In effect, West Germany resumed in 1950 the orientation that Stresemann had worked to secure in the 1920s. Perhaps it was easier for Adenauer than for Stresemann to impose this course, for there were fewer alternatives. Under Stresemann a powerful nationalist alternative course did exist, whereas under Adenauer the nationalist alternative would mean a feeble effort to tack between East and West. Both statesmen understood the importance of reconciliation with France and of forging a connection with the United States. Reconciliation with Paris meant overcoming the political vetoes to German participation in a Western concert. Forging a connection with Washington brought Germany the economic support needed to fulfill the obligations to the other European countries, including France. Over the long run, American aid to Adenauer's Germany was more predictable and steady than the private investment assistance that was mobilized between 1924 and 1929. The United States proved more willing to act as a responsible great power, with continuing obligations toward Western Europe, after the second war than after the first.

In both cases acting as a responsible great power meant investing in the future prosperity of Germany. Examining the German-American relationship of the 1950s reveals both the German role and the American architecture of leadership. Washington's primacy in a Western international system rested upon American economic resources and not just military power. If the Soviet Union exploited its military preponderance in part to transfer resources from its bloc to its own society, the United States secured its allies' loyalties by providing the capital for their economic reconstruction. More specifically, the United States

finally took up the task of funding Europe's balance-of-payments deficit either by covering Germany's reparation payments to Britain and
France, as after 1924, or by replacing reparation transfers after World
War II with Marshall Plan aid. American policy and welfare required
closing the cycle of payments and trade that drained Europe by rein-
fusing Europe and especially Germany with direct grants. This is not
to argue that it was not ultimately in American self-interest to make
the investment. Still, it demanded a farsighted concept of self-interest
to balance future rewards against present demands. From 1947 on,
once the Morgenthau concept of a Europe without an industrial Germany was shelved, Americans advanced the concept of a Europe with
Germany as the major industrial partner. The Marshall Plan was designed to move Europe to that plateau of economic exchange. By the
late 1950s West Germany could even begin to play the role of the major continental military power within the North Atlantic Treaty.

For postwar Western Germany the influence of the United States
obviously became fundamental, as military protector, economic inves-
tor, and ideological model. Each of these roles made possible the other
two. Obviously, without the bedrock of military security, the 50 million
West Germans would not have rested content and relatively unani-
mously within the ambit of American cultural influence. They would
not so easily have imported the model of a relatively pluralist and mer-
itocratic society, although the destruction of their older hierarchies left
them little choice. They would not have believed that they were importing American models of industrial relations with their less confrontational style. But the economic content of the relationship was
fundamental in the postwar years because German political institutions had been devastated. Production promised a surrogate for politics at a point when West Germany was not entrusted with politics.
Indeed, the American model was attractive because Germans felt
Americans had substituted economic rationality and administration
for many of the areas that still seemed to be governed in the Old World
by political ideology. These included class relationships, allocation of
material welfare, and power in the workplace. Social science theories
of modernization and of conflict-free industrial relations were generated in postwar America but adopted by Germans to describe the new
basis for their postwar society.

Were there scope in this essay, one could provide an ironic intellectual history showing how the reigning social science theories imported from America in turn depended upon a partial and selective
reading of German concepts of modernization from a prior generation;

how, to cite two figures, Talcott Parsons took Max Weber but adopted only the portions that stressed rationalization and deemphasized the darker Weberian tonalities of political domination and constraint. In a sense it was Max Weber "sunny side up" that was reimported back into Germany in the 1950s to provide models of a society in which economic optimality displaced political irrationalism and charismatic appeal.

If, as I believe, the shared West German and American concepts of a postwar world led by the United States with Germany playing the role of chief European industrial producer rested on a certain economic reductionism, then it was natural that the collaboration must ultimately be sensed as less satisfying than it was originally. For the flagging of economic success in the 1970s and the decline of United States investment in Western Europe coupled with extraction of more European resources with an overvalued dollar were bound to call into question the beneficial nature of the relationship. At that point, too, Germans would recollect the resonances of their national existence that they had suppressed in the 1950s, such as the seductiveness of cultural appeals to nonmaterial values, the role of landscape and environment, the return of a search in politics for satisfactions of community and wholeness, and the awareness of a wider and a deeper Germany. Germany now stands again at the crossroads of political conceptions, weighing the calculable benefits of the West, of prosperity, and of a functioning republic against the uncertain allure of a more inclusive but potentially disastrous political wager.

Because this essay originated as part of a commemoration of German-American connections, I will close with a personal recollection. My first direct exposure to Germany was my visit as an American high school student of sixteen to a family in Bonn in the summer of 1955. In a sense I arrived just as the country was leaving the first postwar decade that both Günter Grass and Rainer Werner Fassbinder have evoked so mordantly. It is Germany as producer that I know firsthand. But it is a Germany that responded to more romantic and sometimes more brutal yearnings that I know from my historical studies. I am no longer so certain as I was that these appeals can no longer evoke a response. And although for a child of the 1950s this possibility is somewhat frightening, it must be even more frightening for a German who senses the emotional and material bases of his national existence begin to shift. Nonetheless, students of Germany should contemplate this alternative future. For the task of the coming generation, insofar as German-American relations are concerned, may be to preserve understanding in an era when economic success no longer suffices as the basis of the two countries' relationship and when contending political visions once again become autonomous and compelling.

Notes

1. James Bryant Conant, *Germany and Freedom: A Personal Appraisal* (Cambridge, Mass.: Harvard University Press, 1958).

2. Lutz Niethammer, *Die Mitläuferfabrik. Entnazifierung am Beispiel Bayern* (Berlin: J. H. W. Dietz, 1982); John Gimbel, *A German Community under American Occupation: Marburg, 1945–1952* (Stanford: Stanford University Press, 1961).

3. Friedrich Meinecke, *The German Catastrophe* (Boston: Beacon Press, 1963), 38.

4. These debates, available in the Koblenz Bundesarchiv, Aktenbestand Z/3, have now been published, at least in part. See Walter Vogel, Christoph Weisz, et al., eds., *Akten zur Vorgeschichte der Bundesrepublik Deutschland, 1945–1949*, 5 vols. (Munich: Bundesarchiv and Institut für Zeitgeschichte, 1976–).

5. See U.S. Treasury Memorandum, "Is European Prosperity Dependent upon German Industry?" September 7, 1944, in Harry Dexter White Papers, Box 7, F. 22e, Mudd Library, Princeton University; and for the struggle over Morgenthau's ideas, John Morton Blum, *From the Morgenthau Diaries: Years of War, 1941–1945* (Boston: Houghton Mifflin, 1967), 323–47.

6. John Gimbel, *The American Occupation of Germany: Politics and the Military, 1945–1949* (Stanford: Stanford University Press, 1968), 1–22; Paul Y. Hammond, "Directives for the Occupation of Germany: The Washington Controversy," in Harold Stein, ed., *American Civil-Military Decisions* (Birmingham, Ala.: University of Alabama Press, 1963), 311–464.

7. Franz Neumann, *Behemoth: The Structure and Practice of National Socialism* (New York: Oxford University Press, 1942; rev. ed., 1944); Robert A. Brady, *The Spirit and Structure of German Fascism* (New York: Viking Press, 1937).

8. On the antitrust background, see Ellis Hawley, *The New Deal and the Problem of Monopoly* (Princeton: Princeton University Press, 1966), 420–71; James Stewart Martin, *All Honorable Men* (Boston: Little, Brown, 1950). The materials for the Sachs case and the shake-out of the Decartelization Element are in the National Archives: Record Group 200, Johnston Avery Papers, and Record Group 335, Ferguson Committee Records.

9. For the contending currents of the Truman administration, see Alonzo L. Hamby, *Beyond the New Deal: Harry S. Truman and American Liberalism* (New York: Columbia University Press, 1973).

10. For the level-of-industry dispute see the reports in U.S. Department of State, *Foreign Relations of the United States*, 1947, 2:983–1067.

11. See "Vorschlag . . . der August-Thyssen-Hütte," February 9, 1950, in Akten des Verwaltungsamtes für Eisen und Stahl, Z 41/23, Bundesarchiv, Koblenz.

12. See the Byroade Memorandum, May 6, 1950, in U.S. Department of State, *Foreign Relations of the United States*, 1950, 3:933–34.

13. Acheson telegram, May 12, 1950, ibid., 1046.

6.
From Nazism to NATOism: The West German Miracle According to Henry Luce

JOST HERMAND

IN THE YEARS 1943 to 1945, as it became increasingly evident that the Allies would vanquish the Axis powers, the question of Germany's fate after the war became an urgent one. Although the governments of the United States, England, and the USSR were at one in their antifascism, they were thoroughly at odds on the German question because their starting points were different. A final decision on this question was therefore postponed from one conference to the next. Yet it was not only among the three Allies that grave differences of opinion existed regarding Germany's future; there was anything but consensus on this point even within the United States. At the risk of generalizing, we can distinguish three basic attitudes toward Germany that had existed since 1941: first, a hard line based on the necessity of punishment that sought to eliminate Germany's military might so that it would never again launch a world war; second, a middle line that likewise called for punitive measures but simultaneously envisioned reassimilating Germany within the community of peace-loving nations after a long process of reeducation; and third, a soft line demanding the immediate political and economic bolstering of Germany to transform that country into a "bulwark against communism" as rapidly as possible.

The supporters of the hard line were a highly mixed group of understandably embittered Jews, old Germanophobes from the era of World War I, and a consortium of industrialists who wanted to wipe out Germany permanently as a competitor on the world market. Because of its diverse composition, this hard-line bloc perforce made highly varied proposals in editorials and essays. These proposals ranged from dividing Germany into several states, dismantling all factories, and redistributing land, as suggested, for example, in Louis Nizer's *What to Do with Germany?* (1944),[1] to harsher schemes for the forced resettlement, genetic reprogramming, or sterilization of all Germans so as to strike the word "German" from the page of history for all time.[2] And as the opinion polls from the time show, a majority of the American population firmly backed this hard line—as it had in World War I.

It is scarcely surprising that the U.S. government largely supported the then popular hard line, especially since 1944 was an election year. Franklin Delano Roosevelt already mistrusted the Germans—this "monstrous nation," as he put it[3]—and in 1943 and 1944, he spoke out in favor of a hard peace. Yet punishing Germany seemed to FDR a concern of the European nations, not of the Americans, who were supposed to withdraw from Europe after the war and to strive for a global order of peace within the framework of the United Nations.[4] Roosevelt's views were seconded by his trusted aide, Bernard Baruch, who considered Germany much more dangerous than the USSR and favored massive economic aid to Russia. Sumner Welles, Roosevelt's undersecretary of state, took up the hard-line cause just as vigorously, and in his 1944 book, *Time for Decision*, wrote in favor of dividing Germany, weakening its heavy industry, liquidating the Prussian general staff, and ceding parts of its eastern territories to Poland.[5]

All of these proposals first became well known through the so-called Morgenthau Plan. Henry Morgenthau, Roosevelt's secretary of the treasury, had mistrusted Germany ever since World War I and since the mid-1930s had considered it the United States's chief foe. Morgenthau, FDR asserted, was "the man I admired and loved second only to my father."[6] As early as 1943, Morgenthau and his undersecretary, Harry Dexter White, had written a *Program to Prevent Germany from Starting World War III*, in which they, like Sumner Welles and Lord Vansittart, advocated dividing Germany, reducing its industrial capacity, resettling large parts of the German work force in neighboring countries, internationalizing the Ruhr region, and introducing strict French, Polish, and Russian supervision of a "pastoralized" Germany.[7] Such proposals were by no means considered extreme or bizarre. "Morgenthau's desire for a strong Russia as an alternative to an aggressive Germany," wrote the American historian John L. Snell at a later date, "was shared by a vast number of non-Communists in the year 1944."[8] This approach was termed the "Carthaginian peace settlement"—and many politicians believed that Germany deserved nothing less after unleashing two world wars. In any case, this hard line was considered at that time the liberal one, indeed that of the left, and was backed not just by Roosevelt, Morgenthau, and White but also by politicians such as Henry A. Wallace and James F. Byrnes.

To be sure, adherents of the middle line existed even within Roosevelt's cabinet during those years, and they openly declared their opposition to such drastic measures. They, too, favored severely punishing Germany, but they firmly rejected both the ideas of dividing Germany and of completely dismantling German industry. Instead, they held that Germany could surely be reintegrated into the circle of peaceful nations after a period of international supervision, democratic reeducation, and the selection of new political leaders—among whom the name of Konrad Adenauer emerged as early as September 1944.[9] The secretary of war, Henry Stimson, and his undersecretary, John J. McCloy, were the chief advocates of this approach, for although they considered the Germans aggressive by nature, they believed they deserved one more chance after the war. The same line was advocated by Secretary of State Cordell Hull and by James P. Warburg in the Office of War Information, who likewise placed their trust in a thoroughgoing catharsis, out of which a "different, better Germany" would arise.[10] At the behest of this middle-line group, Roosevelt dismissed his undersecretary of state, Sumner Welles, and replaced him with Edward R. Stettinius. As chairman of the Post-War Programs Committee, Stettinius issued a position paper in August 1944 that opposed the division of Germany, advocated only a limited supervision of the German economy, and foresaw an "eventual reabsorption of Germany into the world economy" after a brief period of reparations payments.

The activity of this middle-line group put Roosevelt in a difficult position in the fall of 1944. Although he was personally more inclined to the Morgenthau-White-Welles line and was interested in the continued development of relations with the Soviet Union, the critical editorials that appeared in the U.S. press when the Morgenthau Plan became known vividly demonstrated the strength of the circles pushing for a restoration of free trade with Germany and a concomitant anti-Soviet line. Roosevelt therefore chose his tactics on this point somewhat more cautiously during the weeks preceding his reelection in November of 1944. Although Roosevelt continued to cling to the collective guilt thesis and declared that "the German people as a whole must have it driven home to them that the whole nation has been engaged in a lawless conspiracy against the decencies of modern civilization," he also professed during the campaign that he did not intend "to enslave the German people" or "to harm the common people of the Axis nations."[11] Indeed, in December 1944 he even declared that after the war Germany should be allowed "to come back industrially to meet her own needs."[12] FDR never failed to add, however, that the Germans would have to earn their return "into the fellowship of peaceloving and law-abiding nations" through arduous effort.[13] On the whole, then, Roosevelt held to a middle line between Morgenthau and Stettinius, who was appointed secretary of state on December 1, 1944, to replace the seriously ill Cordell Hull. FDR maintained this line until his death on April 12, 1945. Indeed, this remained the official position of the Democratic party and of the new president, Harry S. Truman, long after the Potsdam Accords, that is, until the beginning of 1946.

The third approach to Germany, the soft or right-wing line, was at first represented primarily by the spokesmen of the Republican party. These circles, who still ideologically backed Herbert Hoover, had resisted not only U.S. diplomatic recognition of the Soviet Union, Roosevelt's New Deal, and the wartime partnership with the USSR in the struggle against Nazi Germany, but also all other evils of the "Red Decade." Indeed, voices had been repeatedly raised on the far Right in favor either of isolationism or of forming an alliance with the Nazis against the Soviet Union. They regarded the New Deal era and World War II as a mere Democratic interlude, to be followed after the end of hostilities by a return to normalcy, namely an antagonistic relationship with the Soviet Union. Apart from a few important men on Wall Street, the chief representatives of this course include John Foster Dulles and Republican Senator Arthur H. Vandenberg, who had campaigned against Roosevelt in 1941 as a strict isolationist,[14] but who started passing himself off as a "realist" beginning in 1943–44 and who dismissed any talk of future world peace guaranteed by the United Nations as naive claptrap.

Following Roosevelt's death and the victorious conclusion of the war, the United States emerged as the leading world power because of the immense growth of its economic and military potential as well as the collapse of the British Empire and widespread destruction in Europe. Under these circumstances, right-wing circles naturally enjoyed a boost and unleashed a media campaign against the USSR and communism that contributed to the victory of the Republicans in the 1946 congressional elections. From this time on, the so-called Cold War was virtually unavoidable. Even President Truman, who had always identified with the "realists," openly advocated this course after 1946. Most members of his cabinet, such as Dean Acheson, Robert Lovett, George

C. Marshall, and James F. Byrnes, did the same. But naturally it was the Republicans who were most prominent in this anticommunist backlash, including such congressmen as Richard M. Nixon and senators such as Joseph McCarthy, whose most important soapbox in this increasingly virulent witchhunt was the House Un-American Activities Committee. All this led—as is well known—to the Truman Doctrine, to the policy of containment, to active support of Greece and Turkey against the Reds, to the Korean War, and finally to the Republican electoral victory in 1952 under General Dwight D. Eisenhower. In the course of these years, many right-wing political commentators deplored more and more openly the error of Roosevelt and Morgenthau in making too many concessions to the Russians at Teheran and Yalta.[15]

For Germany, these Cold War trends quickly led to the integration first of the three Western zones and later of the Federal Republic into the Western economic and military alliance system. This policy would have been unthinkable under Roosevelt, but it enjoyed wholehearted support from businessmen and military leaders who had either always taken an anticommunist stance or were now being urged in that direction. A 1947 pamphlet entitled *American Policy toward Germany* for example, stated that 89 percent of the leading U.S. businessmen favored a "rapid development of German industry"[16] because West German competition on the world market ultimately seemed a lesser evil than the strengthening of communism. Thus by 1947 the first hints had begun to appear of a power constellation that Eisenhower was to label the "military-industrial complex" in the late 1950s, cautioning the nation to be on its guard. But just how are the powerless supposed to protect themselves from the powerful? Let us leave this question unanswered and concentrate on the political paradigm shift of the immediate postwar period, that is, on the ideological maneuvers by which the good Russians were transformed into the evil Russians and the bad Germans into the benign Germans with the aim of getting the overall global situation back on the right track after its derailment by Nazi aggression and the topsy-turvy alliance between the United States and the USSR. How was it that an overwhelming majority of the U.S. populace favored the Morgenthau Plan in 1944 and a few years later dismissed it scornfully and suddenly advocated the exact opposite, indeed was prepared to go to war for these new-found convictions? What machinations within the mass media did this shift require?

Clearly, these are all highly complex and contradictory processes. To avoid further generalizations, I have singled out within the scope of this development one figure, albeit a highly influential one: the media czar Henry Luce (1898–1967), who became editor and publisher of *Time* in 1923 and whose strictly Republican and anticommunist em-' pire also included *Life, Fortune,* and *Sports Illustrated.* From early on, Luce was one of the most forthright representatives of the "free enterprise interests against communism" in the United States, and consequently he despised the Democrats, above all Roosevelt. As early as 1944 editorials in his journals attempted to counteract opinion poll results showing that 81 percent of Americans agreed that "the United States should work with Russia as equal partners in the coming peace." Luce was therefore highly critical of the outcome of the Teheran and Yalta conferences; indeed, he seldom missed an opportunity to rail against the "godless" Russians.[17] To broaden his political influence, he bought 12.5 percent of the National Broadcasting Corporation's Blue Network in 1944. With this purchase he was able to spread his outlook not just through magazines but also through more than one hundred radio stations, thus reaching more than one-third of all adult Americans every week with the gospel of Americanism according to Luce. His chief slogan was "I am biased in favor of God, the Republican party, and free enterprise." Luce pinned his political hopes above all on the elite of big businessmen, whom he regarded as America's aristocracy. But this ideology was most powerfully expressed in his 1941 essay *The American Century,* in which he contrasted his form of "liberalism" with the conservative isolationism still adhered to by many Republicans at that time. This interventionist Republicanism extended far beyond America's borders and aimed at granting to the entire world the blessings of the American free enterprise system. Luce called upon his party "to develop a vital philosophy and program for America's initiative and activity as a world power," and he countered "isolationism" with a "truly American internationalism." "It is our century," he exulted. "It is ours not only in the sense that we happen to live in it but ours also because it is America's first century as a dominant power in the world."[18]

Unswerving in his perception of the Soviet Union as the chief adversary of the American dream, Luce emerged in 1945 as one of the most influential opinion makers in what was first termed the "Cold War" in 1946. To this end, he supported any and all politicians who advocated a rigidly anticommunist line, be it General Douglas MacArthur, Chiang Kai-shek, Winston Churchill, Francis Cardinal Spellman, or the Shah of Iran. Luce and his friends regarded the Roosevelt era as a regrettable interlude during which American policy had gone seriously off course because of its alliance with the Russians. Indeed, even Truman and Byrnes were "too soft on communism" for these circles. They generally draped a moral or religious cloak over the plainly political orientation of their "new course," dressing their desire for global hegemony in the guise of a crusade. In his essay "Christianity and War," Luce in 1948 scored the pacifism of several church leaders, arguing that it could only contribute to Europe's falling to communism.

Luce stuck to this militant line throughout the 1950s. Again and again he drummed into his readership: "We must win, and the sooner the better," as in his 1960 essay, "National Purpose and Cold War." Indeed, he stressed that to achieve the goal of victory over the Soviet Union, even "the great foreseeable risk of total war" might be necessary.[19]

The strength of this Cold War strategy warrants a closer look at the reporting on Germany that appeared in *Time* and *Life*, beginning with Germany's collapse in May 1945 and continuing up to the year 1955, when the Federal Republic achieved sovereignty, a status that Luce had favored and worked as hard as anyone to achieve.

Shortly after the end of the war, the Luce press regretted the mistakes of Yalta and Potsdam, that is, American assent to the decartelization and partial dismantling of Germany's heavy industry, and demanded instead rapid reconstruction in the service of U.S. interests in Europe. Rather than advocating a new ordering of German relationships, as had been foreseen in the Potsdam Accords, *Time* and *Life* flatly favored a restoration of previous conditions. Protracted reeducation and transformation measures seemed to be mere obstacles along this path. Speaking of vanquished Nazi Germany, Luce laconically remarked in 1945: "Take drastic measures to destroy the Nazi government and system. Kill a number of people. Heavily penalize a number of more people. This job ought to be completed in a very few months."[20] He did not regard these tasks as very important. What was truly important, according to Luce, was developing Germany as quickly as possible into a bridgehead of U.S. interests in Western Europe, that is, the establishment of a bulwark against communism.

What, then, do we read in *Time* and *Life* about Germany in the fall of 1945? On August 13, the Potsdam Accords received a relatively brief report in *Time*. Apart from the necessary facts, the article primarily emphasizes what it terms Russia's "intention to dominate Eastern Europe." On the same day, *Life* published a short human interest story about the illegitimate children at the SS "Lebensborn" Institute Hohenhorst, and then, two weeks later, a somewhat longer photo report on the Krupps. In it *Life* portrays Alfried Krupp as one of the chief war criminals, claiming: "The Krupp family is, at least as much as Adolf Hitler, responsible for the casualties of Allied soldiers in World War II. With other German industrialists they first made Hitler and then made his guns." But these truths are not followed by further-reaching consequences. On December 10, *Time/Life* coverage of the Nuremberg trials is just as superficial and expressly absolves "the Germans" of any collective guilt so as to keep open the possibility of a rapid reconciliation with this nation in the near future. Thus it is consistent that in its issue of July 16, 1945, *Time* had already attacked Lord Vansittart's book *Bones of Contention*, which portrays the Germans as "savage" by nature and as collectively guilty, and which threatens them with a Carthaginian peace, that is, a division and deindustrialization of their territory. Predictably, *Time* rapped Henry Morgenthau's book *Germany Is Our Problem* on October 15, dismissing its advocacy of a "hard peace" as mere "rhetoric," indeed as a "tautology."

The Luce press spoke more plainly yet in the year 1946, when it embraced the Cold-War line wholeheartedly. *Life* attacked the Morgenthau Plan again on January 28, citing the division of Europe into Eastern and Western zones as evidence in support of this criticism, while challenging the U.S. government to contribute to the economic bolstering of the three West German occupation zones. The same demand "to make Germany economically strong" was repeated in the July 23 issue of *Life*. On September 16, *Time* reported on James F. Byrnes's speech in Stuttgart after the abortive foreign ministers' conference in Paris in which he urged the West Germans to get involved in the Cold War on the side of the "Western democracies" and promised them the possibility of "running their own affairs." Byrnes's pronouncement was hailed by *Time* as "bold," indeed "America's boldest move yet toward leadership of the world." Byrnes offered such assurances as "German industry will be restored" and "We will not shirk our duty. We are not withdrawing," positions which were sharply criticized by the Poles and the French but which Luce found to be "American" in the best sense. On October 21, *Life* printed a sweeping attack on "unscrupulous Soviet tyranny" in Eastern Europe by the American theologian Reinhold Niebuhr, who—citing Byrnes's speech and dripping with sarcasm against pinkos like Henry Wallace—demanded the immediate economic integration of the three Western occupation zones into the free economy of the Atlantic nations to halt Russian expansionism. Indeed, on December 9, 1946, Luce followed up in *Life* with a longer photo report that showed how the best "Nazi brains"—such men as Wernher von Braun, Alexander Nippisch, Anselm Franz, and Theodor Knacke—were helping the United States with the construction of airplanes and rockets.

In 1947, the Luce press continued to describe the "revival of German industry" as the most pressing problem of future American foreign policy, stated in *Life* on January 13. The February 10 issue of *Life* featured a long cover story entitled "US Occupation of Germany," in which we read: "Germany should be given an opportunity to rebuild peacetime trade under democratic self government." Apart from "industrial recovery," German reunification, including the return of territory occupied by Poland, was emphasized as the second chief aim of U.S. foreign policy. On December 15, after the breakdown of the foreign ministers' conference in London, *Life* demanded that all concessions made to the Russians at Yalta and Teheran be rescinded. *Life* summarized the outcome of the London Conference in blunt language: "The fact is that an old war ended and a new one began." Thus *Life* recommended a new strategy that would finally put an end to punitive measures such as dismantling, reparations, and what it termed the "overemphasis on denazification," all of which smacked of the Morgenthau Plan. This new strategy would entail developing West Germany into a bulwark of anticommunism. According to *Life*, the Russians had failed in their first attempt to "steal Europe." But such an expansionist system was not easily stopped. "Later, no doubt, they will try again," *Life* wrote at the time.[21] And precisely in Germany that attempt would have to be countered with a policy of strength.

The Cold War mentality was even more aggressively evident in the Luce press in 1948, when the Western Allies carried out a separate currency reform in their zones and the Soviets responded with the Berlin blockade, making the prospect of a third world war ever more threatening. "Aggressive firmness," according to the July 12 issue of *Life*, "is the only way to peace." What the Luce press had in mind when it spoke of "aggressive firmness" is revealed in the demand for a "West European federation that is capable of extension to the east." Reinhold Niebuhr's contribution to the German question appeared in *Life* on September 20 with the intentionally provocative title "For Peace, We Must Risk War." In all these articles, the sole aggressor responsible for all danger was the USSR, as was made clear again in the October 4 issue of *Life*. The American position, on the other hand, was presented as uniquely justified morally and religiously. Thus in the elections of 1948, *Life* supported not only Thomas E. Dewey but also John Foster Dulles, Dewey's choice for secretary of state, because

Dulles, as a lawyer for cartels, possessed sufficient experience in Germany, was a pious Christian, and would certainly advocate strengthening the West German economy.[22]

In 1949, in the course of preparations for the founding of a separate Western state on German territory, the Luce press from the outset backed the conservative-Christian group around Adenauer while seeking to discredit all other political groups in West Germany as dangers to U.S. foreign policy. Not only the West German communists under Max Reimann were categorized as political opponents but also the Social Democrats under Kurt Schumacher, who according to the April 4 issue of *Time* was seeking to pave the way for national bolshevism. The Luce press was relieved when the Christian Democratic Union (CDU) emerged as victor in the elections for the first Bundestag on August 14. In an interview with Adenauer published two weeks later in *Life*, this victory was portrayed as a triumph of the "free enterprise system" over socialism, indeed as a decision of the West Germans "for the Christian world of the West." Adenauer, the very model of a "free enterprise Christian" according to *Life*, was quoted: "Germany's industrial power is still considerable. It should be integrated with that of the Western world and linked with the great industrial centers in the U.S." *Life*'s response, of course, was "Amen." On December 5, *Time* published a story on Adenauer entitled "A Good European." Thanks to him, we read here, Germany had regained its proper place among the "free nations." In Adenauer's view, the article states, much "decency" was still to be found in Germany despite the period of fascism, so that "something good" could doubtless be made of "the Germans." And *Time* fully agreed, although—as it restrictively added—"the Germans have never shown any talent for democracy." Thus Adenauer was called upon to turn those authoritarian Germans into good democrats by leading them with a strong hand into the "Christian world of the West," a task totally beyond the abilities of the "sardonic and fierce" Schumacher and his "Socialists" (who are termed "Social Democrats" only in exceptional instances). And in a striking anticipation of future developments, Luce in 1949 demanded rearmament of Germany as quickly as possible because an unarmed Germany was certainly to fall into the clutches of the communists. The same notions appear in the December 12 issue of *Life*, which states the issue even more bluntly: "Rearmament will come: The (only) question is when." Germany is no longer the main danger, we read here, but the USSR. Therefore, any "double-talk" on the matter, as was customary with the Democrats, must finally cease.

The Luce press pounded home the same points in the following year. On February 13, 1950, *Time* hailed the Stuttgart speech of U.S. High Commissioner John J. McCloy, who announced a policy shift returning confiscated factories to their original owners. McCloy stated, and *Time* agreed, that not the German people but Hitler was guilty of the crimes of the Third Reich. On May 15, *Life* praised West Berlin Mayor Ernst Reuter's brave struggle against the Eastern threat. Toward the end of that year, *Life* also published a longer report, entitled "West Sector Shows Brave Gaiety," about the first signs of a new lust for life in West Berlin.[23]

On March 26, 1951, *Life* contrasted the growing prosperity in West Germany with the terrible conditions in the part of Germany behind the Iron Curtain. On July 16, *Life* reported in particular detail on General Eisenhower's NATO mission in Europe, which it termed "a colossal task not merely of physical reconstruction or military rearmament but primarily of moral and psychological regeneration," indeed "a historic enterprise without parallel." On August 6, *Time* wrote in praise of Adenauer and Ludwig Erhard for their reconstruction achievements: "The 'German danger' today is not that the Germans will dominate or desert the West. The danger is rather that the Germans will not be put into the position to do their proper share for the West." By "proper share," *Time* naturally meant rearmament, which was now finally due. To make this step easier for the West Germans, *Time* quoted Eisenhower, who publicly declared that "the German soldier [had] never lost his honor." The same rehabilitation of the military underlies a report in the October 8 issue of *Life* about a reunion in Iserlohn of the former Afrikakorps. Perversely, *Time* on December 3 termed Schumacher's objection to rearmament a "violent stand." *Time* claimed that it was obvious that the Germans would side with Adenauer on the rearmament issue. "The Germans are not rebels by nature," the same article states, "by long standing they respect effective authority." That may be true. But whether this authoritarianism aided the cause of democracy in Germany is another story.

In 1952, the Luce press reported almost exclusively on the growing prosperity in West Germany. In a feature article entitled "The Germans on Our Side," which appeared on July 9, *Life* presented "Postwar Germany" principally as what it termed "a businessman's country." The reporter meant these words as the highest praise. The pressures of the election campaign in 1953 led to many stories on the Federal Republic in the Luce press. On March 30, *Life* commended Adenauer for forcing through the Bundestag his rearmament proposal in spite of what

Life termed "communist rioters." On April 20, *Life* was able to report on Adenauer's first visit to the United States, during which he met such figures as Eisenhower, Dulles, Cardinal Spellman, Nixon, and even a group of midwestern businessmen. On August 10, *Time* and *Life* once again supported the plan for rearming West Germany. Indeed, on August 31, *Time* published a lengthy cover story on Adenauer supporting his reelection, which was equated with a flat "no" to communism. Here once again the Luce press championed a strikingly authoritarian vision of democracy. Ultimately, Adenauer was mainly portrayed as the man with the strong hand. "He seems to tower above them," the magazine wrote of his relationship to the Germans, "not to be argued with, only to be obeyed." *Time* lavished special praise on Adenauer's conviction that "Christianity is the answer to all ideologies." In contrast, *Time* ridiculed his Social Democratic opponent as "tubby little Erich Ollenhauer." On September 10, *Life* presented Adenauer once again as the only conceivable chancellor for Germany, most of all because he stood firmly for rearmament, "knowing that only an armed Germany could put muscle into the European Defense Community." Indeed, the September 14 issue of *Time* quoted Dulles—who had just cautioned that the defeat of Adenauer would be "disastrous" for Germany—and went on to report on Adenauer's reelection. *Life* celebrated Adenauer's victory on September 21 under the title "New Leadership in Europe." Thanks to him, it wrote, Germany had become "the most stable country in Europe." Here was a man who knew what he wanted. He was a "father whose word is the law in his own house." Thus on January 4, 1954, Adenauer appeared on the cover of *Time* as its "Man of the Year," hailed as a "firm-handed democrat" who had led Germany back into the circle of "great powers." His electoral victory, we read here, was "the West's biggest cold-war success of 1953."

And with that, the advocates of what I described at the outset as the "rightist" course had finally achieved their goal. Germany had been successfully transformed into a mighty industrial state, a trustworthy alliance partner, a sturdy bulwark against communism. On May 10, 1954, *Life* published a special issue entitled "Germany: A Giant Awakening," in which the Federal Republic was portrayed as "hopeful" and "healthy" by virtue of its trust in both God and the free enterprise system. The sole concern that continued to trouble the Luce press was wondering how quickly the idea of a new army could be put into practice. Anyone who objected to this concept remained a subversive, a leftist, as can be seen in a *Time* story dated December 6,

1954. When the Social Democrats once again opened a parliamentary debate on the new Bundeswehr in early 1955, they were attacked in the February 24 issue of *Time* as "reckless," indeed as "doctrinairly Marxist." There were especially vehement attacks on Herbert Wehner, whom *Time* called the "evil eminence on the left." By contrast, *Life* had nothing but praise for General Adolf Heusinger, whom it portrayed as the ideal "new-model boss" for the West German army. But the Luce press was fully mollified only when West Germany was admitted into the North Atlantic Treaty Organization (NATO) in the spring of 1955, finally making the Federal Republic a "full partner of the West," as *Time* wrote on May 16.

So much for the reporting of the Luce press on the immediate postwar period and the first six years of the Federal Republic. Admittedly, many grotesqueries can be attributed to journalistic exaggeration, without which such magazines—dependent on sensational news coverage despite their "objectivity"—probably could not hold their own against the competition. Yet when reading through such magazines, it is disconcerting to find how, over and over again, not just profits are being made but also opinions that lead to those profits. To influence opinion, any critical, liberal, or leftist voices were excluded from such publications—or were dismissed as utopian, unrealistic, crackpot, communistic, or simply absurd. And in the case of *Time* and *Life*, these were all the American and West German critics of the dominant Cold-War mentality, who were squelched by the era's conservatives as oddballs, godless commies, or misguided fellow travelers. The American critics of the Cold War, let us recall, included such honorable people as the Democratic senators Claude Pepper of Florida and Glen Taylor of Idaho, the Democratic presidential candidate Adlai Stevenson, the journalist Walter Lippmann, and many others such as W. E. B. DuBois, Freda Kirchwey, David Dellinger, and Grenville Clark, all of whom firmly believed that "reconciliation with the Soviet Union was possible without sacrificing the national interest.[24] The cold warriors, on the other hand, advocated a "Get Tough with Russia" policy that proceeded from the concept of containment ultimately to liberation and massive retaliation.[25] In West Germany, too, critics of the Cold War were not just marginal gadflies or communists, but primarily honorable antifascists, Social Democrats, members of the Confessing Church, and labor leaders who had spent part or all of the Third Reich in exile, in prisons, penal brigades, and concentration camps, and most of whom were not particularly friendly to the communists—we need only think of Martin Niemöller, Kurt Schumacher, Erich Ollenhauer, Gustav Heinemann, or Willy Brandt.

By rejecting any concept of neutrality, the Luce press failed to serve the cause of true internationalism, namely, a policy of peace based on understanding among nations. Indeed, in view of the special problems of West Germany one must add that Luce publications performed a distinct disservice to the concept of a democracy based on pluralism, contradiction, and differences of opinion. They recommended that the West Germans strengthen the country's industry and rearm as quickly as possible. And as the best guarantor of such a policy, they supported Adenauer with his iron hand, inflexible rigidity, and lonely decisions—as if the Germans had not already encountered precisely such authority figures who, time and again, had blocked their path to democracy.

Notes

I would like to thank Jim Jones for the translation.

1. Louis Nizer, *What to Do with Germany?* (Chicago: Ziff-Davis, 1944), 55–109.
2. See John L. Snell, *Wartime Origins of the East-West Dilemma over Germany* (New Orleans: Pauser Press, 1959), 8–13.
3. Ibid., 31.
4. Cf. Bruce Kuklick, *American Policy and the Division of Germany: The Clash with Russia over Reparations* (Ithaca: Cornell University Press, 1972), passim.
5. See John H. Backer, *The Decision to Divide Germany: American Foreign Policy in Transition* (Durham: Duke University Press, 1978), 23–24.
6. Snell, *Wartime Origins*, 65.
7. See Backer, *Decision to Divide Germany*, 25–27.
8. Snell, *Wartime Origins*, 82.
9. See ibid., 11.
10. See Hans W. Gatzke, *Germany and the United States: A "Special Relationship?"* (Cambridge, Mass.: Harvard University Press, 1980), 146–47.
11. Snell, *Wartime Origins*, 74, 19.
12. Gatzke, *Germany and the United States*, 148.
13. Snell, *Wartime Origins*, 102.
14. See Roger Morgan, *The United States and West Germany: A Study in Alliance Politics* (London: Oxford University Press, 1974), 13.
15. See the examples in George Shaw Wheeler, *Who Split Germany?* (Berlin: Verlag Tribüne, 1962).
16. See Joseph Barker, ed., *American Policy toward Germany: A Report of the Views of Community Leaders in Twenty-Two Cities* (New York: Council on Foreign Relations, 1947).
17. William A. Swanberg, *Luce and His Empire* (New York: Scribner, 1972), 209, 211.

18. John K. Jessup, ed., *The Ideas of Henry Luce* (New York: Atheneum, 1969), 7, 113, 115.

19. Ibid., 132.

20. Swanberg, *Luce and His Empire*, 239.

21. *Life*, January 13, 1947.

22. See *Life*, October 4, 1948.

23. *Life*, December 4, 1950.

24. Thomas C. Paterson, ed., *Cold War Critics: Alternatives to American Foreign Policy in the Truman Years* (Chicago: Quadrangle Books, 1971), 4.

25. See Hugh Ross, *The Cold War: Containment and Its Critics* (Chicago: Rand McNally, 1963), 2–4.

PART II:

The State of the Alliance: An Assessment in 1983

7.
German-American Relations in the Postwar Decades

WOLFRAM F. HANRIEDER

IT WOULD BE IMPOSSIBLE and therefore pretentious to offer, in a few pages, more than tentative reflections on a subject as broad and complex as the nature of German-American relations during the last three and a half decades. The subject is especially intractable because German-American relations not only ranged over a wide spectrum of concerns—political, economic, military-strategic—but were also connected, for both parties, with other bilateral and multilateral foreign policy issues: East-West relations, the global and regional military balances, the question of German unity, the political and economic dimensions of the European order, and the nature of the global economic and monetary regimes, to mention just a few. Although the centrality of German-American relations is unquestioned, certainly for the Federal Republic, this issue nonetheless needs to be placed in the larger context of the global and European-regional political order.[1]

The Formative Phase: The First Decade

A central feature—perhaps a paradox—of Allied and especially American policies toward the Federal Republic in the early 1950s was the intention to make the West Germans free and, at the same time, not free. The Germans were to be made free with respect to the personal liberties and constitutional safeguards that are the essence of a democratic political order; but they were not intended to be free with respect to formulating and implementing an independent foreign policy. In its early years, the Federal Republic had neither the power nor the legitimacy to conduct its own foreign policy. When the Federal Republic was created in 1949, it was not a sovereign state (this did not come about until 1955, when the Federal Republic joined NATO, and even then was hedged with restrictions); and the Allied High Commission, which succeeded the military governors of the occupation regime, for all practical purposes controlled the Federal Republic's political and economic relations with other countries and also had the power to regulate, or at least supervise, domestic political, and economic developments. The German government had only limited and provisional authority over domestic and foreign policy. Its first, and indispensable, foreign policy aim was therefore to obtain the right to conduct foreign policy.

Although the Western powers, and especially the United States, were ready to make political and economic concessions in return for West Germany's willingness to rearm, these concessions did not allow Bonn to pursue an independent foreign policy because the diplomatic-political, economic, and military instruments of policy were securely embedded within the structures of the Western alliance. In the Bonn Conventions (1952) and Paris Agreements (1954), Bonn traded rearmament for the restoration of legal sovereignty and the Western commitment to support the reunification of Germany and to recognize the Bonn government as the only legitimate spokesman for all of Germany. But the elements of legal sovereignty that were being restored to the Federal Republic were immediately frozen in the international organizations Germany joined. When this happened—as in the Organization for European Economic Cooperation, the European Payments Union, NATO, the Western European Union, and the European Coal and Steel Community—the primary benefit for Bonn was a gain of equality rather than independence.

The restraint of the Federal Republic through international organizations and contractual commitments was of course the result of conscious policy, for double containment was at the core of Washington's postwar European policy: the containment of the Soviet Union, at arm's length; and the containment of Germany, with an embrace. Every major event in the postwar history of Europe follows from this policy: the rearmament and economic reconstruction of the Federal Republic within the restraints of international organizations; the development of NATO from a loosely organized mutual assistance pact into an integrated military alliance; American support for West European integration; and the solidification of the division of Germany and Europe. So long as the two components of America's double-containment policy were mutually reinforcing, America's European diplomacy was on a sure footing; in later years, when tensions and contradictions developed between the two components, German-American relations became increasingly strained—a subject that shall concern us at a later point.

From the perspective of the German government, and especially of Chancellor Konrad Adenauer, "diluting" gains of sovereignty by joining integrative organizations was intrinsically unobjectionable. His sense of priorities inclined him in the same direction. Adenauer's version of the goal of political recovery—the integration of the Federal Republic in a tightly knit Western European community—could be achieved even with the curtailing of Germany's freedom of action, so long as it brought gains of equality. In fact, it would have been much more difficult for Bonn to extract concessions from the Western powers if the restored elements of sovereignty had not been subject to international surveillance. The creation of integrative West European and Atlantic structures thus had a decisive influence on the speedy political and economic recovery of West Germany. They provided mechanisms for controlling Germany, and they made the restoration of sovereignty less risky for the Western powers, especially France. In turn, the mounting pressures to grant West Germany political and economic concessions provided a powerful impetus for establishing integrative structures that could supervise the Federal Republic. In this two-way interaction, Adenauer's Europe-oriented policy was an essential precondition for successful political and economic recovery. The pursuit of the goal of security—implemented as it was by close alignment with the West and the decision to rearm—thus not only was compatible with the goal of political recovery but was its prerequisite. The quest for security and the aim of political recovery, with the meaning attached to recovery by Adenauer, were mutually reinforcing.

The Social Democratic opposition's cutting characterization of Adenauer as "the chancellor of the Allies" was therefore impertinent (in both senses of the word), for what was involved was not complicity between the German and Allied governments at the expense of German interests, but rather Adenauer's assent to a course of Western diplomatic action that he favored himself. For him choice coincided with necessity. America's double-containment policy was complemented by German self-containment: Adenauer, who was deeply skeptical about the political maturity and circumspection of his compatriots, was determined to tie them to the West and thus prevent his successors from following a seesaw policy between East and West or—perhaps a better metaphor—from carrying water on both shoulders. Moreover, the pro-

Western course the German government charted could count on the political assent and electoral support of the Federal Republic's citizens, in large part because Adenauer's policies promised rapid progress toward economic reconstruction and political rehabilitation. Although rearmament was not popular it was widely, and correctly, perceived as the cornerstone of Adenauer's Western policy that enabled the Federal Republic to gain immediate economic and political benefits. Indeed, economic and political recovery were themselves highly complementary. A weak West German economy would have been a liability for the Western alliance, undermining political stability and opening up opportunities for Soviet maneuvers. Because of the integrative features of the Western alliance, the faltering economy of one alliance partner would have weakend the bloc, with negative consequences for military preparedness. The tensions of the Cold War created an atmosphere in the West that was generally in sympathy with German aspirations to restore a viable economy.

The achievement of economic recovery was skillfully complemented and underpinned by Bonn's policy on political recovery and, by extension, its policy on security and rearmament. In such mixed political-economic ventures as the Schuman Plan (and later the European Economic Community [EEC]), political and economic gains went hand in hand with and were achieved through a coordinated strategy that advanced German demands in the name of European and Atlantic unity rather than that of a discredited German nationalism. The German government's determination to liberalize domestic and international trade was in the long run advantageous politically as well as economically because it underlined Bonn's commitment to political internationalism. By foregoing traditional protectionism, Bonn rejected the economic corollary to political nationalism, a policy strongly pushed by Washington. In sum, the Federal Republic's foreign policy goals of security-rearmament, political recovery, and economic recovery were interdependent, complementary, and mutually reinforcing—as was clearly reflected in the interlocking provisions of the Paris Agreements.

As a consequence, there existed during the 1950s, in the formative stage of the Federal Republic's development, a striking correspondence between the principles of Germany's domestic economic order and those of the international economic order guided by the United States and supplemented by the institutions of West European integration. The German penchant for low inflation rates, budgetary discipline, and trade liberalization was reciprocated in the United

Konrad Adenauer as *Time*'s "Man of the Year" in 1953. The fact that *Time* chose the Chancellor of the four-year-old Federal Republic for this honor was generally viewed as being indicative of a new attitude in the United States toward the defeated enemy of 1945. The only previous German accorded this honor was Adolf Hitler in 1938, who was followed by Josef Stalin in 1939. *Time* dated the return of Germany to international politics from 1953. Because of Adenauer's conservative leadership and uncompromisingly Western sympathies, the magazine noted, Germany once again assumed a place among the great powers. (Reprinted by permission from TIME.)

States; the Bretton Woods monetary regime came to full implementation in the late 1950s with the free convertibility of currencies, ushering in a period of equilibrium between past dollar shortages and future dollar gluts; and such ventures as the Schuman Plan and the EEC yielded Germany political as well as economic gains. In addition, Washington's and Bonn's attitudes on how to contain the Soviet Union, as well as the personality traits of German and American leaders, were more congenial than at any time thereafter.

In subtle but fundamental ways, these developments assured the solidification of the American sphere of influence in Western and central Europe and thus assured as well the viability of Washington's double-containment policy. The West Germans, in contrast to their East German compatriots, became persuaded that their superpower protector showed them the way toward political, economic, and perhaps even moral rehabilitation. Military victories are always harsh on the vanquished. But the American military victory over Germany at the end of World War II was soon followed by a more gentle and leisurely conquest, accomplished by economic inducements, political prodding, and diplomatic persuasion. It is not necessary to speculate about the precise mix of purposes that motivated American diplomacy—altruistic considerations, enlightened self-interest, hegemonic aspirations, or the determination to enlist the Germans as allies against the Soviet Union—the fact remains that in those years the foundations were laid for a remarkably stable German-American relationship that was to obtain, in both countries, a solid measure of bipartisan domestic political support. The infiltration of Western Europe by the transatlantic imperial power, accomplished through the benevolent and irresistible invasions of the American economy and way of life, established for the United States a sphere of influence every bit as pervasive as the one that the Red Army secured for the Soviet Union in Eastern Europe. To put it in even starker terms, by 1955, America's policy of double containment had succeeded in both its Soviet and German aspects. The Soviet Union had become contained within the political and geographical limits of influence it had gained at the end of the war, and the Federal Republic had become securely emplaced in the Western alliance system.

Given the principles of a democratic order that prevailed in the Federal Republic and the opportunities they afforded for the expression of political preferences in free elections, the incorporation of the Federal Republic in the Western alliance took place in political and moral circumstances that were fundamentally different from those in which the German Democratic Republic became part of the Eastern bloc of socialist countries. But in terms of *Realpolitik*, the consequences of integrating the two German states in their respective Cold War alliances were similar and mutually reinforcing: the division of Germany, and hence of Europe, became a major stabilizing element in the global contest between the United States and the Soviet Union, which neither side was ready to question fundamentally lest the regional and global balances of power be upset.

Chancellor Adenauer was fully aware of these realities, and his long-range reunification policy for Germany was based on two central assumptions: that Washington and Moscow held the key to the German question and that with the passage of time the balance of power between the two Cold War blocs would shift in favor of the West, thus allowing negotiations "on the basis of strength," which would induce the Soviet Union to settle the German question on terms acceptable to the West. The first of these assumptions was correct, the second, false; but given the limits of Federal Republic's influence, German diplomacy could in any case only hope to deal with the ramifications of the first.

From the first assumption it followed that Bonn would need political leverage within the Western alliance in order to gain the support of the Western powers, especially the United States, for the cause of German reunification and to ensure that the West would not trade off the German issue in an overall settlement of the Cold War. Adenauer realized that the Western powers viewed the prospect of a unified Germany with apprehension. Thus Bonn's unification policy required increasing German influence within the Western alliance so as to solidify on the political plane the legal and moral commitment of the Western powers to support reunification and acknowledge the Bonn government as the only legitimate spokesman for all of Germany. Yet the only way that Bonn could increase its leverage within the Western alliance was by becoming an indispensable partner in it. This partnership was, however, directed against the Soviet Union and thus ill-suited for inducing the Kremlin to settle the German question on terms acceptable to the West. As a consequence, Adenauer's Moscow-oriented reunification policy was much more passive and negative than his Washington-oriented policy—merely an appendage to his Western policy, formalistic and unimaginative. It was in essence a policy of denial, couched in legal terms, through which Bonn refused to recognize the German Democratic Republic and the Oder-Neisse line—in short, the existing state of affairs in central and Eastern Europe.

Both Cold War camps considered it politic to give at least verbal support to German aspirations for reunification. But neither the United States nor the Soviet Union wanted a unified Germany that would be genuinely free to conduct its external affairs because that would upset the balance of power in Europe, with adverse effects on the cohesion of either Cold War alliance. Securing the allegiance and power potential of the part of Germany that each Cold War camp already controlled promised a substantial increase of strength for each side. After failing to prevent West Germany's membership in NATO, the Soviet Union shifted to a "two Germanies" policy, symbolized in the Kremlin's readiness to establish diplomatic relations with Bonn. By 1955 the Soviet Union had come to accept the status quo in central Europe, and from then on its primary aim was to solidify the existing state of affairs politically and contractually—a process that culminated almost two decades later in Bonn's Eastern treaties and the Helsinki Accords of the Conference on Security and Cooperation in Europe.

This shift in Moscow's policy toward Germany had important consequences for the Western base of Bonn's reunification policy—a base that Adenauer feared was eroding as the Western powers sought to move away from Cold War confrontation toward a more relaxed period of coexistence. After 1955, Bonn's major unification efforts necessarily became limited to denying the Soviet Union and East Germany de jure recognition of the existing state of affairs—there was little hope of bringing about unification—and Bonn expected its allies to support this policy of denial diplomatically. On the verbal level this support was forthcoming, especially from the United States. But Adenauer remained suspicious, fully aware of the fundamental paradox of the German question. Bipolarities of tensions, interests, and power were not conducive to German reunification: that was the lesson to be drawn from the international circumstances of the pre-1955 period. But the developing nuclear balance of terror, the gradually changing perceptions of the Soviet threat, the Gaullist pressures on the Western alliance, and the general reconfiguration of power and interest from a bipolar into a multipolar pattern were equally unfavorable to prospects for unification. Without an easing of East-West tensions, neither side could afford to allow German unification on the opponent's terms—yet an East-West accommodation contained the likelihood that the division of Germany would get not only a tacit political but also an explicit legal blessing.

Transitions and Incongruities: The Second Decade

In the second stage of the Federal Republic's foreign policy development—in the decade from the late 1950s to the late 1960s—the central dilemma of West German foreign policy was the necessity of making difficult choices between Washington and Paris, or to put it in equally stark terms, the dilemma of choosing between its perceived security interests and its desire to construct a viable European community. The striking complementarities that existed in the 1950s between the goals of security and political and economic recovery—complementarities that rested on Bonn's willingness to rearm and that became the foundations of the Federal Republic's emplacement in the Western alliance—began to unravel in the 1960s. Tensions developed between Bonn's Washington-oriented security policy and its Paris-oriented Europe policy; the connections between German security policy and economic policy, although as close as in the first decade, were becoming politically troublesome; the economic and monetary controversies within the Atlantic alliance required awkward and costly diplomatic maneuvering; and the correspondence between American and German monetary policies began to dwindle. These tensions within the Western alliance affected not only Bonn's Western policy but also its Eastern policy because Washington and Paris pursued divergent policies toward the Soviet Union and Eastern Europe and Bonn found it difficult to adjust its rigid Eastern policy to the more accommodating stance of the Western powers. Above all, neither Washington nor Paris pursued foreign policy programs that were fully congruent with German interest, forcing Bonn to choose between alternatives that were intrinsically flawed.

To be sure, the disagreements between Washington and Paris did not begin with General Charles de Gaulle's return to power in 1958; they had posed serious problems for Adenauer from the beginning. Whereas Washington wanted to expedite the Federal Republic's membership in the Western military alliance and an integrated Western Europe, France understandably was reserved and sought to curtail West German influence in these international bodies. Although this situation was at times awkward for Bonn, it was manageable as long as the Western alliance was fairly cohesive, the United States could threaten France with "agonizing reappraisals" of American diplomacy, and Bonn could advance its interest in the name of an integrated Western alliance. But these problems of the early years foreshadowed the much more serious dilemma that the German government had to face later, after Charles de Gaulle returned to power in 1958, when taking sides with either the United States or France sharpened the developing tensions within the Atlantic alliance.

Although the security dependence of the Federal Republic on the United States remained as inextricable in the 1960s as it had been in the 1950s, it was subject to increasing strains. During the 1960s, as American nuclear superiority began to diminish with the development of Soviet nuclear strategic capabilities, an intense doctrinal debate took place within NATO which revolved essentially around the question of how the credibility of the American nuclear commitment to Western Europe could be sustained as the United States gradually became vulnerable itself. This issue (which remains to this day) had special significance for the Federal Republic because of its exposed geographical and political position and because Bonn became increasingly dependent on NATO's deterrent capabilities over which the Germans had no control. Moreover, the Kennedy administration aimed for a more flexible American strategic doctrine, which was designed to multiply Washington's strategic and tactical options and required the European NATO allies to build up a conventional force. This doctrine of "flexible response," which became official NATO doctrine in 1967, required higher German defense expenditures although its stress on conventional troop buildups by Europeans was viewed with apprehension in Bonn because it seemed to undermine the credibility of the American willingness to extend its nuclear umbrella over the European NATO members. Although the Federal Republic had no alternative to its transatlantic security connection—which became the backbone of NATO after the French withdrawal in 1966—it became increasingly clear in the 1960s that the security interests of the United States and the Federal Republic were no longer as congruent as they had appeared to be in the 1950s.

But opting for Paris (which was not seriously considered on security issues) meant opting for a French foreign policy agenda that conflicted with German purposes on a number of centrally important questions, including the future shape of the European order. Both Adenauer and de Gaulle preferred a "little Europe" integrative structure; but de Gaulle opposed genuine political integration because that would curtail the national independence of France, and he expected Germany to help the French regain their position in world politics by providing economic and political support. De Gaulle wanted the economic benefits of the Common Market without paying a political price; Adenauer was ready to pay an economic price for political benefits. De Gaulle sought a European base for his global political ambitions; Adenauer sought an Atlantic base for his European ambitions.

The conflicts that developed between the Anglo-American powers and France during the late 1950s and early 1960s immensely complicated Adenauer's aim of integrating the Federal Republic in a cohesive West European community. While the United States remained the indispensable partner of Germany's security policy, de Gaulle, the indispensable partner for Germany's Europe policy, was determined to shut out Anglo-American influence on the Continent. As a result, during the 1960s Germany's security policy no longer meshed with its Europe policy—in contrast to the 1950s, when the complementarity of Bonn's Atlantic and European policy was the cornerstone of Adenauer's foreign policy program. By that time there were, in effect, two German foreign policies, not one. The first was Adenauer's, which resulted in the Franco-German Friendship Treaty of 1963 and allowed de Gaulle to blackball Britain's membership in the EEC with Germany's implicit acquiescence. The second policy direction was preferred by Economics Minister Ludwig Erhard and Foreign Minister Gerhard Schröder, who advocated a more flexible course and tended to support the Anglo-American position not only on the Common Market and the Atlantic alliance but also on a more imaginative Eastern policy.

When Ludwig Erhard succeeded Konrad Adenauer in the fall of 1963, the policy differences among the Federal Republic, France, and the United States were aggravated. Almost every item on de Gaulle's agenda opposed German foreign policy at a time when the new chancellor in Bonn was much less sympathetic to French projects than Adenauer had been. The EEC crisis of 1965 over the political future and membership of the Common Market pitted Bonn against Paris (although it ultimately strengthened Germany's position in the EEC), and Franco-German disagreement over political fundamentals was further aggravated by clashes over economic and monetary specifics. But Erhard's relations with Washington were troubled as well. The hapless scheme of the multilateral nuclear force (MLF), which had no military-strategic value (President John F. Kennedy called it "something of a fake") and which was designed primarily to give European NATO members the appearance of nuclear ownership without providing it in reality, led to serious tensions between Bonn and Washington when the Johnson administration scrapped it in 1965. In the face of strong domestic objections, Erhard had consistently supported American policy (on NATO, Vietnam, higher conventional troop levels for central Europe, and monetary matters); and he had relied on Lyndon Johnson's readiness to reciprocate by supporting the MLF. But tensions developed between fundamental American interests and the major political purposes that Bonn sought to advance through sharing nuclear control. Throughout, an important reason for Bonn's interest in the MLF was the hope that it could be traded for Soviet concessions on the German question—a point explicitly made by Foreign Minister Gerhard Schröder in the summer of 1965. This anticipated leverage, which was probably illusory to begin with, obviously required continued American support for the MLF, which President Johnson was unwilling to provide because the implied anti-Soviet dimension of Bonn's MLF policy jeopardized two of Washington's most cherished foreign policy goals—a détente with the Soviet Union and an arms control agreement. Negotiations for a nuclear nonproliferation treaty were already well under way, and the Soviet Union had repeatedly made it clear that Washington would have to choose between the treaty and the MLF. Sacrificing the MLF was relatively easy for Johnson because most NATO members had shown no real interest in it. The Germans, however, felt that their suspicions about a possible Soviet-U.S. deal at the expense of German interests were confirmed by Washington's about-face on the MLF.

Economic and monetary controversies within the Atlantic alliance also compelled Bonn to make choices it wished to avoid. At issue between the Europeans and Americans were a wide range of questions— the enlargement of the Common Market, the European Community's plan to establish a common currency area, and the overall political-strategic and economic relationships between the United States and Europe. As American economic hegemony declined relative to Europe and Japan, America's allies—especially France—felt increasingly restive about American political and economic-monetary privileges and began to push for an alteration of the framework (such as the Bretton Woods international monetary regime) within which these political and economic arrangements had been made. The sources of Washington's displeasure with EEC practices were also manifold but focused largely on three related areas: the EEC's preferential trade agreements with an increasing number of countries, which tended to violate the most-favored-nation principle; its protectionist agricultural policy; and the unloading of its large agricultural surpluses in traditional United States markets, especially the Far East and North Africa. The Europeans felt that the central economic issue between themselves and the United States was money rather than trade, especially since the United States enjoyed a consistently favorable balance of trade with the EEC. In the European view, the United States was acting irresponsibly as well as selfishly in not taking steps to remedy its chronic balance-of-payments problems and in shifting a major part of the resulting burden of adjustment onto its European partners.

All this put the Germans in an awkward position. France insisted on Germany's support for the EEC's Common Agricultural Policy because it was the keystone of the Franco-German economic compact made upon entering the community framework, which provided that France would accept an open-market arrangement for German industrial goods in return for agricultural price supports. The United States insisted on Germany's monetary support (including military offset payments, military purchases in the United States, and other burden-sharing arrangements within NATO) to ameliorate the tensions that had developed among the Bretton Woods system's three central principles—the dollar-gold parity, fixed exchange rates, and free convertibility of currencies. The myth that Bretton Woods still worked could be maintained only because the German Bundesbank committed itself in

1967 not to convert dollars into gold and refrained from otherwise shaking the regime, as the French did with great relish. But although the Federal Republic made greater efforts in the 1960s and early 1970s than any other country to cushion the United States against constant onslaughts on the dollar, Bonn-Washington differences over monetary matters were serious because they stemmed from opposing views of what constituted responsible monetary and fiscal practices. A relationship of mutual dependency had developed: the United States supplied the Germans with security benefits (which Washington considered a major source of its balance-of-payments problem) and the Germans reciprocated with direct and indirect monetary support until the formal offset arrangements were terminated in 1976.

The central dilemma of the Federal Republic's Eastern policy in the 1960s was Bonn's inability to reconcile the political and legal aspects of that policy. The Germans realized that international developments (in Western as well as Eastern Europe, in Washington as well as Moscow) called for a revision of Bonn's sterile Eastern policy, but the legalistic inhibitions that had been placed on that policy in the 1950s had become increasingly self-defeating and stood in the way of an adequate response to the political imperatives of the 1960s—an impediment that explains also why Bonn's Eastern policy could not be attuned to that of its major allies.

From the German perspective, American diplomacy was too conservative and French diplomacy was too innovative. Washington's European policy was too conservative in the sense that both the Kennedy and Johnson administrations sought an accommodation with the Soviet Union that had a pronounced bilateral quality and that tended to stabilize the European status quo. American coexistence policy was based on the assumption that the shared dangers and responsibilities of the two nuclear superpowers required a stabilization of the nuclear military balance and that the stability of the European order required the continuance of the Soviet as well as American spheres of influence on the Continent. For Washington, the gradual loosening of the Warsaw Pact alliance (a process that was partially arrested in August 1968) was less a cause for exultation than a source of concern. The fragmentation of the Soviet empire in Eastern Europe might escalate the Cold War conflict and would, at best, lead to the unraveling of the relatively stable and tolerable postwar European order: in short, to the unraveling of Washington's double-containment policy. The Kennedy administration had revamped NATO strategy despite German misgivings, showed little resolve on the question of German unity, and apparently aimed at an accommodation with the Soviet Union in Europe at the expense of German interests, if necessary. The policies of the Johnson administration were hardly more reassuring. The president seemed uncomfortable with European matters and tended to ignore them; and Washington became increasingly preoccupied with Vietnam and with fashioning an arms control arrangement with the Soviet Union—all of which made the Johnson government a politically and psychologically distant ally for the Federal Republic. The possibility that the United States would assent to the legitimization of the division of Europe and Germany—the central foreign policy aim of the Soviet Union in the 1960s—was a nightmare for both Adenauer and Erhard and a continuing source of concern during the years of the Kiesinger-Brandt government, although the latter itself reflected conflicting views on the German question.

Whereas American policy was too conservative for Bonn because of its implicit readiness to solidify the European status quo, French policy was too innovative and dynamic because it aimed, at bottom, at the dissolution of the American and Soviet spheres of influence in Europe. In light of his suspicions of American motives, Adenauer felt obliged to turn to Paris for support of Bonn's rigid Eastern policy, although de Gaulle had recognized the Oder-Neisse line in 1959 (a prerequisite for his overtures toward Eastern Europe) and although the chancellor must have known that de Gaulle could only support a solution of the German question that would fall short of actual reunification. To be sure, de Gaulle wanted the German issue defused: he considered it the major cause (and justification) of the superpowers' continued presence in Europe, a cause that would evaporate with a solution of the German question and would lead to the dissolution of the two Cold War military alliances and speed American and Soviet withdrawal from Europe. "Europe from the Atlantic to the Urals," led by France, would supplant the dual hegemony that the United States and the Soviet Union had imposed on the postwar European order. But de Gaulle, in reaching out toward Eastern Europe and the Soviet Union, went far beyond what the Bonn government thought appropriate; and the fundamental shift of French policy toward the Soviet Union, with its implied Franco-Soviet accommodation, had a profound impact on Franco-German relations, which were soured already in the area of transatlantic and European politics.

In short, Washington's policy undermined the political dimensions of Bonn's Eastern policy because it implied the solidification of the existing spheres of influence in Europe and portended their future legitimization; French policy undermined the legal dimension of Bonn's Eastern policy because it approached, in contrast to Bonn, Eastern European capitals as full diplomatic partners and it conflicted with Bonn's NATO-based security policy as well. The choices between Washington and Paris that were imposed on the Adenauer, Erhard, and Kiesinger governments in the 1960s were not choices between policy alternatives that these governments themselves favored. In contrast to the 1950s, when the Adenauer government could implement only one of two mutually exclusive but inherently desirable alternatives—a viable *Westpolitik* and a viable *Ostpolitik*—the alternatives of the 1960s amounted to a choice between an eviscerated European option and an equally tattered Atlantic option and between American and French Eastern policies that were, for different reasons, equally objectionable to the German government. As postwar German-American relations matured in the 1960s, they also reflected increasing strains over a wide range of military-strategic, economic-monetary, and political issues.

Frictions Amid Transformations: The Nineteen-Seventies

In the 1970s, the global and regional balances of power were changing, creating new possibilities as well as problems for German-American relations. The sources of many of these changes were rooted in events of the 1960s or, in some cases, the early postwar years, but their manifestations became clearly visible in the 1970s and provided a significantly reshaped international environment for German-American diplomacy, with consequences also for the domestic political foundations of the German-American connection.

Above all perhaps, there was the relative devolution of American power. At the end of World War II and at the beginning of the Cold War, the United States wielded unchallengeable economic power, controlled the international monetary system it had created, stood at the peak of international prestige and political influence, and possessed an invulnerable nuclear force that guaranteed America's security and that of its allies. Three decades later, the United States was sharing its predominant economic and monetary position with Western Europe and Japan; was compelled to acknowledge the Soviet Union as its equal in nuclear capabilities; and had suffered a decline in prestige and influence because of mismanagement of foreign and domestic affairs.

These developments, along with the growing self-assertion of

Western Europe, became connected with the realization, on both sides of the Atlantic, that American and West European interests were no longer as congruent as they appeared to be in the immediate postwar period—a realization that was reflected in a number of centrally important aspects of German-American relations.

The Brandt-Scheel government that came to power in the fall of 1969 realized that a German rapprochement with the East and the coordination of German diplomacy with the détente efforts of the Western powers required Bonn's formal recognition of the European status quo. By attuning West German foreign policy to the dynamics of détente—the outstanding foreign policy aim of most members of the Warsaw Pact as well as of the Atlantic Alliance—Bonn hoped to convey a more constructive attitude toward the East, keep pace with international developments, and retain German leverage in an East-West diplomatic setting in which various political, strategic, and economic issues were coupled in multilateral connections. For reasons of history, geography, and the abiding question of German unity, the aspirations and hopes reflected in a Western policy of détente were especially pertinent to the Federal Republic; and the Brandt government was prepared to make the indispensable contribution to its success—acceptance of the European status quo.

The Brandt-Scheel government's *Ostpolitik* also became a complementary part of the Federal Republic's security policies—not because it lessened the Federal Republic's strategic dependence on the United States or its allegiance to NATO but because Bonn's readiness to accept the territorial status quo tackled German security problems at their political roots. In contrast to the 1950s and 1960s, when Bonn's security policy conflicted sharply with its Eastern policy, *Ostpolitik* overcame these stark contradictions. By recognizing the territorial and political realities stemming from World War II, the Germans meshed their security policy and their Eastern policy, developed a more constructive attitude toward arms control, and adjusted West German foreign policy to the dynamics of East-West détente.

Adjusting German diplomacy to the Western powers' détente policies of the early 1970s was not an easy matter, however. Even though Bonn's *Ostpolitik* followed rather than preceded other dynamic Western approaches to the East, their partners' initial response to *Ostpolitik* (especially in Washington) demonstrated to the Germans that their own approach called for a delicate balance of movement and restraint. Too little readiness to support East-West accommodation had in the past brought charges of obstructionism (especially when Bonn dragged its feet on arms control); too much enthusiasm for détente raised fears that Bonn would weaken its ties to the West to improve the prospects for German unity. The suspicion that the Federal Republic was an actual or potential revisionist European power, prepared to unhinge the status quo if given the opportunity, was close to the surface of many of the issues—political, military-strategic, economic—that were contested between Bonn and other capitals.

Moreover, in the late 1970s, after the issues of Afghanistan and

Facing page. Willy Brandt as *Time*'s "Man of the Year" in 1970. By honoring Adenauer's earlier political opponent, *Time* reflected the extent to which American thinking about the Federal Republic had changed. The "Ostpolitik" of the Brandt-Scheel coalition government of 1969 steered the Federal Republic away from Adenauer's one-sided Western orientation. Under the heading "On the way to a new reality," *Time* credited Brandt's new policy toward Eastern Europe with attempting to bridge the differences that divided Europe after World War II.

An important part of *Time*'s cover story on Brandt was a photo of the Chancellor's symbolic gesture of kneeling before the memorial to the 500,000 Jews killed by the Germans in the Warsaw ghetto in World War II. *Time* compared Brandt's gesture with the proclamation of a united German Reich by Kaiser Wilhelm I ninety-nine years earlier in the Mirror Room of Versailles. (Reprinted by permission from TIME.)

Poland beclouded East-West relations, it became increasingly apparent that the results of détente were assessed differently in the United States and Western Europe, in part because the expectations that sustained the détente process in the early 1970s had been different. The expectations of the superpowers, had they been fully articulated, were unmatched to begin with—the United States expected Soviet restraint in most areas of the East-West contest, while the Soviet Union sought primarily the solidification of the European status quo and the East-West military-strategic balance, coupled with increased economic relations with the West. The Germans were perhaps the main beneficiaries of détente because their expectations of enlarged and intensified human contacts between the two Germanys were at least partially fulfilled, and the Federal Republic managed as well to enhance its international prestige and diplomatic leverage. As a consequence, throughout the 1970s the Germans remained committed to the evolution of a European order that would secure and broaden those benefits, and they tended to view détente as a divisible process that could and should be shielded from extra-European disturbances. On the other hand, both the United States and the Soviet Union were, for different reasons, disappointed with the results of détente; their commitment to the development of a dynamic European order was, again for differing reasons, questionable; and the United States sought to impress upon the Bonn government that the process of détente was indeed indivisible and connected with the global East-West contest.

In addition to differing interpretations of the meaning and results of détente, a series of U.S.-German disagreements over economic and monetary matters occurred in the 1970s.

The world monetary crisis of the summer of 1971 was the culmination of the economic-monetary controversies between the United States and the Common Market countries that had developed in the 1960s. The crisis heralded a long overdue reorganization of the world monetary system and revolved, in part, around the economic, strategic, and political role of the United States in world affairs and what part of this role her allies were willing to continue financing. The need to alter this framework was made more pressing by the emerging primacy of economic-monetary matters relative to military-strategic matters, growing economic interdependence, and the special political and economic difficulties posed by the enlargement of the European Economic Community and its arrested integrative dynamics.

Although these developments increased German diplomatic leverage because they shifted elements of power in a direction in which the major sources of German capacity were located, their political, economic, and psychological ramifications became especially trouble-some after Helmut Schmidt took over the chancellorship from Willy Brandt in 1974—not so much because of the change in German lead-ership as because German *Ostpolitik* had largely run its course and the worldwide recession brought economic matters to the foreground. In the mid- and late 1970s, West Europeans were not as preoccupied with the dramatic "high politics" of the preceding years as they were with the much more technical economic and political tasks that con-fronted them: economic growth and monetary stability, security of en-ergy and other raw material supplies, dealing constructively with the Third World, and adjusting European Community structures so as to implement much-needed reforms and accommodate new members. In all those tasks, which required coordinated and therefore incremental steps, it became apparent that economic policy played a steady, funda-mental, and perhaps decisive role, with large opportunities for the Federal Republic to translate economic and monetary capacity into po-litical leverage.

This translation could not be accomplished without some diffi-culties. The Bonn government resisted American suggestions for a Washington-Bonn political-economic "axis" or a locomotive role for the German economy, complained about the international monetary poli-cies of the United States, and generally took a dim view of the style as well as the substance of Washington's foreign policies. The Schmidt government also took a much tougher stand than previous German governments toward the European Community, calling on the mem-ber states to exercise fiscal responsibility and to support reforms of the community's entrenched bureaucracies. Bonn made it clear that it would agree to monetary demands by EEC members only if they would seek to solve the larger structural problems of the community. Although Schmidt was willing to be a "good European"—his generally harmonious relationship with French President Giscard d'Estaing en-abled France and Germany to launch the European Monetary Sys-tem—he also believed that the economic and monetary plight of some EEC countries was in large part the result of fiscal and political irre-sponsibility and that the sense of drift in the community could be over-come only by political leadership that faced up to the challenges of the future and was more resistant to the day-to-day pressures of political expediency.

Germany's growing political and diplomatic leverage also affected the style of the Federal Republic's economic diplomacy. Economic and monetary language had traditionally provided the West Germans with an excellent opportunity to translate political demands, which might still have been suspect because of Germany's past, into respectable economic demands. This compensated the Germans for not being able to translate political demands into military-strategic language, as de Gaulle had managed so dramatically with the *force de frappe*, which was, above all, a supremely political instrument. Had the Germans couched political aspirations in terms of arms, they would have been accused of being unreconstructed militarists; instead, they viewed economics as the continuation of politics by other means. But as economic issues became more directly charged with political meaning, especially when they touched upon the framework conditions of economic and monetary regimes, economic language also became less neutral and more subject to being interpreted as an expression of power politics.

The articulation of German interests was complicated by yet another development. Bonn had always been highly effective in multilateral organizational settings (in contrast to France, whose foreign policy derived its vitality from a separatist line) and had frequently succeeded in turning international cooperation to national advantage. This had the added benefit, and that is the point I want to stress here, that Bonn could express German aspirations in the language of Europe and the Atlantic alliance rather than of German national interests. Being a good German was the same as being a good Atlanticist or a good Europeanist. But as the two alliances increasingly diverged in purpose, and as the Federal Republic gained a role of leadership in the EC, Bonn's opportunities to advance national interests in the name of general international cooperation were becoming less ample and less convincing. The legitimizing ecumenical language in which German purposes could be expressed in the past became less suited to the new circumstances and required the Germans to learn a new diplomatic vocabulary. This was a delicate matter because other European powers, especially France, were highly sensitive to the Federal Republic's translation of economic power into political leverage. As the views of the Federal Republic gained more and more authority, the Germans had to become mindful of the psychological fact that authority, although more than advice, is less than a command. As Helmut Schmidt put it: "We are not small enough to keep our mouth shut, but we are too small to do more than talk"—perhaps a succinct definition of a middle power.

By the late 1960s, the Soviet Union was approaching parity with the United States in long-range missile capabilities, which forced Washington to qualify its automatic nuclear guarantee to Europe, impaired the credibility of that guarantee, led to the institutionalization of U.S.-Soviet parity in the Strategic Arms Limitations Talks (SALT) agreements, and ultimately brought the strategically distinct positions of America and Europe into clear focus.

Nonetheless, in the early 1970s the intense debates of the 1960s over how the alliance should adjust to the waning American nuclear superiority began to abate—for reasons that are highly instructive for America's diplomacy of the 1980s. On the German side, the incentive to question the American commitment to Europe decreased not only because of the changing perception of the Soviet threat but also because the transatlantic security partnership (symbolized by NATO) had been reduced in many respects to a bilateral German-American understanding—and the Brandt-Scheel government was not about to burden that understanding with doctrinal disputes at a time when it needed to demonstrate unequivocally its continuing loyalty to the alliance so as to allay the suspicions that its *Ostpolitik* had initially raised in Washington. But the American side contributed to the defusing of NATO's doctrinal debates as well. There was, compared to its predecessors and successors, a remarkable self-assurance about the Nixon administration's posture toward the nuclear balance, which recognized its centrality to the Soviet-American relationship but accepted also its marginality for affecting the day-to-day conduct of diplomacy. This did not mean of course that the underlying contradictions that had plagued the German-American security relationship had gone away, but it did demonstrate that the reassurance aspect of American national security policy could be sustained with the appropriate diplomacy even after the advent of nuclear parity, precisely because that reassurance depended more and more on political rather than purely military-strategic assessments by the Germans of Soviet intentions and American diplomacy. When American security policy and alliance diplomacy were passed on to the less competent hands of the Carter administration, and when German policy was guided by the more assertive and abrasive style of Chancellor Helmut Schmidt, political disagreements, couched in strategic doctrinal terms, quickly reemerged.

In large measure, the transatlantic security debate of the late 1970s revolved around the perennially troublesome question of forward defense and the related issue of the "conventional pause." President Jimmy Carter, to be sure, reaffirmed the American commitment to the principle of forward defense and did not exclude the use of tactical nuclear weapons on principle. The central question, however—

the timing of a tactical nuclear response—remained as ambiguous as ever. Since many German military figures viewed tactical nuclear weapons as an essential link in the chain of escalation from a conventional response to a strategic nuclear exchange between the Soviet Union and the United States, American ambivalence as to when (or even if) tactical nuclear weapons would be used was seen as undermining the totality of NATO's ladder of escalation and leading to a decoupling of the American nuclear guarantee for Europe. The European NATO members, and above all the Federal Republic, saw their security interests best maintained by the threat to use nuclear weapons in the early stages of a conventional war, but the United States wanted their use postponed as long as possible. European strategists saw American tactical nuclear weapons as the essential link between United States strategic nuclear forces and American theater capabilities in Europe, symbolizing Washington's determination to risk escalation for the sake of its European allies, but American strategists saw tactical nuclear weapons in a backup role should NATO's conventional defenses fail and as a means of limiting conflict to the Continent and preventing escalation. America's NATO partners at the forward line of defense could not accept a strategy that implied sustained conventional warfare at the expense of their population and territory, but the United States needed to take into account the potential nuclear devastation of America and therefore sought to delay the use of nuclear weapons. These differing perspectives, which stemmed from the not fully coterminous security interests of the United States and Western Europe, were underlined by the flap caused within NATO when President Carter vacillated over the decision to develop and deploy neutron weapons, since some European strategists saw such "enhanced radiation" weapons, which could be deployed effectively against tanks and armored vehicles, as a compensation for NATO's weakness in the area of conventional forces. Nor were the Germans reassured when American columnists published excerpts from the so-called Presidential Review Memorandum 10, which included a suggestion to President Carter that, among other options, Western Europe might not be defended along the West-East German border but along the Weser and Lech rivers in the Federal Republic. Although NATO planners had all along questioned the military feasibility of defending Europe along the Federal Republic's border with the German Democratic Republic and Czechoslovakia, it was politically imperative to assure the Germans that their geographical position would not condemn them to being the first (and perhaps only) victims of a conventional war.

In the late 1970s, the twenty-year-old issue of the East-West nuclear balance in Europe, dormant for a decade, became reconnected with the thirty-year-old issues of forward defense, the timing of an American nuclear response, and the general nature of the American nuclear commitment to Europe. Toward the end of the Carter administration and at the beginning of the Reagan administration, the complementarity of aiming for both détente and deterrence—which was the core of the Federal Republic's security policy in the 1970s—was being called into question. The major problem revolved around the question of the eurostrategic (intermediate-range nuclear forces) balance between NATO and the Warsaw Pact. This balance was being undermined by the deployment of a large number of Soviet SS-20 intermediate-range missiles, to which NATO responded in December 1979 with the so-called "double-track" decision, calling for the deployment by the end of 1983 of 572 modernized American Pershing II missiles and cruise missiles unless an arms control agreement with the Soviet Union would make that deployment unnecessary.

This is not the place to deal with the technical complexity and political controversy attached to the question of the eurostrategic balance. But the euromissile controversy—important as it is in its own right—takes on a meaning, on both sides of the Atlantic, that goes far beyond its military-technical import and extends into fundamental questions about the future shape of the transatlantic alliance and the European political order. German attitudes are formed, or hardened, on the issue of the eurostrategic nuclear balance in a way that will reverberate and extend into adjacent issues of German-American relations and affect them for years to come. The highly technical discussions over arms control measures, and the highly emotional responses that these discussions often evoke, are both related to fundamental political attitudes (in the Federal Republic as well as in the United States) about the nature of the East-West conflict, the shape of a desirable regional and global world order, and the principles that govern German-American relations. As security issues have reemerged as major concerns of the Atlantic alliance, it is essential to realize that these concerns, even more than in the 1960s, reflect and portend political purposes that go far deeper than weighing the regional or global military balance or redefining the meaning of security for the 1980s and beyond.

Above all perhaps, the eurostrategic missile debate demonstrated that there was no longer a broad consensus among the populations of the Western countries about the nature and intensity of the Soviet threat and about the appropriate Western diplomacy toward the Soviet Union and toward the political challenges that face the West in the 1980s. Many West Germans, although convinced that German security interests required the Federal Republic's continuing support of NATO, were not eager to see additional nuclear weapons installed on their territory: relative to its size, the Federal Republic already contained more nuclear weapons than any other country in the world; the Soviet Union repeatedly stated that it considered the anticipated deployment of new intermediate-range nuclear weapons as a major threat, leading to increased East-West tensions; and there was a nagging suspicion, fueled by statements made in Washington, that the United States aimed for nuclear superiority over the Soviet Union and that deployment of missiles capable of reaching the Soviet Union from Western Europe was one way of implementing that intention. All this highlighted the central paradox in the West Europeans' attitude toward their transatlantic nuclear protector: they seem equally afraid that the United States would resort to the use of nuclear weapons or that it would not. They seem to fear in equal measure lack of American circumspection or lack of American resolve; they worry about confrontational American policies toward the Soviet Union, but they also fear the possibility of American unilateralism and disengagement from Europe.

Considering the Germans' concern over the eurostrategic missile issue, and its wide-ranging political implications, it should not be surprising that this concern finds expression in shrill as well as measured tones. It is essential for Americans to understand that the more guarded view that many Europeans have developed of their transatlantic partner does not, for that reason, move them closer to Moscow or make them unreliable alliance partners. The pejorative metaphor of "equidistance," with its implication that the Europeans' reservations about American diplomacy place them at one corner of an equidistant political and moral triangle, can be sustained only if one holds a zero-sum view of the East-West contest, with one's loss becoming the other's immediate and automatic gain. There is a broad and deep reservoir of goodwill toward the United States in the Federal Republic that stretches across the incremental and porous boundaries of age, socioeconomic status, or political awareness. But the translation of that goodwill into the practical policies that ultimately determine the nature of German-American relations does not proceed automatically. It requires circumspection and nurture on both sides of the Atlantic, especially on security matters that are perceived to be central to the respective national interests. Most Europeans are not "neutralist" or "anti-American," but their confidence in American diplomacy must be continually earned in the day-to-day conduct of American foreign policy. It has to be earned as well in the conduct of American domestic policy, for many Europeans connect their view of Washington's foreign policy with their assessment of the political process in the United States; their long-run expectations about the political reliability and circumspection of their transatlantic partner evolve as much from their perception of America's future domestic political order as from their perception of current American diplomacy.

If the Federal Republic hopes to help shape a European order congenial to German interests and not lose American support in the process, German diplomacy must realize that the domestic political foundations for a consistent, long-range European policy are no longer as secure in the United States as they were in previous decades and that Washington will most likely persist in linking its political, military-strategic, and economic policies not only in its dealings with adversaries but with its allies as well. If the United States hopes to influence the evolution of the European community in a constructive way, American diplomacy must accept the inevitability of this evolution and the unavoidable ambiguities that accompany it. What is needed, and what many Europeans would welcome, is a reconfiguration of America's political landscape in which an enlightened, responsible economic conservatism is decoupled from a preoccupation with arms and joined with a stance on military-strategic matters that accepts their centrality for American security but realizes their marginality for the day-to-day conduct of American diplomacy. Without such a reconfiguration, it will be difficult to persuade allies in Europe that American policies reflect a mature consideration of common and conflicting interests. Rocky ground must be traversed in the 1980s, but it is also common ground that need not remain totally uncharted, even if both sides head in somewhat different directions.

Note

1. This historical reality makes it difficult to provide the reader with a working bibliography that might assist in exploring the subject matter through further reading. The literature on German-American relations in the postwar period is vast if these relations are conceived as broadly as they should be; and a critical and selective bibliography would be as long (and every bit as interpretive) as this essay. For useful bibliographies of the historical dimension of German-American relations, see Hans W. Gatzke, *Germany*

and the United States: A "Special Relationship?" (Cambridge, Mass.: Harvard University Press, 1980); Roger Morgan, *The United States and West Germany, 1945–1973* (London: Oxford University Press, 1974); James L. Richardson, *Germany and the Atlantic Alliance: The Interaction of Strategy and Politics* (Cambridge, Mass.: Harvard University Press, 1966). A useful guide for the literature between 1974 and 1981 is provided in *Literaturrecherche: Bundesrepublik Deutschland-USA*, prepared by Kai Schellhorn for the *Stiftung Wissenschaft und Politik* (Munich-Ebenhausen: Series B, No. 49, May 1984). For a more detailed explication of my own analysis of German-American relations in the postwar period, which refers to the appropriate literature, see Wolfram F. Hanrieder, *West German Foreign Policy, 1949–1963: International Pressure and Domestic Response* (Stanford, Calif.: Stanford University Press, 1967); *The Stable Crisis: Two Decades of German Foreign Policy* (New York: Harper and Row, 1970); and *Fragmente der Macht: Die Aussenpolitik der Bundesrepublik* (Munich: Piper, 1981).

8.
How Real Is German Anti-Americanism? An Assessment

KURT SONTHEIMER

THE COMMEMORATION OF THE BEGINNING of German immigration into the United States three hundred years ago is no doubt a propitious occasion to assess the quality of German-American relations in the present. That the governments of our two countries consider this anniversary a fortunate opportunity to demonstrate their partnership and allegiance to the common values of Western civilization indicates, at least on the official level, a common interest in and endeavor to preserve and further develop good and friendly relations between the American and German people. Although the positive relationship between our two countries cannot be put in doubt, there is a certain fear—more on the American than on the German side—that this relationship, which was enormously strong and reliable in the 1950s and 1960s, is presently undergoing a change and suffering a setback the cause of which is commonly attributed to a growing sentiment of anti-Americanism in Western Germany.

It is necessary to define at the outset what we mean by anti-Americanism. There are two main forms of anti-Americanism: one cultural and one political. Cultural anti-Americanism considers the dominant American values and their practical implementation in social life as being somehow inferior to one's own cultural standards. It is motivated by the fear that the spreading of American values and lifestyles to other cultures would eventually weaken or even destroy these cultures and deprive them of their national substance.

There has always been a tradition of culturally motivated anti-Americanism in German society, but it was as a rule an isolated social phenomenon, a high-brow attitude restricted to middle- and upper-class intellectuals and combined with the search for German identity characteristic of the era of nationalism. As Fritz Stern has shown in his book *The Politics of Cultural Despair*, there was a real danger that such cultural motivations might be turned into politics. Such an eventuality is, however, history and a matter of the past, not of the present. Cultural anti-Americanism, still significant during the Weimar Republic, has until recently not played an important part in West German society after 1945. On the contrary, on almost all levels—economic, scientific, cultural, and political—German society exhibited an obvious interest in reaching the standards set by American civilization. America not only became the world's forerunner in technical, scientific, and other achievements; it was at the same time the country most Germans looked up to, and it furnished the standard by which other Western countries judged their own success and progress. Cultural anti-Americanism was overcome after 1945 and is still a secondary phenomenon. It appears today mostly in combination with political anti-Americanism and usually supports a previously developed anti-American position on political matters.

Political anti-Americanism manifests itself in two directions. It can repudiate or condemn the nature and the workings of the political institutions and the values they embody—for example, by judging American democracy as an institutional arrangement unable to cope with the problems of the time—or it can severely criticize particular policies of the American government which appear detrimental to the national interests of one's own country. Most of what has been viewed as anti-Americanism in the context of German-American relations over the last two or three years has to do with apprehensions about policy, not with negative attitudes toward the American political system.

It is my thesis that anti-Americanism, whether cultural or political, does not play a significant role in today's political system in Western Germany. But it is evident that negative reactions to American policies regarding the East and Europe have increased considerably in the last years, beginning with Vietnam and ending, for the time being, with bitter disputes about security policies in the East-West conflict.

Different views about policy should, however, not be too quickly interpreted as manifestations of anti-Americanism. Such critical views can very often be found in the United States, where they are part of the political debate. It is therefore misleading to call the articulations of protest or concern about the wisdom and effectiveness of particular policies of an American administration anti-American. One can be a good friend and even an admirer of America and still not support particular policy measures or share the ideological views of a given administration. My preliminary answer to the question, How real is anti-Americanism in West Germany? must therefore be: it is not real. There is no significant wave of anti-American feelings and attitudes in the population, but there is—although restricted to intellectual and political minorities—a remarkable amount of skepticism and mistrust with regard to certain American policies, especially in the field of nuclear armament and East-West relations.

Throughout our history German opinion with respect to America has never really been unfriendly. No verse has been quoted more frequently by Germans in past essays about German-American relations than Goethe's famous "Amerika, du hast es besser, hast keine Basalte, keine Schlösser" (America, yours is a better lot, you have no basalt rocks nor castles). That is, America had the great privilege of not being tied to the fetters of the past as Europeans were, and she was therefore able to move more freely and openly into the future.

After 1945, with the help of the Allied powers, including the Soviet Union, Germany at last was made "safe for democracy"—this time for good, but unfortunately only in the Western part. After a period of hesitation in the first years of military occupation, the United States put her full confidence in the democratic evolution of the new Germany, and her trust and encouragement were not disappointed. As the result of a continuous positive common experience, German-American relations rested for more than twenty years on the firm ground of mutual respect if not sympathy. The Federal Republic of Germany saw in her close friendship and alliance with the United States not only the necessary guarantee for her military security; it beheld in the American people a reliable and good friend for the foreseeable future. German-American relations were certainly never without problems or differences of outlook and opinion, but they seemed, on the whole, positive and unshakable. Has all this come to an end? Has German-American friendship lost the foundation that was so well prepared in the era after 1945?

I do not believe that the foundation on which German-American relations was based in the past has been substantially altered in the last years. All West German governments from those of Konrad Adenauer through Willy Brandt and Helmut Schmidt up to the present new chancellor of the Christian Democratic and Liberal government, Helmut Kohl, have been conscious that Germany, and Western Europe as a whole, owe their present security—and therefore their free existence—to the support of and the military alliance with the United States. They are convinced that this alliance is necessary not only for security reasons but also for the intellectual and emotional support of our free system of government.

When the American president Ronald Reagan spoke in the German Bundestag in the summer of 1982, he was full of praise for West German democracy. He said that Americans admire the achievement of the German people in establishing within the last thirty years what he called a "dome of democracy" in Germany. We should, however, not have to resort to poetry and flattery to make clear that German-American relations in the last thirty years have rested not only upon considerations of security and common interests in the world struggle between East and West but also on a common and unequivocal commitment to the ideas and ideals of Western civilization. Although this commonality is not in doubt between the two governments or our two peoples, we all know that there is very often a discrepancy between the ideals we profess and the deeds we do. This holds true for America as well as for Germany. The recurring conflict between the ideal and the real explains to a certain extent why the Germans, especially younger, university-educated Germans, find it more difficult to look up to America than in the years right after the end of the war. And they have similar difficulties with the existing democracy in their own country. After Vietnam, after Watergate, after the many problematical experiences with the American presidential system and some of its leading representatives, it has become difficult for an informed and critical observer to view the American system of government and the overall situation of American society today as a perfect embodiment of the great ideals of Western civilization. Thus in the eyes of many Europeans and of a great number of Germans the United States has lost some of the glamor and radiance that surrounded it for many of us who belonged to the postwar generation.

Nevertheless, it is important to note that in a public opinion poll conducted in 1981, in answer to the question, "Do you like the Americans or do you not particularly like them?" a much larger number of respondents liked Americans than in an earlier poll. The proportion of positive answers was 56 percent in September 1981; it had been 42 percent in 1975 and was at its lowest point with 37 percent in 1957, which was during the height of the Adenauer's pro-American foreign policy. Although I do not think that such figures are of great help in explaining some of the slight ups and downs of German-American relations, they at least indicate that there is no growing anti-Americanism among the German population; rather the contrary. There is, as far as I can see, less overt admiration for the American political system and for

American society in general; there is a higher level of critical awareness of America's role and position in world politics; there is, especially
since the Reagan administration, a greater insecurity about the continuity and reliability of America's foreign policy; and there are more
and more issues on which European governments and the German
government in particular have other views and favor policies different
from those of the United States and her present administration. It is
often said that the recent political changes in America, which have
diminished the once leading role of her pro-European eastern establishment, have brought about a lack of awareness of the particular problems of Europe and its geopolitical setting. But Europeans sometimes
tend to forget that the United States is a world power with global commitments and interests.

I would conclude, in summing up my argument, that the foundations of the German-American partnership and friendship which were
laid in the years immediately following the war have essentially not
been seriously shaken and that, on the whole, the friendly attitude of
the German people toward the American people has remained constant. On the other hand, the number of political issues on which European governments and the American government, the West German
government and the Washington administration, are not in tune with
each other has notably increased. This is why greater efforts of coordination between the two countries are necessary; this is why German-
American relations have, despite declarations of the two governments
to the contrary, become more difficult; this is why a greater effort toward mutual understanding between the two nations is deemed necessary to consolidate and deepen the partnership that remains, at least
from the German point of view, to strengthen our political existence as
a free country in the future. Former Chancellor Helmut Schmidt once
declared: "There is no doubt: Americans and Europeans are not identical twins who have to behave always and everywhere in an identical
fashion. They are partners, share common ideals and central interests,
but they have in many individual cases different perspectives and interests. They are partners who have to coordinate their policies time
.and again and who are able to do so because they are not only historically and politically, not only economically and militarily tied to each
other, but because they share the common values of democracy and
freedom."

There exists in the present discussion about European-American
relations the fear that the two continents and our two countries could
move away from each other, that the spirit of cooperation and partner-

ship could be replaced by a spirit of mutual diffidence and competition, and that, on the whole, the ideals of Western civilization which have resulted in the intellectual and moral superiority of the West in this world have lost some of their validity and vitality. I do not want to speculate about the decline of the West ("den Untergang des Abendlandes"), which the antidemocratic German philosopher Oswald Spengler announced immediately after World War I. But there is doubtless in my own country and in other Western countries as well a growing disbelief in the values of Western civilization as they have been practiced so far; there is a vague search for new values and new forms of living which are in overt opposition to the dominant life patterns and standards in Western society. But this is a common problem intriguing both countries.

What is often called anti-Americanism is primarily a political phenomenon, which gained importance in Western Germany in a direct causal relationship to the changes in American politics and policies since the last years of the Carter administration and even more so during the Reagan presidency. It is true that criticism of American policies and of the American political system became widespread among leftist intellectuals in Germany, especially since the student protest movement of the late 1960s, but I would not call this anti-Americanism. It was rather a feeling of delusion that the leading power of the West seemed unable to stick to the high principles and ideals of American democracy, as was demonstrated by Vietnam and Watergate. It is understandable that leading German writers and intellectuals such as Günter Grass and Walter Jens appealed sometimes to the other, the "better" America: "the land of civil rights workers and reformers, of peace-loving and nonviolent people, not the land of social Darwinists, war speculators and hegemonists" ("das Land der Bürgerrechtler und Reformer, der Friedfertigen und der Gewaltlosen, nicht das Land der Sozialdarwinisten, Kriegsspekulanten und Hegemonisten"—Jens). But this evocation of another America proves that this was no general anti-Americanism but rather a selective criticism of conservative political orientations and tendencies that marked the new Reagan administration.

Criticism of American policies has indeed become a phenomenon of some magnitude in the German intelligentsia and in left-leaning political parties and movements in West Germany, especially in the so-called peace movement. Again, it is not directed against America as such but against American policies that are considered to be dangerous or motivated by imperialist attitudes and ideologies. There is a marked difference in outlook between the American perception of the nature of the Soviet threat as it is expressed by the Reagan administration and the views of the German minorities that oppose current military and strategic policies. I can understand that this opposition can be taken by Americans as an expression of anti-Americanism, but I think this is a shortsighted and misleading interpretation. Fears that this criticism could build up and eventually bring about a loosening of the ties between the United States and the Federal Republic of Germany are not justified, yet it is necessary to develop a deeper understanding between the two countries. It is illuminating that Klaus Harpprecht, a longtime German television correspondent in the United States, chose as the title for his recent book on contemporary America *Der fremde Freund* (The unknown friend, 1982), perhaps even more so in the case of the American relationship with Germany.

How real is anti-Americanism in West Germany? There is no basic change in the positive attitudes toward the United States in general, and there is no marked change in our official policy toward the United States. But there is a notable decline in admiration for the American political system as compared to the postwar decades, and there is a feeling of uneasiness among significant political minorities about the leading Western power, which sometimes becomes a bitter criticism of certain features of American politics and particular policies, especially since the Reagan administration. If the basically sound relationship between our countries is to be continued—a point on which most Americans and Germans certainly agree—continuous efforts are needed to keep this alliance free from wrong perceptions and misunderstandings. The differences of national interest that do exist should not make us forget, as President Reagan himself underlined during his visit to Bonn, "that our partnership rests on the same Western tradition: that democracy constitutes the best hope for the future."

9.
German-American Relations: Learning to Live with Our Differences

THEO SOMMER

I AM AFRAID I HAVE BEEN HANDED the difficult end of the topic: German-American relations during the past three centuries. All the other contributors to these Tricentennial volumes are free to wallow in the heady hyperbole befitting the occasion. I have been asked to deal with the real world, where interests differ and sometimes clash, where unity of purpose is not a state of nature but the result of much consuming effort, and where we must learn to live with our differences whenever we find ourselves unable to overcome them.

Let me begin by making two remarks. The first is very personal. It has been thirty-three years since I first set foot on American soil as an exchange student privileged to spend two years in this country—first at a small Indiana college and then at the University of Chicago. It was the first of forty or fifty stateside trips. I came to love America; and I have never since wavered or wobbled in my affection and respect for your country. In a way, I am the paradigmatic product of your "re-education," Care parcels and Hoover school lunches, the Marshall Plan, the airlift to Berlin during the blockade, American solidarity in the second Berlin Crisis, (1958–62)—all these events are indelibly etched into my memory, along with many marvelous personal recollections: of the University of Chicago and Henry Kissinger's Harvard Summer Seminar, of rafting down the Colorado river, of conferences, seminars, symposiums, of horseback expeditions into the high mountains around Aspen, and of many friends and acquaintances. As a journalist, I have become used to being called an Atlanticist. Although I frequently criticized particular policies pursued by successive U.S. administrations, I always felt that our quarrels were family quarrels.

This leads me straight to my second remark. The vast majority of my fellow countrymen feel the same way. They want to be friends with you; there is no anti-Americanism to speak of. They want to continue the alliance with the United States; there is no creeping neutralism. And they want to keep the American garrison in West Germany and in Berlin; there is no Ami-go-home movement. All serious polls agree that America's popularity is undiminished. For twenty-five years between 50 and 60 percent of the German people have without fail professed that they like the Americans. In recent polls, 89.1 percent said that NATO was indispensable for the maintenance of peace (SPD voters: 85 percent). Unlike the British (of whom 53 percent feel that American bases should be removed), they want the 230,000 GI's to stay; 60 percent would regret their leaving, more than during the period 1969–76 (59 percent). So do not be deluded by sensational headlines. There is no sensation. The West Germans are not turning their backs on the United States (not even Petra Kelly, the leading lady of our peace movement; she is very proud of her American stepfather, although the present incumbent in the White House is certainly not her favorite American). They are not on the verge of evicting the Seventh Army. And they are not about to bolt from the Western stable.

I wanted to make these two prefatory remarks to put what follows in the proper perspective: my analysis of the German-American differences that have come to dominate the front pages in recent years—differences of interest, differences of perception, and differences of rhetoric. And never mind the show of tricentennial concord. Those differences exist, they will continue to beset our relationship, and they are to a large extent independent of who happens to govern in Washington or Bonn.

Such differences of perception and interest are particularly striking in four specific fields: East-West relations; arms and arms control; North-South relations; and economic policies. I suggest we take a look at them one by one.

Bonn and Washington have been at loggerheads for some time about the value and the prospects of détente. The Americans, especially after Ronald Reagan moved into the White House, tended to discount and discard détente. To them it appeared devoid of any reality, a gigantic fraud, a smoke screen behind which the Soviets embarked on a relentless arms buildup and a determined geopolitical advance across the globe. Their first reflex was to quit talking to the Russians, to rearm massively, and to use economic relations as an instrument to punish the Russians.

The Germans—in fact, most West Europeans—took a different view. For them, détente—though limited—has become a reality, up to a point at least. Détente, they feel, has paid in humanitarian ways: it eased and multiplied contacts, especially between the two Germanys. It paid politically by lowering the frequency of crises in Europe, particularly around Berlin; and it provided some cover, however thin, to reformers in Eastern Europe. It also paid economically, providing a much appreciated business outlet in a difficult period—and Eastern trade, we feel, rather than making us dependent on the Soviet Union, gave us some political leverage. The West Germans, like the rest of the people of Western Europe, agree that it is important to maintain Western security. But at the same time, despite Afghanistan and Poland, they think that it is equally important to search out possibilities for accommodation and cooperation.

Our view is pragmatic, not ideological. Russia did not swim into our ken in 1917; we have been sharing a continent with it for some five hundred years. We realize that much of the international behavior of the Soviet Union bears the imprint of czarist traditions rather than that of world-revolutionary Marxism—the Russian people are 80 percent Russian and only 20 percent communist. We realize full well what monstrosities the Soviets are capable of; no one need lecture us about that—after all, they were the ones who brutally implemented the partition of Europe and Germany. But we do not feel that a return to the Cold War would serve anyone's interest, that an across-the-board trade war would force the Kremlin leaders to their knees, or that constant rhetorical badgering would incline them toward cooperation.

Our point is very simple. Of course, détente did not abolish confrontation, but it supplemented and mitigated it by cooperation. Of course, we cannot ignore what is happening in Afghanistan or elsewhere beyond the confines of NATO. Yet it would be foolish to import tension from outlying areas; for the task of diplomacy is to keep tension divisible and to try to extend the rules of détente to the peripheral regions. Confrontations must be mastered as they are forced upon us, but cooperation must not be lightly thrown to the wolves. The Soviet Union is a shrewd and sometimes ruthless adversary. It is not the antichrist or the originator of all international turmoil; and it should not be treated as an outlaw by the West. The two world powers need to remain in close touch. They must be able and willing to put themselves in each other's shoes if predictability and calculability are to be maintained in international affairs.

In this regard there is little difference between previous Social Democratic governments and the present Christian Democratic government of Helmut Kohl. The explanation is very simple. We have not renounced the option of reunification, but we no longer conceive it as an objective of operational policy. We leave its achievement to the tides of history, recognizing full well that these tides may not necessarily work in favor of national unity. But since it is impossible to overcome the partition of the country, it becomes imperative to end the separation of the people. No German chancellor can leave a single stone unturned in the endeavor to improve the lot of 17 million East Germans, to facilitate contacts between East and West Germany, and to make the border more permeable precisely because it cannot be abolished. Every chancellor must attempt to insulate German-German relations from outside turbulence. And every chancellor will plead for a permanent, honest, and serious dialogue between Washington and Moscow, for there cannot be any fruitful relationship between Bonn and East Berlin while the superpowers are at loggerheads. These are basic West German interests. They explain why Helmut Kohl (and even Franz Josef Strauss) faithfully continue the *Ostpolitik* of Helmut Schmidt.

Regarding arms and arms control, even a superficial glance at the situation easily reveals the constitutive facts that shape our interests: The first fact is obvious. In any armed conflict between East and West, Germany would be the battlefield. The supreme task, then, must be deterrence. NATO's strategy and posture must center on deterring war, not on fighting war. Recent ruminations by American analysts about making nuclear war fightable, even winable, have inevitably set German teeth on edge. So have stray noises coming out of Washington about limited nuclear war in Europe. Nuclearization and regionalization of warfare are the two contingencies we dread. Every Bonn government is duty-bound to object to such notions, as it is duty-bound to insist that in the event deterrence fails there must be adequate means and strategies of defense—means and strategies that do not destroy what is meant to be protected.

The second fact is equally obvious. In the two Germanys we have today the largest concentration of military power anywhere in the world. There are about 1.4 million men stationed in the Federal Republic of Germany and the German Democratic Republic. In West

Panel discussion on "300 Years of German-American History" at the Tricentennial Conference in Philadelphia on October 6, 1983. American and German experts from various disciplines present their views in the Zellerbach Theater of the University of Pennsylvania. At the podium is the discussion leader, Hans Gatzke, Professor of History at Yale. (Randall Schilling, Tricentennial Conference)

Germany alone, a country roughly the size of the state of Oregon, there are 900,000 soldiers from seven nations. In addition, 4,000 nuclear weapons are already deployed on West German soil, (two-thirds have ranges under twenty miles and will, if they are ever used, annihilate what they are supposed to defend), 1,700 launchers for these weapons, and 100 "special ammunition sites." East Germany has 380,000 soldiers, 3,500 nuclear weapons, and 1,500 launchers.

American administrations may discount or discard arms control; they may toy with the idea of linking it to Russia's behavior elsewhere; they may talk loosely about outspending and outgunning the Soviets; they may want to rearm before disarming. No incumbent of the Palais Schaumburg could go along with any of these notions. We feel, like most Europeans, that the arms control process between the two superpowers is an indispensable ingredient of present-day international relations. We fear that linkage would only intensify an arms race that in itself exacerbates existing conflicts. We argue that building up military strength is not sufficient to obtain security but that winding down the arms race is equally necessary. And we are convinced that creating economic and societal stability is just as important as accumulating ever more horrible weapons in our arsenals. We mean it when we say double-track: arming if necessary, disarming if possible.

There are or were wide differences and divergences with regard to the Third World. The Germans, like the other Europeans, accept it on its own merits. They do not regard it only or even primarily as an arena of superpower rivalry, and they think it is wrong to superimpose the pattern of East-West conflict on the North-South relationship. Unrest in the Third World, in their view, has its origins in social and economic ills of long standing, rarely in Soviet machinations. We agree with the Americans that we should try to keep the Third World at a distance from the Soviets, but we argue that we should do so by winning them over politically, by helping them economically, and by seriously negotiating with them—not so much by impressing them militarily or by ranting at them. The Germans do not fear genuine nonalignment. They back reforms in the Third World rather than uniforms. They prefer political solutions to internal problems rather than geopolitical ones. They are in favor of foreign aid, in favor of multilateral institutions like the World Bank or the International Monetary Fund (IMF),

Participants of the panel "300 Years of German-American History." From left: Hans Gatzke, Kathleen Conzen, Günter Moltmann, Hans Trefousse, Peter Demetz, and Theo Sommer. (Randall Schilling, Tricentennial Conference)

President of the Federal Republic of Germany Karl Carstens giving the closing address of the Tricentennial Conference on October 6, 1983, in the Zellerbach Theater of the University of Pennsylvania. (Randall Schilling, Tricentennial Conference)

and in favor of patient negotiations with the young nations of the developing world.

There is a strong feeling in German government circles as well as in public and published opinion that the Reagan administration has been focusing far too narrowly on places like Nicaragua and El Salvador at a time when Brazil and Mexico are approaching financial collapse. It maligned the World Bank and the IMF as "seedbeds of communism" instead of supporting them as crucial instruments to prevent a worldwide banking crash. Its obsession with Soviet expansionism made it blind to the necessities and opportunities at hand.

It is striking that underlying the differences and divergences in these three fields is one central question: How is the West to handle the Soviet Union? Before attempting to answer this question, I must say a few words about a fourth bone of contention that has nothing to do with the management of the East-West conflict: our divergent economic policies.

I am not talking about Reaganomics in general; I am addressing myself only to one of its salient features which has all of Western Europe worrying: the high American budget deficit. It amounts to about $200 billion this year and is expected to stay in this order of magnitude for some years to come. For a Europe saddled with 12 million unemployed and attempting to struggle out of a protracted recession, this U.S. fiscal policy has crippling consequences. It keeps American interest rates at a deliriously high level—higher than ever before in the twentieth century. It siphons off capital from Europe which is badly needed there to crank up the economy. It drives the value of the dollar up beyond any realistic measure. This cheapens European exports to the United States, which in turn provokes American manufacturers and labor unions to clamor for protectionist measures, which triggers European countermeasures—a vicious circle from which no one stands to gain. There is a pervasive feeling in my part of the world that Reagan's deficit spending will continue to incarcerate Europe in recession. His neglect of the dollar can no longer be called benign. At any rate, it makes nonsense of meetings like the Williamsburg summit.

Considering this array of difficult problems it may seem surprising that the alliance still holds together. Many of our recent disagreements are much less pronounced than they were a year ago. We have been moving closer together. There has been more convergence than divergence. In Washington, realism has increasingly triumphed over rhetoric. The policy actually pursued by Reagan turned out to be much more pragmatic than his language suggested. The adage might be applied to it that Mark Twain coined about Richard Wagner's music: "It is not as bad as it sounds."

We have always had our difficulties with each other; we have always overcome them; we shall overcome them this time, too. In fact, many of our recent disagreements are less pronounced today than they were a year ago; just think of the gas pipeline deal. We are learning to live with our differences and to manage our disagreements. But it will take sustained effort. It presupposes a renunciation of Manichean rhetoric as well as of U.S. unilateralism. It requires, in short, a return to centrist positions.

It is clear that the West must be able to hold its own when challenged. The objectives of Western policy are also obvious: to avoid war, to contain communist expansion, to domesticate and ultimately change the Soviet-Marxist system, and to steer its evolution in a direction more favorable to Western interests. There is contention among Western statesmen about the methods to be pursued in this endeavor. My own view is very close to that propounded by Lord Carrington in this year's Alastair Buchan Memorial Lecture: We need a positive political strategy for dealing with the Soviet Union. We should realize that Moscow is already a decaying Byzantium, but we should not rejoice too much or too soon. We cannot significantly accelerate the process of decay; decaying empires have a way of eluding collapse for a long time; there is no question of taking a bulldozer to the Soviet Empire. We must talk to the Russians because "talking to an equally heavily armed but far less scrupulous adversary is not a concession: it is common prudence." Arms control is in everyone's self-interest, not only economically but to preserve security. The democracies have a duty to themselves to be true to their own first principles: dialogue, openness, sanity, and a nonideological approach to the dangerous business of international affairs. We must not resort to crude, one-dimensional moralism. We should realize that indiscriminate economic sanctions are neither feasible nor desirable. The Soviet leaders must be offered a clear choice: both disincentives against continued obstreperousness and incentives for a more positive relationship. Recently there has been too much stick and too little carrot. We should not overreact. We should not shun personal contacts between the top statesmen. "We must deal with the Russians simply because they are there." On such hardheaded realism, I suggest, a new transatlantic consensus could be built.

My conclusion is unambiguous. In the 1980s Europe needs the American connection no less than in the past four decades. The relationships may not be trouble-free; in fact, it is likely to become more conflict-ridden as priorities and preoccupations change. The shift of topics in world politics since 1973 has no doubt infused a new element of competition and rivalry into transatlantic relations. This shift should not, however, overshadow the basic truth that close and good relations with the United States remain absolutely essential to Western Europe.

Conversely, the United States could hardly survive in isolation in a world of hostile powers. Whatever the grounds for mutual discontent and occasional spitballing may be, there is no hope of maintaining a military equilibrium unless Europeans and Americans work closely together, no hope of setting the world economy right, no hope, finally, of coming to terms with an increasingly assertive, even rebellious Third World. The historic rationale of the American-European alliance is as valid today as ever; and it applies more than ever to the German-American relationship.

10.
U.S.-German Relations: An Alliance Turned Normal

FRITZ STERN

EVEN IN OUR CENTURY OF UPHEAVALS, the turbulence of German-American relations stands out as exceptional, swinging twice from desperate enmity to spectacular amity. In 1917, Germany, recklessly reaching for world power, brought America to Europe; American troops turned the tide in the Great War, and in the same year that America entered the global stage, the Bolshevik Revolution challenged America's claim to moral leadership. In the intervening decades, German ambition, American power, and the Soviet challenge have dominated world politics. In 1941, German power, driven to still greater frenzy and perfection, once more brought America to Europe, this time to liberate it from the Nazi terror and in alliance with the Soviet Union. In the 1920s partially and fitfully, and since 1947 consistently and forcefully, the United States turned from being Germany's enemy to being its chief friend, ally, and protector—and the reversals of role, from enemy to friend, brought a reversal of sentiment. Both countries are unusually adept at sentimentalizing foreign relations. When the United States was fighting Germany in World War I, caricatures of the brutal Hun and the evil Junker abounded; in the second war, the reality of Nazi horror exceeded Western imagination. But at war's end, the Soviets became our chief opponent, and our image of the Germans grew more benevolent. Moreover, a defeated Germany fell under America's spell in a reversal that began a celebration of friendship and harmony that lasted until recent times.

By speaking of "an alliance turned normal," I mean to suggest that the overexuberance of recent years seems to have waned: the new German-American relationship has turned sober, *sachlich*, except at moments of national celebration. Lord Palmerston once said that Britain had no permanent friends, only permanent interests. In 1849, after the Russians had helped Austria to crush the Hungarian revolt, an Austrian statesman vowed: "By our ingratitude we will astonish the world." Seven years later, the Austrians attacked Russia. Palmerston's dictum is memorable and misleading: even interests are rarely permanent, and for nations, as for individuals, the recognition of true interests is not always easy. But Palmerston's main concern was to warn against sentimentalizing politics and against assuming permanent congruence in a world of change.

For decades we assumed, on both sides of the Atlantic, that the United States and Germany were permanent and exemplary friends, held together by a common threat from the USSR. The United States, moreover, assumed that the Germans would be permanently grateful and compliant. I believe we are now discovering that we are allies bound by common interests and threatened by divergent ones, that the rhetoric of sentiment will not dispel the reality of conflict, and that we had best recognize the differences among ourselves and search for means of coping with them. We are allies with differences, friends with reservations.

By claiming that the alliance is turning normal, I do not for a moment wish to suggest that sentiment plays no role in statecraft; it does. At times nations do sense a special affinity or a special distance and even hostility for another. In the nineteenth century the British felt a great enthusiasm for Greeks and Italians, and their poets were partisans of liberation. At the same time the British harbored the deepest suspicion of the Russian bear, who was forever pawing at the gates of India; it was a historic moment when British suspicion shifted from Russia to imperial Germany. Sentiments rise and fall, and the new German-American alliance after 1945 was burdened by an exceptional baggage of feelings.

A special bond between the United States and the Federal Republic of Germany has lasted for nearly four decades. In this period there have been immense changes, and we now view the alliance more coolly; it has become an alliance among more equal partners, under more critical conditions, with increasingly divergent interests and perceptions and mounting suspicions. It would be dangerous to allow special occasions or extravagant rhetoric to becloud reality.

And yet reality includes the long-standing cultural relations between our two countries: memories and family ties. Prevailing stereotypes are significant even as a relationship becomes more *sachlich*, more matter-of-fact. There is more than antiquarian interest involved in celebrating the three hundredth anniversary of German immigration to this country. In two years the Germans will celebrate the three hundredth anniversary of Huguenot immigration to Brandenburg-Prussia. In the aggregate that immigration—no less important to Germany than the German immigration to the United States—consisted essentially of one wave of exceptionally talented and disciplined people, who maintained their separate identity for at least as long as did the Germans in America. In the American experience, what started as a trickle to Germantown became a torrent, and the Germans not only contributed greatly to the development of the United States but had a profound effect on America's perception of German life. On both sides, impressions hardened into stereotypes; some of these have been explored in other contributions to this volume. German-Americans were thought to be hardworking, honest, and a trifle humorless. When Max Weber visited the United States, Columbia University organized an evening of events to make him feel at home: German-speaking students, relentlessly guzzling beer, took to the sabers and dueled all evening. Weber could hardly have thought the spectacle caught the heart and soul of German student life. Most Germans, I think, were even more distant from America than Americans were from Germany. Bismarck was an exception: he once thought of emigrating to the United States, though what he would have done here is a puzzle. He prudently sent his funds to this country, investing in U.S. bonds right after the Civil War. In the nineteenth century German images ranged from a sense of America as a utopia, a classless society of unlimited opportunities, to the fear which the eminent scientist Emil Du Bois-Reymond expressed in 1873 that Germany was threatened by Americanization, that is, by all the evils of commercialism, capitalism, and materialism. In the early 1870s, in the so-called *Gründerjahre*, many Germans came to blame the excesses of capitalism—or their own spectacular skill at developing an industrial capitalist society—on outsiders corrupting them, most especially on Jews, Manchesterites, and Anglo-Saxons. Let me cite one last astounding example of German perceptions of the United States. In his *Civilization and Its Discontents*, Sigmund Freud speaks of "certain difficulties inherent" and ineradicable in culture, a principal one being "'la misère psychologique' of groups: "This danger is most threatening where the bonds of a society are chiefly constituted by the identification of its members with one another, while individuals of the leader type do not acquire the importance that should fall to them in the formation of a group. The present cultural state of America would give us a good opportunity for studying the damage to civilization which is thus to be feared."[1] It is arresting that in 1929 Freud would call this diminution of authority an American malaise; in some ways it was a prophetic insight.

There was also great diversity in the way Germans and Americans viewed each other. German learning and science were always cherished in America; in the 1920s Germans came to appreciate American technology, Taylorism, and jazz. Despite appreciation, however, the pre-1945 German spirit harbored a sense of unambiguous cultural superiority—a nationalist feeling that German culture was the best. By 1945 all notions of superiority, of a distinct German as against a Western culture, vanished.

The Germans have called 1945 "Stunde Null," and however inappropriate the implied suggestion of a complete break and a new beginning was, that year did mark the moment when Germany was at its nadir and the United States at its zenith: The new friendship began between victor and vanquished at a time when Germany was in shambles, morally devastated, economically ruined, intellectually bankrupt—and America was at the height of its power. It was not only the victorious world power, unchallengeable by any other power, but it was self-confident that it excelled in all realms; it had no peer. At that point the Germans were enraptured by all things American; they looked upon America as sole protector and provider, as model and as guide. Never again was the gap between the two countries to be so great: Germans came to the United States in droves, as students, as tourists, as vagabonds; they came for their requisite year in America, and it was in America that the true reeducation took place. Our efforts inside Germany were largely unsuccessful and often risible. But by and large—despite clouds of misunderstanding or lingering prejudice—Germans were enchanted by the United States, by its Care packages and its music, by its material power and its writers. It was inevitable that sooner or later enchantment would turn to disenchantment, that the German fascination with America would turn to excessive disillusionment. A different generation of Germans now sees a different America, and the disenchantment has something of the bitterness of the disappointed lover. But postwar Germans had no doubt whatever that their country was "Western" and that the long tradition of anti-Westernism had died with Nazism.

I am suggesting here that Germans did us or themselves no favor by embracing us so uncritically; their need was clear, and they saw us not as we were, even then, but as how we wanted to be and how they would have liked us to be. To be sure, America was self-confident, but in the year of our most constructive statesmanship, 1948, a young American historian, destined to become the greatest of his generation, Richard Hofstadter, wrote that American "culture has been intensely nationalistic and for the most part isolationist; it has been fiercely individualistic and capitalistic."[2] By 1948 America was facing an unprecedented historic challenge: to assume—more or less suddenly and by default—world leadership while preserving and enlarging democratic practices at home. To reconcile global imperium and isolationist, democratic tradition was a gargantuan task that could never be mastered, only fitfully attended to.

For the last decade or longer, the special glow by which Germany saw the United States has faded. The United States is no longer seen as the model society. Indeed, for many Germans—and for many Europeans—the United States and the USSR have been reduced to a moral equivalency: both are superpowers that evoke fear and distrust. Americans resent this charge and see it as ingratitude. To a large extent, however, after Vietnam and Watergate, after the faltering of so many of our domestic programs and hopes, the Europeans are only echoing the doubts that pervade America itself: do we think of ourselves as we did in 1945? Americans revel in self-criticism, but as a nation we resent foreigners who echo such criticism. For a global power, we are remarkably, prohibitively, thin-skinned.

Before I discuss common and divergent interests, let me recall the fundamentally changed conditions in world politics since 1945: the Western alliance remains intact—the most enduring alliance of free partners in history. The United States is still the mainstay of that alliance, the nuclear deterrent is still the assumed guarantor of peace, but fundamental changes have taken place: the United States has lost its strategic superiority vis-à-vis its principal opponent, and it has become relatively weaker as compared to its West European allies. The United States is still the world's greatest economic power, but it has lost its unambiguous lead in science and technology; in many realms it is no longer competitive with its chief rivals. Nor does it exert the cultural magnetism it once did. Finally, America has not provided the steady leadership in the alliance that it once did—or that we nostalgically remember it once did. Being top nation in an alliance with ancient historic states, jealous of their once unquestioned autonomy, is no easy task, and the Europeans have always criticized us for being either too strong or too weak, too close or too distant in our dealings with the Soviet Union. But since the middle years of President Carter's administration the criticisms in Europe and in Germany have hardened into an almost permanent mood of carping and unease.

For decades we have assumed that even within the alliance we have a special relationship with West Germany. The Federal Republic was an American offspring; we fathered and protected it. It has been the most exposed member of the alliance; America alone was the guarantor of its endangered security. Under our benevolent protection, the Federal Republic enjoyed an unmatched period of economic prosperity and political stability. The Federal Republic excelled in what may be called Europe's greatest postwar achievement: a pacification of Europe at home and abroad. For decades, the Federal Republic has enjoyed not only political stability and uniquely favorable labor relations but a social cohesion that even the outbreak of student revolts, terrorism, and hostility to foreign workers could not seriously shake. Until very recently, the much-vaunted class struggle seemed to have disappeared entirely. Abroad, the Germans have relentlessly worked toward the integration of Western Europe and have built their own bridges to Eastern Europe. Helmut Schmidt's deep personal commitment to achieve a reconciliation and a partnership with Poland, despite all historic obstacles and rival ties, demonstrated the will of the late government to carry forward the task of pacification.

The United States has watched with mounting apprehension as its most compliant client pursued its own détente policy, its own *Ostpolitik*—even as the United States backed away from détente. Both the United States and the Federal Republic tend to have expectations for each other's foreign policy that often ignore the realities of domestic pressures. So successful was Germany's integration and so close its relations with the United States that many people in this country forgot that German interests—beyond the fundamental interest in the preservation of peace—were necessarily dictated by geopolitics, by the presence of some 2 million *Volksdeutsche* in Eastern Europe and 17 million East Germans, all of them in some sense hostages to détente. Their fortunes are linked to Soviet-German relations with an immediacy that many in the United States fail to understand. The well-being of Berlin also depends on the faithful execution of the Four-Power Agreement, and trade with Eastern Europe has become ever more critical in a period of protracted recession. But above all many people in the United States—and perhaps some people even in the Federal Republic—forget what Germans could never forget: that Germany is the one country in Europe, perhaps the one major country in the world, with a deep national grievance. That the division of Germany was self-inflicted, the consequence of Hitler's war, does not lessen the German hope that someday—in the framework of a general pacification of Europe from the Atlantic to the Urals—the German nation will be reunited. Until recently, the issue of reunification was muted; it was almost as if the Germans had adopted the old French slogan from the post-1871 period concerning the loss of Alsace-Lorraine to Germany. The French followed the injunction: "Speak of it never, think of it always." No German statesman can even for a moment forget the tie to the German Democratic Republic or the ultimate hope of reunification. It is striking that Chancellor Kohl on the occasion of his recent trip to Moscow brought the issue openly to the fore. Franz Josef Strauss has also learned to fish in Eastern waters. Helmut Schmidt's admiration for the Poles was partially shaped by his awe for a people who regained statehood after 125 years of extinction. The dream of a united German nation is not going to disappear, regardless of which party is in office. It is the ultimate reason why the Federal Republic favors détente; but there are many more immediate reasons for preserving a policy that once had its wise analogue in Washington.

A chief difference between the Federal Republic and the United States—even on the governmental level—was and is a divergent perspective on the power and intentions of the USSR. The Germans tend to minimize the Soviet threat, the Americans periodically to exaggerate it—the vision of each influenced by respective interests. A divergent perspective necessarily leads to differences in policies, the latter also being attuned to divergent interests. There have been many U.S. officials who are convinced that the USSR is bent on an aggressive course, as exemplified by the relentless advance in its armaments and by its aggressive conduct in various parts of the world. Convinced of Soviet power and fearful of Soviet intentions, these officials seek ever greater armaments and favor a tough course against a system that President Reagan in his Orlando speech branded as "the source of all evil." Hence America's impatience with what it regarded as European reticence in meeting the challenge of Afghanistan, the pressure on Poland, or Soviet adventurism elsewhere. Hence, too, America's wish to punish the Soviets with economic sanctions and hence the bitter dispute over the pipeline. Many Germans—following general European perceptions—are more impressed by Soviet prudence, by the Soviets' efforts always to expand their power with minimal risk. The Germans, in addition, have become apprehensive lest their protectors have come to speak loudly but carry a weak stick, a fear that first hit them at the time of the overthrow of the Shah of Iran. The Germans see a paradox in America's insistence that the Soviets are immensely powerful and immensely dangerous—but that their system could be toppled by imposing an arms race on them. The Germans see further selfish contradictions in U.S. preaching of economic restraint while concluding essential grain deals with the USSR and demanding of its allies greater military preparedness, especially in conventional weapons, without itself instituting conscription.

Like many Europeans and Americans, the Germans regret President Reagan's rhetoric; at best, they think it imprudent and dangerous. They are appalled by the return to political Manicheanism—with the Soviets the incarnation of evil and the United States presumably, by definition, the source of virtue. Many critics also fear that the rhetoric either is intended to bespeak a defiant policy or will result in one as a self-fulfilling prophecy. Not a wild member of the peace movement but the eminent physicist-philosopher Carl Friedrich von Weizsäcker wrote a couple of years ago: "While Soviet policy is uniformly concerned with power, American policy moves in waves, with swings of the pendulum, and the present pendulum swing aims at the recapture of America's hegemonial position in the world."[3] There is a widespread apprehension in Germany that the United States is pursuing a provocative course; Germans fail to notice that in the 1970s the Soviets augmented their military potential far beyond Western efforts.

Sentiment is not always explicable by precise rational causes. We cannot ignore the emergence of a sentiment of fear and insecurity in the Federal Republic and elsewhere—more ominous than anything that has existed in the postwar world. In the Federal Republic, there are additional reasons for this sentiment: a country that had grown accustomed to economic well-being is confronted by a worsening and seemingly endless economic crisis that has already sharpened a social antagonism that in prior decades had been successfully dampened. In recent years Germany found an important element of strength and security through its codominion with France. That relationship has weakened, not just because of the disappearance of the two personally close leaders, Giscard and Schmidt, but because of the precariousness of the French economy. Above all, an existential insecurity has gripped many people in the West as a result of the more or less sudden awakening to the terror of the nuclear threat and to the catastrophe of an ever-spiraling arms race. At a later time perhaps we will be able to understand better the political-psychological fact that the nuclear danger became immediate and anguished only in recent years and the reasons why a peace movement has sprung up in most of our countries at this time. I am merely contending here that the Germans see themselves as especially vulnerable by virtue of their exposed geographic position and their total reliance on America's nuclear protection—at a time when authoritative experts on both sides have called the effectiveness of that protection into question. Many, often logically incompatible, apprehensions crowd the psychic-political scene: some Germans fear that a bellicose America, unwilling for its own domestic reasons to engage the USSR in serious negotiations, will provoke the Soviets into a move that would turn Europe into a nuclear battlefield while perhaps preserving the American sanctuary. Logic or reason is not enough to dispel these and similar fears; they exist, and they constitute a liability to the alliance.

In the United States—in the government, among some members of the Congress, and probably in a growing section of public opinion—there is a sense that the Europeans, but most especially the Germans, are showing ingratitude and political myopia; the United States expected a permanently compliant Germany. There is an American impatience with what is viewed as inadequate military efforts on the parts of the Europeans, again with a particularly high standard for the Germans. Why should the Europeans not make the supreme effort to defend themselves conventionally or at least do much more in that direction—even at the huge social sacrifice that that would entail? Just as American speeches are taken as bellicose, so German speeches and marches are taken as signs of incipient appeasement, of creeping neutralism—and there is no doubt that a small but growing German minority would favor a bloc-free, more or less neutralized Europe. A tiny but ever-growing minority of Germans favor unilateral disarmament. The overwhelming majority of the Germans continues to favor NATO.

The two countries trust each other, and yet within each there are groups that view the other with deep apprehension. Americans are afraid that the Federal Republic might drift away from the alliance in an easterly or neutralist direction, and there are Germans who fear that the United States is seeking to regain its hegemonial position, trying to force the Soviets to their knees, or conversely that the United States might return to a sullen, protectionist isolationism. Specific events, when seen in the perspective of fear, can be read as confirmatory evidence: German *Ostpolitik* or an American Senate that threatens to cut off funds from the United Nations.

Fears are exacerbated by ever-growing difficulties. Is it too much to say that for the Federal Republic the economic and political miracles have ended all at once? The protracted recession signals the end of an unprecedented period of prosperity. The political scene in the Federal Republic may also turn less stable, and however much some Americans find Chancellor Kohl's amiability more pleasing than Helmut Schmidt's always instructive acerbity, they will find that he speaks for a more troubled polity. The emergence of the Greens as a fourth party, or rather the emergence of a fourth party that claims to be an antiparty, the leftward drift of a Socialist party in opposition, the difficulties that Chancellor Kohl will encounter in balancing demands for social services, for investment, and for military purposes; all of these elements will complicate the political scene in the Federal Republic. For thirty-five years it has benefited from greater political stability, better political leadership at all levels, and a higher degree of social cohesion than any other regime in German history. But now the Federal Republic may also be turning more normal.

The context within which alliance issues have to be resolved has grown more difficult. In the economic realm—as in so many others—the two countries need each other, have common international interests and aims, and benefit from the open markets they both believe in. But there are divisive issues as well: the Germans are troubled by America's ever-growing fiscal deficit, which a conservative administration is amassing; their economists, as ours, see in that deficit the cause either for continued high interest rates or for renewed inflation. The Germans are not alone in wondering how future historians will judge a nation that could recklessly and with seeming oblivion defy economic prudence and tacitly admit that the immediate political price for fiscal responsibility is too great to pay—hence burdening an unknown future with present debts. The United States in turn is apprehensive about Germany's Eastern trade. The two countries are competitors in some fields, and both are threatened by the appearance of new rivals, especially in East Asia, where capitalism, unexpectedly, has apparently found its last and most congenial home. Unemployment is the most serious challenge in the Federal Republic today.

We need to acknowledge as well that we live with what is often called the successor generation—a generation that hardly remembers the halcyon days of the alliance, the early days of America's abundance. Its political education was formed in Vietnam, and it fears American involvement in Lebanon and Central America, in the Philippines and Chile. Of their own past, many young Germans are relatively ignorant; Hitler's crimes are distant in every sense. In truth, they are an unhistorical generation and know nothing of John Dos Passos's warning that "In times of change and danger when there is a quicksand of fear under men's reasoning, a sense of continuity with generations gone before can stretch like a lifeline across the scary present. . . ."[4]

The younger generations on both sides are drifting apart and have no a priori sense of affinity. The governing elite of America is also changing, and the predominance of what we called the eastern or liberal establishment is a thing of the past. We can no longer count on an automatic affinity or on people feeling at home in each other's country.

We all know that one dramatic issue dominates the scene today: the implementation of the double-track decision. As in many historic moments, that issue has substantive and symbolic importance. It is the burning issue of the day and touches on every other aspect of our relationship. It began as a military issue, raised by Helmut Schmidt as an answer to a Soviet deployment of medium-range SS-20s that had altered the existing military balance in Europe to such an extent that it opened the prospect of political blackmail. NATO's response, the Brussels double-track decision, was a compromise, and no one could have predicted that that compromise would have to be carried out in the face of a new and pervasive peace movement that would bring together in most Western countries the dignitaries of the church, the leaders of responsible professions, the young, the ordinary citizens, and the committed left. Experts of equal wisdom disagree now on the military necessity for deployment; some now argue that sea-based alternatives could offer equal security. But the issue has become political—it has become an issue of credibility and prestige. Deployment threatens the political decorum in the Federal Republic and offers the Soviet Union its most important instrument for dividing the alliance. The German and the American governments are determined to go ahead with deployment if the Geneva negotiations yield no satisfactory results. Not to deploy would suggest intolerable weakness within the alliance and that in the face of Soviet threats and internal dissension the alliance is no longer able to stick to its decisions or to defend its own acknowledged needs. Most leaders agree that such abnegation under duress would be catastrophic. It would open the way for further Soviet blackmail; the issue, as I have said, has become principally one of credibility.

But for many Germans—and for many Dutch and English as well—the deployment issue signifies something much larger. To many people it has become an existential question of whether the arms race is going to become ever more dangerous, ever more absurd. It raises questions about the ultimate intentions of the United States; it suggests a further escalation of hopelessness and helplessness, an abdication of human and political responsibility. There are those who argue that the Pershing II missiles—which can reach to the suburbs of Moscow, where the Germans were once before—are a provocation to the Soviets and thus weaken rather than strengthen Western security. The opponents of deployment come from many quarters, including supporters of the alliance, who on this issue turn against the alliance. Washington might think all opponents are alike: who is not for us is against us, and thus unless there is a last-minute agreement in Geneva, and President Reagan has made some important new proposals, the deployment issue will harm the spirit of the alliance.

I have tried to suggest that the alliance has turned normal and that as normal it will survive. It will survive because of our common interests and common values—and it will survive because there is no alternative. But given the new differences and difficulties, the health of the alliance will need greater tending and greater understanding than hitherto. Traditional pieties will not suffice; the future of the alliance requires the commitment not only of the two governments but of concerned citizens of both countries. Our continued friendship and cooperation require domestic constituencies that include citizens from all professions and all walks of life.

Notes

1. Sigmund Freud, "Civilization and its Discontents," in James Strachey and Anna Freud, eds., *The Standard Edition of the Complete Psychological Works of Sigmund Freud*, 24 vols. (London: The Hogarth Press, 1961), 21 : 115–6.

2. Richard Hofstadter, *The American Political Tradition and the Men Who Made It* (New York: Knopf, 1948), x.

3. Carl Friedrich von Weizsäcker, *Der bedrohte Friede. Politische Aufsätze, 1945–1981* (Munich: Hanser, 1981), 595.

4. John Dos Passos, "The Use of the Past," in John Dos Passos, *The Ground We Stand On: Some Examples From the History of a Political Creed* (Boston: Houghton Mifflin, 1941), 3.

PART III:
Political Relations: Research Perspectives

11.
Twentieth-Century German-American Relations: Historiography and Research Perspectives

HANS-JÜRGEN SCHRÖDER

RESEARCH OPPORTUNITIES IN GERMAN-AMERICAN RELATIONS in the first half of the twentieth century have long been a privileged area and have been affected by the defeat of Nazi Germany in 1945. Most German documents up to 1945 became available for research only a few years later. Washington established a relatively liberal policy for the use of American records. Most State Department files covering the period up to 1945, for example, were accessible by the mid-1960s. Less than ten years later, by the early 1970s, State Department records were opened through the year 1949; these files are now open through 1954. Until the introduction of a thirty-year rule in Great Britain in 1967, the excellent availability of source material for historical research on German-American relations was indeed unique. This special situation was also reflected in document series published both in the United States and in the Federal Republic of Germany.

But despite the availability of printed and archival source materials, both American and German historians were slow to discover German-American relations, which have oscillated between confrontation and cooperation since the beginning of this century, as a major field of research. Two primary reasons might be cited for this delay: historians first wanted to document the Third Reich's responsibility for the beginning of hostilities in 1939 and the Nazi plans to dominate Europe and ultimately the entire world; and in the immediate post–World War II period historical writing concentrated on the description of visible diplomatic actions rather than on indirect or informal influences in the international system, which are characteristic of American diplomacy, particularly in the interwar period.

Since the late 1960s research on German-American relations has intensified, first concentrating on the interwar period (which will be discussed below) and more recently also on the post–World War II years. The growing interest in the latter period needs no explanation. Interest in the interwar period reflects a shift in the methodological approach to the interpretation of international relations, both in the United States and in West Germany. Since the late 1960s attention has increasingly focused on the role of domestic constellations in the formulation of a nation's foreign policy and the interdependence of foreign and domestic policies. In addition, economic factors have become more and more recognized as being of central importance when interpreting twentieth-century international relations. This school of thinking, which tends to emphasize structural elements rather than personal factors, could be characterized by mentioning the names of two exponents of the approach: William Appleman Williams and Hans-Ulrich Wehler. The latter contributed to the reception of the so-called "Williams school" in the Federal Republic, especially by his publications on American imperialism.[1] The debate within Germany as to whether Williams's approach could be regarded as a useful concept not only for the interpretation of American foreign policy but also for a better understanding of specific German-American problems obviously served to intensify research in the latter of these.

Although special attention has hitherto been given to the interwar years and to the reestablishment and development of German-American relations after World War II, the early twentieth century has been neglected. In 1958 Erich Angermann drew our attention to the major importance of the so-called second Venezuelan crisis of 1902–3, interpreting it as a turning point in German-American relations,[2] but we lack more recent publications, especially on the first decade of the twentieth century. Therefore it is good news that two contributions covering this period will be published in the not too distant future. Ragnhild Fiebig just finished a dissertation on German-American competition in Latin America during the 1890s and the first years of the twentieth century. Extensive archival research made it possible to analyze the emergence of antagonistic forces that ultimately shaped German-American relations before World War I.[3] The author convincingly proves the central importance of the Venezuelan crisis of 1902–3 as a decisive factor in the further development of relations between

Berlin and Washington. As suggested by Angermann,[4] Fiebig points out that the outcome of the Venezuelan crisis predetermined American intervention in 1917, and it was certainly important in explaining the deterioration of German-American relations during the following years. The rise of this German-American antagonism undoubtedly is an important research topic that needs further attention, especially in the larger context of the rise of antagonism between Great Britain and Germany and the emergence of a "special relationship" between Great Britain and the United States during the years following the Venezuelan crisis of 1895–96.[5] The forthcoming study by Reiner Pommerin should contribute to this end.[6] Both an analysis of bilateral relations and their interpretation in the context of the shifting balance in the international sphere since the 1890s are necessary to put American intervention of 1917 into a long-range historical perspective.[7]

The issues that led to a continuing deterioration of German-American relations from the eve of World War I to American intervention have been well documented.[8] Reinhard Doerries's studies on bilateral relations are of particular value. In his book on Count Bernstorff and in various articles Doerries shows that the ambassador was one of the few officials in imperial Germany who did not underestimate the economic, strategic, and political importance of the United States. But the ambassador's opinion could neither influence his government's view of the United States nor its amateurish ambitions in Mexico.[9]

For more than fifty years, historians have been preoccupied with the issues of responsibility for World War I, American intervention, and the German "problem." A vast number of publications have been devoted to German war aims, American peace proposals, and Woodrow Wilson's struggle for a stable order in postwar central Europe. Terms such as "imperialism of idealism," "higher realism," "Puritanism and liberalism," "response to revolution," and "containment and counter-revolution" characterize the driving forces of Wilsonian diplomacy and at the same time indicate the wide range of divergent historical interpretations.[10] The military defeat of imperial Germany turned out to be relatively easy when compared with the task of determining how to influence the internal political structure of Germany and how to integrate a "new" Germany into the international system or, more precisely, into a Western community challenged by Bolshevik revolution. This is the central theme of Klaus Schwabe's voluminous book *Deutsche Revolution und Wilson-Frieden* (German revolution and Wilson peace, 1971) in which he gives a detailed account of German-American relations from October 1918 through June 1919. In supplementing Gordon Levin's interpretation, Schwabe makes a clear distinction between short-range and long-range aims in Wilsonian diplomacy toward the German problem. Germany was first to be punished before it could be reintegrated into a community of states, the author argues when discussing certain inconsistencies of Wilson's policy at Versailles.[11]

By interpreting Wilson's domestic defeat on the Versailles Treaty as an American retreat from Europe, Schwabe—explicitly repudiating Williams's thesis on U.S.-European policy in the 1920s—by and large follows the traditional interpretation of American foreign policy after World War I.[12] But did Washington really retreat from Europe? Was the United States of the 1920s isolationist? Can one make a distinction between economic diplomacy and foreign policy in general or between economic isolationism and political isolationism in particular?[13] The way these questions are answered is necessarily of great significance for the interpretation of German-American relations in the interwar period. In following the approach of the Wisconsin school, I am inclined to reject the thesis that American policy toward Europe in general and Germany in particular was isolationist in the 1920s.[14]

Many historians still hesitate to accept any economic interpretation—and the resulting political implications—of American foreign policy that stresses the importance of overseas markets and defines an expanding American export trade as a necessity for the United States because of its economic structure. But there has been a consensus among historians for a long time that American financial involvement in postwar Europe was considerable, despite an alleged retreat from the Old World. And there is a growing list of publications dealing with America's involvement in the reparation problem. Dieter Bruno Gescher published his dissertation covering the years 1920–24 in 1956. This primarily chronological account of events was taken up by Eckhard Wandel in his book on the period 1924–29, which was limited to the description of the financial mechanisms.[15] More recent publications leave no doubt that this American financial involvement in Europe—through both reparations and war debts—had far-reaching political implications.[16] But what exactly was the political significance of this American financial involvement? Did the Dawes Plan, for example, inaugurate the end of French predominance in Europe, as Stephen Schuker has suggested in his important book? In the context of German-American relations, Werner Link presented an epoch-making analysis in 1970 of American stabilization policy in Germany and its political dimensions.[17] Link's book is of central importance in

explaining the origins and mechanisms of German-American cooperation of the 1920s. His interpretation of American foreign policy follows
the approach of William A. Williams and his students. By applying this
interpretation to German-American relations after World War I the author convincingly proves that Germany was of central importance for
the United States both as a market and as a partner in the struggle to
establish a worldwide open-door policy. Special attention is given to the
German-American commercial treaty of 1923, which was based on the
unconditional most-favored-nation clause and must be regarded as a
model for American commercial treaties concluded with other states.
In evaluating the importance of the German market Carl-Ludwig
Holtfrerich goes a step further than Link does. In analyzing the effects
of German inflation on foreign trade, Holtfrerich's quantitative analysis not only confirms the importance of the German market for some
key United States products; in addition, he is convinced that inflation-
ary expansion in Germany decisively contributed to overcoming the
worldwide depression of 1920–21.[18] Therefore it cannot be surprising
that Germany became the cornerstone of Washington's policy toward
Europe: "There can be no economic recuperation in Europe unless
Germany recuperates," as Secretary of State Charles Evans Hughes
put it in December 1922.[19]

The various steps of American stabilization policy as most clearly
evidenced in the Dawes Plan and the influx of American capital into
the German economy are extensively analyzed by Link.[20] The overwhelming empirical evidence presented proves that Washington not
only realized important economic goals but that the American government was also in the position to influence political developments in
Europe. This political dimension of American stabilization policy occurred primarily because after the war the United States became the
decisive factor in German foreign policy planning. For Berlin close cooperation with the United States was essential for both economic and
political reasons. The influx of American capital was vital for the reconstruction and stabilization of the German economy. This economic
reconstruction process was also defined in political terms: a strong
economy and particularly an active trade policy were regarded as the
most important levers to further German revisionist aims against the
Versailles Treaty, a strategy that had already been formulated during
the years 1918–19.[21] The resulting German dependence on the
United States offered Washington various opportunities to influence
German economic and political decisions informally. The abortive
Stresemann-Briand talks at Thoiry (1926) might be cited as an ex-

ample. Because of its great dependence on the United States the
Weimar Republic is described as a "penetrated system."[22]

The German-American parallelism was brought to an end by the
collapse of the Weimar Republic. The dissolution process of the close
German-American cooperation needs further examination.[23] Was the
shift from cooperation to confrontation the result of Hitler's "Macht-
ergreifung"? Were there any long-established structural divergences
between Washington and Berlin that came to the surface during the
Great Depression? Is the development of German-American relations
during the depression just part of dissolving international politics?[24]
Can the "penetrated system" thesis still be defended, if one takes into
account how quickly the German-American cooperation of the 1920s
actually ended? What influence did the Hoover administration still
have in Europe in the early 1930s?

Although the process of the dissolution of German-American cooperation during the Great Depression needs further investigation,
our information about German-American relations during the Nazi
years seems to be excellent. A large number of books, articles, and dissertations are available covering a wide spectrum of important problems, such as bilateral diplomatic and economic relations,[25] the United
States as a factor in the strategic and political thinking of the Nazi
elite,[26] Nazi propaganda in the United States and the *Deutschtum* of
Nazi Germany,[27] American reactions toward the prosecution of Jews,[28]
the impact of German immigrants in the United States,[29] and the challenge to the U.S. government's interests by National Socialist ideological, economic, and finally territorial expansion.[30] This Nazi threat
manifested itself dramatically in the Third Reich's policy vis-à-vis
Latin America, which developed into an important zone of conflict between Washington and Berlin.[31] This already long list of research topics could easily be expanded. Clearly, the main problem one faces
when interpreting German-American relations during these years is
not the lack of information but a determination of the relative importance of these factors for the development of the German-American
confrontation in the 1930s and for the entry of the United States into
World War II.

Because of the close economic cooperation between the two states
in the 1920s, the dissolution of German-American parallelism during
the Great Depression hurt economic relations between Berlin and
Washington. It was not primarily the dramatic reduction of bilateral
trade between the two countries but the competition in underdeveloped
areas such as Latin America and southeastern Europe that alarmed

the Roosevelt administration, as Lloyd Gardner has pointed out in his *Economic Aspects of New Deal Diplomacy.*[32] Although aggressive German export drives reduced the U.S. share in the import trade of various countries, especially in Latin America, there was an even more important matter of principle involved: German autarky and bilateral trade schemes (with Japan and Italy practicing similar methods) seriously challenged the Roosevelt administration's concept of an "indivisible world market"—to use a phrase of Detlef Junker's.[33] In Washington many decision makers regarded this challenge to America's open-door concept not only as a matter of foreign economic policy or foreign policy in general; they also stressed the domestic consequences for the United States: "Every blow at our foreign trade is a direct thrust at our economic and social life," as Assistant Secretary of State Francis B. Sayre put it in 1936.[34] How did Washington react to this German challenge? Were there any active elements in U.S. policy toward Nazi Germany before 1938? What did it really mean when Secretary of State Cordell Hull and others talked about "economic appeasement"?

The lack of diplomatic activity in Washington's relations with Hitler's Germany up to the end of 1938, when President Roosevelt stated on November 15 that the Nazi pogroms "had deeply shocked public opinion" in the United States and that he himself "could scarcely believe that such things could occur in a Twentieth Century civilization,"[35] has given historians occasion to define United States policy vis-à-vis Germany as a policy of appeasement. Arnold Offner, for example, has repeatedly maintained that the overriding aim of Washington's European policy was "to appease Germany during 1933–1940." Offner titled his important work on American policy toward Germany in the 1930s *American Appeasement.* In his survey on the origins of World War II, Offner, referring to various similarities in British and American policy, speaks in general terms of an "era of appeasement." And he concludes that during the year 1938 "American diplomacy floundered in the sea of appeasement." But was there anything like a general appeasement of Nazi Germany by the English-speaking world, as British historian Ritchie Ovendale has formulated?[36]

Both a comparison of British and American policies toward Nazi Germany and the inclusion of economic factors into this comparative approach offer opportunities to challenge these interpretations and to describe American policy before the outbreak of hostilities in Europe as a more active one than a general appeasement formula might suggest. Recent historiography on British appeasement policy has stressed the close interdependence of economics and politics in London's approach toward Germany. Bernd-Jürgen Wendt and others have demonstrated in great detail that the British policy of economic appeasement was not only aimed at reducing economic tensions in bilateral relations with Germany but was also seen in London as a means of pacifying Europe politically and therefore regarded as an integral part of overall foreign policy.[37] Economic agreements with Germany would obviously have great possibilities as "a stepping stone to political appeasement," as was repeatedly stressed by British diplomats.[38]

Like the British policy toward Germany, the United States administration similarly based its policy on the realization of the close interdependence of economic and political problems. But the American concept of economic appeasement diverged fundamentally from the British approach. The Roosevelt administration shared the view that international cooperation in the economic field would reduce political tensions, but this did not mean agreement with British political strategies. Most members of the State Department advocated an uncompromising line toward the Third Reich: any concept of economic appeasement was to be applied on American conditions, namely, on the basis of an open-door policy as formulated in the reciprocal foreign trade program. Because this trade agreement system was expanding, it was argued, Germany would increasingly be subject to economic pressure in the field of foreign trade, which would be the basis for finally exerting political pressure on the Third Reich.[39] As the chief of the European desk put it: "The development of our trade agreement program will automatically put economic pressure on Germany, and in this we have a ready forged weapon in hand to induce Germany to meet general world trade and political sentiment."[40] According to the hard-liners in the State Department, trade concessions similar to those granted by London would only make it easier for the National Socialist regime to gain hegemony in Europe and to carry out its plans for world domination. Assistant Secretary of State George S. Messersmith stressed again and again that a hard line in the economic field would offer the opportunity to weaken National Socialist Germany both economically and politically.[41] Ultimately the Reich would be forced to accept compromises both in the economic sphere and in foreign affairs. This active element of American policy toward Europe—which had been developed at a time when there was no question of a German military or strategic threat to U.S. security interests—is best evidenced in the Anglo-American trade talks of 1937–38.

The Anglo-American Trade Agreement of November 1938 was

a cornerstone of the economic "containment" strategy.[42] The combined political-economic function of the agreement was repeatedly emphasized—by the State Department in particular. In the context of German-American relations the political significance of the trade agreement can hardly be overemphasized. In view of the isolationist trends in American public opinion and the neutrality legislation passed by Congress, the only instrument available for the Roosevelt administration in the field of foreign affairs up to 1939 was trade policy, specifically, the reciprocal trade agreements program. Even if one rejects the assumption that there were significant economic driving forces behind U.S. foreign policy, focusing instead on the political and ideological aspects of Roosevelt's prewar diplomacy, the instrumental use of trade policy nevertheless remains unaffected.

The importance of American trade policy in foreign affairs was clearly diagnosed by both the British government and the Nazi leadership. The British records clearly reveal the political relevance of the 1938 trade treaty with the United States. The delegates to the Imperial Conference of 1937 were informed by Neville Chamberlain that "the moral and psychological effects of such an agreement throughout the world would be tremendous, that it was through economic cooperation that American sympathy was to be won and that that sympathy would be of an incalculable value if we were once again involved in a great struggle." In July, the cabinet members agreed "to place on record the importance that they attached, from a political and international point of view, to the conclusion of a Trade Agreement with the United States of America."[43]

In Berlin, the Anglo-American Trade Agreement was also interpreted as a political step directed against Germany. For the Nazi leadership it was therefore of utmost importance that these foreign policy aspects should not be discussed in public. Before the agreement was concluded the Ministry of Propaganda had confidentially given journalists an indication of its political significance; but at the same time instructions had been given that the trade agreement "should not give rise to speculation about a close political alliance of the western democracies."[44] When the trade agreement was signed, the German press was again expressly forbidden to indulge "in polemics about the agreement so as not to create the impression that we consider this as a victory of the democracies."[45] The Nazi leadership, however, was well aware that the conclusion of the trade agreement was of major political importance.

The example of the Anglo-American Trade Agreement clearly

demonstrates the integration of economic factors into American foreign policy toward Nazi Germany. A comparison between British and
American foreign policy strategies might add new dimensions to the
historical evaluation of relations between the United States and the
Third Reich. The British and American files on the 1937–38 Anglo-
American trade talks—which were not included by David Reynolds in
his study on Anglo-American relations during the years 1937–41 [46]—
contain impressive empirical evidence that should encourage such an
approach. In taking account of these materials it is possible to go
much further than did Callum MacDonald in his book *The United
States, Britain, and Appeasement.* MacDonald states in his criticism
of Offner's appeasement thesis that "a shift from appeasement to containment . . . took place in October 1938." [47] I would like to emphasize,
however, that American policy toward Germany must be described as
a containment strategy long before Munich. Further research on the
political, strategic, and economic elements in Anglo-American relations
in the late 1930s and early 1940s will certainly contribute to clarifying
American policy toward the Third Reich and make clear that there
never was an American appeasement of Nazi Germany. [48] From the
Roosevelt administration's perspective, any compromise with the Third
Reich would have undermined not only basic principles of American
foreign policy but also the president's aim of an "indirect U.S. world
leadership." [49] The projected Pax Americana as outlined in the Atlantic
Charter implied serious threats to the British Empire. One can hardly
imagine how Roosevelt could have been prepared to tolerate a Nazi
Empire (collaborating with Japan) while he set about the task of dismantling the British Empire—despite the long-standing "special
relationship" between Great Britain and the United States.

   The extent to which National Socialist expansion was regarded
as a major threat to America's global interests is also reflected in the
Roosevelt administration's postwar planning. One of the main problems was to deal with defeated Nazi Germany in a manner that would
eliminate the danger of future German aggression. [50] The most extreme approach was suggested by Secretary of the Treasury Henry
Morgenthau, who wanted to deprive Germany of the industrial capacity that had enabled it to upset the international status quo twice
within a quarter of a century. [51] But these discussions about a harsh approach toward Germany were soon to be reduced to a historical episode by a series of events that shaped the postwar international order
in general and American policy in particular. Within two years after
the defeat of the Third Reich the part of Germany under the immedi-

ate control of the Western powers had again emerged as a cornerstone of American stabilization policy toward Germany, which is symbolized in both the "destructive" Joint Chiefs of Staff directive 1067 of April 1945 and the "constructive" directive JCS 1779 of July 1947. This focus on the Western sectors was certainly a key factor in bringing about the economic revival of West Germany and finally the founding of the Federal Republic of Germany.

The reconstruction of West Germany during the years 1945 to 1949 and the consolidation of the Federal Republic in the early 1950s has become a major field of historical research. The broad range of projects is perhaps best reflected in a number of essay collections,[52] as well as in the excellent edition of documents on the *Vorgeschichte der Bundesrepublik Deutschland*.[53] Because of the key role the United States played in the West German reconstruction process, American policy toward the Western zones of occupation and the Federal Republic has been of particular interest to both historians and political scientists.[54] This special interest is also evidenced in the impressive OMGUS project undertaken jointly by the Institut für Zeitgeschichte and the Bundesarchiv, which made many files of the American military government available for research in West Germany.[55]

There is general agreement that the reconstruction of West Germany has to be seen in the context of international relations, particularly in the context of growing East-West tensions. There is no doubt that Germany was "a major theatre in the 'cold war.'"[56] But what exactly was the role of the United States concerning these growing East-West tensions in Germany, which resulted in the partition of the former Reich?[57] The debate on the reparation problem might be taken as just one example of the wide spectrum of divergent interpretations which are represented in the works of Bruce Kuklick and Otto Nübel and which is part of the ongoing controversy about the origins of the Cold War.[58]

Although most commentators agree in principle on the interdependence between these international developments and German domestic issues, we are confronted with differing interpretations of the relative importance of external factors for specific developments in West Germany. Two questions might be raised here which are closely connected with American reconstruction policy in Germany and in particular with the Marshall Plan: (1) When did the reconstruction process actually start? and (2) Did the United States insist that West German recovery take place in the framework of a restored private capitalist system?

It has long been taken for granted that the beginning of the economic reconstruction process was brought about by foreign aid (particularly the Marshall Plan), currency reform, and the introduction of the social market economy to West Germany. This traditional interpretation has been repeatedly challenged by Werner Abelshauser, who argues that "the deadlock of German industry was broken and a substantial beginning was made before currency reform took place in June 1948" and that the social market economy had already been significantly modified toward corporatism by the time the ultimate breakthrough took place in the early 1950s. But Abelshauser also confirms the leading role of United States policy in Germany for the beginning of the economic recovery by drawing our attention to the paradox that although specific American contributions seem to have been less crucial for this breakthrough, "the U.S. Military Government was quite successful in priming the German economy with German means and resources at a very early stage of postwar development."[59] This early priming of the German economy must certainly be seen as part of General Lucius Clay's pragmatic stabilization policy before the inauguration of the Marshall Plan.[60] And such a development could not have taken place against the declared will of the U.S. government.

Another controversial issue is the question whether the U.S. government's policy toward postwar Germany was guided by the assumption that the restoration of democracy and capitalism in West Germany necessarily went hand in hand. Significant political forces in postwar Germany were bent on establishing different socioeconomic systems as alternatives to capitalism, but they failed to realize their anticapitalist objectives. The so-called revisionists take it for granted that a major aim of the Truman administration was to reintegrate West Germany into a Western capitalist system and to revamp the German economy according to the American model of free enterprise. Lloyd Gardner, for example, described policy toward Germany as being reactionary: "What actually took place in Western Germany . . . was an American counterrevolution—against the policy of . . . German social democrats, and, finally, European radicalism." In challenging the revisionist interpretation, Dörte Winkler even went so far as to speak of the American policy of socialization in Germany. More recently, Werner Link in his article on the Marshall Plan supported Winkler's approach. Link is convinced that "the American Government would not have rejected a [German] democratic decision to socialize basic industries." But this interpretation has to be revised again in light of the British files. As Horst Lademacher and Rolf Steininger were able to prove, the Attlee government's plans to socialize the Ruhr mines were blocked by the U.S. government. Financial difficulties forced the British government to accept the American position. As General Robertson put it: "He who pays the piper calls the tune."[61]

The debate on the motives and the failure of British socialization policy in Germany is more than just another example to underline the vital role of the United States in the West German reconstruction process. This debate also makes clear that the results and mechanisms of United States policy toward postwar Germany cannot be exclusively understood by a purely bilateral view. Again, the inclusion of the British factor and in particular research in the British archival material open new dimensions for the interpretation of America's role in the West German reconstruction process. Continued research on the Marshall Plan would offer an excellent opportunity to advance such a multilateral approach.

Although a number of publications deal with the Marshall Plan, many questions concerning its impact on Germany have yet to be satisfactorily answered.[62] What exactly was the impact of the Marshall Plan on economic growth and the shaping of the economic order in West Germany? Can the Marshall Plan be interpreted as a "crash program"[63] or was it part of long-range policy planning? What is the function of West Germany in the context of Washington's European policy and the origins of the Cold War? Can the significance of the Marshall Plan for the various European countries be compared? How were the economic interests of the United States defined when the plan was inaugurated? And, finally, what were the elements of continuity in the American stabilization policy in Europe during the 1920s and the late 1940s?

There are obviously striking similarities between American stabilization strategies in Europe after both world wars. In both periods Germany became the cornerstone of American policy toward Europe, and as in the late 1920s, the problem of how to stabilize Germany and Europe was primarily defined in economic terms. This interpretation is convincingly presented by Werner Link in his comparison of United States reconstruction policies during the two postwar periods.[64] Both in the 1920s and after World War II American stabilization policies in Germany formed the basis for extraordinarily close German-American cooperation in the political field as well. It is important to emphasize the continuities of the cooperative phases in German-American relations and to report their "success." But it is also necessary to explore the causes of conflicts of the past to become more sensitive to potential frictions between the two powers in the future. A reexamination of German-American relations during the first half of our century (a period for which a vast number of unpublished sources are available) might not only contribute to a better understanding of developments during the second half of the twentieth century; it might also aid in recognizing divergences between the two powers more quickly. And this could be a first important step in solving actual and potential problems in German-American relations. Because of the experiences of the past, such a reexamination of various phases in German-American relations should give more attention to the political dimensions of economic factors and above all follow a multilateral rather than a bilateral approach. As history shows, the relations between the two powers since the beginning of this century have had far-reaching implications for the international system and have been vital for both Germany and the United States.

Notes

1. William Appleman Williams, *The Tragedy of American Diplomacy* (Cleveland: World Publishing Co., 1959; 2d rev. ed. New York: Dell, 1972). See especially Hans-Ulrich Wehler, *Der Aufstieg des amerikanischen Imperialismus. Studien zur Entwicklung des Imperium Americanum 1865–1900* (Göttingen: Vandenhoeck & Ruprecht, 1974), and his earlier article, "1889—Wendepunkt der amerikanischen Aussenpolitik. Die Anfänge des modernen Panamerikanismus—Die Samoakrise," *Historische Zeitschrift* 201 (1965): 57–109; on the reception of the Williams school in West Germany, Werner Link, "Die Aussenpolitik der USA 1919–1933. Quellen und neue amerikanische Literatur," *Neue Politische Literatur* 12 (1967): 343–56; Link, "Die amerikanische Aussenpolitik aus revisionistischer Sicht," ibid. 16 (1971): 205–20; Hans-Jürgen Schröder, "Ökonomische Aspekte der amerikanischen Aussenpolitik, 1900–1923," ibid. 17 (1972): 298–321.

2. Erich Angermann, "Ein Wendepunkt in der Geschichte der Monroe-Doktrin und der deutsch-amerikanischen Beziehungen. Die Venezuelakrise von 1902/03 im Spiegel der amerikanischen Tagespresse," *Jahrbuch für Amerikastudien* 3 (1958): 22–58.

3. Ragnhild Fiebig, "Lateinamerika als Konfliktherd der deutsch-amerikanischen Beziehungen, 1890–1903," (Ph.D. dissertation, Cologne, 1984).

4. Angermann, "Wendepunkt," 57–58.

5. Paul M. Kennedy, *The Rise of the Anglo-German Antagonism, 1860–1914* (London: George Allen & Unwin, 1980); Kennedy, "British and German Reactions to the Rise of American Power," in Roger J. Bullen et al., eds., *Ideas into Politics: Aspects of European History, 1880–1950* (London: Croom Helm, 1984), 15–24.

6. Reiner Pommerin, *Deutsch-amerikanische Beziehungen zwischen Realität und Perzeption, 1890–1917* (forthcoming).

7. See Alfred Vagts, *Deutschland und die Vereinigten Staaten in der Weltpolitik*, 2 vols. (New York: Macmillan, 1935).

8. Hans W. Gatzke, "The United States and Germany on the Eve of World War I," in Imanuel Geiss and Bernd-Jürgen Wendt, eds., *Deutschland in der Weltpolitik des 19. und 20. Jahrhunderts* (Düsseldorf: Bertelsmann, 1973), 271–86.

9. Reinhard R. Doerries, *Washington-Berlin 1908/1917. Die Tätigkeit des Botschafters Johann Heinrich Graf von Bernstorff in Washington vor dem Eintritt der Vereinigten Staaten von Amerika in den Ersten Weltkrieg* (Düsseldorf: Pädagogischer Verlag Schwann, 1975; American ed. forthcoming); see also Doerries's articles: "Imperial Berlin and Washington: New Light on Germany's Foreign Policy and America's Entry into World War I," *Central European History* 11 (1978): 23–49; "The Politics of Irresponsibility: Imperial Germany's Defiance of United States Neutrality during World War I," in Hans L. Trefousse, ed., *Germany and America: Essays on Problems of International Relations and Immigration* (New York: Brooklyn College Press, 1980), 3–20; see also Jürgen Möckelmann, *Deutsch-amerikanische Beziehungen in der Krise. Studien zur amerikanischen Politik im ersten Weltkrieg* (Frankfurt: Europäische Verlagsanstalt, 1967); Kennedy, "British and German Reactions," 24.

10. Williams, *Tragedy*, chap. 2; Arthur S. Link, *The Higher Realism of Woodrow Wilson and Other Essays* (Nashville: Vanderbilt University Press, 1971); Klaus Schwabe, *Woodrow Wilson. Ein Staatsmann zwischen Puritanertum und Liberalismus* (Göttingen: Musterschmidt, 1971); N. Gordon Levin, *Woodrow Wilson and World Politics: America's Response to War and Revolution* (New York: Oxford University Press, 1968); Arno J. Mayer, *Politics and Diplomacy of Peacemaking: Containment and Counter-revolution at Versailles, 1918–1919* (New York: Random House, 1969).

11. Klaus Schwabe, *Deutsche Revolution und Wilson-Frieden. Die amerikanische und deutsche Friedensstrategie zwischen Ideologie und Machtpolitik 1918/19* (Düsseldorf: Droste, 1971).

12. Ibid., 658.

13. See Melvyn P. Leffler, "Political Isolationism, Economic Expansionism, or Diplomatic Realism? American Policy toward Western Europe, 1921–1933," in *Perspectives in American History* 8 (1974): 413–68; Klaus Schwabe, *Der amerikanische Isolationismus in 20. Jahrhundert. Legende und Wirklichkeit* (Wiesbaden: Steiner, 1975).

14. An excellent survey of differing interpretations of American foreign policy in the 1920s is given by John Braeman, "American Foreign Policy in the Age of Normalcy: Three Historiographical Traditions," in *Amerikastudien/American Studies* 26 (1981): 125–58.

15. Dieter Bruno Gescher, *Die Vereinigten Staaten von Nordamerika und die Reparationen, 1920–1924. Eine Untersuchung der Reparationsfrage auf der Grundlage amerikanischer Akten* (Bonn: Röhrscheid, 1956); Eckhard Wandel, *Die Bedeutung der Vereinigten Staaten von Amerika für das deutsche Reparationsproblem, 1924–1929* (Tübingen: J. C. B. Mohr, 1971).

16. See discussion of the literature by Peter Krüger, "Das Reparationsproblem der Weimarer Republik in fragwürdiger Sicht. Kritische Überlegungen zur neuesten Forschung," *Vierteljahrshefte für Zeitgeschichte* 29 (1981): 21–47.

17. Stephen A. Schuker, *The End of French Predominance in Europe: The Financial Crisis of 1924 and the Adoption of the Dawes Plan* (Chapel Hill: University of North Carolina Press, 1976); Werner Link, *Die amerikanische Stabilisierungspolitik in Deutschland 1921–32* (Düsseldorf: Droste, 1970), summary: "Die Beziehungen

zwischen der Weimarer Republik und den USA," in Manfred Knapp et al., eds., *Die USA und Deutschland 1918–1975. Deutsch-amerikanische Beziehungen zwischen Rivalität und Partnerschaft* (Munich: C. H. Beck, 1978), 62–106.

18. Carl-Ludwig Holtfrerich, "Die konjunkturellen Wirkungen der deutschen Inflation auf die US-Wirtschaft in der Weltwirtschaftskrise 1920/21," in Gerald D. Feldman et al., eds., *Die Deutsche Inflation. Eine Zwischenbilanz* (Berlin: de Gruyter, 1982), 207–34.

19. Quoted in Link, *Stabilisierungspolitik*, 174.

20. On American stabilization policy in Germany see also Frank Costigliola, "The United States and the Reconstruction of Germany in the 1920s," *Business History Review* 50 (1976–77): 477–502; Manfred Jonas, "Mutualism in the Relations between the United States and the Early Weimar Republic," in Trefousse, ed., *Germany and America*, 41–53, with further references.

21. Peter Krüger, *Deutschland und die Reparationen 1918/19. Die Genesis des Reparationsproblems in Deutschland zwischen Waffenstillstand und Versailler Friedensschluss* (Stuttgart: Deutsche Verlags-Anstalt, 1973).

22. Werner Link, "Der amerikanische Einfluss auf die Weimarer Republik in der Dawesplanphase (Elemente eines "penetrierten Systems")," in Hans Mommsen et al., eds., *Industrielles System und politische Entwicklung in der Weimarer Republik* (Düsseldorf: Droste, 1974), 485–98; Link, *Stabilisierungspolitik*, 348ff. The impact of the United States on the Thoiry talks was pointed out by Robert Gottwald, *Die deutsch-amerikanischen Beziehungen in der Ära Stresemann* (Berlin: Colloquium, 1965).

23. On German-American relations during the Brüning government see the excellent dissertation by Robert C. Dahlberg, "Heinrich Brüning, the Center Party, and Germany's 'Middle Way': Political Economy and Foreign Policy in the Weimar Republic" (Johns Hopkins University, 1983).

24. Gustav Schmidt, "Dissolving International Politics?" in Gustav Schmidt, ed., *Konstellationen internationaler Politik 1924–1932. Politische und wirtschaftliche Beziehungen zwischen Westeuropa und den Vereinigten Staaten* (Bochum: D. N. Brockmeyer, 1983), 348–428.

25. On the years 1933–39: Josef E. Heindl, "Die diplomatischen Beziehungen zwischen Deutschland und den Vereinigten Staaten von Amerika von 1933–1939" (Ph.D. dissertation, Würzburg, 1964); Joachim Remak, "Germany and the United States, 1933–1939" (Ph.D. dissertation, Stanford University, 1965); Peter Schäfer, "Die Beziehungen zwischen Deutschland und den Vereinigten Staaten von 1933 bis 1939. Unter besonderer Berücksichtigung der handelspolitischen Beziehungen und der Boykottbewegung der Vereinigten Staaten" (Ph.D. dissertation, Humboldt Universität Berlin, 1964); Thomas H. Etzold, "Fair Play: American Principles and Practice in Relations with Germany, 1933–1939," (Ph.D. dissertation, Yale University, 1970); Alton Frye, *Nazi Germany and the American Hemisphere* (New Haven: Yale University Press, 1967); Arnold A. Offner, *American Appeasement: United States Foreign Policy and Germany, 1933–1938* (Cambridge, Mass.: Belknap Press of Harvard University Press, 1969); Hans-Jürgen Schröder, *Deutschland und die Vereinigten Staaten 1933–1939. Wirtschaft und Politik in der Entwicklung des deutsch-amerikanischen Gegensatzes* (Wiesbaden: Steiner, 1970); on the crucial years preceding America's entry into the war: Hans L. Trefousse, *Germany and American Neutrality, 1939–1941* (New York: Bookman, 1951); Jürgen Rohwer, "Das deutsch-amerikanische Verhältnis 1937–1941," vol. 1, "Vom Neutralitätsgesetz zur Englandhilfe" (Ph.D. dissertation, Hamburg, 1954); Saul Friedländer, *Hitler et les Etats-Unis, 1939–1941* (Geneva: Librairie Droz, 1963); Günter

Hass, *Von München bis Pearl Harbor. Zur Geschichte der deutsch-amerikanischen Beziehungen 1938–1941* (Berlin: Akademie, 1965); Thomas A. Bailey and Paul B. Ryan, *Hitler vs. Roosevelt: The Undeclared Naval War* (New York: Free Press, 1980); see also the review articles by Ernest R. May, "Nazi Germany and the United States: A Review Essay," *Journal of Modern History* 41 (1969): 207–14, and Werner Link, "Das nationalsozialistische Deutschland und die USA 1933–1941," *Neue Politische Literatur* 18 (1973): 225–33.

26. See especially Andreas Hillgruber, "Der Faktor Amerika in Hitlers Strategie 1938–1941," in *Aus Politik und Zeitgeschichte*. Beilage zur Wochenzeitung *Das Parlament* (May 11, 1955): 3–21, reprinted in Andreas Hillgruber, *Deutsche Grossmacht- und Weltpolitik im 19. und 20. Jahrhundert* (Düsseldorf: Droste, 1977), 197–222; also Joachim Remak, "Hitlers Amerikapolitik," *Aussenpolitik* 6 (1955): 706–14; Joachim Remak, "Two German Views of the United States: Hitler and His Diplomats," *World Affairs Quarterly* 28 (1957–58): 25–35; Gerhard L. Weinberg, "Hitler's Image of the United States," *American Historical Review* 69 (1963–64): 1006–21; Harald Frisch, "Das deutsche Roosevelt-Bild (1933–1941)" (Ph.D. dissertation, Freie Universität Berlin, 1967); James V. Compton, *The Swastika and the Eagle: Hitler, the United States and the Origins of World War II* (Boston: Houghton Mifflin, 1967).

27. Joachim Remak, "'Friends of the New Germany.' The Bund and German-American Relations," *Journal of Modern History* 29 (1957): 38–41; Arthur L. Smith, *The Deutschtum of Nazi Germany and the United States* (The Hague: Martinus Nijhoff, 1965); Klaus Kipphan, *Deutsche Propaganda in den Vereinigten Staaten 1933–1941* (Heidelberg: Winter, 1971); Gernot Heinrich Willy Graessner, "Deutschland und der Nationalsozialismus in den Vereinigten Staaten von Amerika 1933–1939. Ein Beitrag zur Deutschtumspolitik des Dritten Reiches" (Ph.D. dissertation, Bonn University, 1973); Sander A. Diamond, *The Nazi Movement in the United States, 1924–1941* (Ithaca: Cornell University Press, 1974).

28. Henry L. Feingold, *The Politics of Rescue: The Roosevelt Administration and the Holocaust, 1938–1945* (New Brunswick: Rutgers University Press, 1970); Saul S. Friedman, *No Haven for the Oppressed: United States Policy toward Jewish Refugees, 1938–1945* (Detroit: Wayne State University Press, 1973); Arthur D. Morse, *While Six Million Died* (New York: Random House, 1968); Moshe R. Gottlieb, *American Anti-Nazi Resistance, 1933–1941: An Historical Analysis* (New York: KTAV Publishing House, 1982).

29. Joachim Radkau, *Die deutsche Emigration in den USA. Ihr Einfluss auf die amerikanische Europapolitik* (Düsseldorf: Bertelsmann, 1971).

30. Detlef Junker, *Der unteilbare Weltmarkt. Das ökonomische Interesse in der Aussenpolitik der USA 1933–1941* (Stuttgart: Klett, 1975).

31. On National Socialist ideological and economic penetration into various Latin American countries and resulting conflicts between Washington and Berlin see Manfred Kossok, "'Sonderauftrag Südamerika.' Zur deutschen Politik gegenüber Lateinamerika 1938 bis 1942," in *Lateinamerika zwischen Emanzipation und Imperialismus 1810–1960* (Berlin: Akademie, 1961), 234–55; Heinz Sanke, ed., *Der deutsche Faschismus in Lateinamerika, 1933–1939* (Berlin: Humboldt Universität, 1966); Frye, *Nazi Germany*; Arnold Ebel, *Das Dritte Reich und Argentinien. Die diplomatischen Beziehungen unter besonderer Berücksichtigung der Handelspolitik* (Cologne: Böhlau, 1971); Hans-Jürgen Schröder, "Hauptprobleme der deutschen Lateinamerikapolitik 1933–1941," *Jahrbuch für Geschichte von Staat, Wirtschaft und Gesellschaft Lateinamerikas* 12 (1972): 408–33; Stanley E. Hilton, *Brazil and the Great Powers, 1930–*

1939: The Politics of Trade Rivalry (Austin: University of Texas Press, 1975); Reiner Pommerin, *Das Dritte Reich und Lateinamerika. Die deutsche Politik gegenüber Süd- und Mittelamerika 1939–1942* (Düsseldorf: Droste, 1977); Stanley E. Hilton, *Hitler's Secret War in South America, 1939–1945: German Military Espionage and Allied Counterespionage in Brazil* (New York: Ballantine Books, 1982).

32. Lloyd C. Gardner, *Economic Aspects of New Deal Diplomacy* (Madison: University of Wisconsin Press, 1964).

33. Two important State Department documents dealing with German economic penetration into Latin America are published by Hans-Jürgen Schröder, "Die 'Neue deutsche Südamerikapolitik.' Dokumente zur nationalsozialistischen Wirtschaftspolitik in Lateinamerika von 1934 bis 1936," *Jahrbuch für Geschichte von Staat, Wirtschaft und Gesellschaft Lateinamerikas* 6 (1969): 337–451, and "Die Vereinigten Staaten und die nationalsozialistische Handelspolitik gegenüber Lateinamerika 1937/38," ibid. 7 (1970): 309–71. Junker's phrase appears in his *Der unteilbare Weltmarkt*.

34. Francis B. Sayre, *Our Problem of Foreign Trade* (Washington, D.C.: Government Printing Office, 1936).

35. Statement by Roosevelt, November 15, 1938, in Donald B. Schewe, ed., *Franklin D. Roosevelt and Foreign Affairs*, 2d ser., January 1937–August 1939, vol. I (New York: Clearwater Publishing Co., 1979), 83.

36. Arnold A. Offner, "Appeasement Revisited: The United States, Great Britain, and Germany, 1933–1940," *Journal of American History* 64 (September 1977): 373; Offner, *American Appeasement: United States Foreign Policy and Germany, 1933–1938* (Cambridge, Mass.: Belknap Press of Harvard University Press, 1969); Offner, *The Origins of the Second World War: American Foreign Policy and World Politics, 1917–1941* (New York: Praeger, 1975), 104ff., 124; Ritchie Ovendale, *Appeasement and the English Speaking World: Britain, the United States, the Dominions, and the Policy of "Appeasement," 1937–1939* (Cardiff: University of Wales Press, 1975).

37. Bernd-Jürgen Wendt, *Economic Appeasement. Handel und Finanz in der britischen Deutschlandpolitik 1933–1939* (Düsseldorf: Bertelsmann, 1971), summary in English, "'Economic Appeasement'—a Crisis Strategy," in Wolfgang J. Mommsen and Lothar Kettenacker, *The Fascist Challenge and the Policy of Appeasement* (London: George Allen & Unwin, 1983), 157–72; see also the important book by Gustav Schmidt, *England in der Krise. Grundzüge und Grundlagen der britischen Appeasement-Politik, 1930–1937* (Opladen: Westdeutscher, 1981).

38. Hudson minute, July 8, 1938, Public Record Office, Kew, FO 371/21647.

39. See especially the debate within the State Department on the German trade agreement offer of October 1937 in Record Group 59, 611.6231/998ff., National Archives, Washington, D.C.

40. Moffat memo, January 31, 1938, ibid. 1002 1/2.

41. Numerous documents in the Messersmith Papers, University of Delaware Library, Newark, Delaware, and in the relevant files in the Franklin D. Roosevelt Library, Hyde Park, and the State Department records.

42. The Roosevelt administration was, however, confronted with the problem of bringing private enterprise into line with government policy. This question needs to be examined in the context of German-American relations; see, for example, the remarks by Bernd Martin, "Friedens-Planungen der multinationalen Grossindustrie (1932–1940) als politische Krisenstrategie," *Geschichte und Gesellschaft* 2 (1976): 66–88.

43. Cabinet 36 (38), in Public Record Office, Kew, Cab. 23/94.

44. Bundesarchiv Koblenz, collection Brammer, vol. 10.

45. Ibid., collection Traub, vol. 10.

46. David Reynolds, *The Creation of the Anglo-American Alliance, 1937–41: A Study in Competitive Cooperation* (London: Europa Publications, 1981).

47. Callum A. MacDonald, *The United States, Britain, and Appeasement, 1936–1939* (London: Macmillan, 1981), ix.

48. Important contributions are Warren F. Kimball, *The Most Unsordid Act: Lend-Lease, 1939–1941* (Baltimore: Johns Hopkins Press, 1969); James R. Leutze, *Bargaining for Supremacy: Anglo-American Naval Collaboration, 1937–1941* (Chapel Hill: University of North Carolina Press, 1977); Reynolds, *Creation of the Anglo-American Alliance,* and his *Lord Lothian and Anglo-American Relations, 1939–1940* (Philadelphia: American Philosophical Society, 1983).

49. Andreas Hillgruber, *Der Zenit des Zweiten Weltkrieges, Juli 1941* (Wiesbaden: Steiner, 1977); see also Bernd Martin, "Amerikas Durchbruch zur politischen Weltmacht. Die interventionistische Globalstrategie der Regierung Roosevelt 1933–1941," *Militärgeschichtliche Mitteilungen* 2 (1981): 57–98.

50. For an early German contribution see Günter Moltmann, *Amerikas Deutschlandpolitik im Zweiten Weltkrieg. Kriegs- und Friedensziele 1941–1945* (Heidelberg: Winter, 1958).

51. On the Morgenthau Plan in the context of international relations see Warren F. Kimball, *Swords or Ploughshares? The Morgenthau Plan for Defeated Nazi Germany, 1943–1946* (Philadelphia: J. B. Lippincott, 1976).

52. See, for example, *Westdeutschlands Weg zur Bundesrepublik 1945–1949. Beiträge von Mitarbeitern des Instituts für Zeitgeschichte* (Munich: C. H. Beck, 1976); Claus Scharf and Hans-Jürgen Schröder, eds., *Politische und ökonomische Stabilisierung Westdeutschlands 1945–1949. Fünf Beiträge zur Deutschlandpolitik der westlichen Alliierten* (Wiesbaden: Steiner, 1977); Heinrich August Winkler, ed., *Politische Weichenstellungen im Nachkriegsdeutschland 1945–1953,* Sonderheft 5 *Geschichte und Gesellschaft* (Göttingen: Vandenhoeck & Ruprecht, 1979); Josef Becker et al., eds., *Vorgeschichte der Bundesrepublik Deutschland. Zwischen Kapitulation und Grundgesetz* (Munich: Fink, 1979); Claus Scharf and Hans-Jürgen Schröder, eds., *Die Deutschlandpolitik Frankreichs und die Französische Zone 1945–1949* (Wiesbaden: Steiner, 1983), with a bibliography on West German development in the context of international relations during the years 1945–49; for an excellent survey of the recent literature on the German problem see *Bibliographie zur Deutschlandpolitik 1975–1982,* edited by the Bundesministerium für Innerdeutsche Beziehungen (Frankfurt: Alfred Metzner, 1983).

53. *Akten zur Vorgeschichte der Bundesrepublik Deutschland 1945–1949,* 5 vols. (Munich: R. Oldenbourg, 1976–83).

54. On American occupation policy in Germany and German-American relations during the formative years of the Federal Republic see, for example, Harold Zink, *The United States in Germany, 1944–1955* (Princeton: Princeton University Press, 1957); John Gimbel, *The American Occupation of Germany: Politics and the Military, 1945–1949* (Stanford: Stanford University Press, 1968); Wolfgang Schlauch, "American Policy towards Germany, 1945," *Journal of Contemporary History* 5 (1970): 113–28; Bruce Kuklick, *American Policy and the Division of Germany: The Clash with Russia over Reparations* (Ithaca: Cornell University Press, 1972); Lutz Niethammer, *Entnazifizierung in Bayern. Säuberung und Rehabilitierung unter amerikanischer Besatzung* (Frankfurt: Europäische Verlags-Anstalt, 1972); Roger Morgan, *The United States and West Germany, 1945–1973: A Study in Alliance Politics* (London: Oxford

University Press, 1974); Manfred Knapp, ed., *Die deutsch-amerikanischen Beziehungen nach 1945* (Frankfurt: Campus, 1975); Edward Norman Peterson, *The American Occupation of Germany: Retreat to Victory, 1945–1952* (Detroit: Wayne State University Press, 1977); John H. Backer, *The Decision to Divide Germany: American Foreign Policy in Transition* (Durham: Duke University Press, 1978); Werner Link, *Deutsche und amerikanische Gewerkschaften und Geschäftsleute 1945–1975. Eine Studie über transnationale Beziehungen* (Düsseldorf: Droste, 1978); Hans-Jürgen Grabbe, "Die deutsch-alliierte Kontroverse über den Grundgesetzentwurf im Frühjahr 1949," *Vierteljahrshefte für Zeitgeschichte* 26 (1978): 393–418; Ekkehart Krippendorff, ed., *The Role of the United States in the Reconstruction of Italy and West Germany, 1943–1949* (Berlin: John F. Kennedy-Institut, 1981); Hans-Dieter Kreikamp, "Die amerikanische Deutschlandpolitik im Herbst 1946 und die Byrnes-Rede in Stuttgart," *Vierteljahrshefte für Zeitgeschichte* 29 (1981): 269–85; Hans-Jürgen Grabbe, *Unionsparteien, Sozialdemokratie und Vereinigte Staaten von Amerika 1945–1966* (Düsseldorf: Droste, 1983).

55. James J. Hastings, "Die Akten des Office of Military Government (US)," *Vierteljahrshefte für Zeitgeschichte* 24 (1976): 75–101; John Mendelsohn, "The OMGUS Records Project," *Prologue* 10 (1978): 259–60; Wolfgang Benz, "Das OMGUS-Projekt. Die Verzeichnung und Verfilmung der Akten der amerikanischen Militärverwaltung in Deutschland (1945–1949)," *Jahrbuch der Historischen Forschung in der Bundesrepublik Deutschland*, Berichtsjahr 1978 (Stuttgart: Klett, 1979), 84–88; see also Wolfgang J. Wittwer, "Deutschland nach 1945. Entstehung und Entwicklung der Bundesrepublik und der DDR. Ein neuer Förderungschwerpunkt der Stiftung Volkswagenwerk," *Vierteljahrshefte für Zeitgeschichte* 27 (1979): 151–54; Christoph Weisz, "Politik und Gesellschaft in der US-Zone 1945–1949. Geschichte der Nachkriegszeit aus amerikanischen und deutschen Dokumenten: Ein Projekt des Instituts für Zeitgeschichte," in Winkler, *Weichenstellungen*, 290–97.

56. Department of State Policy Statement, Germany, August 26, 1948, in U.S. State Department, *Foreign Relations of the United States, 1948 II* (Washington, D.C.: Government Printing Office, 1973), 1315.

57. Limited space does not permit a discussion on the vast amount of literature on the origins of the Cold War. On problems relating to Germany see the *Bibliographie zur Deutschlandpolitik*.

58. Kuklick, *American Policy and the Division of Germany*, and "American Policy on Reparations," *Western Political Quarterly* 23 (1970): 276–93; Otto Nübel, *Die amerikanische Reparationspolitik gegenüber Deutschland 1941–1945* (Frankfurt: Alfred Metzner, 1980).

59. See, for example, Werner Abelshauser, *Wirtschaft in Westdeutschland 1945–1948. Rekonstruktion und Wachstumsbedingungen in der amerikanischen und britischen Zone* (Stuttgart: Deutsche Verlags-A., 1975); "Die Rekonstruktion der westdeutschen Wirtschaft und die Rolle der Besatzungspolitik," in Scharf and Schröder, eds., *Politische und ökonomische Stabilisierung*, 1–17; "Wiederaufbau vor dem Marshall-Plan. Westeuropas Wachstumschancen und die Wirtschaftsordnungspolitik in der zweiten Hälfte der vierziger Jahre," *Vierteljahrshefte für Zeitgeschichte* 29 (1981): 545–78; *Wirtschaftsgeschichte der Bundesrepublik Deutschland 1945–1980* (Frankfurt: Suhrkamp, 1983); the quotations are from a paper Abelshauser presented at a symposium, "The United States and European Recovery after Two World Wars" at Berkeley in July 1982.

60. John H. Backer, *Priming the German Economy: American Occupational Policies, 1945–1948* (Durham: Duke University Press, 1971).

61. Lloyd C. Gardner, "America and the German 'Problem,' 1945–1949," in Barton J. Bernstein, ed., *Politics and Policies of the Truman Administration* (Chicago: Quadrangle, 1972); Dörte Winkler, "Die amerikanische Sozialisierungspolitik in Deutschland, 1945–1948" in Winkler, *Politische Weichenstellungen*, 88–110; Werner Link, "Der Marshall-Plan und Deutschland," *Aus Politik und Zeitgeschichte*, Beilage zur Wochenzeitung *Das Parlament*, no. 50 (1980): 14; Horst Lademacher, "Die britische Sozialisierungspolitik im Rhein-Ruhr-Raum 1945–1948" in Claus Scharf and Hans-Jürgen Schröder, *Die Deutschlandpolitik Grossbritanniens und die Britische Zone* (Wiesbaden: Steiner, 1979), 51–92; Rolf Steininger, "Reform und Realität. Ruhrfrage und Sozialisierung in der anglo-amerikanischen Deutschlandpolitik 1947–1948," *Vierteljahrshefte für Zeitgeschichte* 27 (1979): 167–240; Robertson, Memorandum, July 5, 1947, in Public Record Office, Kew, FO 371/64514.

62. On Germany and the Marshall Plan see, for example, Manfred Knapp, "Deutschland und der Marshallplan: Zum Verhältnis zwischen politischer und ökonomischer Stabilisierung in der amerikanischen Deutschlandpolitik nach 1945," in Scharf and Schröder, eds., *Politische und ökonomische Stabilisierung*, 19–43; Erich Ott, "Die Bedeutung des Marshall-Plans für die Nachkriegsentwicklung in Westdeutschland" in *Aus Politik und Zeitgeschichte*. Beilage zur Wochenzeitung *Das Parlament*, Supplement no. 4 (1980): 19–37; Link, *Der Marshall-Plan und Deutschland*; Manfred Knapp, "Reconstruction and West-Integration: The Impact of the Marshall Plan on Germany," *Zeitschrift für die gesamte Staatswissenschaft* 137 (1981): 415–33.

63. John Gimbel, *The Origins of the Marshall Plan* (Stanford: Stanford University Press, 1976); see also the comment by Manfred Knapp in "Das Deutschlandproblem und die Ursprünge des Europäischen Wiederaufbauprogramms. Eine Auseinandersetzung mit John Gimbels Untersuchung 'The Origins of the Marshall-Plan,'" *Politische Vierteljahresschrift* 19 (1978): 48–65.

64. Werner Link, "Zum Problem der Kontinuität der amerikanischen Deutschlandpolitik im zwanzigsten Jahrhundert" in Knapp, ed., *Die deutsch-amerikanischen Beziehungen nach 1945*.

12.
Research on American-German Relations: A Critical View

ARNOLD A. OFFNER

HANS-JÜRGEN SCHRÖDER HAS PROVIDED an excellent survey of the major scholarly efforts to discern the primary reasons the United States and Germany have both waged war against each other and cooperated to work toward a peaceful world order in the twentieth century. In this essay I will focus first on American-German relations in the 1920s, then on the United States's confrontation with Nazi Germany in the 1930s, and finally on American wartime planning and subsequent postwar reconstruction policy for Germany. I believe that there are recurrent problems and themes in these periods which provide significant insight into American-German relations in particular, United States foreign policy in general, and the dilemmas of our own era.

In reviewing assessments of American-German relations in the 1920s, Schröder denotes as especially impressive the "economic expansionist" theses propounded by William Appleman Williams and his followers in the United States and by Werner Link in Germany.[1] These scholars demonstrate, Schröder asserts, that after World War I American statesmen neither abandoned the tenets of President Woodrow Wilson's internationalism nor retreated from Europe but instead pursued a foreign policy that presumed that Germany was of central importance to the United States both as a market for goods and capital and as a partner in the persistent effort to establish a global Open-Door policy based on convertible currencies, equal access to markets and materials, and most-favored-nation trade treaties. Indeed, at first glance the historian might conclude that such a policy seemed more necessary than ever because World War I had produced—or accelerated—a massive shift in the international economic order: the United

States, previously a debtor nation, was now the world's greatest creditor; the Wilson administration's Edge and Webb-Pomerene legislation permitted American banks to establish foreign branches and corporations to combine for export trade free from antitrust restrictions; and the United States now produced nearly one-half of the world's industrial goods, more than Germany, France, and England combined.

Surely Schröder and others are correct to contend that in the 1920s the United States was not isolationist, in the sense of being totally withdrawn from European affairs. But it is also indisputable that American leaders were chastened by the bitter domestic political debates over the Treaty of Versailles and the League Covenant and by public disaffection with European affairs, including the prewar alliances, arms races, and balance-of-power considerations. If President-elect Warren Harding would say with typical hyperbole in November 1920 that the League of Nations was as "dead as slavery," so too would Franklin D. Roosevelt, seeking the Democratic nomination in 1932, capitulate to the influential isolationist publishing magnate, William Randolph Hearst, by precluding American entry into the League.

It is equally important to recognize, however, that American policy makers doubted the efficacy of traditional political-military means to preserve peace. Typically, Republican Secretary of State Frank B. Kellogg insisted in 1928 that history tragically demonstrated that neither treaties nor military alliances sufficed to maintain European or world peace; liberal Republican Senator William E. Borah contended that no international organization could preserve peace so long as economic justice was absent from the international order; and leading bankers and businessmen who played key roles in public-international affairs—such as Owen D. Young, board chairman of RCA and General Electric—argued that peace and prosperity could not be sustained in the face of major adverse economic forces. And as Norman H. Davis, prominent businessman and diplomat who served Presidents Wilson and Roosevelt, advised the new secretary of state, Charles Evans Hughes, in 1921: "Through the highly industrial developments of Europe prior to the war, Germany had become the axis, and the rehabilitation of Europe and its continued prosperity is most dependent upon that of Germany. Unless Germany is at work and prosperous, France cannot be so, and the prosperity of the entire world depends upon the capacity of industrial Europe to produce and purchase."[2]

This bipartisan consensus about the interconnectedness of the world political and economic order and belief that Germany was the economic axis of the United States and Europe—if not the entire world—led American diplomats to conclude that the primary task confronting statesmen was to resolve the inextricably intertwined problems of German reparations and ultimate German reconstruction and reintegration into the Western political and economic mainstream while also satisfying French claims for political and economic security—but not hegemony, as Washington officials often suspected was the Paris government's real objective.[3] From the American perspective, European peace—or détente—depended upon establishing a proper Franco-German balance. In recent years, spurred by economic expansionist arguments, historians have carefully reappraised American foreign policy in the 1920s and developed a persuasive postrevisionist thesis, which is reflected, for example, in Melvyn Leffler's writings about American policy and the quest for stability in Europe, Frank Costigliola's studies of American efforts to reconstruct Germany economically, and the assessments by Kenneth Paul Jones and others of the role of American businessmen-diplomats in Europe's recurrent political and financial crises.[4] These historians confirm that United States officials sought to promote a liberal-bourgeois Germany able to absorb American dollars and goods, disposed to peaceful treaty revision, and perhaps able to play a countervailing role in Europe with respect to the Soviet Union. But these historians also stress that American policy was not premised entirely on political isolationism or economic expansionism but on a judicious mixture of pragmatism, realism, and deliberately conceived minimal political-military commitment in Europe, which derived as much from the policy makers' preferences as it did from public and congressional constraints.

The Ruhr crisis of 1923 provided American diplomats with an almost welcome challenge to resolve the vexing Franco-German reparations conflict, which was of immense political as well as economic significance. This effort has been scrutinized not only by analysts of American policy toward Germany but by scholars of European diplomacy who are proponents of the new international history, the role of private and central banking in international affairs, and the diplomatic use of monetary, trade, and financial policy as means of power politics.[5] Virtually every assessment has accorded American officials high marks. Thus the critical American-inspired Dawes Plan of 1924— which Owen Young played a key role in shaping—is no longer perceived as merely establishing a fruitless circular track for the flow of American dollars to Germany, reparations to England and France, and war debts back to the United States. Rather, it is recognized as a shrewd effort to promote German reconstruction by confining reparations payments in marks chiefly to credits (rather than freely transferable currency) for German goods, thus stimulating German industry. In turn, Great Britain and France would be forced to choose between accepting German exports (which would compete with British and French manufactures) as reparations or have German reparations reduced annually by the amount that reparations marks deposited in the Reichsbank accumulated above a fixed level. American loans meanwhile fostered German recovery, the German government ostensibly levied taxes to pay reparations, and an American agent general oversaw German economic stabilization measures and retained a veto over declaring Germany in default on reparations, thus precluding another French march on the Ruhr.

During the latter half of the 1920s American "dollar diplomacy" provided the atmosphere necessary for the Stresemann-Briand talks, the Locarno Pacts (the political expression of the Dawes Plan), the Kellogg Pact, and France's early evacuation of the Rhineland. The Young Plan in 1930 fixed Germany's total reparations bill at a modest $8 billion, payable over fifty-nine years, with the last twenty-two German annuities approximating British and French war debts. Further, by permitting the German government to commercialize reparations through bond sales, the bankers and businessmen seemingly had taken iniquitous politics out of the reparations and assured the French of their payments while easing the German government's financial burdens but discouraging it from default, which would jeopardize its credit rating and rouse the ire of American bondholders.

Obviously, not everything worked as intended. American tariffs hindered international trade, and both American bankers and German officials encouraged too great a flow of dollars to Germany, which led to the "transfer" crisis of 1927–28. Then the stock market crash in late 1929 quickly dried up international credit, revealing that the outflow of American dollars was more critical to the war debts–reparations tangle than anyone had realized. There followed bitter political recriminations on both sides of the Atlantic, not to mention the Nazi party's vitriolic campaign against ratification of the Young Law in 1930. During 1930–32 Chancellor Heinrich Brüning's government pursued a risky deflationary policy at home and adamant demands abroad for further revision of the Versailles Treaty, including equality of arms, return of the Saar, and reductions in reparations, all of which culminated in Adolf Hitler's accession to power in 1933.[6]

Overall, postrevisionist historians have criticized American statesmen for seeking to maintain the benefits of the Versailles Treaty without incurring its obligations, for failing to link war debts and reparations directly and perhaps canceling both, and for seeking economic profit without a correlative political commitment in Europe. But scholars have also praised American policy makers for recognizing their country's growing economic primacy and corresponding political influence and attempting to apply this power adroitly and judiciously rather than dissipating it through unlimited global commitments. Thus American officials sought to maximize their legitimate national interests and minimize unwanted foreign entanglements. In so doing, they managed, with considerable success, to reintegrate a peaceful and liberal Germany into the Western mainstream while moderating France's ostensible drive for predominance and providing greater sense of reassurance to all involved through a peaceful and prosperous European order.

Ultimately, the American quest for security in Europe proved elusive, as historians have noted, in part because American officials put too much faith in the good works of private parties, overloaded them with responsibilities more appropriately assumed by government, and could not control the parochial-nationalist pressures of the 1920s. Finally, the center everywhere was unable to hold against the Great Depression's rising torrents. As Costigliola has concluded, American officials' highly admirable sense of restraint in the use of power ironically made them less able than ever to sustain the stable world order that they had envisioned.[7]

The ensuing confrontation between the United States and Nazi Germany in the 1930s has recently drawn great attention, with Schröder in particular making highly significant contributions with numerous scholarly articles and his notable book, *Deutschland und die Vereinigten Staaten 1933–1939: Wirtschaft und Politik in der Entwicklung des deutsch-amerikanischen Gegensatzes.*[8] Schröder and others have argued that American hostility toward Germany resulted less from Nazi militarism and expansionism than from German economic policies that challenged the Open-Door policy, especially in Latin America and eastern Europe. In particular, Americans objected to Germany's 1934 "New Plan" and later autarchic policies that emphasized barter agreements and bilateral trade treaties to ensure Germany a favorable balance of trade, blocked and "ASKI" marks usable to purchase only German goods, nonconvertible currency and nonrepatriation of foreign firms' profits, and export subsidies for business and industry.

Schröder has documented the sharp decline in the 1930s of

German-American trade and underscored that Germany made strong inroads, often at American expense, in Central America (Costa Rica, Guatemala, and Nicaragua) and South America (Bolivia, Brazil, Chile, and Peru). He has argued further that whereas the British sought to appease Germany by proferring bilateral economic concessions—especially in eastern Europe—to moderate German political demands, American reciprocal trade agreements and global economic appeasement policies were intended to contain Germany and force it to conform to America's liberal norms. In short, the commercial rivalry engendered by two distinct economic systems established the basis for war between the United States and Germany long before the first shots were fired.

The theory is impressive, but my analyses of the realities of the 1930s provide a different perspective—and different conclusions.[9] For example, the major decline in German-American trade first came during the Great Depression in 1929–33. Although thereafter German-American trade recovery lagged behind world trade recovery, the United States still ranked first in value of exports (especially strategic materials and wheat) to Germany in 1933, 1934, and 1938. Liberal trade maxims notwithstanding, the State Department allowed American businessmen to use clever bookkeeping devices to barter goods, which accounted for 50 percent of German-American trade in 1938–39. And the American diplomats who in 1934–35 successfully opposed renewal of the German-American trade treaty (because the Germans refused to include the most-favored-nation provision) did so for political reasons—their contention that Germany sought credits and raw materials for rearmament and then war to redraw the map of Europe. Throughout the decade, many American diplomats (including Ambassadors Norman H. Davis, William C. Bullitt, Hugh R. Wilson, Joseph P. Kennedy, and even Undersecretary of State Sumner Welles) believed that Germany should be allowed special economic preferences in eastern Europe. Moreover, even the most thorough critique of American reciprocal trade policies in Latin America has concluded that the Roosevelt administration "never came to a commercial detente with Nazi Germany, Japan, or Italy mainly because of political considerations."[10] In short, American hostility toward Nazi Germany derived chiefly from political opposition to Nazi barbarism at home and abroad, especially the German invasion of western Europe in the spring of 1940, which led the Roosevelt administration to sustain countervailing duties on German imports, use trade licenses and subsidies to induce American firms to sever ties with German businesses in Latin America and the Balkans, and take over vital communications and transportation facilities.

United States policy toward Germany is best understood by realizing that Americans had two competing views of Germany, or thought there were two competing Germanys. The traditional view, shared by many, including Roosevelt and even the outspoken anti-Nazi ambassador in Berlin, William E. Dodd, perceived Germany as a highly efficient, organized, and productive society, although occasionally moved by its Prussian influence to militarism and efforts to dominate its neighbors. But fundamentally Germany was a heavenly city for American trade, investment, and cultural exchange and the model for American universities and scholarship. As late as October 1939 Roosevelt spoke admiringly of German family life and property-holding traditions, which were preferable to Russian "brutality."[11] Simultaneously, Americans were horrified by Germany's increasingly authoritarian or totalitarian behavior and soon became fearful that its Nazi dictators were determined upon war or that the dynamics of the Nazi state and an overheated economy would demand war. By mid-decade even diplomats as favorably disposed toward Germany as Ambassador Davis insisted that it was governed by a "Frankenstein" who did not know how to stop, and Assistant Secretary of State Adolf A. Berle contended in 1938–39 that Germany was governed by "madmen" whose "Napoleonic machine" was bent on conquest. He added that whereas Europe could be reorganized geographically and economically to accommodate Germany, "the real question is the moral and philosophical concept within any of these areas."[12]

Despite persistent anxieties, American diplomats had hoped to preserve peace through political-economic revision of the Versailles system. They acquiesced in German rearmament and the Rhineland occupation, and although they were increasingly angered by Hitler's saber-rattling diplomacy and ambivalent about the consequences of appeasement, they also acquiesced in the *Anschluss*, the Munich Conference, and German claims against Poland. Indeed, during 1936–39 Roosevelt and his emissaries explored numerous conference proposals intended to revise Versailles to Germany's favor or to encourage German moderates to remove Hitler if he remained intransigent about negotiations.

But these efforts bore no results, partly because Roosevelt was indecisive, the British resisted surrendering their role as Europe's arbiter, and Hitler disdained every overture. Undersecretary Welles made a final effort at political-economic negotiations during his mission to Europe in the winter of 1940 but returned convinced that no conference could succeed as long as the Hitler regime remained in power and the German people continued to live on "another planet, where lies have become truth; evil, good; and aggression, self-defense." Or as the young diplomat George F. Kennan wrote in March 1940, the German "colossus" was determined to dominate—or destroy—Europe, and peace was impossible because "the Nazi system is built on the assumption that war, not peace, is the normal condition of mankind."[13]

After Hitler's invasion of western Europe, the Roosevelt administration abandoned public mention of Germany and spoke only of a Nazi state: totalitarian, unappeasable, locked in an "unholy alliance," and seeking "universal empire" by force. Americans thus had no choice, Roosevelt insisted, but to become the "great arsenal of democracy," and peace could not come until the Nazi hammerlock on Europe was broken, after which the United States would decide how to deal with a defeated Germany.[14]

Schröder's review of American-German relations after 1945 has raised vital but not yet fully explored questions about American planning for postwar reform or the reconstruction of Germany and its prospective role in the new world order. Roosevelt's wartime planning was ambiguous, but he unquestionably wanted the German people to bear the burden of their responsibility—or guilt. Thus he demanded "unconditional surrender," wished to rid Germany of the Nazis and "the Prussian military clique," and made occasional visceral comments about curbing the Germans' "war-breeding gangs" through castration and thin daily diets from army soup kitchens.[15]

Roosevelt's formal policy proposals derived from the sharp views expressed in Sumner Welles's writings, Secretary of the Treasury Henry Morgenthau, Jr.'s famous "Program to Prevent Germany from Starting a World War III," the harsher aspects of JCS 1067, and the Yalta agreements. As a composite, these programs presumed heavy reparations (Yalta estimated $20 billion); dismemberment of the Reich, with Poland's cessions in the east to Russia of its historical regions compensated by gains in the west at Germany's expense; and—above all—Anglo-American-Soviet accord.[16]

Conservative critics of this "Welles-Morgenthau-Yalta" approach have alleged that it was unworkable because it was too politically vengeful and likely to create chaos in Europe and to encourage further Soviet expansionism. Critics on the Left have insisted that American abrogation of Yalta, especially the German terms, precipitated the Cold War. In particular, Bruce Kuklick's *American Policy and the Division of Germany* has charged that American liberal capitalism ("multi-lateralism") caused the United States to deny the Russians a fixed sum of reparations to be taken from all of Germany and instead to institute a restrictive zonal reparations policy, which implied economic spheres and led in turn to political spheres in Germany, thus presaging the political-economic division of Europe.[17]

Critics of Roosevelt's allegedly harsh dismemberment-reparations policy have ignored or obscured the larger issues he wished to address thereby: the Soviet Union's historical-national security quest for boundary changes and the prospect that reparations might provide the Soviets with compensation for war losses and resuscitate the British economy through their taking over Germany's former export trade. And Roosevelt might avoid having to ask Congress, already reluctant about Lend-Lease appropriations, for huge postwar loans for Great Britain and the Soviet Union. Overall Roosevelt's German policy sought to minimize the American commitment of dollars and troops to post-war Europe and to secure what he perceived as retributive justice and lasting political and economic security—or balance—in the Old World.[18]

At Potsdam in July 1945 the United States largely abrogated Roosevelt's approach to Germany, but not entirely for the reasons economic revisionists have posited. Indeed, in 1944 Secretary of War Henry L. Stimson powerfully and eloquently stated to Roosevelt his opposition to the Morgenthau Plan, insisting that ten European countries, including Russia, depended upon Germany's export-import trade and production of raw materials and that it was inconceivable that this "gift of nature," populated by peoples of "energy, vigor, and progressiveness," could be turned into a "ghost territory" or "dust heap." Yet Stimson also envisaged major transfer of territory (East Prussia, Upper Silesia, Alsace, and Lorraine) and perhaps further north-south partition of Germany and internationalization of the Ruhr. What he most feared, however, was that too low a subsistence-level economy would turn the anger of the German people against the Allies and thereby "obscure the guilt of the Nazis and the viciousness of their doctrines and their acts." Stimson pressed similar arguments on President Harry S. Truman in the spring of 1945, and William Donovan's Office of Strategic Services (OSS) advised Truman that since neither the United States nor the Soviet Union could allow the other to dominate Germany, which should not be partitioned, the best solution would be "the establishment and maintenance of a democratic-socialist Germany balanced between Eastern and Western blocs but aligned with neither."[19]

In preparing for Potsdam, State Department officials frequently opposed dismemberment and heavy reparations, but often for reasons inspired by recent history and humanitarian concerns. They warned against repeating "the history of Versailles," were fearful of policies that would require German "Quislings and Vichyites" to effect them (any "anti-Nazi parties should be spared the odium of this collaboration"), and believed that a "poor house" standard of living for Germany meant the same for Europe and ultimately—once again—the German people would revolt against a system and allies who would be weak and divided.[20] At the same time, American officials also advised against a British proposal to merge the three Western zones because that would create an "economic wall" between East and West, and they also warned against France's "obsession" with detaching western Germany's coal and industrial regions, which seemed too reminiscent to the Americans of French policy after World War I.[21]

At Potsdam the Americans initially pressed their "first charge" principle but abandoned this when they secured zonal reparations, which included an exchange-transfer of 25 percent of the capital equipment from the Western zones to the Russians but no final, fixed reparations figure. Undoubtedly Truman's reparations negotiator, Edwin M. Pauley, and the new secretary of state, James F. Byrnes, could have been more accommodating to the Russians, especially when they appeared ready to accept significantly reduced reparations. But the Americans were too parochial, too much the horse-traders, and too determined to impose their principles on Russia in Germany.

There is no evidence, however, that the Americans intended the permanent division of Germany. Indeed, historian John Gimbel has documented that in succeeding years American policy was as bedeviled by French reparations and separatist policies—and resistance to creation of central agencies—as by Soviet policies.[22] This situation was duly reported by Truman's special emissary, Byron Price, in his extensive report on Germany in November 1945 and in like commentaries by traveling War Department officials in succeeding months.[23] French intransigence, Gimbel has shown, underlay General Lucius D. Clay's decision to halt reparations transfers from the American zone in May 1946. Byrnes's Stuttgart speech in September calling for a self-sustaining Germany and the economic merger of the Anglo-American zones in December 1946 derived from many concerns, including denazification, decartelization, democratization; countering both French and Russian policies; rehabilitating Germany and Europe; and preserving American tax dollars. These steps, combined with the harsh winter of 1946–47, rising occupation costs, and the "dollar gap," led to the Marshall Plan and European Recovery Program of 1947–48, which led to the further, or political, division of Germany and Europe and intensification of the Cold War.

It is also possible to argue, however, that just as American policy in Germany in 1945–46 derived from many concerns, so too the Marshall Plan was more than an anti-Soviet measure or stabilizer of international capitalism. Obviously American officials began their planning with powerful, culturally ingrained presumptions about the preeminent rationality and efficiency of private enterprise and with an official commitment to the tenets of a global, liberal-capitalist order, which they pressed too hard—along with their bias against nationalization—as the basis for Marshall Plan membership. And in "selling" the Marshall Plan to the public and Congress they used too much anticommunist rhetoric and too often raised the specter of containing the Soviet Union. The United States ought to have done more to encourage Soviet membership, although it is unlikely that the Russians would have joined or allowed the East European states to do so.

But as Gimbel has argued, although it is indisputable that containment of the Soviet Union was a feature of the discussion concerning European recovery, the Marshall Plan also evolved into an attempt to contain Germany within a larger economic structure and to create a nascent Atlantic community, which would minimize France's obstructionism or repetition of its hegemonic efforts of the early 1920s yet would satisfy French claims for political and economic security. In this respect American Open-Door rhetoric served to defuse the politically charged issue of German rehabilitation, while incipient European cooperation or integration would provide the means to effect and contain German economic recovery. Or as both Edwin Pauley and John Steelman, President Truman's special adviser, said in the spring of 1947 in opposing the unlimited industrial recovery of Germany, revival of that "German colossus" would lead to militarization and a repeat of the consequences of the 1930s.[24]

The Marshall Plan thus was, as Stalin later insisted, more than the Truman Doctrine with dollars, although it is not surprising that economic division encouraged further political, and later, military division in Germany and in Europe as a whole. But before we condemn out of hand the political and economic division of Germany, we might pause to ask if these divisions did not—ironically—serve a larger purpose.[25] Or stated otherwise, neither the United States nor the Soviet Union was prepared to risk that the other might wholly control a unified Germany, which the French also resisted. And conceivably, a unified and economically powerful Germany might have presented the same revisionist threat to Europe that it did during the interwar era. Hence the political-economic division of Germany helped to resolve an American-Soviet (and French) dilemma in the sense that if there were twenty years of peace between the two world wars, there have been forty years of peace since the end of World War II. And perhaps in ways not imagined at the time, the division of Germany has resolved Europe's "German problem" by providing a framework whereby Germany's immense repository of human talent and natural resources might help its own and other societies flourish without threatening either the balance of power on the Continent or the balance between the two superpowers that first confronted one another over prostrate Europe in 1945. The division of Germany thus might be said to have spurred development of long-imagined integrative efforts in Western Europe and perhaps even helped to create the conditions whereby Germany, or the two Germanys, might now further conditions conducive to achieving lasting détente.

This is not to argue that statesmen in the mid-1940s moved by grand design rather than haphazardly, or at least by indirection. But it is to say that the new state system that emerged in postwar Europe has at least provided the Western world with the semblance of peace for four decades. Perhaps one might suggest that given what statesmen knew and feared about the past—French intransigence, German revisionism, the collapse of the world economic order—there was more logic or inevitability to the division of Germany than politicians, and even historians, would ever care to admit. And perhaps as we come to know more about the political, economic, and bureaucratic pressures that influenced Soviet diplomacy, we shall come to conclude that both sides, or all sides, share responsibility for having imposed upon us so many cold, and hot, wars. And similarly we shall hold all sides responsible for reducing the balance of terror that now threatens our existence, and we shall assert more forcefully than ever the oneness of our humanity that transcends the boundaries of any nation, military alliance, or regional group and unites all of us in a common quest for peace and prosperity.

Notes

1. William A. Williams, *The Tragedy of American Diplomacy*, 2d ed. (New York: Dell, 1972), and Werner Link, *Die amerikanische Stabilisierungspolitik in Deutschland 1921–32* (Düsseldorf: Droste, 1970). See also Manfred Knapp, Werner Link, Hans-

Jürgen Schröder, and Klaus Schwabe, *Die USA und Deutschland 1918–1975: Deutsch-amerikanische Beziehungen zwischen Rivalität und Partnerschaft* (Munich: C. H. Beck, 1978).

2. Davis to Hughes, March 12, 1921, Box 27, Norman H. Davis Papers, Manuscript Division, Library of Congress, Washington, D.C.

3. Melvyn P. Leffler, "Political Isolationism, Economic Expansionism, or Diplomatic Realism: American Policy toward Western Europe, 1921–1933," *Perspectives in American History* 8 (1974): 441.

4. See ibid., 413–61, and Melvyn P. Leffler, "American Policy and European Stability, 1921–1933," *Pacific Historical Review* 46 (May 1977): 207–28, and *The Elusive Quest: America's Pursuit of European Stability and French Security, 1919–1933* (Chapel Hill: University of North Carolina Press, 1979); Frank C. Costigliola, "The Other Side of Isolationism: The Establishment of the First World Bank, 1929–30," *Journal of American History* 59 (December 1972): 602–20, and "The United States and the Reconstruction of Germany in the 1920's," *Business History Review* 50 (Winter 1976): 477–502; and Kenneth Paul Jones, ed., *U.S. Diplomats in Europe, 1919–1941* (Santa Barbara: ABC-Clio, 1981).

5. For an overview see Jon Jacobson, "Is There a New International History of the 1920's?" *American Historical Review* 88 (June 1983): 617–45. Important studies include Marc Trachtenberg, *Reparations in World Politics: France and European Economic Diplomacy, 1916–1923* (New York: Columbia University Press, 1980); Stephen A. Schuker, *The End of French Predominance in Europe: The Financial Crisis of 1924 and the Adoption of the Dawes Plan* (Chapel Hill: University of North Carolina Press, 1976); Charles S. Maier, *Recasting Bourgeois Europe: Stabilization in France, Germany, and Italy in the Decade after World War I* (Princeton: Princeton University Press, 1975); and Dan P. Silverman, *Reconstructing Europe after the Great War* (Cambridge, Mass.: Harvard University Press, 1982).

6. On German policy see Edward W. Bennett, *Germany and the Diplomacy of the Financial Crisis, 1931* (Cambridge, Mass.: Harvard University Press, 1962), and Wolfgang J. Helbich, *Die Reparationen in der Ära Brüning: Zur Bedeutung des Young-Plans für die deutsche Politik, 1930 bis 1932* (Berlin: Colloquium, 1962).

7. Frank C. Costigliola, "United States and Reconstruction of Germany," *Business History Review*, 50 (1976): 501–2.

8. Hans-Jürgen Schröder, *Deutschland und die Vereinigten Staaten 1933–1939: Wirtschaft und Politik in der Entwicklung des deutsch-amerikanischen Gegensatzes* (Wiesbaden: Steiner, 1970). See also Schröder's "Das Dritte Reich und die USA," in Knapp et al., *Die USA und Deutschland*, 107–52, and "The Ambiguities of Appeasement: Great Britain, the United States, and Germany, 1937–9," in Wolfgang J. Mommsen and Lothar Kettenacker, *The Fascist Challenge and the Policy of Appeasement* (London: George Allen & Unwin, 1983), 390–99, and "Economic Appeasement: Zur britischen und amerikanischen Deutschlandpolitik vor dem Zweiten Weltkrieg," *Vierteljahrshefte für Zeitgeschichte*, 30 (January 1982): 82–97. See also Callum A. MacDonald, *The United States, Britain, and Appeasement, 1936–1939* (London: Macmillan, 1981).

9. Arnold A. Offner, *American Appeasement: United States Foreign Policy and Germany, 1933–1938* (Cambridge, Mass.: Belknap Press of Harvard University Press, 1969); *The Origins of the Second World War: American Foreign Policy and World Politics, 1917–1941* (New York: Praeger, 1975), 104–32, 165–72; "Appeasement Revisited: The United States, Great Britain, and Germany, 1933–1940," *Journal of American History* 64 (September 1977): 373–93; and "The United States and National Socialist Germany," in Mommsen and Kettenacker, *Fascist Challenge*, 413–27.

10. Dick Steward, *Trade and Hemisphere: The Good Neighbor Policy and Reciprocal Trade* (Columbia, Mo.: University of Missouri Press, 1975), 283.

11. Roosevelt to Joseph P. Kennedy, October 30, 1939, in Elliott Roosevelt, ed., *F.D.R.: His Personal Letters, 1928–1945*, 2 vols. (New York: Duell, Sloan and Pierce, 1947–50), 1:942–44.

12. Norman H. Davis to Cordell Hull, November 17, 1936, Box 40, Cordell Hull Papers, Library of Congress; Berle diary entries for May 16 and November 15, 1939, in Beatrice Bishop Berle and Travis Beal Jacobs, eds., *Navigating the Rapids, 1918–1971: From the Papers of Adolf A. Berle* (New York: Harcourt, Brace, Jovanovich, 1973), 199–201, 270.

13. George F. Kennan, *Memoirs, 1925–1950* (Boston: Little, Brown, 1967), 117–18; for Roosevelt's peace efforts, see Offner, "Appeasement Revisited," 378–93.

14. Samuel I. Rosenman, comp., *The Public Papers and Addresses of Franklin D. Roosevelt*, 13 vols. (New York: Random House, 1938–50), 9:161, 638–39, 643.

15. Raymond G. O'Connor, *Diplomacy for Victory: FDR and Unconditional Surrender* (New York: Norton, 1971), 50–56; Rosenman, comp., *Public Papers of Roosevelt*, 12:391; and John Morton Blum, *From the Morgenthau Diaries: Years of War, 1941–1945* (Boston: Houghton, Mifflin, 1959–67), 341, 348–49.

16. Sumner Welles, *The Time for Decision* (New York: Harper, 1944), esp. 306–61; on the Morgenthau Plan, JCS 1067, and Yalta, see Blum, *Years of War,* 327–414, and Warren F. Kimball, *Swords or Ploughshares? The Morgenthau Plan for Defeated Nazi Germany, 1943–1946* (Philadelphia: J. B. Lippincott, 1976). Morgenthau originally intended to limit reparations to existing German resources and territories, but at Yalta Roosevelt also included payment from current production.

17. For criticism—usually of a conservative nature—of the harsh approach to Germany, see Hanson W. Baldwin, *Great Mistakes of the War* (New York: Harper, 1950); Chester Wilmot, *The Struggle for Europe* (New York: Harper, 1952); Anne Armstrong, *Unconditional Surrender: The Impact of Casablanca Policy upon World War II* (New Brunswick: Rutgers University Press, 1961); Gaddis Smith, *American Diplomacy during the Second World War, 1941–1945* (New York: Wiley, 1965); and Sir John W. Wheeler-Bennett and Anthony Nicholls, *The Semblance of Peace: The Political Settlement after the Second World War* (London: Macmillan, 1972). For revisionist studies that argue that American "reintegrationist" policy toward Germany helped to precipitate the Cold War, see Bruce Kuklick, *American Policy and the Division of Germany: The Clash with Russia over Reparations* (Ithaca: Cornell University Press, 1972); Lloyd G. Gardner, *Architects of Illusion: Men and Ideas in American Foreign Policy, 1941–1949* (Chicago: Quadrangle Books, 1970); and Diane Clemens, *Yalta* (New York: Oxford University Press, 1970). For postrevisionist assessments, see John Lewis Gaddis, *The United States and the Origins of the Cold War, 1941–1947* (New York: Columbia University Press, 1972); Tony Sharp, *The Wartime Alliance and the Zonal Divison of Germany* (Oxford: Clarendon Press, 1975); and John H. Backer, *The Decision to Divide Germany: American Foreign Policy in Transition* (Durham: Duke University Press, 1978).

18. Arnold A. Offner, "FDR Remembered: Statesman of Peaceful Means," *OAH* [Organization of American Historians] *Newsletter* 2 (May 1983): 23–25.

19. Henry L. Stimson and McGeorge Bundy, *On Active Service in Peace and War* (New York: Harper, 1947), 571–83; Donovan to Truman, May 5, 1945, Office of Strategic Services Files, Box 15, Harry S. Truman Papers, Truman Library, Independence, Missouri.

20. Department of State, Briefing Book, "Policy toward Germany" [June 29, 1945], in U.S. Department of State, *Foreign Relations of the United States: The Conference of*

Berlin (The Potsdam Conference), 2 vols. (Washington, D.C.: Government Printing Office, 1960), 1:435–49.

21. Ibid., State Department Briefing Papers, "The Ruhr" and "The Rhineland," June 30, 1945, ibid., 1:586–89, 591–92.

22. John Gimbel, "On the Implementation of the Potsdam Agreement: An Essay on U.S. Postwar Policy," *Political Science Quarterly* 87 (June 1972): 242–69, and "The American Reparations Stop in Germany: An Essay on the Political Use of History," *Historian* 37 (February 1975): 276–96.

23. Price to Truman, November 9, 1945, Official File 198, Box 687, Truman Papers, Truman Library; see also Gimbel, "On the Implementation of the Potsdam Agreement," 250–54.

24. John Gimbel, *The Origins of the Marshall Plan* (Stanford: Stanford University Press, 1976); Pauley to Truman, April 15, 1947, and Steelman to Truman [late April 1947], President's Secretary's Files, Box 122, Truman Papers, Truman Library. Pauley and Steelman were responding to former President Herbert Hoover's proposals for unlimited German reindustrialization.

25. See, for example, Anton W. DePorte, *Europe between the Superpowers: The Enduring Balance* (New Haven: Yale University Press, 1979).

PART IV:

The German-Americans in the Twentieth Century

13.
Elusive Affinities:
Acceptance and Rejection
of the German-Americans

CHRISTINE M. TOTTEN

IN 1911, THE GERMAN HISTORIAN HERMANN ONCKEN regretted that the impact of German immigrants on the United States had been so slight relative to their numbers.[1] Three years later, when the German-Americans did assert themselves, their struggle to preserve American neutrality in World War I prompted violent rejection of their group.

The force of this backlash was without precedent. Previous political involvement of the German-descended, like their stand against the blue laws, their support of the abolitionist cause, and their role in the early labor movement, had caused only minor ruffles on the surface of prevalently placid attitudes toward them in the United States.

Tracing majority sentiment toward an ethnic group through statements made by politicians, journalists, and scholars is likely to be seen more as subjective theorizing than as the recording of factual history. This assessment was true at least until the 1940s, when systematic surveys lent quantitative respectability to such tasks. Specialists in image research have found, however, that public opinion is simplistic and repetitive and that the expansion of sources beyond judiciously chosen samples replicates the results already found.[2] The difficulties of summary group appraisals do not justify their neglect; sentiment not only reflects but tangibly influences historical development.

The Germans formed a sufficiently substantial and ubiquitous sector of the American people to invite considerable scrutiny by their neighbors and by politicians concerned about their vote. In a bird's-eye view of three centuries of German immigration, a dividing line can be drawn between two images: first, an evaluation based upon impressions of relatively simple and clear outlines; later, a more diverse and contradictory picture, which developed after the onset of mass migration in the 1830s.

William Penn's affinity for the congenial Mennonites and Quakers from the Rhineland paved the way for friendly reception of the Germantown pioneers. In his description of Pennsylvania, the *Umständige Beschreibung*, Francis Daniel Pastorius reports with satisfaction that the proprietor recommended goodwill toward the Germans: Penn had emphasized at a meeting "that he was very fond of me and the High Germans, and that he wanted his councilors to follow suit."[3]

The cordial relations between Germantown and Philadelphia suffered in 1688, when Pastorius and three other leading citizens explained to the monthly meeting of the Quakers why they were "against the traffick of men Body." Their protest against slavery was put aside by the quarterly and yearly meetings with embarrassment. The Quakers resented the holier-than-thou stance of settlers from a Continental country that had not shared British colonial experiences.

Divergent sensitivities, this time toward the native Americans, had caused friction between Captain John Smith and his German carpenters in the Jamestown colony of 1607. He cursed the Germans as the "damned Dutch" when they chose to remain with the Indian King Powhatan after they constructed a house for him. Nevertheless, Captain Smith preferred the Dutch and Poles, who knew what a day's work was, over the poor English gentlemen, who were "more fit to spoyle a Commonwealth, than . . . to begin one."[4]

A century and a half later, in 1753, Benjamin Franklin arrived at a similar appraisal. He stated that the English tended to get lazier in the New World, whereas the German laborers retained their "habitual industry and frugality." In his eyes, productivity was the saving grace of the coarse and uncouth "boors of the Palatinate," "the most stupid of their own nation."[5] Yet he had enough trust in their literacy to print the first German books in America in 1730 and the first German-language newspaper two years later.

The aversion of the sectarians in Pennsylvania to secular education contributed to two contradictory impressions about the Germans both as low-brow and as avid readers. The early appearance of the Germans as awkward simpletons became one of the most permanent strands in the changing patterns of their image, along with the contradictory concept of them as learned and bookish.

The tenor of Franklin's disparaging remarks about the Germans was determined largely by nativist fears that they would "soon so outnumber us that all the advantages we have will . . . not be able to preserve our language, and even our government will become precarious."[6] Such concerns, plausible at a time of bilingual advertising and street signs in Philadelphia, were not put to rest when following waves of immigrants "Anglified" as readily as Franklin demanded. In times of crises and following influxes of new arrivals from Germany, fears of their linguistic and cultural ascendancy burdened relations with the German-Americans.

It is a matter of debate whether the paranoia caused periodically by the German element's permanent fate of being the second largest national group in the United States was intensified by their "clannishness" or modified by their remarkably swift and thorough assimilation.[7] In any case, the closeness of this group in appearance, values, and socioeconomic background to other Atlantic European groups constituting the bulk of the American people served to neutralize the potential irritant of their large numbers. Yet within the family likeness of central and West European immigrant groups, individual traits such as remarkable diligence could be singled out since colonial times as specifically German ingredients of the American melting pot.

The consensus on the productivity of the Germans found ever more frequent expression in the era of national consolidation. The Pennsylvania Germans received inordinate praise for their industry and frugality. Their best-known eulogist was Benjamin Rush, the respected Philadelphia physician and statesman. In 1789, he used sixteen examples to show how the Germans had brought prosperity to Pennsylvania, favorably comparing their farmers' conscientious care for livestock with the practices of their English and Scotch-Irish neighbors.[8] Later French and English travelers agreed with Rush's observation that German pioneers cleared the virgin land in a superior way.[9]

The didactic flattery of this bright picture earned Rush the title of a "Tacitus" of the Pennsylvania Germans. Rush omitted the darker side of the picture—widespread criticism of the farmers' miserly materialism and exploitation of their women through hard outdoor work. But the positive aspects of Rush's appraisal were repeated by later observers. Henry Clay spoke in 1832 about the "honest, patient, and industrious German."[10] Recent quantitative content analysis of popular antebellum literature confirms "continuity, industry, persistence, and direction" as substantial German-American traits.[11] The German-Americans themselves joined the chorus praising their position in the vanguard of American productivity. In his *Festschrift zum deutschen Pionierjubiläum* in 1883, Oswald Seidensticker quoted statistics in support of his statement that "German immigrants represent a much larger percentage of efficient people than the general population."[12] The cliché of the hardworking German survived the vilifications of two world wars[13] and is applied routinely in journalistic reports to this day on both sides of the Atlantic, even though its continued applicability has been doubted in the Federal Republic.[14]

The *New Yorker Staats-Zeitung* has been published continuously since 1834. As the flagship of the German-language press in North America, which numbered almost 800 daily, weekly, and monthly newspapers at the end of the nineteenth century but which has shrunk to just 14 newspapers today, the *Staats* cele-brated its nostalgic 150th anniversary in 1984. Its long history reflects that of the German-language press in general, which was shaped in its early phase by the Forty-Eighters and the grow-ing readership accompanying the mass immigration of the late nineteenth century. Since its decline during the First World War, the German press has shifted its concentration to reporting pri-marily on German-American organizations and regional news. The *Staats-Zeitung* merged with the *New Yorker Herold* dur-ing the Second World War and changed from a daily to a weekly publication. Today, the German-language travel agency "Staats-Herold Tours" plays an important role in the survival of the news-paper. (C. J. Zumwalt, Mecki McCarthy, *New Yorker Staats-Zeitung und Herold*)

From Jamestown to contemporary public opinion polls, the stereotype of German industry prevailed. Another old, once firmly entrenched notion, that of the unobtrusive, quiet German, was overlaid with the diametrically different picture of the noisy and assertive German who arrived with nineteenth-century immigrant groups. The pious, pacifistic sectarians and solid church-oriented families of the early German immigration had not crossed the Atlantic on their own ships like the Spaniards, English, or Dutch. They came without arms, and they projected images of inwardness and serenity.

The comfortable uniformity of impressions created by these homogeneous groups was first shattered by the arrival of intellectual newcomers from the revolutionary uprisings in Germany after 1830 and 1848–49, then by the diversity of mass immigration from the German-speaking countries.

The Germans were originally easy to live with as political followers. In 1703, Pastorius complained in a letter to William Penn about the unwillingness of Germantown's citizens to accept public office.[15] Benjamin Franklin recalled with satisfaction the days when the Germans "modestly declined meddling in our elections" but later resented them as unpredictable, independent voters.[16] The first group of politically motivated German immigrants, the Forty-eighters, shared the general assessment of the German-Americans as politically listless, as "Stimmvieh" in the words of Julius Froebel. The efforts of the German revolutionaries to arouse their apathetic countrymen, enlisting them for the abolitionist cause, winning them for the Turner's socialist ideals, even opposing organized religion, went against the grain of all preconceived notions about the Germans in America. The discomforting juxtaposition of radical German leaders and their conservative followers produced antagonism against the agitators, who were "working upon the feelings of the brave, noble, simple, honest-hearted Germans."[17]

The new highly diverse picture of the Germans became most obvious in the wider spectrum of their religious preferences. The older German immigration had been entirely Protestant, easily labeled as coming from the "land of Luther," a friendly name for Germany at the time of strong American self-appreciation as a Protestant country.[18] The arrival of Forty-eighter freethinkers and Reform-minded Jews, and especially the large contingent of Roman Catholics in the later nineteenth-century migration, changed the previous denominational uniformity.

The concentration of the German-born population in the Midwest made visible a specific way of life that became part of the German image. The sociability and conviviality of innumerable German *Vereine* created a powerful stereotype of the German beer drinker, beer brewer, and antiprohibition beer promoter. The same attributes generated rejection and acceptance in different constellations of America's Zeitgeist: the noisy "damn Dutch" arousing Know-Nothing nativists to violent anger at the Sabbath-desecrating, beer-guzzling picnics of "hare-lipped, red Republican" Turner associations in the 1850s.[19] But the German concept of "Gemütlichkeit," of merrymaking as balance for hard work, had caught on a century later both in rural and urban America.[20] Oktoberfest celebrations became a popular attraction of American mainstream life beyond events organized by German-American associations.

By the mid-nineteenth century, an important new factor complicated the process of forming opinions about the Germans in America. Approval and disapproval of the political behavior of the Germans in Europe entered the consciousness of the American public through increased press reports from the Continent. Up to the Napoleonic Wars, the German powers had remained at the periphery of American attention, which was absorbed by government interaction with London and Paris. Yet the revolutionary movements in southwestern Germany, beginning in the 1830s, found resonance in the United States.[21] In politics as in religion, similarities stimulated affinities. Even before the influx of German revolutionary refugees, American journalists could relate to forces calling for unification, for a federation of German states, and, above all, for a republic replacing a conglomerate of tyrannical principalities. But the revolution collapsed in 1849, and disappointed American observers saw confirmed the notion of German incompetence in politics, which had been nurtured by American experience with German immigrants for a century and a half.[22]

When German unification came about more than twenty years later—not based upon a republic after the American model but as a bond between princes hailing an emperor—American public opinion underwent a series of dramatic shifts. These events primarily affected sentiments toward the new German Reich but eventually also touched the German element in the United States.

Reflections in the American press of attitudes before, during, and after the Franco-Prussian War have been well researched.[23] In 1866, a characteristic journalistic statement summed up the Germans as "the most learned, patient, industrious, civilized people on the face of the globe, which has attained the highest distinction in arts, in science, in arms, in literature, in everything, in short, but in politics."[24]

At the outbreak of hostilities in 1870, most American newspapers warmly supported the Prussian cause.[25] But when Paris suffered under the Prussian blockade, the American press reversed itself. Now the French monopolized American sympathies, not only as the underdog but also as "innately liberty-loving" Republicans. In contrast, the Germans were characterized as "innately subservient to their rulers, out for war and conquest, vainglorious and immoral."[26] Attributes of abhorrence which emerged again in the two world wars made their first appearance at this time, when Prussia was depicted as "the most relentless and malignant of conquerors that the Old World had seen since Attila and his Huns."[27]

Resentments between nations can remain buried beneath the ashes of passing time until a gust of turbulence fans them again to an open flame. The antagonism against the new German Reich which had been smoldering since 1871 was fed surreptitiously by a series of economic and naval rivalries between the United States and Germany at the turn of the century.[28] But public opinion was set on fire only when the partisanship of American leaders for England and France put an end to U.S. neutrality in 1917.

The immediate effect of German unification on the status and prestige of the German-American community gave no clue to its long-range consequences. Disregarding a few disappointed and warning voices of liberals, the majority of the German-Americans basked in an upsurge of ethnic self-confidence and pride in the military and economic successes of their old country.[29] The German-Americans' position was strengthened by the well-being of their cousins across the ocean during the period when their reputation received the greatest benefit from American affinities for contemporary German culture. At this time, the appraisal of the Germans as outstanding scholars, teachers, musicians, and artists and as ingenious inventors crystallized into a potent, long-lasting stereotype.

The experience of Americans in German-speaking countries was confirmed by contributions of German immigrants to American life. Close to ten thousand young Americans studied at German universities up to World War I. Their reasons for choosing German schools reflect the two nations' cultural compatibilities in the nineteenth century.[30] The image of Britain still suffered from animosities toward the "hereditary enemy" of the wars of independence and 1812. Oxford and Cambridge were considered too conservative and flawed by British class-consciousness. Waterloo marked the end of half a century of preference for French culture, personified by Thomas Jefferson. Ameri-

Steuben, the monument. Friedrich Wilhelm von Steuben (1730–99) became the representative figure of German-American identity in the late nineteenth century, although this role was not recognized as such by all German-Americans. "Washington's Drillmaster," as the Prussian officer became known, represented the positive role of Germans in the American Revolution. The Steuben Monument in Washington, D.C., stands out among the monuments to the general which were constructed in many American cities before 1914. Erected near the White House with money from Congress and dedicated in 1910, the statue represents America's recognition of the German contribution to the building of America. In 1919, when the American image of the Germans had reached its lowest point, a new political organization known as the Steuben Society was founded to use Steuben's prestige to advantage. After the Second World War, the Steuben name served the same purpose. The Steuben Parade began in New York in 1958. (National Park Service, Capitol Region)

can parents hesitated to expose their sons to the frivolities of Parisian life, to the Revolution's lingering heritage of atheism, and to an atmosphere of sensuous aesthetic values which they felt were foreign to American—as well as German—sensibilities. German independence of thinking was exemplified by Martin Luther, the modernity of educational ideals propounded by the brothers Humboldt, and the preeminence of the natural sciences represented by such men as Wilhelm Bunsen, Hermann von Helmholtz, and Robert Koch.

German literature found its first major resonance in America not in the works of Goethe, whose personal morality was regarded with suspicion. Rather, it was Schiller's lofty philosophy which agreed perfectly with American concepts of ethics and poetry when in 1859 the hundredth anniversary of his birth was celebrated from coast to coast.[31] The spirit of the bard of freedom was also recognized in the idealism of German émigré scholars such as Franz Lieber and Karl Follen.

The German immigrants' musical heritage was not always accepted without reservation. Both New England's Puritans and Pennsylvania's Quakers looked askance at the integration of singing and worship. But admiration for the German sectarians' musical innovations prevailed: the choirs of Ephrata and the orchestral music of the Moravian Brethren set new patterns. In the nineteenth century, the small German band at the street corner, the elaborate competitive events of the *Männerchöre*, the concert tours of the Forty-eighters' Germania orchestra, and outstanding conductors such as Theodore Thomas and Leopold Damrosch captivated all levels of the American people. Bach, Beethoven, and Brahms became mainstays of the concert hall.[32]

Affection for German composers and musicians marked the initial as well as the final phase of American receptiveness to the cultural contributions of German immigrants. It survived the esteem for German-American artists of the Düsseldorf school. The grandiose paintings by Emmanuel Leutze and Albert Bierstadt plummeted as fast in the public's appreciation as they had risen in the 1860s, after American tastes turned to Paris and the delights of French impressionism.[33]

This shift in preferences was symptomatic as one of many signals announcing replacement of Teutonic cultural models with enthusiasm for French elegance and English flair toward the end of the century. Kuno Francke, the nationalistic high priest of Germanism, tried to stem the tide by initiating moves for a Germanic museum at Harvard in 1897. According to Henry Adams, Harvard had been dominated by an admiration for Germany in the 1850s.[34] Half a century later, Francke felt beleaguered by "overwhelming English and French influence." Compared to the "measured refinement of the French" and the "cosmopolitan vigor of the English," Francke found that the "amorphism, volatility, exaggeration, and sentimentality of the German character" were regarded as inferior. Only "the unique grandeur of German music" received full recognition in New England.[35]

The gradual fall of German culture from American favor coincided with the first signs of disintegration in German-American ethnic coherence, as the United States moved closer to England and France politically in the period before World War I. U.S. entry into the alliance stressed primary bonds with England. Slogans that popularized the concept of the "sister nations of the Anglo-Saxon race" urged the joining of "hands across the sea."[36] The counterpart to the promotion of pro-English sentiment was the dismantling of old affinities for the Germans. The rapport with them had only recently become brittle, but its decline was accelerated by distaste for the political assertiveness of associations like the German-American Alliance and fear of the "hyphenates'" disloyalty to the war effort. It was also helped along by overbearing, defensively shrill utterances of German-American cultural chauvinism.[37] Since the turn of the century, America had begun to shed the skin of her German orientation. Instead of continued gradual decline, wartime emotions cut every German sector out of the American way of life in one radical operation.[38]

The German-Americans faced their most devastating rejection in 1917–18. After this, the attention of the American public to their idiosyncrasies diminished in direct proportion to their decreasing visibility. Their image became static, no longer subject to alteration. Illusions of modification were created by the reflection of changing American attitudes toward the Germans in Europe: the mixed appeal and skepticism evoked by the Weimar Republic, the aversion to Hitler's dictatorship, the revulsion at the postwar disclosures of Nazi genocide, and eventually renewed acceptance in the course of unprecedented cooperation between the governments of the United States and the Federal Republic of Germany.

Even after the German-Americans ceded the limelight to their cousins overseas, they continued to exert some direct and indirect influences. They vented feelings of solidarity in the voting booth.[39] They activated family ties in relief actions after both wars. Their charity triggered traditional American sympathies for the underdog as a first step toward the recovery of goodwill for the defeated enemy. Above all, impressions created by the German-Americans in more than two centuries did not fade overnight. When a public opinion survey in 1942 indicated that 28 percent of the respondents personally hated the Japanese as against 12 percent who hated the Germans, the ratio was explained not only by cultural differences but also "by the fact that the traditional friendly, favorable stereotypes of the Germans were lacking in the Japanese case." In September 1944, when Americans were asked who should be "blamed for the cruelties in this war," only 2 percent blamed the German people, 58 percent blamed the Nazi leaders, and 38 percent blamed both leaders and people.[40]

New waves of immigration from Germany to the United States after 1918 served to reinforce major traits of the old image. The exodus of brilliant minds from Hitler's persecutions in the 1930s made Germany's loss more clearly America's gain than ever before. Past historical experience with intellectually creative German immigrants was surpassed by contributions of the refugees in philosophical thought, letters, science, music, the arts, and architecture. In the late 1940s and 1950s, members of immigrant groups lumped together under designations such as "Operation Paperclip" and "brain drain" revived preconceived notions about the ingenious Germans, which had been nurtured in the nineteenth century by inventors such as Ottmar Mergenthaler and Charles Proteus Steinmetz and by wizards of bridge-building such as the Roeblings. Wernher von Braun and his team of rocket specialists received attention from the media that was tinged with controversy, ever-present in the juxtaposition of old positive stereotypes of the constructive German with the new powerful image of the Nazi villain.[41]

Spouses and children made up a large part of the postwar immigration of three-quarters of a million Germans up to 1970. The war brides fitted into the category of quiet, unobtrusive, rapidly assimilated immigrants.[42] Another sizable sector of this group, wartime refugees and those expelled from former borderlands with Russia and Poland or from German ethnic enclaves in Eastern Europe, imported an ethnic frontier mentality that had earlier been characteristic of the Russian Germans. Their injection of a new active spirit into declining German-American organizations contributed to a revival of German Day traditions.

Since the Bicentennial celebrations of German immigration in 1883, periodic stocktaking at conventions of ethnic Germans in the United States had served as a barometer of their standing in American society. At the yearly assembly of the Deutscher Pionier Verein of Philadelphia in April 1883, its president, Oswald Seidensticker, accepted a proposal by Kellner to honor two hundred years of German immigration. The festival lasted four days, from October 6 to 9, and was summed up as "glänzend" (magnificent).[43] Its luster was derived to a great extent from the high scholarly caliber of publications prepared for the gathering. More examinations of German-American history followed in its wake, prepared by Germanists and historians including Seidensticker, Friedrich Kapp, Heinrich Rattermann, and the later governor of Pennsylvania, Samuel Pennypacker.

The Bicentennial marked the beginning of celebrations of October 6 as German Day, Pastorius Day, or Settlers' Day in irregular sequence, not only in Philadelphia but also in the Midwest, New York, and New Jersey. The next major milestone, the 225th anniversary of German immigration, was again marked by participation of eminent scholars and the publication of a Pastorius biography by Marion Dexter Learned, the successor to Oswald Seidensticker as chairman of the German Department at the University of Pennsylvania.[44] But the festivities of 1908 stood out as a demonstration of self-confidence of the German-Americans' rank and file that was never again matched in spirit and numbers. The main organizer was Charles J. Hexamer, an engineer and son of a Forty-eighter, who had been instrumental in the unification of German-American associations and who became president of the National German-American Alliance when it was founded on October 6, 1901. Seven years later, twenty thousand participants in the German Day parade were joined by thousands of onlookers in Vernon Park to listen to the choir of the United Singers of Philadelphia and a children's choir. Georg von Bosse, pastor of the German Lutheran St. Paul's church and later president of the National Alliance, gave the main address in German. Theodore Roosevelt sent good wishes for the "Americans of German birth," and representatives of the German emperor tried to use the occasion for the generation of goodwill at a time of rising distrust and dislike for Wilhelm II in the United States.

The unveiling of the cornerstone for a Pastorius monument was the highlight of the day. Its fate was symbolic for the vicissitudes of fortune awaiting the German-American community.[45] The monument's cost of $50,000 was shared by the National Alliance and an appropriation of Congress. The War Department had hardly completed construction in the spring of 1917 when protesters interpreted the allegorical figure holding a lamp on top of thirty feet of Tennessee marble as Germania triumphant. Although designer Albert Jaegers explained that "the figure portrayed Civilization, the light bearer, the ideal in the hearts of the German pilgrims," the monument was encased in a huge box.

The controversial lady again saw the light of Vernon Park at dedication ceremonies on November 10, 1920. She became the rallying point of German-American associations that survived the war. The next major gathering at her feet, for the 250th anniversary of German immigration in 1933, reflected a surprising continuity of established traditions, although on a much diminished scale. On October 6, 7, and 8, members of the Second German-American Congress of Philadelphia and New York, the Steuben Society, and the German-American War Veterans were joined by close to twenty clubs of singers, Turner, and churches celebrating in a folk-festival atmosphere. October 6 was devoted to a cultural conference, organized by A. Busse, with lectures by five professors and two ministers. The only mention of the ominous political changes in Europe was the listing of the Friends of New Germany as the last of the associated societies. Hitler's ambassador, Hans Luther, was a member of the Honorary Committee along with President Franklin Delano Roosevelt, senators, and congressmen. Speeches were in both English and German. Advertisements of German-language newspapers, churches, butchers, bakers, and brewers created a familiar ambience. The officers of the Columbia Pinochle Club exemplified this spirit. Their notice in the program extended good wishes for the success of the tireless efforts in preparation of the festival, in line with Goethe's exhortation "Noble be man, helpful and good," before it turned to a recommendation of their "first-class meat, sausage, grocery and delicatessen store on 4th Street."

A few weeks later, the Pastorius Celebration in Cincinnati on October 29 was distinguished by an address by Albert Faust. He tried to recover bygone verve, citing old, well-known virtues of the law-abiding, hardworking, and peaceful German-Americans, but admonished his audience to use their "large, silent, independent vote," which was "the terror of politicians but the safety and backbone of the nation."[46]

Like the festivities in 1933, their sequel in 1958 arrived at a time of recovery from blows dealt to the German-American community almost two decades earlier. The 275th German Settlers Day, sponsored in Philadelphia's Town Hall by the Pastorius Day Association and twenty-seven member organizations, was limited to October 6. The historical, musical, and theatrical program was conducted entirely in English. Congressmen, the governors of Pennsylvania and Maryland, and President Eisenhower sent congratulatory messages stressing the marks left by the German immigrants' "industry, hard work, and their culture."[47] The ambassador of the Federal Republic to the United States, Wilhelm Grewe, delivered the main address.

The year 1958 saw new German-American initiative with the organization of the first Steuben Parade on New York's Fifth Avenue on September 20. Side by side with New York's Governor Averell Harriman, New Jersey's Governor Robert Baumle Meyner, and New York City's Mayor Robert Ferdinand Wagner, both of second-generation German lineage, reviewed the paraders from the grandstand. It was decorated with a flag sent by President Eisenhower from the White House and a German flag presented by President Theodor Heuss. The parade, deliberately fashioned after the model of the Irish St. Patrick's Day parade and the Polish Pulaski parade, attracted 10,000 participants and an estimated 150,000 onlookers.[48] The response to the

Steuben Parade on Fifth Avenue in New York, 1981. In the foreground: Frank Bolz, a famous local police officer of German descent.
In the background on the white line: Richard von Weizsäcker, then
Mayor of Berlin and later President of the Federal Republic, and his
wife Marianne. Right: Ed Koch, Mayor of New York, without a jacket
and with his arm raised. Next to him the Consul General of the Federal Republic, Hartmut Schulze-Boysen, and his wife Marita. (C. J.
Zumwalt, *New Yorker Staats-Zeitung und Herold*)

show encouraged continued efforts for cooperation among German-
American clubs: such was the goal of the German-American National
Congress, which was founded in Chicago in 1958, and other coordi-
nating organizations.

In the quarter of a century following 1958, the continued struggle
against decline in the membership of German-American organizations
and in German-language periodicals was balanced to a certain extent
by factors favoring the German-American community: a benign climate of relations between Washington and Bonn, attention for German contributions at America's Bicentennial stocktaking in 1976, and

increasing public interest in folklore, ethnicity, and the search for German family roots. A resurgence of scholarly concern was reflected in the expansion of the Society for German-American Studies.

These developments point to characteristic aspects of the Tricentennial celebrations in 1983. Hundreds of folk festivals all over the United States fulfilled popular expectations of the German-American talent for merrymaking. At the University of Pennsylvania in Philadelphia, a four-day conference on German-American history, politics, and culture was organized. It surpassed earlier symposia in range of topics and speakers, especially with the inclusion of a large number of scholars from West German universities. At the University of Wisconsin at Madison the Max Kade Institute for German-American Studies was founded "as a national center for the study of German immigration and German ethnic culture in America." The Johns Hopkins University established the American Institute for Contemporary German Studies in Washington.

The pomp and circumstances of the ceremonies on October 6, 1983, set them apart from previous anniversaries through an unprecedented degree of high-ranking executive involvement both from the United States and the Federal Republic. The appointment of a Tricentennial Committee by President Ronald Reagan, the extension of official events to Krefeld, the participation of Vice-President George Bush and of the Federal Republic's President Karl Carstens raised the occasion to a level of mutual acknowledgment with undertones of political concern that had been missing in times of greater detachment. Underlying strains in the alliance, apparent in the October 6 peace march of American and German protesters against missile deployment in Europe, were the major point considered worthy of mention by the American press, if they took any note of the Tricentennial at all.[49]

Looking ahead to the possibility of German Days in the years 2008 or 2033, the apparently final drying up of German immigration in the 1970s might reduce them to a mere evocation of historical memories. Degrees of acceptance or rejection of the German-Americans might cease to be a factor in American-German relations. The preservation of concord between successor generations of young Americans and young Germans, threatened even now by indifference and resentment, will demand close attention if the benefits of the German-American legacy are to be preserved.

Facing page. Tradition and the German-Americans. The diversity among German-speaking immigrant groups in the United States provides a fascinating parallel to the fragmentation of German-speaking Europe. However the term "German-American," widely used in the nineteenth century, particularly by the Forty-Eighters, is not completely adequate as an expression of this diversity. Within the realm of American ethnic representations, it shows strong traces of the "Schaukultur" of the Wilhelminian age. Groups that have shown the strongest identification with a regional ethnic culture are the South German-Austrians, the German-Hungarians, the Danube Germans, and the Volga Germans. The photos show both the "Prussian" image (top: "Die Langen Kerls" of the Philadelphia Steuben Parade, 1981) and the "Bavarian" image (bottom: parading the colors on German Day in Highland Park, St. Paul, Minnesota, 1983). (Max A. Frei, Steuben Day Observance Association, Philadelphia; Hugo Skrastins, *Voyageur*)

Notes

1. Hermann Oncken, "Die deutsche Auswanderung nach Amerika und das Deutschamerikanertum vom 17.Jahrhundert bis zur Gegenwart," in *Jahrbuch des Freien Deutschen Hochstifts* (1912), 3–25.

2. Introduction to John Gerow Gazley, *American Opinion of German Unification* (New York: Columbia University Press, 1926), 16. I arrived at the same conclusion pursuing the American image of the Germans in the decade before 1963: Christine M. Totten, *Deutschland—Soll und Haben, Amerikas Deutschlandbild* (Munich: Rütten & Loening, 1964), 11–16.

3. Francis Daniel Pastorius, *Umständige Geographische Beschreibung Der zu allerletzt erfundenen Provintz Pensylvaniae* (Frankfurt and Leipzig, 1700), quoted in Oswald Seidensticker, *Die erste deutsche Einwanderung in Amerika* (Philadelphia: Globe Printing House, 1883), 52.

4. Albert Bernhardt Faust, *The German Element in the United States*, 2 vols. (Boston: Houghton Mifflin, 1909), 1:8, 9.

5. Carl Wittke, *We Who Built America: The Saga of the Immigrant* (Cleveland: Case Western Reserve University Press, 1964), 81.

6. Faust, *German Element*, 2:153–55.

7. A chain reaction can be traced from stress on "clannishness" by John Arkas Hawgood, *The Tragedy of German-America* (New York: G. P. Putnam's Sons, 1940), esp. 93–224, to Richard O'Connor, *The German-Americans: An Informal History* (Boston: Little, Brown, 1968), esp. 67–97, to journalists who use O'Connor's readable and plausible clichés. Among scholars who have recently singled out rapid assimilation as characteristic, the work of Kathleen Neils Conzen stands out: *Immigrant Milwaukee, 1836–1860: Accommodation and Community in a Frontier City* (Cambridge, Mass.: Harvard University Press, 1976), and "The Paradox of German-American Assimilation," *Yearbook of German-American Studies* 16 (1981): 153–60.

8. Faust, *German Element*, 2:130–35.

9. Wittke, *We Who Built America*, 82.

10. Ibid., 232.

11. Dale T. Knobel, *"Hans" and the Historian: Ethnic Stereotypes and American*

Popular Culture, 1820–1860, Occasional Papers of the Society for German-American Studies, 10 (1980): 63.

12. Seidensticker, *Die erste deutsche Einwanderung in Amerika*, 11.

13. For comparative surveys see Manfred Koch Hillebrecht, *Das Deutschenbild, Gegenwart, Geschichte, Psychologie* (Munich: C. H. Beck, 1977), 213.

14. Helge Pross, *Was ist heute deutsch? Wertorientierungen in der Bundesrepublik* (Reinbek: Rowohlt, 1982), 13, 93ff.

15. Seidensticker, *Die erste deutsche Einwanderung*, 67.

16. Faust, *German Element*, 2:154.

17. Wittke, *We Who Built America*, 216.

18. Norbert Muhlen, *Germany in American Eyes: A Study of Public Opinion* (Hamburg: Atlantik Brücke, 1959), 12; Gazley, *American Opinion of German Unification*, 100, 125.

19. Horst Ueberhorst, *Turner unterm Sternenbanner* (Munich: Moos, 1978), 48, and Wittke, *We Who Built America*, 215.

20. John F. Kennedy observed that "we owe the mellowing of the austere Puritan imprint on our daily lives . . . to the influence of the German immigrants in particular" (*A Nation of Immigrants* [New York: Harper & Row, 1964], 53).

21. Gazley, *American Opinion of German Unification*, 26–33; Hans W. Gatzke, *Germany and the United States: A "Special Relationship?"* (Cambridge, Mass.: Harvard University Press, 1980), 28–29.

22. Gazley, *American Opinion of German Unification*, 35, 80–86.

23. Gazley's ample documentation is complemented by Clara Eve Schieber, *The Transformation of American Sentiment toward Germany, 1870–1914* (Boston: Cornhill, 1923). For recent research on the period see La Vern J. Rippley, "German Assimilation: The Effect of the 1871 Victory on Americana-Germanica," in Hans L. Trefousse, ed., *Germany and America: Essays on Problems of International Relations and Immigration* (New York: Brooklyn College Press, 1980), and Trefousse's article in Vol. 1 of this book, "German-American Immigrants and the Newly Founded Reich."

24. In the Germanophile *Nation*, August 16, 1866, quoted in Gazley, *American Opinion of German Unification*, 227.

25. Pro-Prussian sentiment rested largely on admiration for its free common school system, emulated by Horace Mann and Henry Barnard. See Gazley, *American Opinion of German Unification*, 40–41, 322ff.

26. Muhlen, *Germany in American Eyes*, 19.

27. *New York Times*, quoted in Gazley, *American Opinion of German Unification*, 398.

28. Schieber, *Transformation of American Sentiment*, 39–136; Gatzke, *Germany and the United States*, 43–45.

29. Rippley, "German Assimilation," 128–30.

30. President Charles Franklin Thwing of Western Reserve University gives a detailed comparative evaluation in *The American and the German University: One Hundred Years of History* (New York: Macmillan, 1978), 46–47, 66, 69–70, 75.

31. Henry August Pochmann, *German Culture in America: Philosophical and Literary Influences, 1600–1900* (Madison: University of Wisconsin Press, 1957), 329–32.

32. Wittke, *We Who Built America*, 368–75; Wallace Brockway and Herbert Weinstock, eds., *Men of Music: Their Lives, Times and Achievements* (New York: Simon and Schuster, 1950), 469–70.

33. Anneliese E. Harding, *America through the Eyes of German Immigrant Paint-*

ers (Boston: Goethe Institute, 1975–76), and contributions to Klaus Wust and Heinz Moos, eds., *Three Hundred Years of German Immigrants to North America* (Munich: Moos, 1983), 143.

34. Gazley, *American Opinion of German Unification*, 140.

35. Richard C. Spuler, "Mediating German Culture: American Germanistik at the Turn of the Century," *Yearbook of German-American Studies* 16 (1981): 9–25, esp. 22.

36. Muhlen, *Germany in American Eyes*, 14.

37. Schieber, *Transformation of American Sentiment*, 251, 277.

38. The superior account is Frederick C. Luebke, *Bonds of Loyalty: German-Americans and the World War* (De Kalb: Northern Illinois University Press, 1974).

39. For the German-Americans' fate between the wars consult La Vern J. Rippley, *The German-Americans* (Boston: G. K. Hall, 1976), esp. 190, 193–95.

40. Muhlen, *Germany in American Eyes*, 33, 35.

41. Totten, *Deutschland*, 63–65, 100.

42. Ibid., 141, 338. For statistics see Robert Henry Billigmeyer, "Recent German Immigration to America," in Dennis Laurence Cuddy, ed., *Contemporary American Immigration* (Boston: Twayne, 1982), 117.

43. Described in *Nachtrag zur 250jährigen Gedenkfeier der Landung der ersten deutschen Einwanderer und Gründung von Germantown. Unter den Auspizien des Deutsch-Amerikanischen Zentralbundes von Pennyslvanien und anderer angeschlossener Vereinigungen. Zweiter Deutsch-Amerikanischer Kongress, Philadelphia, Freitag, Samstag und Sonntag, den 6., 7. und 8. Oktober 1933*. The program is not paginated.

44. Ibid. In the following year, 1909, two of the basic works on the German-Americans were published, Faust's *The German Element in the United States* and Rudolf Cronau, *Drei Jahrhunderte deutschen Lebens in Amerika* (Berlin: Dietrich Reimer).

45. Edward W. Hocker, *Germantown, 1683–1933* (Germantown, Pa.: Published by the author, 1933), 300–301.

46. Albert B. Faust, *Francis Daniel Pastorius and the 250th Anniversary of the Founding of Germantown* (Philadelphia: Carl Schurz Memorial Foundation, 1934), 19, 21.

47. In a letter of September 25, 1958, from Congressman Hugh Scott to Herman Witte, president, Pastorius Day Association, printed in the program of the 275th German Settlers' Day.

48. Gerhard Hirseland, ed., *Steuben Parade am 20. September 1958. Ein Bericht in Wort und Bild* (New York: German-American Committee of Greater New York, 1958), 1–2.

49. In contrast to extensive coverage by the *Philadelphia Inquirer*, the *New York Times* published only one substantial feature on October 4 (D 26), followed on October 6 by a picture and brief note (A1, 5) and review of the German-American TV documentary (C 31). A more detailed report on October 7 (A 14) mentions the peace rally to which the *Washington Post* devotes twice as much space (October 7) as to Carstens's visit on October 6 (A 14, E 3).

14.
The Rhetoric of Survival: The Germanist in America from 1900 to 1925

HENRY J. SCHMIDT

THE DOCUMENTS THAT CHRONICLE THE HISTORY of German studies in the United States between 1900 and 1915—the professional journals, the publications for specialists and for mass audiences, the speeches and memoirs—reveal an apparently healthy, self-confident profession. Seen in retrospect, conditions were indeed enviable. Since the late nineteenth century, German had been considered the second language of the republic, and by 1915, it was taken by 24 percent of all public high school students, compared to 9 percent in French and 2 percent in Spanish. (Today the high school enrollment in German is 1.5 percent.) The teaching of German was actively supported by the newspapers, organizations, churches, and financial enterprises of what was then the largest ethnic group in the United States: in the year 1910 more than 8 million Americans were either German-born or of German parentage. The teaching profession seemed firmly united behind its primary objectives: to preserve the German language and to transmit the cultural heritage and moral idealism of Wilhelminian Germany.

Under such circumstances, one would expect to find a profession complacent in its success. The question therefore arises why, long before the outbreak of World War I, instructors of German were so strident and immodest in their praise of all things German. Book-length studies and countless speeches and essays extolled the German national character and its allegedly formative influence upon the development of American democracy. Explicitly or implicitly, Germans were considered superior to other nationalities in qualities ranging from discipline and thoroughness to the love of music, family, and pets. A simple rearrangement of the familiar catalog of virtues exposes, through contradiction, its fundamental meaninglessness: the Germans turn out to be a proud, humble, serious, lighthearted folk; they are daring and obedient, manly and soulful, aristocratic defenders of democracy and individualistic defenders of the collective will. Clearly this rhetoric signifies something beyond its vapid substance. As I intend to demonstrate, such chauvinistic utterances signify an intense struggle for legitimacy: a struggle for professional recognition within the academic sphere and a struggle for a secure position for German-Americans within American society.

German immigrants who taught at American universities helped popularize the concept of the professor as a spiritual leader. Like their colleagues in other fields, Germanists at German universities regarded themselves as high priests of culture, as builders of character, and as interpreters of ultimate moral values. These academic mandarins, as Fritz K. Ringer calls them,[1] were a homogeneous social class: male, affluent, Christian, politically conservative. They defended their privileged status against the less well-educated masses as well as against women, Jews, and foreign influences by claiming to be the guardians of the nation's cultural heritage, which they fashioned into an instrument of support for the monarchy.

The American university in 1900 was receptive to this educational ideology because it too subscribed to a trickle-down theory of culture. The American-born Germanist Marion Dexter Learned, for example, urged the educated German classes to unite with American academicians to ensure that German culture would be represented by German-American intellectuals, instead of by the "German communities representing the uneducated classes," in which the German element was "so objectionable, not only to the English population, but to the better German classes as well."[2] His comment reflects the antagonisms within the German-American community between the so-called soul Germans and the stomach Germans. Academic humanists attempted to distinguish themselves not only from the uneducated but also from plutocrats, the well-born, and the military on the basis of their classical learning. The prestige and authority deriving from a classical education implied the mastery of a prescribed set of subjects as well as familiarity with the prevailing canon of classical works. To fulfill their mission to influence the moral upbringing of American students, Germanists had to find models for spiritual uplift within their own cultural heritage. In doing so, they were obliged to confront the

Pastorius Redivivus, 1908, as portrayed by the Germanist Marion Dexter Learned (1857–1917), who in the same year published his biography of the founder of Germantown. Learned's admiration for Francis Daniel Pastorius, of whom no known pictures exist, and his interest in the culture of the German immigrants created a firm basis for the field of German-American studies around the turn of the century. Like Oswald Seidensticker, who was also a professor at the University of Pennsylvania and a scholar of German-American culture, he generally pursued a positivistic approach in his work. (Roughwood Collection)

traditional dominance of Greek and Latin classicism and to compete in the educational marketplace against Anglo-American, French, and Hispanic cultural missionaries—a competition that has never ceased. This pursuit of academic territory was reflected in an essay published in 1887 by Julius Goebel, who attempted to put the teaching of idealism on a German footing: "It is a wrong assumption of some of the classic philologians . . . that 'idealism' can only be attained by the reading of the ancient classics. Would not a careful study of Schiller's 'Anmut und Würde' or 'Aesthetische Briefe' enrich the mind of the student at least as much as one of the easier dialogues of Plato?"[3] As literature emerged as a curricular commodity, culture was similarly instrumentalized; Kuno Francke, for example, considered his efforts to establish a Germanic museum at Harvard in 1903 "a necessity, if the discipline that I represent is to stand its ground against the overwhelming influence of England and France."[4] Germanists justified their cultural expansionism by insisting that they were operating in an intellectually backward country. Charles J. Hexamer, the American-born president of the Deutschamerikanischer Nationalbund, said in 1915 that "no one . . . will ever find us prepared to step down to a lesser *Kultur*; no, we have made it our aim to draw the other up to us."[5] His polemic was motivated by ethnic protectionism; as Goebel remarked in 1910, the primary target group of the cultural chauvinists was the second and third generations of German-Americans: "We must prevent them from drowning in a mediocre culture and instill in them a justified pride in their heritage, instead of cowardly shame."[6] The solidification of ethnic ties would assure a constant and possibly expanding clientele for educators, the clergy, the German-language press, and any entrepreneurs who profited from the maintenance of German identity.

Not surprisingly, therefore, the spirit of "am deutschen Wesen soll die Welt genesen" (the German spirit will heal the world) within the German-American community was often as intense as in the Fatherland itself. To promote ethnic goals, Germanists spoke out against prohibition, puritanism, women's suffrage, American materialism, mass culture, and—most important—Germany's enemies. German-language newspapers sold German flags and pictures of Kaiser Wilhelm to their readers,[7] and the editor of *Monatshefte für deutsche Sprache und Pädagogik*, the official journal of the Nationaler Deutschamerikanischer Lehrerbund, devoted a full page in 1913 to congratulate the Kaiser upon the twenty-fifth anniversary of his coronation.[8] Even Kuno Francke, the leading Germanist of his time and an opponent of ethnic extremists in his own camp, was moved to confess that he thought the Kaiser to be a combination of Richard Wagner's Parsifal and the Nietzschean superman.[9] Already in 1900 Francke had described the German struggle for cultural dominance as a holy war.[10] It is little wonder, then, that this crusading spirit eventually caused some Germanists to welcome the outbreak of hostilities in 1914. Heinrich Hermann Maurer announced in *Monatshefte*: "We want Germany's victory. . . . We need Germany's victory as a badly needed guarantee of the victorious influence of a superior German culture."[11]

When the war began, many Germanists continued to defend the German cause. (Others holding different views either did not attempt to voice their opinions or were not granted a forum, as far as I have been able to determine.) The greatest threat to their ethnic status lay in America's pro-British bias. In response, prominent academicians from America and Germany spoke to mass meetings and thousands of copies of books and pamphlets were distributed to counter atrocity stories about the German armies, to justify the invasion of Belgium, and to protest misrepresentations of the German position in the American press. American Germanists helped revive the ancient fear of the "barbaric Slavic hordes" overrunning the Fatherland and its culture. But as anti-German sentiment grew, so did the willingness of German-Americans to cast off their ethnicity and disappear into the great melting pot. The Deutschamerikanischer Nationalbund campaigned desperately against such assimilation; those who differed from its extremist views were branded as traitors. Kuno Francke, for example, incurred its wrath when he publicly rejected its political lobbying efforts for the sake of cultural diplomacy. He argued that if the Nationalbund had limited itself to the cultivation of German music, literature, and art, the American public would have been more receptive to its cause.[12] His idealistic stance reflected the tendency among academic humanists to defend their interests in terms of morality and fair play rather than political expediency, rendering them vulnerable to the charge of naivete.

After 1914, the German-American community was split essentially into four camps: the pro-Germans, the pro-Americans, the neutralists (out of religious conviction or the desire for anonymity), and the socialists, who opposed the war from the start as a manifestation of capitalistic imperialism. Germanists who continued to publish had two options: they either lent their expertise and rhetorical skills to the battle for German ideals being waged by *Monatshefte* and the German-language press, or they published "neutral," "apolitical" scholarship in the pages of *PMLA, Modern Language Notes, The Journal of English and Germanic Philology*, and *Modern Philology*. The nationalists continued to mine the classics for confirmation of the German cause. Thus the German people were seen as being on the verge of fulfilling the prophecy of *Nathan der Weise*'s parable,[13] Goethe and Schiller were employed as heroic prophets of a mighty German national state,[14] but Heinrich Heine was cast aside as "a morally unstable person."[15] "Neutral" scholarship had an entirely different goal; it was to legitimate German literary criticism and philology as academic disciplines governed by principles of scientific objectivity. At this time, American *Germanistik* was not dominated by one particular school of criticism; the eclecticism of critical method resembles that of the post–World War II era, as a small sampling of article titles, all published during the war, will indicate: "Kleist at Boulogne-sur-mer," "Goethe's Theory of the Novelle," "English Translations of *Werther*," "Isoldes Gottesurteil," "The Influence of Hans Tolz on Hans Sachs," and "Concerning the German Relatives 'Das' und 'Was,' in Clauses Dependent upon Substantivized Adjectives, and upon Neuter Indefinites, as Used in Schiller's Prose." With the exception of *PMLA*, World War I had no visible effect on journals of "pure" research. Having shielded their scholarship from the war, they were able to continue publishing without interruption, whereas *Monatshefte* disappeared completely from 1918 to 1920 and did not resume its monthly publication until 1928. These other journals regularly published comparative studies by Germanists, which appear to have had a function antithetical to the cultural separatism of *Monatshefte*. The comparatists attempted to integrate German literature into European culture, to strengthen its bonds with other national literatures. It is revealing that even during a period of protracted hostility, English and Germanic philology would willingly coexist under the roof of the same journal, especially considering that the journal's long-term editor and one of its most prolific contributors was Julius Goebel, who was also one of the most rabidly militant, anti-Semitic, unreconstructed German nationalists on the academic scene.[16] Obviously, the integrationist and segregationist alternatives were not mutually exclusive; numerous Germanists besides Goebel practiced both simultaneously. I would theorize that their adaptability is paradigmatic for the institutionalization process of German studies in America: the profession attempted to acquire recognition and status through several institutionalized modes of discourse at the same time. Historical events proved nationalistic rhetoric to be in the last analysis a transitory and ineffective method to achieve institutional permanence. The future, in short, belonged to assimilation.

The first major setback for the pro-German campaign in the United States was the sinking of the *Lusitania* in May 1915. Thereafter, German teachers began to lower their collective profile, and voices critical of rabid partisanship were heard, even in *Monatshefte*.[17] Looking beyond the war's end, German teachers began to realize that their professional stability was now at odds with their cultural identity. Especially after the United States declared war on Germany in April 1917, the profession underwent a full-scale ideological metamorphosis. This transformation is most vividly recorded in *Monatshefte*. In early 1915, a prominent contributor had ended an article about the war with the words, "and therefore hail and victory to German and Austrian weapons on and under the water, on land and in the air";[18] by May 1918 the journal was advising its readers—now in English rather than German—about survival techniques in the classroom. In a lengthy article titled "Adjusting Instruction in German to Conditions Imposed by the War," J. D. Deihl urged that teachers "combine a sympathetic appreciation of the values of German with an uncompromisingly American opposition to those forces in Germany which have helped make this war possible." He instructed teachers to employ "Yankee ingenuity and grit" as they readjusted their classroom procedures, for, in his opinion, the profession could afford to be optimistic: "There is no reasonable doubt that the present war will stimulate to a hitherto undreamed-of degree the interest in modern foreign language study."[19] The wholesale substitution of pro-Americanism for pro-Germanism becomes less startling the more one realizes that the patriotic attitude had not changed, merely its content.

In self-preservation, teachers cast about for "safe" literary texts. (Deihl recommended Paul Heyse, Friedrich de la Motte Fouqué, Joseph von Eichendorff, and Adelbert von Chamisso, and he urged that instructors emphasize literature's formal and stylistic beauties.)[20] Textbooks that glorified Kaiser and Fatherland were removed, and one German teacher in Cincinnati was commended by his superintendent of schools for censoring "with absolute fidelity" textbooks he himself had written.[21] Literary criticism in *Monatshefte* underwent a similar transformation. For example, in May 1916, C. H. Handschin published an essay titled "Gottfried Keller und Deutschland," in which he eulogized Keller as a "Seher des Germanentums" (prophet of the Germanic heritage). Although having to argue around the inconvenient fact that Keller was Swiss, Handschin nevertheless saw in him "the primary traits of the German character: loyalty, integrity, profundity, diligence, and depth of feeling."[22] Less than two years later, Handschin published another article on Keller in *Monatshefte*, but this time the title was "Kellers Tierliebe" (Keller's love of animals). Keller was now no more nor less than a "passionierter Tierfreund" (impassioned friend of animals).[23] Although I cannot prove that the changing Zeitgeist affected Handschin's perspective, the contrast is symptomatic of the profession's reaction to the war.

But the profession's shift of allegiance must also be seen against the background of the anti-German hysteria that seized America after it entered the war. The spirit of vengeance was directed at anything and everything German, from Beethoven and Schiller to hamburger and sauerkraut. University professors were dismissed for unpatriotic utterances, and textbooks were burned at public ceremonies. Linguistic chauvinism was as rabid among the anti-Germans as among the pro-Germans: German was denounced as a barbarian language "in which it is impossible to think clearly,"[24] a language whose sound "reminds us of . . . the driving of about 100,000 young French, Belgian, and Polish women into compulsory prostitution."[25] As a consequence, the teaching of German was banned in approximately half the states of the Union. The precipitous drop in student enrollment decimated the ranks of the profession, and, although there is not conclusive proof, it apparently traumatized the mandarins of American *Germanistik*. The profession was under fire not primarily because of its cultural aspirations and humanistic ideals but because it taught the German language. To comprehend the consequences adequately, we must consider briefly the institutionalization of foreign culture studies as a whole in the American university up to that point. The best indicator of this development is its main journal, *PMLA*. Its earliest issues after its founding in 1884 contain a mixture of pedagogical and philological research, as well as literary criticism. But as universities increasingly emphasized professional training and allowed the graduate school to rise to a dominant position, these disciplines divided into well-defined areas of specialization. Philology eventually gravitated from *PMLA* to other journals. Pedagogical studies disappeared from *PMLA* before the turn of the century, and in 1902 the pedagogical section of the Modern Language Association (MLA) was eliminated. In his presidential address to the MLA in 1914, the Wisconsin Germanist Alexander Hohlfeld applauded this development, claiming that it had been necessary "to repress narrowly and specifically pedagogical interests." He hailed the "final victory of scholarship" and praised those "who, in this struggle for supremacy, held high the banner of learning."[26] Note that pedagogy is excluded from "scholarship" and "learning." Pedagogues retaliated by expanding their own organizations and founding the *Modern Language Journal* in 1916. As a result, the MLA's remaining hierarchy that set the standards of professional achievement was dominated by a highly specialized elite of literary critics.

But this state of affairs did not jibe with the expectations of American society—a difference of opinion that still prevails today. Whereas the humanist aspired to influence moral values and instill ideals, society demanded training in functional skills.[27] When many Germanists—those who still held jobs, that is—were reduced to teaching "der-die-das" to small classes, the true base-superstructure relationship of the profession in America was revealed. The self-image of the Germanist as an intellectual leader never reached its inflated prewar proportions because never again could enrollment be taken for granted. Falling enrollment, in other words, tended to reduce class distinctions in German departments and in the German-American community.

To be sure, not every Germanist chose the course of self-protective adaptation. Kuno Francke and other regular contributors to *Monatshefte* made a virtue out of necessity by conjuring a new myth out of the ashes of the old myth of German invincibility. Since the Germans had failed to achieve grandeur in victory, they were to be allowed grandeur in martyrdom, idealized as a folk with a superhuman ability to endure suffering. This theme occurs in much of Francke's inspirational poetry, which was published regularly in *Monatshefte* and in American newspapers. His poem "Deutsches Volk," which appeared on the first page of the January 1917 issue of *Monatshefte*, is typical of the genre; I quote the final stanza:

> O du Volk, schicksalsgestählt,
> O du Volk, gnadenerwählt—
> Neue Menschheit hast du begründet,
> Neuen Glauben hast du entzündet,
> Mitten aus Schrecken und Donner der Schlacht
> Hast du den Heiland der Zukunft gebracht!
> Deutsches Volk![28]

> O you folk, fate-hardened
> O you folk, chosen by God's grace—
> You have founded a new human race,
> You have ignited a new faith,
> From the midst of battle's terror and thunder
> You have brought the Savior of the future!
> German folk!

Elsewhere he wrote that German history and culture were branded with a "Signatur des Tragischen" (tragic mark), causing the Germans to endure a recurrent *Götterdämmerung* out of which they would again arise to new heights of idealism.[29] Meanwhile, other Germanists and the German-language press blamed the war on Germany's rulers, who, it was claimed, had led the German people astray. This scapegoat deflected attention from their own complicity, and once again the moral superiority of Germans—and by extension, German-Americans—was assured. By focusing, as before, on spiritual rather than material values, the revisionists were able to hail the end of the war as a victory of American ideals, while at the same time they were urging their audiences to protest Germany's so-called dishonor at Versailles.

Between 1920 and approximately 1925, a number of former cultural crusaders and ethnic politicians attempted to rebuild their prewar influence and prestige. In German studies, this brief Age of Restoration was spearheaded by *Monatshefte*. Publishing almost exclusively in German again, *Monatshefte* resurrected the definition of the German teacher as a missionary for the German language, *Geist*, and culture. That the journal chose this form of coming to terms with the past may be attributable to its founding editor, Max Griebsch, who was appointed in 1899 and was still in office after the war and would remain so until 1934—an editorship of thirty-five years. In his preface to the first *Monatshefte* yearbook in 1920, he announced: "The yearbook intends to announce to the world . . . that our belief in the cause that we represent is not shaken."[30] The laws of competition in the educational marketplace appeared to have reinstated nationalism once again as an acceptable quality; Griebsch noted approvingly that French and Spanish teachers were producing textbooks imitating the prewar *Im Vaterland*, one of the favorites of the bookburners.[31] To underscore its ideological heritage, *Monatshefte* created a series called "Sie waren unser" (They were ours) to commemorate the extremists who had fought for the German cause. For further moral support, a regular feature called "Stimmen von drüben" (Voices from across the sea) broadcast the political opinions of German academics who were nostalgic for the Second Reich. With a sigh of relief, contributors welcomed back the old values: "It's right after all—that indestructible idealism, that German sense of duty: work and do not despair."[32] A Führer ethos predominated, and the rhetoric was at times frighteningly prophetic: "What is now felt as a gentle breeze will soon blow across the land as a storm, as a purifying thunderstorm. The healthy will conquer the sick and decrepit, community spirit will prevail over selfishness, the spirit of truth over the delusion of lies."[33] But no contributor was able to match the brazen unrepentance of Julius Goebel in 1922: "The time will come when people will thank us for saving the true spirit of the republic from destruction . . . personally, I think that we were rather modest in our praise of things German."[34] A further indication of the political direction behind this campaign appeared in a polemic in the same yearbook against "the masses of workers blinded by the idea of the proletarian International." The conclusion was that "salvation lies not in the International, but in the national!"[35]

But the ethnic lobbying of yore and the calls for the mystic rejuvenation of the German spirit lacked popular support. Although many German-Americans may well have shared the pro-German sentiments of the *Monatshefte* contributors, they now preferred to remain within the national consensus, avoiding public attention and criticism. In German studies, the moderates began to prevail, and *Monatshefte* again lowered its volume. After the Supreme Court ruled in 1923 that the ban against teaching German was unconstitutional, German departments accelerated their rebuilding of language programs, and by 1932 the mission of the profession had become, according to Alexander Hohlfeld, "purposeful German-English mediation." [36] Literary scholarship steered clear of political issues, and German culture was converted into an inoffensive commodity. Claiming to fear a repetition of past errors, the profession took little note of the cataclysms occurring in Europe during the 1930s and 1940s; the impact of World War II was appraised primarily for its effect on pedagogy. Having limited its objectives to strictly academic concerns, the profession, according to Henry C. Hatfield and Joan Merrick in 1948, "failed to make what might have been its greatest contribution in a period of crisis: the interpretation of the German mind to a puzzled nation." [37] I believe their criticism is justified, for the profession had indeed overreacted to the chauvinistic excesses of an earlier era. Its revulsion for politics created a legacy of exclusivity, a preoccupation with aesthetics and existentialist philosophy that survived long into the postwar period.

Notes

1. Fritz K. Ringer, *The Decline of the German Mandarins: The German Academic Community, 1890–1933* (Cambridge, Mass.: Harvard University Press, 1969).
2. Marion Dexter Learned, "The 'Lehrerbund' and the Teachers of German in America," *Pädagogische Monatshefte* 1 (1899): 13.
3. Julius Goebel, "A Proposed Curriculum of German Reading," *Modern Language Notes* 2 (1887): 26.
4. Kuno Francke, *Deutsche Arbeit in Amerika* (Leipzig: Felix Meiner, 1930), 41. All German quotations have been translated by the author.
5. Quoted in Frederick C. Luebke, *Bonds of Loyalty: German-Americans and World War I* (De Kalb: Northern Illinois University Press, 1974), 100.
6. Julius Goebel, "Gedanken über die Zukunft des Deutschtums," *Monatshefte für deutsche Sprache und Pädagogik* (formerly *Pädagogische Monatshefte*) 11 (1910): 154.
7. Carl Wittke, *German-Americans and the World War (With Special Emphasis on Ohio's German-Language Press)* (Columbus: Ohio State Archaeological and Historical Society, 1936), 31.
8. *Monatshefte für deutsche Sprache und Pädagogik* 14, no. 6 (1913): frontispiece.

9. Kuno Francke, *A German-American's Confession of Faith* (New York: B. W. Huebsch, 1915), 6.

10. Kuno Francke, "Goethes Vermächtnis an Amerika," *Pädagogische Monatshefte* 1 (1900): 6.

11. Heinrich Hermann Maurer, "Wir Deutschamerikaner und der Weltkrieg," *Monatshefte für deutsche Sprache und Pädagogik* 16 (1915): 42.

12. Kuno Francke, "Die Deutschamerikaner, die Harvard Universität und der Krieg" (N.p., 1915), reprint in Kuno Francke Papers, Harvard University Archives, Cambridge, Mass.

13. Clara L. Nicolay, "Die Kinder des Ringes," *Monatshefte für deutsche Sprache und Pädagogik* 17 (1916): 89.

14. Julius Goebel, "Goethe und Schiller," *Pädagogische Monatshefte* 2 (1901): 357.

15. O. E. Lessing, "Neuere Literaturgeschichten," *Pädagogische Monatshefte* 4 (1903): 42.

16. See, for example, his *Das Deutschtum in den Vereinigten Staaten von Nord Amerika* (Munich: Lehmanns, 1904).

17. See, for example, Paul E. Titsworth, "The Attitude of the American Teacher of German toward Germany," *Monatshefte für deutsche Sprache und Pädagogik* 17 (1916): 195–96.

18. Ernst Voss, "Zum Weltkriege," *Monatshefte für deutsche Sprache und Pädagogik* 16 (1915): 73.

19. J. D. Deihl, "Adjusting Instruction in German to Conditions Imposed by the War," *Monatshefte für deutsche Sprache und Pädagogik* 19 (1918): 128–34.

20. Ibid., 131, 134.

21. "Umschau," *Monatshefte für deutsche Sprache und Pädagogik* 19 (1918): 236.

22. C. H. Handschin, "Gottfried Keller und Deutschland," *Monatshefte für deutsche Sprache und Pädagogik* 17 (1916): 155–61; quotation, p. 155.

23. C. H. Handschin, "Kellers Tierliebe," *Monatshefte für deutsche Sprache und Pädagogik* 18 (1917): 71–74; quotation, p. 72.

24. Knight Dunlap, "Value of German Language Assailed," reprint from the *New York Times* in "German Department," William Oxley Thompson Papers, Ohio State University Archives.

25. *Throw Out the German Language and All Disloyal Teachers*, published by the American Defense Society, quoted in Luebke, *Bonds of Loyalty*, 216.

26. Alexander R. Hohlfeld, "Light from Goethe on Our Problems," *PMLA* 29 (1914): lxxiii.

27. Richard Ohmann's comment about teaching English composition pertains equally well to elementary courses in foreign languages: "The part of our job that justifies us to others within and outside the university is the part we hold in lowest regard and delegate to the least prestigious members of the profession" (*English in America: A Radical View of the Profession* [New York: Oxford University Press, 1976], 243).

28. Kuno Francke, "Deutsches Volk," *Monatshefte für deutsche Sprache und Pädagogik* 18 (1917): 1.

29. Kuno Francke, *Die Kulturwerte der deutschen Literatur von der Reformation bis zur Aufklärung* (Berlin: Weidmannsche Buchhandlung, 1923), 623.

30. Max Griebsch, "Begleitwort," *Monatshefte für deutsche Sprache und Pädagogik* (Jahrbuch 1920): 1.

31. Ibid., 3.

32. F. Klaeber, "Stimmen von drüben," *Monatshefte für deutsche Sprache und Pädagogik* (Jahrbuch 1920): 37.

33. Ibid., 39.

34. Julius Goebel, "Das Recht auf die Muttersprache und ihre Erhaltung," *Monatshefte für deutsche Sprache und Pädagogik* (Jahrbuch 1922): 24.

35. Heinrich Maurer, "Der Kampf um das Deutschtum in Amerika in seiner kulturgeschichtlichen Bedeutung," *Monatshefte für deutsche Sprache und Pädagogik* (Jahrbuch 1922): 73.

36. Alexander R. Hohlfeld, "Eine Hauptaufgabe der Deutschen in Amerika," *Monatshefte für deutschen Unterricht* (formerly *Monatshefte für deutsche Sprache und Pädagogik*) 24 (1932): 11.

37. Henry C. Hatfield and Joan Merrick, "Studies of German Literature in the United States, 1939–1946," *Modern Language Review* 43 (1948): 354.

15.
Ameliorated Americanization: The Effect of World War I on German-Americans in the 1920s

LA VERN J. RIPPLEY

WORLD WAR I WAS THE CATALYST that jelled the Americanization of the German population in the United States. Progress toward
assimilation had, however, been initiated and in many respects completed well before that event, depending on which groups or regions
one refers to.[1] For example, the areas of earlier immigration—New
York, Maryland, Pennsylvania, Ohio, and Missouri—had seen once-
solid German regions dissolve under the secular, political, social, or
psychological pressures of daily life. In the same sections of the country, however, certain groups held tenaciously to their Germanness for
reasons other than their nationality. Religious tradition was undoubtedly the most powerful factor in restraining assimilation. The Amish in
Pennsylvania, though among the earliest to arrive, are still not assimilated. Marriage traditions likewise impeded the abandonment of ethnicity, and some rural communities tended to be conservative in both
religion and politics and therefore also in regard to ethnicity.[2] Inter-
woven with the rural-urban lag in assimilation during the first third of
the twentieth century were technological and transportation barriers.
For instance, electricity was commonly available in the cities before
the 1930s whereas the Rural Electrification Act (REA) did not reach
outlying nonurban areas until World War II. In turn, rural families did
not have radios and had telephone service only sporadically. Roads
were not paved in the country until the 1930s, and therefore the auto-
mobile did not have its devastating impact for the breakup of rural
America, and with it the ethnic communities, until after World War II.
The war also wrought havoc on ethnic communities. The effect was

not physical and not simply because young men were drawn to far-away fields of battle with the resulting unwillingness to return, but because labor demands in the industrial centers lured entire families from rural to urban centers, where they remained following the peace.

The rural pockets notwithstanding, assimilation of the Germans in American society was progressing, though slowly, until the World War I hysteria accelerated it. In the year 1900, for instance, fifteen cities in the United States had German populations of fifteen thousand or more German-born, or 36 percent of the total German-born population of the United States. An additional 13 percent lived in ninety-four cities with from one thousand to fifteen thousand German-born.[3] In these more than one hundred cities the German population was concentrated enough that neighborhoods were self-sufficient. The intellectual level was high, and sufficient professionals were present to serve the needs of the group if it chose to continue in isolation. German communities with their own doctors, lawyers, bankers, businessmen, political leaders, and, not least, teachers, journalists, and artists were sustainable at levels of high quality. As scholars have shown, an ethnic community that is not large enough and not adequately underpinned by intellectuals who provide high-quality maintenance of traditions, arts, professions, and language is doomed to an early demise.[4]

The Germans were so successful in the professions, in publishing, in journalism, in operating their own schools, and in sustaining their own churches with well-educated clergies that, paradoxically, the youth were only too well prepared to cope with transition to the American mainstream. After successfully facing the threats of nativism in the 1850s, the Germans were drawn into the Civil War in large num-

Facing page. "A slice of American life has a German filling." Popular poster for the Tricentennial. The image of a cake, cleverly combining both the German and American colors, also calls to mind a profession frequently identified as "German" by Americans, that of the baker and confectioner. The text of the poster mentions the early protest against slavery made by the German families in 1688. It also points out that over seven million German immigrants came to America and that more than one-fourth of all Americans today claim German ancestry. The poster was designed by a German organization dealing with German culture abroad and documents the new approach taken by Germans toward such anniversaries. Most such declarations which originated in Germany before 1918 and after 1933 unrealistically considered German-Americans to be merely Germans living abroad (*Auslandsdeutsche*), a position which only exacerbated their unwanted isolation and subsequently hastened their assimilation into American society. (Inter Nationes)

A slice of American life has a German filling.

1683

100 Years of German Immigration

On 6 October 1683, the first 13 German families arrived aboard the small ship "Concord", the "German Mayflower".
They founded Germantown in Pennsylvania and in 1688 issued the first manifesto against slavery.
Over seven million German immigrants followed. Today more than one fourth of the population of the United States claims German ancestry.

bers.[5] They then easily garnered acceptability by touting their role in the war and their previous real or imagined antislavery stance.[6] Building on their Civil War reputation in the United States, the Germans also gained pride and success in the 1870s and 1880s as a result of the unification of Germany under Bismarck in 1871. Overnight Germany had gained a powerful new position in Europe, both in politics (at least until the advent of Kaiser Wilhelm II in 1888), and, even more important, in science, industry, technology, education, city planning, and world trade.[7] In many U.S. cities there were districts referred to almost affectionately and certainly with admiration, even if grudgingly, as "Little Germany," "Over the Rhine," "Little Saxony," "Germantown," and similar appellations.

Because the Germans were neither threatened by nor threatening to the larger society in the 1880s and 1890s, they welcomed impoverished newcomers, often set up societies, training cadres, and employment offices, and generally sent their ethnic members on their way.[8] In some respects there was more solidarity during these decades in the New World communities than in the Old, where the long-standing antagonisms between the North and the South, East and West, the working classes and the intelligentsia, the Protestants and the Catholics were more pronounced. In American rural German communities, homogeneity often prevailed along Lutheran, Catholic, Mennonite, and other boundaries, and in the urban centers ethnicity rather than religion easily became the common backdrop. So large and sophisticated were many of the urban German communities that they accommodated all religions, including Jewish Germans. Prussians, Pomeranians, Bavarians, Bohemian Germans, Austrian Germans, and Swiss Germans could identify by their language and in pride for their felt superiority. Whether university graduate or peasant, atheist or Catholic, nun expelled because of Bismarckian May Laws or Jesuit runaway teacher, a strong common front shielded the urbanized Germans from the blandishments of Americanization.

After the turn of the century, however, these communities waned even though they still presented the appearance of an impregnable solidarity. Almost as an afterthought, the national organization known as Der Deutsch-Amerikanische Nationalbund (the German-American Alliance) was created in 1901 to unite all the Germans in America behind common goals, defined mostly as cultural.[9] The alliance was intended as a federation of all local societies of German-speaking people and excluded from its scope all matters of religion and politics, except when the Germans came under overt political attack. In many respects, the alliance was modeled on the Polish National Alliance and others that had preceded it by at least a decade and that had genuine cultural and political purposes to safeguard. Its real purpose thinly disguised, the German-American Alliance was never needed the way others were during the late 1880s or the early 1900s. Germans were secure, respected, and content. The practical purpose of the alliance was to defend the traditions of the Fatherland regarding alcoholic beverages. Accused during the World War I period of serving as an arm of the imperialist Pan-German Union founded in Berlin in 1897, the German-American Alliance was handsomely subsidized not by the German government in Berlin, as alleged, but by the association of American brewers, which at the time was almost exclusively a German-American profession.[10] Throughout the period of contentment from 1900 to 1915, the beer keg provided a far stronger rallying point for the Germans in America than did the Pan-German cries of the German Kaiser and the Prussian officer class.

The only concrete suggestion made by the alliance for preserving German culture and traditions in the United States was a call for the use of the German language in public and parochial schools. Even here the alliance was not the primogenitor of German-language use, for it had already been sanctioned by public law in many states beginning with Pennsylvania in 1839 and followed by Ohio, Wisconsin, Nebraska, and many others throughout the balance of the nineteenth century.[11] In Nebraska, the state chapter of the alliance instigated adoption of German in the schools by lobbying the legislature to pass the Mockett Law in 1913. This law in turn became the pivotal case for outlawing German in the schools, beginning in 1918 and thereafter despite the war's conclusion, in Colorado, Arkansas, Indiana, Iowa, Kansas, South Dakota, and, of course, Nebraska.[12] Eventually state laws against the use of German and other non-English languages in the schools were overturned by the U.S. Supreme Court, but not until 1923.

When assessing the topic of Americanization, it is important to understand that language is an important, if not the key, factor in ethnicity, as is emphasized by the results of the xenophobia against the Germans during and following World War I. During the war and in the 1920s, the Germans were barely distinguishable from Anglo-Americans; both groups shared many northern European traditions and a common historical language. All the North Europeans looked similar in a crowd. Thus it was not the nationality, the physical features, or the geographic origins but the language that marked Germans as the target of venom during and following World War I.

Although disintegrating as an ethnic bloc in the early twentieth century, the German element was nonetheless numerically the strongest non-Anglo-American group in the United States. In 1910, according to the Thirteenth Census, the total population of the nation stood at 91,972,333, of which 13,345,546 had been born in a foreign country. In their introduction to the volumes on population, the census staff commented, "Among the countries of birth of the foreign-born . . . Germany held first place in 1910, with 2,501,333 or 18.5 percent of the total foreign-born. Next in importance were Russia and Finland (jointly) with 12.8 percent; Austria-Hungary, 12.4 percent; Ireland, 10 percent." [13] If we consider the entire ethnic community, we must include the category of ethnic stock, defined by the census as immigrants and the native-born children of immigrants (at least one parent born abroad). Under this subheading, in 1910 there were 92 million Americans of whom 8,646,402 were of German stock, yielding nearly a 10 percent component of the entire U.S. population.

But even this statistic does not deliver the full impact because, as noted, the language was the primary identifying characteristic of Germanness during and following World War I. Subdividing the U.S. population of 92 million according to the mother tongue, we are fortunate because the census of 1910 was the first to include a complete inquiry about mother-tongue usage. In 1910 there were 9,187,000 mother-tongue speakers of German in the United States, representing 28 percent of all non-English speakers and more than 11 percent of the total population of the nation at that time. During the war and in the decade that followed, a member of an ethnic group was not distinguished by his nation of birth or heritage. Boundaries and nations were in flux. If he spoke German, it mattered little whether he came from the German Empire, Austria, Switzerland, Luxembourg, Bohemia, Hungary, or the German colonies of South Russia. To the man on the street this person was an "enemy alien" even if his Fatherland—Russia, for example— was an ally of the United States in the struggle against the German-speaking Central Powers.

The result was that such organizations as the German-American Alliance were torpedoed at the national level when, following hearings, the U.S. Congress in 1918 revoked its charter. [14] Publication of German-language newspapers also fell calamitously when a law was enacted forcing them to file with the local post office translations of any article dealing with the war, a cost that was too heavy to bear by a press that was already waning from its peak years of 1895–1900.[15] Perhaps the most readily recordable shift of German sentiment can be traced in the balloting results, which show mass switching from the Democrats (the party of Wilson and the war in the German mind) to the Republicans, a switch that was especially noteworthy in 1918 and 1920.[16] More intriguing perhaps, is the statistical picture. In 1920 there were 1,686,108 persons of German birth in the United States, representing 12.1 percent of the foreign-born and 1.6 percent of the total population. Germans were still the largest of the foreign-born groups, followed by persons from Italy, Russia, Poland, Canada, Ireland. In 1920 there were 631,826 fewer German-born or 25.3 percent less than there were just one decade earlier, despite the arrival of 174,227 newcomers during the decade of the teens. As in 1910, however, Germans still constituted the largest foreign-born element in the United States in 1920. A similar pattern emerges when comparing the German stock population in 1920 with that of 1910. In 1920 there were 8,164,111 mother-tongue speakers of German in the United States, a decline of 482,291 or 5.6 percent. Meantime, among all the foreign-born white groups in the United States, the Germans in 1920 were not only the largest but also the one with the highest percentage of persons who had already become citizens of the United States, about 74 percent. Conversely, Germans were the lowest group with only first papers or alien status among all the foreign groups in the United States. Next in line seeking U.S. citizenship behind the Germans in 1920 were the Scandinavians (including Norway, Sweden, and Denmark) with about 68 percent, the Irish with 65 percent, and the English (including Scotland and Wales) with 64 percent. The least likely to take out citizenship in 1920 were immigrants from Mexico, followed by Hungary, Italy, and Poland.[17]

What do these data demonstrate? First, the Germans came to the United States with intentions of remaining,[18] not simply working for a time and then remigrating to the old homeland. Immigrants from countries such as Mexico, Portugal, Greece, Hungary, and even Italy did not especially want citizenship because they harbored intentions of returning once they had saved enough money for a comfortable existence in their country of origin.[19] Second, the data suggest that by 1920 the Germans were so well acclimated to life in the United States that they no longer conceived of a separate Germany across the sea. At most they hoped for a German culture that would persist parallel to, but with full participation in, the American political system.[20] One of the chief objectives of the German-American Alliance had been to promote U.S. citizenship for the Germans to strengthen the chances of German issues at the ballot boxes. Finally, the data indicate that between 1910 and 1920 the German-born as well as the German stock in the United States moved underground. It is not reasonable to believe that there was actually a drop of 25.3 percent in the number of German-born between 1910 and 1920 when there was a continuing flow of German immigrants into the United States between 1910 and the outbreak of war in the summer of 1914. It appears rather that in 1910 persons of German birth readily acknowledged to the census-taker where they had been born. By 1920, however, the stigma of being German appears to have been so severe in certain areas that many Germans denied their origins when asked by government officials. Of all the non-English mother-tongue statistics kept by the census for 1910 and 1920, the only one that showed a decline in that decade was German—by nearly half a million speakers. All others, including Italian, Polish, Yiddish, Swedish, Norwegian, and even French, increased, some significantly, despite the restriction on immigration that beset these groups as well. The only reasonable conclusion is that the Germans underreported both their nation of birth and their mother tongue to the 1920 census-takers. Although more research is necessary to determine the causes, perhaps the decline can be linked to anti-German conditions that prevailed in certain states. The decline of speakers of German from 1910 to 1920 was sharpest in New York, Illinois, Ohio, and Pennsylvania; it stayed about the same in Minnesota and increased slightly in Michigan, California, and Colorado.[21]

After 1920, when it was no longer a matter of pride to identify with German culture, German-language publications also declined precipitously, from 554 in 1910 to 234 in 1920, more than 50 percent. Daily German newspaper circulation in 1920 was only a quarter of what it had been in 1910. The German language was already out of the schools by law, and in the churches the shift to English accelerated rapidly. In 1917 only one-sixth of the Missouri Synod Lutheran churches held one English service per month whereas by 1920 three-quarters were doing so.[22] Epitomizing the shift in attitude is a comment by George N. Shuster, former president of Hunter College in New York: "If you step into the Milwaukee Public Library, you will find a good collection of German drama. All the earlier plays of Hauptmann, Sudermann, and the rest are there. But no titles more recent than 1914 are on the shelves. The interesting fact is not so much that no additional books were purchased after the war but that nobody cared to ask the librarians to buy more."[23] Not only were Germans willing to deny their ancestry to the census-taker, they were also shy, perhaps ashamed, to admit publicly their interest in German culture. Only in the ballot box did they frequently express their common ground with brothers across the seas.

In the relative privacy of the postal windows, too, they risked their identities with large-scale donations mailed for the relief of suffering families in Germany. Likewise, semipublic postwar collections for the hungry in Germany were highly successful when orchestrated by the churches in this country, for then the stigma seemed to be lifted. The German city of Milwaukee reported handling more than one hundred thousand packages of butter, sausage, and flour in the months immediately following the lifting of the blockade around former imperial Germany. An estimated three hundred clubs were started to raise money and foodstuffs for the starving Germans.[24] Enormously generous through their own private organizations, the Germans in the United States were particularly penurious toward Herbert Hoover's officially sanctioned European Relief Council, to which Americans on the average gave twenty-seven cents each yet the 6 million Germans in America gave only an estimated fifteen cents each.

The traditionally Democratic Germans registered a powerfully negative vote in the national election of 1920, solidly rejecting the Democrat James M. Cox of Ohio in favor of Warren Harding, also of Ohio. On principle, the Germans determined in the privacy of the ballot box to reject the Wilson Democracy. They did so not by voting Republican but by switching to third-party candidates, casting many ballots for Nonpartisan Leaguers and for Lafollette Progressives, parties strong in the Upper Midwest. At this time also the new Steuben Society was organized in hopes of replacing the National German-American Alliance, but its membership remained minuscule, never more than twenty thousand in comparison to the approximately 3 million that had signed up in the alliance.

During the 1920s two other threats to the Germans raised their heads, both only obliquely anti-German in nature. One was the Red Scare, essentially a conservative movement in opposition to the threat of communism following the success of the October Revolution of 1917 and of the civil war that swept Russia during 1919–21 with its concomitant famine.[25] What made the Red Scare a problem for the Germans was that in some sections the socialist movement was being squarely led by German-speaking, if not actually German-born, politicians in the United States. The best-known case is that of Congressman Victor Berger from Milwaukee, who maintained his hold on this most German of all American cities throughout most of the 1920s until his death in 1927, in spite of all efforts, even in the Congress itself, to have him ousted for his blatant socialism.[26]

The other threat was the persistent pressure of the temperance movement. Initiated as early as the 1850s, the push for prohibition subsided for a time during and following the Civil War but regained the initiative in 1869, when a national Prohibition party put forth a candidate for the presidency.[27] Candidates ran occasionally in elections throughout the nineteenth century, always vigorously opposed by the Germans and the American brewers, who were synonymous with the Germans. Running parallel to the political party were organizations such as the Women's Christian Temperance Union, begun in Ohio in 1873. Similar to it was the Anti-Saloon League, founded in Wisconsin in 1897 and supported nationwide, especially by the Methodists. In response to the ever-increasing threat to their lifestyles, the Germans enthusiastically supported the National German-American Alliance to counter the temperance movement. Nevertheless, after the turn of the century more and more states adopted prohibition—Maine, Kansas, North Dakota. By 1914, fourteen states had gone dry, by 1916 twenty-three, and a mere two years later, thirty-two. Only such overwhelmingly German states as Wisconsin held out. Always an abomination to the Germans, prohibition became the law of the land when the bill sponsored by Minnesota's Norwegian-American Andrew J. Volstead (Wraalstad) became the Volstead Act. After ratification by forty-five states, the Eighteenth Amendment took effect on July 1, 1919. Prohibition had succeeded, not on its own merits but because German opposition to it had been pounded back by attacks on loyalty, patriotism, and Americanism during World War I. By 1932, when the country had righted itself both with respect to its anti-Germanism and its futile anti-liquor attitudes, it was again the Germans in the congressional delegation from Wisconsin, the nation's most German state on a percentage basis, who sponsored federal legislation to repeal the hated Eighteenth Amendment. Understandably, Wisconsin and Michigan simultaneously became the first states to ratify the Twenty-First Amendment.

The 1920s also witnessed the rise of isolationism and conservativism in politics and with it the birth of a Nazi party in the United States.[28] As early as 1924, while Hitler was serving a prison term for his 1923 beer hall putsch, Kurt G. W. Ludecke began recruiting Germans in America but opposed the outright formation of Nazi cells in the United States. Somewhat later Fritz Gissibl organized some recent

German immigrants in Chicago into a *Sturm Abteilung*, and called it Teutonia. This unit became the parent of Nazi party organizations in New York, Detroit, Milwaukee, Philadelphia, and many other cities. In 1932 Ludecke was appointed official representative of the party in the United States, but after Hitler's accession to the chancellery, Berlin dampened further party growth in the United States. Instead the movement found umbrage in the new organization Friends of the New Germany, which flourished until 1935, when the House Committee on Immigration and Naturalization began investigating it. Its remnants then merged into the German-American Bund, established in March 1936 by Fritz Julius Kuhn, the former head of the Detroit local of the Friends. Although membership of two hundred thousand was at times claimed, there were perhaps twenty-five thousand at any one time, mostly concentrated in the northern industrial cities from Milwaukee to New York. Mostly the Bund was composed of German-born nationals who had arrived in the 1920s. Following large rallies in Madison Square Garden in the late 1930s, always on Washington's birthday, the House Un-American Activities Committee chaired by Martin Dies triggered adverse publicity, which led to the demise of the Bund in 1939.

The weakened image of the Germans led not only to Nazis and prohibition in the 1920s but also to the passage of laws restricting immigration and, for the first time, the enactment of quotas. The Immigration Act of 1924 and its national origins provision favored northern and western European groups. Restriction on immigration had been building ever since the reports by Senator William P. Dillingham in 1910 but did not gain legislative distinction until World War I made such an act feasible. The first Immigration Act to become law passed in 1917, beginning with a literacy test, and expanded in 1921 and again in 1924.[29] Though given impetus by the anti-German feelings aroused during the war, restrictive laws were not directed against the Germans nor did German immigration suffer because a high German quota had already been established.

Rather, church, civic, and educational institutions sought to Americanize those Germans already here. Several states tried to promote citizenship classes through vocational and extension services.[30] Others sought to enlist the giants of industry to furnish classes for their workers in civics and the English language. At times, these blatant efforts were couched in terms of "safety" on the job, and "loyalty" to the cause of higher productivity. Even the Catholic church was enlisted to offer catechetical classes with the ingredients of Americanization. Civil organizations set up county-based councils for Americanization. There were conferences, some sponsored by universities, and conventions to teach cadres how to Americanize their subjects.[31] Women's societies became involved, and motorized libraries were established to bring "good books in English" to workers in factories and mines. In several universities standing professorships on Americanization were funded. Although these efforts were made primarily in response to the perceived threat of the Germans as a result of World War I, as it turned out the Germans were the ones least in need of such campaigns and thus they greeted it with a yawn. The Americanization efforts for civic responsibility, therefore, shifted ever more toward eastern and southern Europeans.

Meanwhile Germans arrived as new immigrants during the decade of the 1920s and were counted in the Fifteenth Census of the United States. Inflation in Germany and a relatively strong economy in North America caused many more Germans to cross the North Atlantic between 1920 and 1930 than during the previous decade, although the war was the chief hindrance during the former period. Whereas only 174,227 or 2.7 percent of the total immigration from Germany came to the United States between 1910 and 1920, well over twice that many, 386,634 or 9 percent, came in the post–World War I decade. Not until the 1950s would there be another large burst of German immigrants to these shores.[32] In 1930 there were 1,608,814 persons of German birth in the United States, a decline of only 4.6 percent from the previous decade, which contrasts sharply with the reported 25.3 percent drop of German-born as enumerated by census-takers in 1920.[33] The German-born in 1930 were the most numerous in New York, Illinois, and Wisconsin, suggesting that they were now settling largely in the cities. The Germans in 1930 had by far the largest foreign stock population in the United States, 6,873,103, followed by Italy with only 4,546,877. Thus the Germans had 17.7 percent of the foreign-stock population; Italians accounted for 11.7 percent of the total.[34] As indicated previously regarding the German-born, there was only a small decline of the German-stock population from 1920 to 1930 (from 7,032,106 in 1920 down to 6,873,103 or 159,000 fewer in 1930) compared to the precipitous fall of German-stock population from 1910 to 1920 (nearly 1 million—949,590—from 7,981,696 in 1910 to 7,032,106 in 1920). These data seem to corroborate the conclusions that the Germans in the years immediately following World War I denied their origins on a grand scale. If so, it is understandable that the process of assimilation was greatly hastened. Changing one's name was one device to mask an identity, but clearly there were many others, one of which was to merge quietly into the anonymous crowd.

The name of Germany or of Deutschland in the 1920s had lost the respect it commanded before World War I, and thus the immigrants were dissociated from the nation of their origin and its language. In the years 1916–19, the Germans were brutally accosted by Anglo-American propaganda machines and by overly zealous local patriots. During the 1920s there was an amelioration of forced assimilation, but it was only an amelioration. Once the mere name "German" spelled success in many circles. For instance, I have just completed a study of the "German" banking system in the state of Minnesota and discovered that the plethora of "German" banks came into being not so much to serve the German ethnic communities but because bank founders hoped to capitalize on a name that communicated solidity, security, and success. What depositor could ask for more? Of the more than two dozen banks with "German" in their names in Minnesota, not one survived past the year 1918. Likewise, in the Midwest there were many clubs, organizations, and even school sports teams that characterized themselves under the appellation "German" or "Germania." There were no such manifestations of ethnic pride during the 1920s, and there is none today. We do have national league teams named after the Vikings and countless apartment complexes that pick up on British, French, and Spanish traditions. None, to my knowledge, play upon the German heritage, although we do have the Milwaukee Brewers. Americanization of the Germans following the World War I period ameliorated considerably, and it has continued on its subtle way down the back roads of the American conscious from that time to ours.

Notes

1. James M. Bergquist, "German-America in the 1890s: Illusions and Realities," in E. Allen McCormick, ed., *Germans in America: Aspects of German-American Relations in the Nineteenth Century* (New York: Columbia University Press, 1983), 1–14. See also Robert Henry Billigmeier, *Americans from Germany: A Study in Cultural Diversity* (Belmont, Calif.: Wadsworth, 1974), 171–79, and La Vern J. Rippley, "Xenophobia and the Russian-German Experience," *Workpaper of the American Historical Society of Germans from Russia*, no. 18 (September 1975): 6–12.

2. See Richard Bernard, *The Melting Pot and the Altar: Marital Assimilation in Early Twentieth-Century Wisconsin* (Minneapolis: University of Minnesota Press, 1980).

3. Kathleen Neils Conzen, *Immigrant Milwaukee, 1836–1860: Accommodation*

and Community in a Frontier City (Cambridge, Mass.: Harvard University Press, 1976), and Conzen, "The Germans," in Stephen Thernstrom et al., eds., *Harvard Encyclopedia of American Ethnic Groups* (Cambridge, Mass.: Harvard University Press, 1980), 405–25.

4. Joshua A. Fishman et al., eds., *Language Loyalty in the United States: The Maintenance and Perpetuation of Non-English Mother Tongues by American Ethnic and Religious Groups* (The Hague: Mouton, 1966), esp. Heinz Kloss, "German-American Language Maintenance Efforts," 206–52; Vladimir C. Nahirny and Joshua A. Fishman, "Ukrainian Language Maintenance Efforts in the United States," 318–57; and Nathan Glazer, "The Process and Problems of Language Maintenance: An Integrative Review," 358–68.

5. Wilhelm Kaufmann, *Die Deutschen im amerikanischen Bürgerkriege* (Munich: R. Oldenbourg, 1911), 118–37, and Albert B. Faust, *The German Element in the United States*, 2 vols. (2d ed., New York: Steuben Society, 1927), 1:526–68.

6. See Frederick C. Luebke, ed., *Ethnic Voters and the Election of Lincoln* (Lincoln: University of Nebraska Press, 1971), and Georg von Bosse, *Das deutsche Element in den Vereinigten Staaten* (New York: Steiger, 1908).

7. La Vern J. Rippley, "German Assimilation: The Effect of the 1871 Victory on Americana-Germanica," in Hans L. Trefousse, ed., *Germany and America: Essays on Problems of International Relations and Immigration* (New York: Brooklyn College Press, 1980), 122–36.

8. John B. Jentz and Hartmut Keil, "From Immigrants to Urban Workers: Chicago's German Poor in the Gilded Age and Progressive Era, 1883–1908," *Vierteljahrschrift für Sozial-und Wirtschaftsgeschichte* 68 (1981): 52–97, and Jentz and Keil, "German Working-Class Culture in Chicago: A Problem of Definition, Method and Analysis," *Gulliver* 9 (1981): 128–47.

9. Max Heinrici, ed., *Das Buch der Deutschen in Amerika* (Philadelphia: Walter's Buchdruckerei, 1909), 781–82.

10. Clifton James Child, *The German-Americans in Politics, 1914–1917* (Madison: University of Wisconsin Press, 1939), 8–21.

11. Heinz Kloss, *The American Bilingual Tradition* (Rowley, Mass.: Newbury House, 1977), chap. 4, 81–106, and Kloss, *Das Volksgruppenrecht in den Vereinigten Staaten von Amerika*, 2 vols. (Essen: Essener Verlagsanstalt, 1940–42), 1:216–17 and 2:615–16.

12. Jack W. Rodgers, "The Foreign Language Issue in Nebraska, 1918–1923," *Nebraska History* 39 (March 1959): 1–22; La Vern J. Rippley, *The German-Americans* (Boston: Twayne, 1976), chap. 8; and Paul Schach, *Language in Conflict: Linguistic Acculturation on the Great Plains* (Lincoln: University of Nebraska Press, 1980).

13. U.S. Congress, Senate, *Thirteenth Census of the United States, 1910* (Washington, D.C.: Government Printing Office, 1913), 1:783.

14. See *National German-American Alliance, Hearings before the Subcommittee of the Committee on the Judiciary* 65th Cong., 1st Session (Washington, D.C.: Government Printing Office, 1918), 1–18.

15. Carl Wittke, *The German-Language Press in America* (Lexington: University of Kentucky Press, 1957), 206–10.

16. John B. Duff, "German-Americans and the Peace, 1918–1920," *American-Jewish Historical Quarterly* 59 (1970): 425–44.

17. U.S. Congress, Senate, *Fourteenth Census of the United States, 1920*, 3 vols. (Washington, D.C.: Government Printing Office, 1922), 2:687–93, 970–75, 803–14.

18. Alfred Vagts, *Deutsch-Amerikanische Rückwanderung* (Heidelberg: Carl Winter, 1960), and Betty Boyd Caroli, *Italian Repatriation from the United States* (New York: Center for Migration Studies, 1974).

19. See, for example, Linda Degh, "Survival and Revival of European Folk Cultures in America," *Ethnologia Europaea* 2–3 (1967–68): 97–108; Degh, "Ethnicity in Modern European Ethnology," *Folklore Forum* 7 (1974): 48–55; and esp. Degh, "Approaches to Folklore Research among Immigrant Groups," *American Folklore* 79 (1966): 551–56.

20. Heinrici, ed., *Das Buch*, 782, point 6.

21. *Fourteenth Census of the United States*, 2:972.

22. Conzen, "The Germans," 423.

23. George N. Shuster, "Those of German Descent," *Common Ground* 4 (Winter 1943): 31–35.

24. Rippley, *German-Americans*, 193–95, and Rippley, "Gift Cows for Germany," *North Dakota History* 40 (Summer 1973): 4–16.

25. Benjamin M. Weissman, *Herbert Hoover and Famine Relief to Soviet Russia, 1921–1923* (Stanford: Hoover Institution Press, 1974), and George F. Kennan, "Our Aid to Russia: A Forgotten Chapter," *New York Times Magazine*, July 19, 1959.

26. Sally M. Miller, *Victor Berger and the Promise of Constructive Socialism, 1910–1920* (Westport, Conn.: Greenwood Press, 1973).

27. A fair summary of the Prohibition movement appears in William Francis Raney, *Wisconsin: A Story of Progress* (Appleton, Wisc.: Perin Press, 1963), 316–24.

28. For a quick summary, see Rippley, *German-Americans*, chap. 15.

29. William S. Bernard, "Immigration: History of U.S. Policy," in Thernstrom et al., eds., *Harvard Encyclopedia of American Ethnic Groups*, 486–95, esp. 492.

30. For example, see Gerd Korman, *Industrialization, Immigrants and Americanizers: The View from Milwaukee, 1866–1921* (Madison: State Historical Society of Wisconsin, 1965).

31. See, for example, Alfred E. Koenig, Committee Chairman, *Proceedings of the Second Minnesota State Americanization Conference at Minneapolis, Minnesota, May 19, 1920* (Minneapolis: Council of Americanization, 1920).

32. United States Bureau of the Census, *Historical Statistics of the United States: Colonial Times to 1970* (Washington, D.C.: Government Printing Office, 1975), 105.

33. *Fifteenth Census of the United States, 1930*, 4 vols. (Washington, D.C.: Government Printing Office, 1933), 2:228–42.

34. *Fifteenth Census of the United States, 1930*, 4:264–86.

16.

An Untidy Love Affair: The American Image of Germany Since 1930

VICTOR LANGE

WHEN CONSIDERING THE IMAGE OF GERMANY held by Americans since the 1930s, it is well to begin with a few commonplaces. What one society thinks of another is an inexhaustible topic not so much of analysis as of speculation, sometimes entertaining, more often condescending, and in times of crisis charged with undercurrents of irritation and animosity. To speak of a body of people, differing from us in their social and intellectual presuppositions, requires a degree of detachment, sensible categories of judgment, and an awareness of the difficulties of intercultural understanding that few of us can command. My impressions are drawn from half a century of life and work as a more or less Americanized German, an American with German roots, a teacher of German who has always thought of his academic as well as his private pursuits as efforts in mutual understanding, interpretation, and mediation.

Such an intention must seek to cope with the cultural stereotype that freezes elusive features, some observed, others derived from books and pictures, others without any concrete frame of reference, in a fixed set of images, picturesque or distasteful beyond argument, and almost impossible to dislodge. I need not elaborate upon the stereotypical image of the Germans. During the half-century of which I speak, its essential characteristics have hardly changed, and I doubt that even the elaborate resources of modern reporting and the brief glimpses of German life which moments of television coverage provide will change it. We are likely, as presumed experts in German social, literary, or even economic life, to engage in the wishful thought that the often declared admiration for certain German achievements past or present—Goethe or Wagner, Kafka or Grass, Gropius, Schönberg, Fassbinder, or Wernher von Braun—might modify a widely held image of the Germans. Alas, such an assumption vastly overrates the effect of these spectacular figures and their accomplishments on the aggregate American impression of the Germans.

Germans and Americans used to think of one another across an ocean that represented distance in space as well as time. Some fifty years ago, five or six days of sea travel separated the two countries, days that meant moving away as well as coming closer, leaving behind as well as discovering what was expected, dreamed about, or feared. This gradual approach to the other side of the Atlantic, to the other society, has given way to rapid transportation from one bleak airport to another, to a sudden plunging—whether as tourist, businessman, or visiting scholar—into another world, which, however different from the one we left, has a visible surface of common and universal features, slogans, facilities, and institutions.

In the American social world of the 1930s, the arrival of a German dignitary, whether Thomas Mann or Max Schmeling, was an event that caused considerable and sometimes noisy excitement, and the arrival of a German newcomer on a college campus, in a factory, or in a farming community was noted and recorded. In the 1930s German immigrants came to an America recently shaken by the Great Depression yet barely aware of what was then happening in Germany. Americans' feelings about those Germans were affected only vaguely by the war that had ended a few years earlier. The kaiser was gone, no longer feared as the despised embodiment of Prussian arrogance and militarism. And Hitler seemed, a short time later, less an ominous threat than an untried political alternative to civil war and chaos in Germany. In the tensions that subsequently emerged, whatever happened in Germany or was reported of German life with its complex admixture of aggressive energy and happy community singing, of awesome efficiency and sentimental attachment to a landscape of enchanted towns and forests, cheerful music (now accenting the goosestep), oceans of flags and garlands, emblems and medals, order and discipline—seemed to confirm established stereotypes. It was no wonder that settled or more recently arrived German-Americans felt and often demonstrated a proud sense of affinity to the Germans at home. It is difficult for us today to recall the self-confidence and the hopes of political activism which in the 1930s galvanized the "German-American element," as it was then seen and called. The spectrum and sentiment that prevailed in the vocal and visible organizations of male and female choruses and *Turnvereine*, of Pfälzer and Bavarians, of *Harugari-Frohsinn* and *Schlaraffia*, but no less among the teachers of German and the recently immigrated businessmen from Elberfeld and Offenburg, was firmly and vociferously in hopes of a reactivated Germany reviving the admiration shattered by the war of 1914–18.

In retrospect we may wonder at the delusion, shortsightedness, political hubris, or blindness of the German-Americans; yet the attachment to their native country, like that of the Italo-Americans or Irish-Americans, remained in important respects founded on the static memories of the Germany they had left, the Germany of their dreams.

Not only their view of Germany but, more profoundly, the generally caustic and reserved American assessment of the Germans, was modified, less by the cataclysm of World War II, than, several years earlier, the astonishing influx of German and Austrian refugees. The two events, taken together, suggested to Americans in all walks of life that there appeared to be two groups of living Germans, one thoroughly hateful, the other oppressed, persecuted, and disenfranchised, largely but not exclusively Jewish, and entitled to the traditional American sympathy for dissenters and underdogs.

We now know how important a contribution these German and Austrian refugees and, later, their children have made to American life and how much the polarization of the American image of the Germans affected American attitudes during and after the war. The integration of these exiles is an involved chapter in the story of shifting sensibilities on both sides. The difficulties of finding a livelihood were for these newcomers greater than can now be easily realized. Some few of them came with sufficient funds, but most were desperately dependent upon finding employment. Cultivated men and women, many of whom had been forced in midcareer to abandon their professions as doctors, lawyers, or academics, begged for menial employment. It is a remarkable phase in the history of American tolerance, self-interest, and humaneness that sooner or later most of these refugees were accepted, even, in a measure, integrated into American society. Their role not only in the cultural life of this country but in the shaping of American policy during and after the war is now a historical fact. The induction of many into the army as American citizens where they shared common dangers and hopes, gave them an attachment to American values and ways of life that far outweighed any residual sentimental attachment to the old country.

The "German-American" of the past ceased at that time to rep-

The young maiden with the beer. Ethnic stereotypes are not always negative. Many stereotypes persist for more than a century, as in these advertisements for German beer. Left: the Bock Beer Maid representing the Phillip Best Brewing Company in 1886. Right: the Beer Maid representing the St. Pauli Girl Brewery in 1985. Only available in America since the 1960s, St. Pauli Girl beer has already captured fifth place among imported beers with its successful advertising campaign. (Library of Congress; Carlton Importing Company)

resent the long-prevailing if somewhat petrified image of the "Germans." Circumstances made "German" an acceptable designation, even though the mistrust of those who had remained in Germany was still strong.

I need not go into detail about the remarkable Germans whose contribution to American life changed the level of tolerance and receptivity in their host society. Some may have reinforced the persistent ethnic stereotype, carrying their sense of order and obedience, their excessive passion for hard work, abstract discourse, and musical and literary emotionalism into their new life. Yet for a number of reasons, they appeared to learn faster than their predecessors to accommodate themselves, to adjust, and to integrate. However paradoxical their circumstances, many of them wanted to forget the immediate reasons for

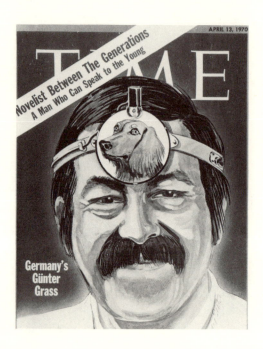

their leaving Germany, though not, perhaps, the deep, subliminal attachment to the culture that had shaped them for thirty, forty, or fifty years.

After the severe measures taken later against the Nazis, after the oppressive display of their destruction and inconceivable inhumanity, after the explicit efforts at urging upon the Germans the prospect of a new, democratic cast of life, and with the return of GIs from close and at that time reasonably relaxed traffic with Germans, German girls, German families, and German hospitality, it seemed only natural that the American stereotype of the Germans in its most rigid form should have been modified. An enormous amount of American money, both that of individuals who sent Care packages and of the taxpayers who helped consolidate the hopes of enlisting Germany in a common political vision, was spent in the expectation that a promising future and not a paralyzing past should be at the core of our thinking about the Germans. For some forty years, almost the span of time altogether given the German Reich between 1870 and World War I, Germany and the Germans have remained a central concern of American foreign policy. For forty years that attachment has been almost axiomatic, and

Facing page. Günter Grass as a doctor. No German writer since Thomas Mann and Hermann Hesse has received as much attention in America as the author of *The Tin Drum* and *The Flounder*. That *Time* should choose the year 1970 and the novel *Local Anesthetic* to praise Grass as the great diagnostician of the Germans who could speak to the younger generation is not without a certain irony. The book was a flop in Germany and the younger reading public began turning away from Grass at that time. Nevertheless, *Time*'s assessment gained wide recognition throughout America since it contrasted sharply with the American public's otherwise general indifference toward German literature (with the exception of Hermann Hesse's cult popularity in the 1960s). The situation was not much better in the 1930s and 1940s when many leading German writers such as Bertolt Brecht, Heinrich Mann, Alfred Döblin, and Carl Zuckmayer came to America as exiles. Only a few, among them Thomas Mann, Lion Feuchtwanger, Emil Ludwig, and Franz Werfel, had success as writers in the American market. (Reprinted by permission from TIME.)

the image of the Germans has, in one way or another—often with an admixture of skepticism—been kept reasonably appealing and positive.

What I have said so far is part and parcel of the recent memory of many of us Americans, and we might conclude with some relief that the time of misunderstanding, mistrust, and antagonism is as thoroughly past as the shallow affection for the provincial charms of Bavarian or Swabian displays in America. But the love affair between Germans and Americans remains untidy; neither suspicion nor sentimental infatuation has sufficiently disappeared, and it may be well to inquire briefly into the reasons for the continuing prevalence of conflicting attitudes, the gravity or equanimity with which we should weigh them, and the considerations that are required for their productive balancing.

The deep-seated and not easily understood divergence of fundamental assumptions and prejudices may be gradually eroded; yet even in the new country Germans remain rooted in their original historical soil; they carry much of their inbred baggage of convictions into the adopted life. Perhaps the most important of these, judged from an American point of view, is the disarming postulate of "Denken macht frei." Whereas the American believes in doing and performance, the German insists upon the priority, drawn from the tradition of Protestant idealism, of reflection, speculation, and thought. It is this difference between two attitudes and their ultimately political consequences— one pragmatic and with an abiding trust in the efficacy of present action, the other skeptical, always with an eye on the binding directives

American and German writers debate at the German Book Fair in New York, 1983. Discussing the topic "The Responsibility of the Writer in an Endangered World" are (from left) Fritz J. Raddatz (who substituted for Max Frisch), Joyce Carol Oates, Ted Solotaroff (discussion leader), John Irving, and Günter Grass. Differences of opinion came to light: while Grass and Raddatz called for increased political involvement on the part of writers, the American writers Oates and Irving supported a separation of literary production and political activism. The German Book Fair, unofficially termed the "Frankfurt-on-Hudson," was unexpectedly successful as both an assessment and as a marketing event of the American-German publishing industry in the anniversary year of 1983. Attracting over 35,000 visitors, the Book Fair gained considerable attention in the American media for the neglected literary relations between the two countries. (Börsenverein des Deutschen Buchhandels)

of history—that defined much of the behavior of the new German-Americans. It is a difference which, brought into creative play, gave and gives the special flavor and fascination to the thinking of so many of the German intellectuals whose work was brought to fruition during their exile in America. Among such diverse minds as Herbert Marcuse, Max Horkheimer, Theodor W. Adorno, Paul Tillich, Erich Fromm, or Erik Erikson, one will easily recognize in all these and many others such as Erwin Panofsky or Walter Gropius an unmistakably German tradition coming to terms with social realities and forms of thought which, before coming to America, they had not recognized in their compelling character. These artists and scholars of a strongly German disposition confirmed and to some extent qualified the view held of Germans by Americans. They represented acknowledged German virtues and ideals; they were "gebildet," orderly, sensitive to aesthetic and historical values; they tended, as Europeans, to accept authority more readily than their American friends and, sooner or later, learned to appreciate the tolerant, pragmatic, libertarian ways of their new life.

In these refugees—and, indeed, in that new breed of Germans who came after the war—the image of Germans in America emancipated itself to a remarkable extent from its petrified stereotype. Moreover, common economic and political interests have converged, and the realities of interdependence have blunted the edges of strangeness or confrontation. From time to time, a residue of the stereotypical views of the Germans surfaces, in its comic as well as its serious manifestations, in the TV series *Hogan's Heroes* as well as in the suspicion that the aggressive impulses in the Germans may reassert themselves—an almost atavistic reaction to what, without an adequate effort at understanding, we assume the other society to be.

To comprehend the psychological makeup, the historical memories, or the unspoken assumptions of another society is difficult. Information and genuine interest are the necessary prerequisites. Do we, as Americans, know enough about the Germans, those in our midst as well as their friends and relatives in Germany? What should we know and who are, for Americans, the most effective interpreters? Are we prepared to accept our fundamental differences? An answer to these questions depends upon the adequacy of our view of the Germans. Are our efforts at understanding sufficiently thorough? It is generally admitted that the media pay only momentary attention to German affairs; they provide little material for an understanding of a society more different from our own than we casually assume. Current German literature is hardly more familiar to the broad spectrum of American readers than Finnish or Portuguese. Two or three novelists—Heinrich Böll, Max Frisch, or Günter Grass—may be known in their chief works by a relatively narrow group of readers. American publishers point with regret to the small sales of German books. Can we hope to galvanize that interest among so literate a society as the American? German films have recently enjoyed exceptional success, not, perhaps, because we view them as documents of life in Germany but because they demonstrate a high degree of craftsmanship and artistic intelligence. Given the abstract character of much contemporary art, we see

Film Reviews

The Marriage
of Maria Braun
Directed by Rainer Werner Fassbinder;
screenplay by Peter Marthesheimer and Pia
Frohlich, with additional dialogue by R. W.
Fassbinder; cinematography by Michael
Ballhaus; edited by Juliane Lorenze; music
by Peer Raben. With Hanna Schygulla,
Klaus Lowitsch, Ivan Desny, Gottfried
John, Gisela Uhlen, Gunter Lamprecht and
Hark Bohm. Color, 120 minutes. A New
Yorker Films release.

The Marriage of Maria Braun is well on
its way to becoming R. W. Fassbinder's
most popular film to date in this country.
The prolific and controversial German
director is by now well-known to people
knowledgeable about film, but *Maria
Braun* may become his breakthrough film
to mass audiences in the U.S. His films have
ranged from the beautifully clear *Ali: Fear*

relatively few examples of German painting and know little about the accomplishments of German architects.

However lively our respect for the remarkable German and Austrian share in modern art, music, and literature may be, however impressive the contributions of Sigmund Freud and Franz Kafka, Hermann Hesse, Robert Musil, Hermann Broch, or Bertolt Brecht, of Arnold Schönberg or Anton Webern, of the Bauhaus or the German filmmakers and painters of the 1920s and 1930s, these cannot be considered witnesses of contemporary life. Much of what we associate with German skill and sensibility, whether in cameras, recordings, or automobiles, is, like their superb music-making, a contribution to an increasingly international technological market but hardly the material for producing more perceptive views of "the Germans."

It is true that interest in German history has during the past two decades been more lively in America than ever before; yet one cannot escape the conclusion that the most popular historians or literary critics have, like the media, concentrated their attention, to the point of fixation, on the 1920s and their aftermath from Hitler's beginnings to the holocaust. Some of that American interest has understandably troubled the younger Germans in America, recent immigrants of a generation that would rather put that history behind than dwell upon it.

It is difficult to say how American writers and teachers could or should devote themselves to further clearer understanding of the Germans whose image past and present is so conspicuous an element in the American experience. Traditionally, the college teacher was assumed to provide access to that image. But with notable exceptions,

Facing page. Rainer Werner Fassbinder's film *The Marriage of Maria Braun* achieved great success in the United States as a fascinating interpretation of Germany's rise from the ashes after World War II. For her portrayal of a successful businesswoman in this film, Hanna Schygulla (pictured here) received rave reviews. Fassbinder's film realized the promise which American film critics had recognized in the "New German Cinema" in the 1970s. The positive reaction in America and the ensuing discussion were decisive factors in the international breakthrough of the German film. The work of directors such as Werner Herzog (particularly for his Kaspar Hauser film), Volker Schlöndorff (whose 1980 film *The Tin Drum* won an Oscar for Best Foreign Film that year), Wim Wenders, and Hans Jürgen Syberberg (particularly his seven-hour film essay on Hitler which is entitled *Our Hitler*) attracted considerable attention which went well beyond that accorded contemporary German literature.

However, with the exception of Wolfgang Petersen's *The Boat*, the acclaim of the New German Cinema did not spread very far beyond interested artistic circles and universities. The image of Germany created by these films differed greatly from the established ethnic clichés, but their emphasis on melancholy, cold romanticism and self-torment tended to awaken some older stereotypes. In the post-Vietnam, post-Watergate period of introspection in America, these films had a stimulating and thought-provoking effect. (Ruth McCormick, Cineaste)

German teachers in America have, on the contrary, tended (by predilection and training) to consolidate rather than dispel stereotypes and prejudices and have overemphasized the role of a splendid tradition of literary genius to the detriment of objective social and political analysis. They have, in the framework of philological studies, drawn dubious conclusions as to language as a mirror of collective behavior and have not always recognized the historical fact that German civilization, like any other European culture, whatever its remarkable features and accomplishments, can no longer claim the status of a privileged, admired, and superior model. One of the essential motives for learning to understand another culture has thus ceased to be compelling.

Yet what we think and feel about the Germans is of overriding consequence for our political judgment and action. "The Germans" are now divided into two distinct societies—are we aware, beyond the shibboleths of West and East rhetoric, of the diverging convictions that determine the two ways of life?

Our present respect for the German partner is the result of a complex economic and political relationship and not primarily of American sympathies for what we may perceive to be the German character or mentality. Understanding is more often urgently required of the stronger of two partners, though much could be said about the shortcomings in the German view of Americans, of stereotypical absurdities, and of emotional bias. Understanding is the means of recognizing where two kinds of social sensibility diverge and where they can be seen to coincide. If it is difficult for Germans to understand America, it should be rewarding for us Americans to see the Germans and to fathom their past and present modes of thought and action, their ambitions and fears, in as unprejudiced and unburdened a fashion as is possible for critical but affectionate eyes.

PART V:

Immigration After 1933

17.
Transplanted and Transformed: German-Jewish Immigrants Since 1933

HERBERT A. STRAUSS

I

PHILADELPHIA IS ONE OF THE HISTORIC PLACES of origin of the American-Jewish community. It was here that Jews from German lands laid many of the foundations for American-Jewish religious, intellectual, and organizational life in the eighteenth and nineteenth centuries. It was from here, too, that one strain of American-Jewish economic life had its beginnings, with Jews starting out as peddlers and wagon-barons and working their way up to retailing in fixed stores, finally taking their place in American economic development as businessmen, manufacturers, or bankers. The Jewish migration to Philadelphia originated in some of the same inhospitable conditions in Germany that drove non-Jewish emigrants overseas. Jews like Gentiles came here for the opportunity to shape their lives without the restrictions imposed by oppressive economic conditions or the as yet semifeudal organization of their societies. Jews in eighteenth-century Germany and the nineteenth-century Deutsche Bund were burdened by age-old discrimination and second-class status. Typically, the nineteenth-century German-Jewish immigrant participated, at least until the 1860s and 1870s, in many German cultural activities together with his non-Jewish fellow immigrant from Germany. When the large-scale immigration of Jews from czarist Russia and Poland began after 1881, German-Jewish institutions were ready to assist what turned out to be the mainstream of the Jewish future in the United States. By the end of the century, German-Jewish immigrants had created the basic framework of Jewish religious life and social service in this country.

The topic of this chapter is the immigration and acculturation of Jews from Nazi Germany beginning in 1933. To deal with this topic in the context of a commemoration of German immigration is not a simple matter and not a matter of continuity with the nineteenth-century pattern. Just as nothing is simple about German history, so, too, nothing is simple about the relationship of Germans and Jews, and Jews and Germans, in our period.

2

To understand the character of Jewish emigration from Germany after 1933—I shall exclude the significant Austrian and German-speaking Czechoslovak Jewish immigration—one needs to focus on several major factors that shaped the relationship of Jews and Gentiles in Germany before 1933. Jewish emancipation in Germany began in the middle of the eighteenth century and became a long, drawn-out process. In contrast to the pattern in France and the United States, legal equality was to follow what can best be called the acculturation of the Jew in German intellectual life, society, politics, and economic life. In fact, this social and cultural integration of the German Jew was the basic condition set by governments everywhere for granting legal and economic equality.

The Jews in Germany satisfied this condition in an exemplary way. The German-Jewish period was an outstanding time for Jewish creativity during which many of the forms that shape Jewish life in the modern world were created and an intellectual, religious, and philo-sophical culture developed that compares favorably to the Hellenistic or Spanish periods of Jewish history. It may be too early, we may be too close in time to this fruitful period, and we may still be too shocked by the way it ended to have a comprehensive picture of the many factors that made this coexistence of Jews and non-Jews in Germany possible. It was never easy. The Christian churches of the nineteenth and twentieth centuries learned the hard way that a true dialogue presupposes that each of the partners has equal weight. It may also be too early to raise the historic question whether the insecurity with which the Jews in Germany were forced to view themselves did not contribute to the cultural and psychosocial energies that fueled their major achievements in this period.

When Hitler struck in 1933, he unleashed the persecution of a community that was characterized by an extremely diversified pattern of integration and acculturation. Its size was infinitesimal compared to the 65 million inhabitants of the German Reich. There were about 525,000 Jews affiliated with Jewish religious communities on January 30, 1933. About 100,000 of them were of foreign nationality, primarily from eastern European countries and the old Austro-Hungarian Empire. Anti-Semitic opinion frequently viewed them as foreign, although their ancient language—Yiddish—derived from the middle high German dialect they had taken East from central Europe when they began to migrate there after the fourteenth century.

Socially, the Jews in Germany were in the middle class, predominantly lower middle class. In some demographic characteristics they differed from their Christian counterparts. More than the Christian population, Jews in Germany had engaged in "Handel und Verkehr" (commerce and transportation, 61.3 percent as compared to 19.4 percent), and in the professions and service sectors of the economy (12.5 percent as compared to 8.4 percent). Fewer Jews had been occupied with industry and crafts (23.1 percent compared to 40.4 percent), agriculture and forestry (1.7 percent compared to 28.9 percent). Almost half of the Jewish population (46 percent) was self-employed, as compared to 16.4 percent of the general population. One-third of all Jews were white-collar workers (as compared to 17 percent among Christians), and only 8.7 percent were classified as blue-collar workers, as compared to 46.4 percent among the general population. (All of the above figures and the classifications used are taken from the German census returns of May 1933.)

Yet this statistical reality was contradicted by a long-established stereotype ascribing to Jews in Germany (and not only in Germany) financial or political roles that were at best self-deceptions or premature generalizations. Following their liberation from premodern isolation, Jews in Germany had joined the ranks of the German bourgeoisie in a social success story that brought some of them to significant wealth and highly visible positions in a few sectors of the economy. Thus relatively more Jews than Gentiles were engaged in the textile trades, especially in such cities as Berlin, which they turned into a center of mass production in this field, or in the metal trades, in retailing (they pioneered the technique of the department store already developed in the United States), in mass-circulation publishing, or in private banking and stock exchange trading. By comparison, Jews played almost no role in the process of industrialization in coal and steel as manufacturers or mine owners. One exception was Upper

Silesia, where coal trading led Jews to mine ownership and iron manufacturing. Another was electricity; Emil Rathenau founded the General Electric Company of Germany, the AEG in Berlin. The progress of the industrial revolution in Germany after 1856 reduced the Jewish role in, for example, banking: when corporate banking and industrial self-financing demanded substantial capital formation, the traditionally small to middling Jewish banker declined, being reduced to a bank employee or board member. In World War I the Jewish bourgeoisie patriotically bought war bonds that were worthless paper after the war, and the runaway inflation of the postwar era affected Jews as much as or more than a population whose income derived from wages. When the worldwide depression struck in 1929–30, the Jewish population was hit not only by economic problems but also by political discrimination because the rise of the depression coincided with the rise of Nazism and anti-Semitism in Germany. Beginning in 1933, Jewish social agencies recorded an annual unemployment figure of about forty thousand until 1938, when Jews were forbidden to be gainfully employed in the general economy and lost every remaining right to do business or follow their professions. This figure gains additional significance if the declining absolute number of Jews in Nazi Germany is taken into consideration. Thus social and economic realities belied the age-old stereotype of the rich and powerful Jew in Germany. Demographically declining, increasingly elderly to an "absurd degree" (Bennathan), economically out of the mainstream of industrialization (as compared to their earlier role in commercial capitalism), Jews were the target of stereotypes that belied their true condition.

In one sector, however, Jews still played a highly visible and significant role in the early 1930s. Government careers and public service jobs had been denied Jews until 1918. Like Gentiles, they had entered universities in growing numbers beginning in the 1880s, but unlike Gentiles, they turned to the professions, journalism, the arts, literature, and other private sector cultural pursuits. Because acculturation in Germany had made considerable progress among Jews since 1815—most were no longer "assimilated Jews" but felt themselves to be Jewish Germans or German Jews—a number of Jews married Christian partners or left the Jewish fold. Before 1918, conversion to the Christian religion served, as Heinrich Heine had put it years earlier, as an "admission ticket" to German culture and to academic or government careers. As a result of this many-tiered process taking place over several generations, persons of Jewish descent, whether of the Jewish or

Christian religion, served as university professors especially in the natural sciences and mathematics, the social sciences, economics, or philosophy, and Jews were represented in the legal and medical professions in percentages that were out of proportion to their ratio of the population, although relatively small in absolute numbers. About 12 percent of physicians and 16 percent of lawyers in Prussia were Jews. If Jews of the Jewish religion and persons who descended from Jews but had left the Jewish community are combined—as the moronic "racial laws" of the Third Reich prescribed as early as April 7, 1933 (Law for the Restoration of Professional Civil Service)—then about one-third of German academic personnel of all ranks (from assistant to full professor) may have been of "Jewish descent" in 1933.

This pattern accounts for the characteristic groupings among refugees but also for the enormous difficulties they faced when forced to flee Germany when Hitler established his government on January 30, 1933. The total number of persons who succeeded in fleeing Germany—before a decree by SS Reichsführer Heinrich Himmler, dated October 1941, forbade all emigration—may be estimated at about 278,000. About 132,000 of these reached the United States before 1945. The bulk was of the Jewish religion and characteristically of lower-middle and middle-class background. This status corresponded not only to the demographic and occupational breakdown cited above but also to U.S. immigration provisions of the time, which called for assurances that an immigrant would not be likely to become a public charge ("LPC-clause"). The law required that assurances by relatives (affidavits of support) be submitted to consulates abroad, which exercised the power to grant or deny immigration visas. The immigration of the 1930s, like that of the nineteenth-century, originated in the southern rural and western sections and in cities like Frankfurt and Berlin, where the Jewish population was strongly lower-middle and middle class.

This group had to bear the brunt of the immigration restrictions of the 1930s, not only in the United States but around the world. In the United States, legislation had provided a system of quotas based on country of birth. The number of immigrants to be admitted from Germany was 25,957, relatively high compared to quotas of 6,000 each for Italy and Poland. Besides the "average," that is, the "quota" immigrant, U.S. immigration law also provided for "preference quota immigrants" (near relatives in ascending or descending lines) and "nonquota" immigrants. The latter category covered clergymen and university professors who had taught for a defined period of time at a foreign university and had an invitation to teach at a recognized American institution of higher learning.

Thus the law suggested some of the occupations of immigrants from Nazi Germany. The largest group was the "Jewish immigration." It was culturally diversified along the lines of emancipation and integration into German society—as described above—and of predominantly lower-middle and middle-class, white-collar, or small entrepreneurial status. It also included a higher percentage of professionals in the legal, medical, teaching, or artistic professions than any other earlier comparable group of immigrants. These professionals, in turn, may be divided into the now well-known "intellectual migration," the political migration, the so-called "Exilliteratur"- and "Kunstexil"- migration, and a younger group of students who would eventually establish themselves as professionals or artists. The intellectual migration included university professors and lecturers hoping to continue scholarly and scientific work interrupted by Nazi persecution and the predominantly left-oriented intelligentsia that had made the Weimar Republic a center of avant-garde culture and a major influence in modern art and literature. The political migration consisted of persons who did not see themselves generally as immigrants but as exiles, who hoped to return to their homelands soon and take part in the post-Nazi development of their governments and societies. Most persons in this group were not of the Jewish religion although a number were of Jewish descent. Especially hard hit by emigration were the German writers who had established reputations and an established public in Germany but who were unable to find a corresponding circle of publishers and readers abroad. They, too, hoped to return to their homelands, where they expected to be honored as the upholders of German culture abroad in dark and satanic times.

According to estimates, Jews may have made up 94 percent of the entire emigration from Germany, Austria, and Czechoslovakia. The total number of émigrés from these three countries between 1933 and 1945 is estimated at 500,000, the number of non-Jews at about 30,000.

3

Although the distinctions made above penetrated the self-understanding of émigrés and their organized life down to a finely tuned, leftist-oriented sectarianism among political émigrés, the American public hardly distinguished between exile, emigration, immigration, religions, or degree of integration into German society and culture. The opposition of the voters, the media, and consequently the Congress to all "refugees" was reflected in the long-term trend of American immigration legislation since the end of the nineteenth century. By the time of World War I, the racist and nationalist Zeitgeist had fixed a quota system whose numbers were dictated by the belief that the "Nordic" immigration from countries located around the North Sea—and thus including Germany—would be superior to southern and eastern European (Slavic, Mediterranean, Catholic, and Eastern Jewish) newcomers. In September 1930 a directive issued by President Herbert A. Hoover had raised legal requirements and financial assurances to be submitted by applicants so high that all immigration was severely curtailed, including refugee immigration from Germany. The directive remained in force, although between 1932 and 1935 the net outflow of aliens was larger than the inflow of new arrivals. (In 1936, the net gain of arrivals over departures totaled 512.) The visa division of the State Department requested consulates to keep as many immigrants as possible out of the country, a procedure that was perceived as chicanery by applicants attempting to flee Hitler's persecution. In the House of Representatives, the Subcommittee on Immigration and Naturalization was controlled by southern congressmen of long service. During the entire period 1933–45, only one small exception (the admission of about a thousand refugees from Italy and Yugoslavia as internees to Fort Oswego for the duration of the war) was made by President Franklin D. Roosevelt, who followed rather than led public opinion. Although the Hoover directive was relaxed beginning in 1937, the quota for immigrants from Germany was filled only in 1939, after the pogroms of the "Kristallnacht" had brought home the seriousness of the persecution of Jews in Germany. Following Pearl Harbor, no "enemy aliens" were admitted. Only with the passage of special legislation admitting "displaced persons," including Catholics and Eastern Europeans, could German Jews also succeed in reaching the United States from countries such as Great Britain, where they had waited for the opportunity throughout the war years.

4

The flight of refugees from persecution in Nazi Germany (since 1933), Austria (since March 1938), and Czechoslovakia (since September 1938) became a "migration emergency" for two basic reasons. The Nazi government impoverished its Jewish citizens through a dismal variety of measures and refused to participate in international efforts to turn flight into an orderly exodus, and most countries—including the United States—continued to restrict immigration. It remains an open question whether more determined efforts by Jewish communities would have changed the perceptions of the national and economic interests that determined these restrictive policies. The record indicates, however, that Jewish communities—primarily in the United States and Britain—and Jewish communal organizations in Nazi-controlled countries mounted a singular effort at voluntary aid for refugees. In Europe, the Jewish communities organized aid committees in every country of refuge. From 1933 on, Jews in Germany turned organizations like the Hilfsverein der Juden in Deutschland, the Palästina-Amt, and the Jüdische Auswanderungshilfe into effective centers to aid the migration process. They could not have worked without the financial (and political) support given to German Jewry by Jewish organizations abroad, especially the American Jewish Joint Distribution Committee, the Hebrew Sheltering and Aid Society, and numerous other voluntary groups not restricted to Jewish communities. In the United States the National Council of Jewish Women, the Jewish Labor Committee, the National Refugee Service, and later the (New York) Association for New Americans organized on national levels to counsel the refugees following their arrival. In every major city established Jewish social agencies received funds from local communities to provide a variety of social services, economic advice, and cultural amenities. The Orthodox and Reform religious denominations excelled in offering religious hospitality, sociability, and personal assistance.

Besides the massive needs satisfied by Jewish assistance, aid given by Christian and nondenominational groups like the Catholic Refugee Service, the American Friends Service Committee, and the Unitarian Service Committee, as well as university, women's, student, and professional organizations of a wide variety and scope often benefited Jewish refugees. This outpouring of voluntary aid tested government restrictionism and limited its damage—alas with negligible legislative effect.[1] This singular voluntary effort of citizens from all walks of life and occupations enabled the Jewish refugees to embark upon the adventure of integration and acculturation in this country.

In the context of American immigration history, the Jewish immigration of the Nazi period can hardly be called a mass migration. Its size—about 132,000—pales in comparison with the 1.5 million Eastern-Jewish immigrants who arrived between 1881 and 1924, or the 750,000 German immigrants who entered in the twenty years between 1950 and 1970. The diversified social structure, relatively high level of education, and professional and artistic orientation of these migrants belie the label "Jewish mass immigration" often used by socialist or communist scholars to set it apart from the allegedly elite group of political exiles. Its cultural component alone distinguishes it from comparable immigrant groups with the possible exception of some colonial groups or the Forty-eighters.

In many ways this immigrant group offers no exceptions to the general pattern of American immigration history. Like other immigrants, German Jews congregated in the large ports of entry and inland metropolitan centers upon arrival. New York gave shelter to up to seventy thousand refugees. Other major points of concentration were the greater New Jersey area, Boston, Chicago, Los Angeles, with San Francisco, Pittsburgh, Cleveland, Cincinnati, and Philadelphia receiving smaller groups. They arrived mostly without cash or mobile assets but often brought their entire apartment furnishings, many in the somewhat heavy style of the German bourgeoisie following the trend of "Neue Sachlichkeit." Nazi law had despoiled them by means of numerous taxes and contributions and prohibited the export of German marks except at ridiculously low rates, but allowed them to transfer "personal belongings," which included furniture. They thus often found instant new occupations as providers of furnished rooms to fellow refugees in large apartments made vacant by the slackening demand of the depression years. Thus for most immigrants, including many professionals and intellectuals, social mobility began at the bottom—the proverbial entry-level job.

As with many other immigrant groups, their integration into American life was supported by their families. In Germany the traditional extended family had still functioned as a center of economic, educational, marital, and social decision making. American immigration law tended to stress family cohesion, because it gave preference to prospective immigrants with assurances of support provided by American sponsors to U.S. consulates abroad. U.S. aid agencies had set up search centers to identify long-lost relatives of prospective immigrants and to help them overcome the hurdles placed in the path of immigration by restrictionism. Having an "uncle in America" provided lifelines and prestige during those years in Nazi Germany.

Interviews suggest, however, that the new-found mutuality between immigrants and American relatives was short-lived: European styles of mutual support among extended family members gave way to the urban pattern of the nuclear family limited in living space and resources, and to the traditional expectation that immigrants should be self-reliant and work their way up as other immigrants had done before them.

Thus the immigrant family became the nucleus of social and cultural change, especially because this immigration was predominantly a family migration of two or three generations. If measured by divorce rates, family stability appears to have been extremely high, possibly in line with the pattern of stability for the older German-Jewish generation. Even among intellectuals and artists of the older immigrant generation, divorce appears to have occurred less frequently than among younger colleagues.[2] Nevertheless, tensions existed under the stress of the immigration situation. There is evidence that immigration continued changes already in progress in Europe as a result of urbanization and similar influences on the relations between the generations and the sexes. Women faced the difficulties of rerooting at a faster pace and apparently with greater adaptability, were much less fearful about speaking faulty English (yet needed to speak it with the corner grocer and the butcher), and had been better prepared for manual labor than men, partly because of their traditional occupations as housewives and partly because they had been retrained by German-Jewish social agencies before emigration to practice such crafts as hat-making, tailoring, the production of artificial flowers, confectionery, or the making of chocolate. Thus women often were the first to earn salaries, helped their spouses to prepare for the resumption of their professional careers, and functioned as daughters, wives, and mothers besides being homemakers.

One study suggests that changes such as these were less influenced by religious differences than by age.[3] The same study provides some evidence that major tensions between parents and children derived from their different perceptions of what constituted a good education. For the older group, the then prevalent progressive pattern of education ("American education") appeared inferior to the more traditional and memory-oriented education of their youth, and this feeling led to friction among the generations. This tension would be more central than some others derived from the strong role played by education in the upwardly mobile aspirations built into working at the bottom of the social ladder as an immigrant, especially after being despoiled of one's middle-class status by persecution and emigration. It is not clear whether the German-Jewish immigrants continued a pattern they had experienced during their integration into German society (where higher education had been one route to acquiring status and economic mobility and part of the prestige system of the "bürgerliche Gesellschaft"), whether this was the classical response of immigrants in the generational sequence (with this group jumping part of the generational change because of its initially higher level of education and language proficiency), or whether these immigrants profited from the extraordinary expansion and democratization of higher education in the United States following World War II. Parents and children alike appeared to have shared this stress on education. One index of its success is that among the outstanding professionals and artists included in the *International Biographical Dictionary*, 28 percent were under nineteen years of age, another 19 percent were between twenty and twenty-nine years of age when they left their countries of origin, and about 48 percent of all persons included in the *Dictionary* settled in the United States as their final destination. People of the Jewish religion accounted for 80 percent of the entries in the *Dictionary*. Whether the "German-Jewish work ethic" was also a factor in the observed absence of widespread social or psychological pathologies among second-generation immigrants from central Europe remains to be analyzed. The traumatization claimed for the second generation of camp survivors has not been observed in this group.

Today, more than fifty years after Hitler's appointment as chancellor of the Reich and almost forty years after his demise, time is running out for a comprehensive study of the economic adjustment of German-Jewish refugees. No such study has been undertaken as yet. Based on interviews collected by the Research Foundation for Jewish Immigration of New York, a variety of studies completed mostly before 1950[4], and the records of immigrant organizations, it appears that, like many other immigrants, this group reached the levels of its preimmigration economic status under the favorable economic circumstances of wartime prosperity, the postwar boom, and expanding educational opportunities; unlike other émigré groups, it contained an extraordinary number of professionals and artists, who succeeded, in the first generation, in doing productive work in their fields.

The records of the Research Foundation for Jewish Immigration and the Institut für Zeitgeschichte in Munich contain some twenty-five thousand files on significant achievements by émigrés in all countries of resettlement, a large majority of them in the United States. They can be found in engineering, management, accounting, banking, export-import trade, textiles, manufacturing, social work, teaching, consulting, the introduction of such new trades as leather goods, toys, and leisure-time industry, in several high-fashion design firms, metal trading, the chemical industry, conglomerates and corporations, and a considerable variety of retail and wholesale trading. In the context of an economy spanning a continent, however, few of these achievements can be classified as pioneering or innovative in the way the German-Jewish immigrants of the nineteenth century ("our crowd") created new economic forms in banking or international trading, for example. German Jews took their places in a developed economy; they did not create it.

In addition, for the bulk of the immigrants, reaching one's pre-immigration economic status meant reaching an essentially white-collar or small entrepreneurial level in the food trades, retailing, or the repair or service industries. Their "embourgeoisement" was of the "petit" variety. Many lived in poverty. The records of the social agencies created by this group suggest that among the estimated seven hundred thousand Jews in New York living at or below the officially defined poverty line in 1983—primarily the aged and physically or mentally handicapped—there have been a sufficiently large number of immigrants, especially of Austrian background but by no means confined to them, to warrant the maintenance of a social service establishment through the postwar decades. In many cases German reparations ("Wiedergutmachung") were not adequate to compensate for the absence of family savings so that supplemental social security payments to the aged are not unknown among this group.

5

This result of immigrant integration into American economic life must not be obscured by the high visibility of the most discussed group among refugees—the intellectuals who migrated, primarily writers, scholars, artists, filmmakers, or university teachers who are becoming a legend in American cultural history—"Hitler's gift to the world." The record of their achievements is detailed in many of the nine thousand biographies (for central European émigrés in *all* immigration countries and of all religions, nationalities, or political persuasion, not only for Jewish immigrants) contained in the *International Biographical Dictionary*. It is a record both of broad achievement and of major pioneering of the older European-trained and the younger ("Kissinger") generation and includes among the twenty-six Nobel Prize winners of all religious backgrounds and all countries such names as Albert Einstein, James Franck, Erwin Schroedinger, Otto Stern, Felix Bloch,

Victor Hess, Max Born, Hans Bethe, and Arno Penzias (physics), Richard Willstaetter, Fritz Haber, Peter Debye, Georg von Hevesy, Max Perutz, and Gerhard Herzberg (chemistry), Otto Mayerhoff, Otto Loewi, Sir Ernst Boris Chain, Sir Hans Adolf Krebs, Fritz Albert Lippmann, Konrad Emil Bloch, Max Delbrueck, Sir Bernard Katz (physiology and medicine), and Henry Kissinger, Elias Canetti, Nelly Sachs, and Thomas Mann. Many, but by no means all, of these men and women were of Jewish background or the Jewish religion. Fifteen winners were immigrants to the United States since 1933.

In mathematics there were Richard Courant, Emmi Noether, and Hans Lowy. Among scholars in Judaistics were Abraham Heschel, Leo Baeck, Julius Guttmann, Ismar Elbogen, Eugen Taeubler, Jacob Katz, and Hans Liebeschuetz. Sociologists included Max Horkheimer, Theodor Adorno, Paul Lazarsfeld, Herbert Marcuse, Karl Mannheim, Adolf Schutz, and Otto Neurath, besides numerous lesser-known but influential teachers and researchers. Political science was enriched by Hannah Arendt, Leo Strauss, Richard Loewenthal, Karl Loewenstein, Hans Morgenthau, Ernst Fraenkel, Franz Neumann, Siegfried Neumann, and Karl Deutsch. Historians included Hajo Holborn, Felix Gilbert, Ernst Kantorowicz, Fritz Stern, and other creative scholars. Among philosophers we count Ernst Cassirer, Karl Loewith, Hans Jonas, and Walther Kauffmann. Especially numerous was the group connected with the several branches or activities of the psychoanalytic movement (both men and women) including Sigmund Freud (who emigrated to the United Kingdom in 1939), Erich Fromm, Erik Erikson, Ernst Kris, Alfred Adler, Otto Lowenstein, Helene Deutsch, Frieda Reichmann-Fromm, Therese Benedek, Heinz Hartmann, Kurt Eisler, Bruno Bettelheim, Wilhelm Reich, and numerous others. There was the Bauhaus. There were economists such as Joseph Schumpeter and Karl Hayek.

Names and disciplines such as these are illustrative of the broad stream of the intellectual talent and achievement of both sexes of the older, European-trained generation and the younger generation of émigrés of 1933 to 1945. Not all of these men and women were of Jewish background, and not all went to the United States. But they are representative of the most influential and historic effect of Hitler's persecution—the transfer of significant knowledge and methods in the persons and minds of refugees more capable and more creative than their persecutors. Nothing in earlier German, Jewish, or other immigrant movements the world has seen compares to this migration in quality and quantity of talent.

From the point of view of German history, the loss of vitality and the self-inflicted decline in scholarship destroyed entire disciplines at German universities (sociology, political science, Gestalt psychology, psychoanalysis, modern architecture, Judaic studies, modern music, modern literature, modern art, applied mathematics, significant aspects of theoretical physics, chemistry, physiology/medicine, liberal and socialist-Marxist history and social theory), and seriously decimated others such as applied engineering, scientific management, film, theater, independent "Publizistik" and journalism, international law and economic theory, to name those most obviously damaged. No other expulsion in modern history, not even the revocation of the Edict of Nantes of 1685 and its consequences, had so lasting an effect on the home country. It would be years before German scholarship would reconnect with international scholarship following 1945. There is still some question whether it has regained its diversity and vitality in certain fields.

For American intellectual history and for acculturation history, this unique group has already given rise to legends. It would be incorrect to say that U.S. universities and academies generously welcomed the refugee scholars. In truth, placement was hard in a period of academic unemployment and concern with training the next generation of American university teachers. Refugee scholars had to adjust to tension between progressive faculty opinion on the defense against conservatives, and to administrators seeking quality without opening their schools to radicals (like Einstein) or minorities (like Jews and women). The behavioral and social adjustment of foreign faculty was seen as a problem because graduate university styles of teaching, collegial behavior, and research at German universities differed from the genteel undergraduate traditions of American colleges. That a considerable number of older scholars and an astonishing number of younger-generation immigrants succeeded in carving out creative careers for themselves in spite of these differences is in part owing to the selfless voluntarism and humanitarianism of scholars, university personnel, and students in the United States and elsewhere who understood this persecution of scholarship as a threat against all free institutions, including their own, and acted on that conviction.

Generally, scholars finding niches in American higher education and scholarship succeeded in areas with an intellectual atmosphere that was prepared to receive and integrate them. Typically, in the major natural sciences, psychoanalysis, modern architecture, sociology, and political science, networks of international communication had developed by the 1920s; ideas had been transferred overseas and received into the proper frameworks of universities or culture. Where this situation prevailed, refugee scholars benefited from American developments and enriched them. The best-known examples are the fusion of the Bauhaus and "Neue Sachlichkeit" styles of design with the International Style developed in the United States from native origins, the synthesis of European psychoanalysis with American trends established since the early twentieth century, and the reception of the works of the greatest German sociologist, Max Weber, by American sociologists (Talcott Parsons) in the 1920s. More temporary, it would seem, was the impact of the German school of Gestalt psychology, although it too had been taught at one or two American colleges since the 1920s. Unique departures created by refugees were the development of considerable literature dealing with Nazism and totalitarianism, the creation of a new center of applied mathematics at New York University, the introduction of phenomenology, the graduate study of progressive social science at the New School for Social Research in New York City, the rise of archival sciences and the iconographic school of art criticism at Princeton's Institute for Advanced Study through Erwin Panofsky. In contrast, some trends were received less permanently into the mainstream of American culture, among them possibly applied social science (Paul Lazarsfeld at Columbia University) and theoretical societal philosophy as represented by the former Frankfurt Institute for Social Research of Max Horkheimer, Herbert Marcuse, and Theodor Adorno.

The best-known example of this function is, of course, the contribution made to theoretical and nuclear physics by German and Austrian physicists with the development of nuclear fission and fusion, leading to the atomic and hydrogen bombs and ushering in the atomic age. The record does not bear out the legend that Einstein or "the refugees" produced the atomic bomb. It was the result of many international developments, culminating in the American political decision to assign scarce wartime resources to the Manhattan Project, a gigantic engineering enterprise. Albert Einstein, contrary to this legend, was kept ignorant of this project during the war years, because he was considered a security risk by U.S. government scientists. Nonetheless, the presence of major theoretical physicists among the refugees contributed knowledge and drive in this area, and American natural science and higher mathematics were considerably enriched by a broad group of talented immigrants of the first and second generations long after 1945. The record of this enrichment still awaits a systematic assessment. Its significance, cleared of legends and exaggerations, is beyond doubt.

6

In addition to these individuals, social agencies, foundations, and institutions directed by volunteers and guided by humane impulses, a contribution was also made by refugee self-help and mutual aid institutions toward the integration and care of the immigrants. Wherever immigrants reached a "critical mass" they organized in several categories of organizations playing the dual function of continuing accustomed patterns of life while preparing the refugee for integration into the reference groups of his choice. Refugees created numerous religious congregations that allowed them to continue the "sacred ethnicity" of ritual and musical offering they had been accustomed to within their group. They organized social service and mutual aid societies that served as employment agencies, counseling and legal aid centers, summer camps for children and vacation homes for adults, and, in the course of time, geriatric institutions. Among these social agencies, some—like the New York Selfhelp Community Services or United Help—pioneered apartment complexes for the aged and homemaker services that have influenced American geriatrics in both concept and style of service. Besides their professionalized services they continued the older pattern of direct and supplemental help to the most indigent (Blue Card), directed a broad range of volunteer services to the aged, and built model nursing homes such as the Margaret Tietz Center for Nursing Care. The community also created cultural institutions that stimulated research and writing as well as archival collections dealing with the defunct German-Jewish epoch of Jewish history (Leo Baeck Institutes) and, in its last phase, the migration period (Research Foundation for Jewish Immigration). In response to the unique attempt made by the government of the German Federal Republic to make at least material amends for the damages inflicted upon those persecuted by the Nazi regime, refugees created legal counseling agencies dealing with restitution and indemnification (United Restitution Organization). For numerous political and communal tasks they formed a central representation on the model of their last Jewish representation in Germany, the Reichsvertretung der Juden in Deutschland, and named it the American Federation of Jews from Central Europe. Most of these agencies had equivalents in the major cities of refugee concentration or, as in the case of the American Federation and the United Restitution Organization, represented American affiliates of international organizations. Through them new working connections on many political and legal-governmental levels were established with the government of the Federal Republic of Germany.

A third type of organization is represented by groups concerned with leisure-time pursuits ranging from serious political and intellectual discussion groups to light entertainment and nostalgic Viennese operetta. Its main prototype was the New York–based New World Club, which also published the most intelligent German-language weekly of the period, *Aufbau*, which still exists in 1984. Most of these groups were adaptations of home-country organizations such as student societies (this time without dueling practices), lawyers' groups, medical societies, veterans' associations, hiking clubs, burial societies, sports clubs, Zionist groups, women's social groups (especially within the religious congregations), and at later stages senior citizen groups.

The significance of this organizational pattern lies in its function as a source of personality integration and a starting point for the acculturation process of individuals as well as organizations. Where enough immigrants congregated, an immigrant subculture developed comparable to that observed in other immigrant movements in the United States. Generally, because emotional and propagandistic tensions rose after Pearl Harbor, the German language was not central to this subculture. Only the group around *Aufbau*, made up of journalists, literary persons, and political exiles, retained the language. Soon after arrival, the community at large conducted its activities in English, including sermons, meetings, lectures, and social activities. Yet language alone does not serve as an index of acculturation. Subjectively, the severity of the persecution in Germany, the apparent absence of effective resistance against Nazism and anti-Semitism, and finally the news of the Holocaust shook the organized Jewish community to its roots to such an extent that young GIs returning from army service in large part determined the attitude toward Germany. These immigrants had had few, if any, organized connections with the German-American community during the Third Reich and for a considerable time thereafter. The steep decline in the teaching of the German language and literature at colleges and universities may reflect a deeper cultural response than that observed here, and refugees may have shared in this response. (In regard to language, the response of Nazi-period refugees in Israel and Latin America appears to have differed from that observed in France, the United Kingdom, and the United States. A comparative study of this observation might throw some needed light on the underlying factors.)

From this low, postwar history suggests a change in attitudes toward the image of a more democratic Germany attempting, however haltingly, to rid itself of the worst of its Nazi inheritance. Still, the return rate to countries of origin remained extremely low even for scholars and artists. (A comprehensive study of this return movement should be undertaken soon.) German reparations, a program unique in migration history, led to fruitful cooperation between refugees and German civil servants and legislators in its political phase. The later phases of implementation of this law often led to dissatisfaction in many cases because of the fiscal harshness of German budgets and ministerial budget cutting. A variety of programs instituted by German agencies as well as the search by this aging immigrant group for personal contact with its roots were further factors in this change. Still, like non-Jewish immigrant groups from Germany, this group exhibited patterns in its integration and acculturation that suggest a psychological readiness to accept the break with the homeland as final, and to adopt new reference groups on individual and organizational levels from the majority

culture surrounding them. Organizationally, most social and mutual aid groups declined or disbanded, and most congregations suffered severe attrition, mainly because their clientele shifted residence with the shifting urban patterns of the American metropolis and left synagogues and community buildings behind in ethnically changed neighborhoods, for example, in areas of the Eastern seaboard. The community also paid a price for its ideology of successful integration: it rarely succeeded in retaining the interest of its younger generations, although here too residential mobility in line with upward social change had a changing influence on memberships. Some organizations, especially the cultural and research groups and the social welfare agencies able to expand their concepts to wider community purposes, succeeded in becoming general community organizations and in showing a healthy age distribution. The shift of social welfare work to government assistance (President Johnson's Great Society program) had the effect of turning sectarian agencies into nonsectarian agencies because one of the conditions for obtaining government grants to volunteer agencies was that open access be provided to all groups. Among religious groups, too, the Orthodox have tended to blend resolutely into general American-Jewish life while retaining their ethnic base. There is not enough hard data about third-generation attitudes toward German-Jewish culture, but some suggest that Hansen's Law (of a return of the third generation to a different perception of immigrant culture)

Facing page. The emigrant newspaper *Aufbau* was one of the first to break the silence surrounding the mass murder of Jews by the Nazis in its edition of July 3, 1942. The article, entitled "The Conspiracy of Silence," appeared a few days after reports surfaced in the London *Daily Telegraph* and caused a sensation even though the paper had previously reported on the extermination of Jews in Eastern Europe. By this time, over a million Jews had already perished.

Aufbau was established in New York in 1934 as a newspaper of Jewish refugees from Germany. Under the direction of editor in chief Manfred George, it grew into an internationally recognized publication which today continues to play an important role for Jewish-German émigrés throughout the world. With the passing of the first generation of émigrés, the paper, which celebrated its 50th anniversary in 1984, has had a steady decline in circulation from a high of 50,000. *Aufbau* was a forum for such important authors in exile as Thomas Mann, Lion Feuchtwanger, Oskar Maria Graf, and Franz Werfel and has maintained its excellent critical reporting on Jewish and German cultural events. After the Second World War, the paper helped to bridge the gap between Jews and Germans. *Aufbau*'s suggestion that previous Jewish residents of German cities be invited back to visit at no cost was actually implemented; Berlin led the way in this program. (*Aufbau*) may operate among some members of that generation. The immigrants as a group have pioneered high professional standards of social service and care for the aged; they have introduced forms such as lecture series, *Lerntage* (all-day conferences on a contemporary topic in historical perspective composed of persons from different walks of life), research organizations that have created new branches of knowledge (German-Jewish history, German-Jewish migration history), and a more objective appraisal of German-Jewish historical relations, a new consciousness.

Although they were unprepared for the historic role into which Nazi persecution projected them, and although they did not play a major role in American or American-Jewish life as a group, their communal spirit and their work ethic provided the framework for the individual achievements of their intellectuals and professionals and for alleviating the suffering caused by the uprooting and resettlement of the community. Even if they failed to leave a lasting mark in their response to harsh circumstances and are today submerged in historiography in the greater shock over the Holocaust, they met their obligations in the sober and distinctly unecstatic spirit that is the bourgeois' defense against turbulent realities. The basis of their success was a condition of their failure.

Notes

1. The history of this aid is chronicled in Herbert A. Strauss, ed., *Jewish Immigrants of the Nazi Period in the U.S.A.*, vol. 1: *Archival Resources*, comp. S. W. Siegel (New York: K. G. Saur, 1978).

2. This is the impression given by the material incorporated in Herbert A. Strauss and Werner Röder, eds., *International Biographical Dictionary of Central European Emigrés 1933–45*, vol. 2 (Munich: K. G. Saur, 1983).

3. Ruth Neubauer, "Differential Adjustment of Adult Immigrants and Their Children to American Groups" (Ed.D., dissertation, Teacher's College, Columbia University, 1966).

4. See relevant items in Henry Friedlander et al., comps., *Jewish Immigrants of the Nazi Period in the U.S.A.*, vol. 2: *Classified and Annotated Bibliography* (New York: K. G. Saur, 1981), 148–51, 170–83.

18.
Cassandras with a German Accent

ANTHONY HEILBUT

IN THE HISTORY OF EMIGRATION TO AMERICA, no other group has had so large and immediate an impact as the German-speaking people who fled Hitler. It is also arguable that no other group tried so hard to maintain its cultural legacy. Yet these refugees would offer a very mixed benediction on a collection that commemorates three hundred years of German-American relations. Unlike the group Leo Schelbert characterizes as a "people of choice," they did not want to come here; as Brecht's poem "Hounded out of Seven Nations" implies, America was not the first choice of most artists and intellectuals.

Upon their arrival, some refugees strove valiantly to become more American than the Americans, veritable chameleons, unwittingly attesting to Heinrich Mann's cynical observation that the actor was the perfect modern type. Others, particularly the artists and intellectuals, remained more loyal to their history, although this loyalty would cause Americans to regard them with extreme suspicion, as Cassandras in spite of themselves.

Although most refugees were Jewish, they were also, as Paul Breines notes, so assimilated and secularized that something other than religion had to provide a common bond of identity. Because there were numerous political disagreements among them, this bond was to become the great tradition of German culture, albeit a tradition continually interrogated and revised by people who were accomplished modernists. While in transit, the émigrés sustained themselves with prodigious feats of memory. We know that in the internment camps there flourished a veritable epidemic of quotations. This was not mere nostalgia; it was also a deliberate assertion that the émigrés were the last, best heirs of Goethe, whose immense range of inquiry and enthusiasm was the model for their own versatility, or of Heine, whose witty depictions of the bourgeoisie and obsessive interest in a Germany he both revered and despised resembled their own ambivalence. Homage to the German language, as well as to German philosophy, led the émigrés to cite Goethe and Heine, Marx and Nietzsche as commentators on their own fate.

Culture worked overtime, in lieu of politics or religion, to provide a common element. But culture was not exclusively the classics; popular culture provided a comparable source of energy, especially for those who had been young in Berlin, growing up amid the literary cafés and movie studios. This is one reason why Brecht became the supreme poet of the emigration. He often noted that a poor refugee could not lug along too much baggage. Thus he sang about the emigration in lyrics as breezy, idiomatic, and disposable as popular songs; in fact, in internment camps such as Gurs in France, Brecht's poems provided the quick charge, the emotional refill one expects from popular music. Refugees turned to lyrics redolent of the streets not in place of but as companions to the poems of Goethe and Heine. They recognized that the culture they brought with them now embraced all forms of modernism, most particularly popular culture. Thus, for such artists as the great film directors, it was a given that American culture comprehended blues, jazz, and gospel music as much as it did Melville, Whitman, and Twain.

The émigrés' alertness to excesses of *Schmus* (sweet-talk) and *Quatsch* (babble) complemented the irreverence inculcated in the Berlin of the 1920s. Max Ophuls's son reports that these words were his father's favorite terms of dismissal, although burghers and bohemians alike used them to deplore a universal atmosphere of banality and deceit. This made them an immensely spirited and engaging group, one superbly equipped to master novelties without losing their bearing. It also made them appear daunting and supercilious: irreverence is not easily dissociable from contempt.

While the refugees maintained this firm if unacknowledged cultural identity, a more circumscribed identity was imposed from without. Hitler's book-burning and dismissal of Jewish scholars served to link radicals and intellectuals. Thus by the time they reached America, refugees found that their representative figure was an unemployed left-leaning college professor, unlike the potato farmers or factory workers who had symbolized earlier emigrations. In America, most of the identifications imposed on them by Jew and Gentile, Left and Right alike, were negative. As a result, refugees often felt themselves endangered on all sides.

During the 1930s, American officials such as the infamous Breckinridge Long had made emigration to this country extremely difficult, predicated on written proofs of character and financial solvency. For the writers particularly, this reduction of a life's meaning to codes and slogans was galling. Long's offenses did not stop in the 1930s; in 1943, he helped suppress reports of the death camps as diversionary and insignificant. But Eleanor Roosevelt's commitment to the refugees was never in doubt; as a result, the émigrés briefly yielded their skepticism and regarded the Roosevelts as idols despite the president's lethargy in attending to their plight: it was not until January 1944 that he set up a War Refugee Board. Political conservatives were never sympathetic to the refugees, whom they saw alternately as fifth columnists, international Jewish conspirators, and unfair competition for American labor. But the left was not much more trustworthy. The Stalinists abandoned the fight against fascism for two years, and during the war Trotskyists opposed the participation of American workers in an "interimperialist conflict." Even American Jews were considered dubious allies. The enduring feuds between East and West European Jews did not help matters. Many American-Jewish leaders feared that an influx of refugees would inflame native anti-Semitism and were perhaps excessively cautious in soliciting assistance for the newcomers or in demanding rescue of those imprisoned in Hitler's camps. In addition, during the war, many émigrés considered Zionism an unconscionable distraction from the European fates of their relatives.

I stress this unhappy history both to suggest that the émigrés' more manic responses were sometimes indistinguishable from simple good sense and to offer a context for the few but provocative assertions of identity provided by émigré writers. As if to confound their enemies, they accepted the full implications of the terms "rootless Jew" and "vanguard intellectual" by conflating the two. Thus during the 1940s, under California skies, three disparate émigré writers arrived at similar conclusions. Theodor Adorno, in *Dialectic of Enlightenment* (Dialektik der Aufklärung, 1947), said the Jews' curse and triumph was to represent "happiness without power, wages without work, a home without frontiers, religion without myth." The first three conditions apply to only some Jews, but absolutely to Adorno and his fellow intellectuals for whom, since work is play in the good Germanic double sense of art and leisure, it cannot be remunerated or translated into power. In Thomas Mann's *Doktor Faustus* (1947), the concert promoter, Saul Fitelberg, begs to be the composer-hero's Jewish mediator between his homeland and the world. He is uniquely able to serve both because as a Jew he is both "international" and "pro-German," although his best attributes are the non-German traits of tolerance and good humor. Otherwise, Fitelberg warns, the self-contained Germans will find themselves in "real Jewish trouble." And the novel ends with the image of an ostracized Germany shut off from its neighbors "like ghetto Jews."

Alfred Döblin, that anomalous combination of fellow traveler and Catholic convert, had a similar vision. In *A People Betrayed (November 1918*, 1948–50), he argued that Jews would be the "race of the future" by providing the apparently "useless" ideas that transformed the Gentiles' lives. Adorno was part Jew (a part he may have deliberately obscured by using his mother's maiden name), Döblin a convert, Mann a Gentile with an early history of anti-Semitic remarks—which he later disowned—now married to a Jewish woman and thus the father of half-Jewish children. They are certainly not the most impeccable arbiters of Jewish identity. But given the peculiar history of German Jews, who could be? The point is that World War II had shocked them all into a common position: the refugee Jews would be vanguard figures, models of postwar life. Hannah Arendt, a most unlikely addition to this already vexed trio, would concur. She believed that the exiled Jews had learned earliest, though not through any luck or talent of their own, that everything had changed in politics and the academy. Thus, logically, she identified herself as a political scientist. To paraphrase Brecht, who now knew whether the "useless" was not in fact the most truly "useful": an insight already granted to the scores of refugees who had kept themselves sane through the repetition of ancient texts.

With this background, the postwar history of émigrés in America becomes more resonant. For the public issues they addressed were invariably linked to their own histories and the political facts of their exile, as well as to philosophical matters that had absorbed their attention in Berlin, Frankfurt, or Vienna. Fritz Lang once declined any prophetic status for having directed *Doktor Mabuse*; it was no pleasure for him that he had guessed the future. Likewise, when refugees criticized elements of postwar American life, it was with deep unhappiness: most of them had once loved the country to excess, and all of them knew that they remained extremely vulnerable, with their most famous figures Einstein and Thomas Mann condemned in the press and Congress. Cassandra is no comedy act.

Elsewhere I have noted that in one of the most exorbitant occupational demands ever placed on immigrants, refugee social scientists were expected to master American life and make sense of it for the natives. Impressionistic writers like Adorno were horrified by our popular culture; and even more objective scholars discovered traces of fascistic propaganda in the mass media. Their conclusions might have been questionable. More interesting is the paradox that their occupation was to explain American leisure. The émigrés were virtually the first scholars to attend to American fantasies (although a few smart-alecks might have declared that "homemade" was usually the same as "store-bought"). As well, and even more ironically, people living on borrowed time became the professional observers of other people's free time. Their agitation over such frivolous matters as radio serials and magazine biographies were not overblown: they anticipated the great modern dilemma of free and wasted time, precisely because it was spectacularly inapplicable to their own condition.

Although Albert Einstein and Thomas Mann had been the leading intellectual opponents of McCarthyism during the 1950s, the fullest opposition of refugee intellectuals to the American government occurred during the Vietnam War. Once again, there were strong echoes of the past. For example, Herbert Marcuse was identified as the intellectual guru of the American student movement, although his works were filled with allusions to that German literary culture I described earlier. His rare and late references to American soul music scarcely balanced the numerous citations of Schiller and Hegel, Walter Benjamin and Karl Kraus. Marcuse's most famous formulation, "repressive tolerance," baffled many Americans. In fact, as Frankfurt School paradoxes go, this was a model of precision. Earlier in Europe, Benjamin and Kraus had observed that the cacophany of the newspaper page, with its noisy collage of text, photo, and advertisement, drowned out any sustained argument. Many refugees were initially bemused at finding that talk in America did not change matters; whatever arguments were advanced and tolerated, the relations of power remained the same. Marcuse was simply giving a left-wing gloss to a universal perception.

Perhaps the most astonishing insertion of refugee conflicts into American public life occurred with the publication of Hannah Arendt's *Eichmann in Jerusalem* (1963). Arendt's famous phrase and subtitle, "the banality of evil," would not have shocked the countless refugees who had discovered vast resources of evil in their neighbors and friends, nor should it startle Americans who have had ample evidence of political corruption attended by platitudes and clichés. Arendt's greatest offense, one for which she has never been forgiven, was her refusal to countenance *Schmus* and *Quatsch*. She vastly offended Germans by dismissing their postwar attitudes as stupid and self-serving: as she saw it, the older, culpable generation had not come clean, and the younger innocents were masochistically relishing an artificial guilt. To Arendt, Adolf Eichmann was both horrible and uproarious when he sprinkled his testimony with references to "geflügelte Worte" (literally "winged words" but also the title of a collection of aphorisms). Her amusement appeared heartless but surely some Americans would laugh if a mass murderer were to interpolate *Bartlett's Familiar Quotations* into his confession.

Ironically, Arendt's most controversial remarks were prompted by the demands of accurate reporting. The Israeli prosecutor brought up the impotence of European Jewish leaders; Arendt believed he did so for tendentious purposes. She regretted his comments but felt obligated to elaborate on them: all over Europe, Jewish leaders had cooperated with the authorities; whether their motives were altruistic or selfish, the results were the same. Arendt was at her boldest and most radical—and also at her most European, for these were arguments familiar to all German-Jewish intellectuals—in rooting the problem in the very nature of an establishment. She deplored privileged categories, whether of national origin, military rank, or education; she was one German Jew who abominated the old "*yid* versus *yekke*" feuds. She also may have remembered that some prominent rabbis had written in the early 1930s that they admired the Nazis' dedication to German culture and Hitler's vehement opposition to atheistic communism.

This is not the place to examine Arendt's analysis or the astonishing public attacks that have continued even after her death—these matters are discussed in detail in my *Exiled in Paradise* (1983). But what should be emphasized is that Arendt's case anticipated many subsequent controversies. For daring to question the Jewish establishment, she was regarded as, at best, lacking in "Herzenstakt" (Gershom Scholem), at worst, a traitor. The experience of this public conflict probably enabled her to criticize the American establishment in later years—she had been much more circumspect during the McCarthy era—particularly over its conduct in Southeast Asia. In 1982, when Israel invaded Lebanon, there was much wider resistance by American Jews to the establishment. One of the first to voice his opposition was Arendt's friend Hans Jonas. Yet again, those Jews who opposed establishment policy were condemned as traitors: the accusers were largely drawn from among Arendt's critics. Somewhat earlier, when Jacobo Timerman had described the ineffectual response of Argentine Jewish leaders, he was dismissed by American neoconservatives as hysterical, as if Argentine anti-Semitism were a chimera. Arendt had seen it all: one either attacked the authorities or one identified with them; either position allowed one a distinctive vocabulary and means of explaining history. (The impudent Brecht might have noted traces of conventional class conflict, made clearer by the right-wing nature of the Israeli and American establishments.)

Apart from Arendt and Marcuse other refugees were active in antigovernment protests, including the politically moderate Hans Morgenthau. In recent years, scientists actively opposing the spread of nuclear weapons have been led by the émigrés Hans A. Bethe, Victor F. Weisskopf, and Konrad E. Bloch. Einstein's role in American politics was extraordinary, whether in his public defenses of political heretics or in his ceaseless agitation for nuclear disarmament; the recent citation of Einstein as an advocate of nuclear strength by the French "nouveau philosophe" André Glucksmann is a scandalous misreading.

Although there were fewer refugee conservatives, they too had a disproportionate impact. The divisions between Right and Left had begun in Europe, frequently as internecine squabbles among left-wing splinter groups. The extremes met most dramatically in one family, the Eislers. When the House Committee on Un-American Activities resumed hearings in 1947, it presented the extraordinary spectacle of Ruth Fischer publicly accusing her brother Gerhard Eisler of monstrous crimes performed in the service of Soviet Russia. Four years later, another former communist, Karl August Wittfogel, testified before the McCarran Committee. Both Fischer and Wittfogel declared that they were finally calling the Stalinists to account for numerous betrayals of their German comrades. America thus became the ground for settling European scores. Likewise, Willi Schlamm, an Austrian ex-Marxist, became a zealous *Time-Life* cold warrior and a presiding intelligence of *National Review*. During the Vietnam War, such refugee intellectuals as Bruno Bettelheim compared the student protesters to young Nazis. Indeed the impact of disillusioned European socialists on American conservatism has not been fully revealed. The close reasoning, the aggressive tone, the merciless attacks on deviationists that once characterized European leftist discourse are all echoed in the contemporary language of American conservatism. What is missing, however, is the historical context that gave those arguments their particular dignity; what remains usually sounds wrongheaded and shrill.

My point is not which side got matters right, but rather that émigré critics helped set the tone and agenda for political argument in postwar America. Their influence has not waned, despite the ravages of age and the continual changes in fashion: witness the continuing debates over Israel or nuclear weapons. Émigrés such as Einstein insisted that their criticisms of America were inseparable from their love of the country and its best institutions, notably the Constitution. Often refugees became fanatic patriots; for them America was right always, wrong never, although a few continued to despise everything about the country, from its financial arrangements to its popular culture. Some chameleons declared that a second nature had replaced their first one; a number of these even insisted that they had stopped dreaming in German.

But the Cassandras lived and died upholding a European cultural tradition. In 1939, Thomas Mann wrote his brother Heinrich that old age "in the Goethean sense belongs to our tradition alone; it is less a matter of vitality than of intelligence and will." Mann neglected to add that in his old age, Goethe delighted in the prospects of an "alleviation of humanity" ushered in by the American Revolution; the idea of a New World revived him. So, too, although America gave such people as Mann grounds to feel like demoralized prophets, it also allowed them the freedom to step forward and declare themselves, Cassandras with a German accent. A surprising result of this German-American relation was that it offered an unprecedented instruction in new ways of growing old.

19.
Neither State nor Synagogue: The Left-Wing German-Jewish Emigré Intellectual as Representative Jew

PAUL BREINES

AMONG MANY JEWS TODAY, the reputations of German-Jewish intellectuals generally and their left-wing circles in particular have fallen on hard times. In their quests for assimilation as "German citizens of the Jewish faith" or for humanist cosmopolitanism outside religion and nationalism, they appear to exemplify what Jean-Paul Sartre called the inauthentic Jew, that tragic specialist in self-evasion. Today's prevalent image of German Jews as Jews is tarnished when placed alongside our highly romanticized pictures of pre-Holocaust *Ostjuden* and post-Holocaust Israelis. Compared to the former's natural *Yiddishkeit* and the latter's hardy Zionism, the *yekkes* (German Jews) look for all the world like Jewish *goyim*.

The main reasons for this poor image are not hard to find. It is, for example, obviously conditioned by Nazi mass murder. The dreams of emancipation and assimilation did, after all, burst horribly in the nightmare of the Final Solution; the Jewish *goyim* turned out to be just Jews, forced to flee or to die with the rest. It is not surprising that, in the aftermath, we take a more critical, often more hostile view of those dreams. But it is not only in relation to the Holocaust that the various Jewish-German programs of minimal Jewishness appear, through the lens of the present, so tragically futile. Today's American context, with its chorus of celebrations of ethnic roots, be they black, Italian, Polish, Jewish, and so forth, also plays a part in the judgment. In this context, the German Jews' failure to announce and affirm their Jewishness more assertively looks unfashionable.

These evaluations do not suffice. I want to try here to defend at least part of the Jewish legacy of German-Jewish intellectuals, echoing some of the impulses of several recent revisionist historians, among them George L. Mosse, Peter Gay, and Michael Marrus, who have argued that it is neither enough nor entirely just to read post-Holocaust perceptions back into the nineteenth and early twentieth centuries in Europe. Before proceeding, though, it is worth lingering another moment, not without sympathy, on the prevalent view. The horrible facts of the Nazi assault on Jews and the quiescence of much of the Christian West do seem to render naive at best and suicidal at worst the hopes of the assimilationist and cosmopolitan Jewish Germans. One could argue plausibly, but, I believe, wrongly, that such events have reduced to rubble cosmopolitanism as such. In any case, although there were some tangible gains for German Jews, they ought to have known better, to have been more clever, to have seen the danger signs, even in the most hopeful years of the early nineteenth century.

Real Jews, more Jewish Jews would have done so. More Jewish Jews did, say the Zionists, who, of course, offer the main case against the assimilationists and cosmopolitans. Thus Gershom Scholem has commented astutely and bitterly on Jewish enthusiasm in the early and mid-nineteenth century for the "German-Jewish Dialogue": "The unending Jewish demand for a home," he has written, "was soon transformed into the ecstatic illusion of being at home"—at home in Germany, amid the culture of *Bildungsidealismus*, of Schiller and of the ideal of humanity. The well-known critical Jewish spirit, Scholem noted further, seemed to vanish when German Jews came to speak of their own situation. As to the outcome of the "ecstatic illusion," Scholem cites an example he considers unsurpassed in its grotesque self-denial. It is from Margarete Susman in 1935, when the poet was aware of the Jewish Germans' desperate straits. "The vocation of Israel as a people," Susman wrote, "is not self-realization, but self-surrender for the sake of a higher, transhistorical goal."

It appears sufficient merely to refer to Auschwitz to reduce to pathos or worse Margarete Susman's program. But it is not sufficient. Susman's 1935 idea has had a recent, tragicomic echo in America. Jewish self-surrender is the subtheme of *Zelig*, a film directed by and starring Woody Allen. The hero, Leonard Zelig, of central European Jewish extraction, suffers from an astonishing psychosomatic disorder—a lack of identity so extreme that it transforms him physically as well as emotionally into whatever person he happens to be in contact with at any moment. He is the assimilationist Jew gone haywire, one whose craving for acceptance and affirmation shoots beyond the point of self-surrender to total self-effacement. His malady begins during grade school years, when, the better to integrate himself among neighborhood youths, Leonard Zelig transforms himself into an Irish Catholic boy, complete with the stereotypical equipment: red hair, green eyes, and a small, turned-up nose. Later he will become a chubby Negro, an Indian chieftain, a professional baseball star, a psychiatrist of great skill and learning, a Chassidic rebbe, and finally a Nazi.

Among the film's various themes there is the Jewish one. Gershom Scholem, in his essay "Germans and Jews," has perceptively and angrily gone near the core of the significance of the character of Zelig by referring to the "widespread current appreciation of Jews as classic representatives of the phenomenon of man's estrangement or alienation from society"—an appreciation, Scholem adds, from which the Jews have never benefited. In Scholem's terms, Leonard Zelig represents the Jew as pure estrangement and self-estrangement. I propose that Zelig is also more than what Gershom Scholem's perspective will allow. As in Margarete Susman's idea of Jewish self-surrender in the cause of a transhistorical goal, Zelig, in his extreme insecurity, lack of identity, and deformity embodies the values and needs which the power of national, religious, and ethnic passions has severely weakened in this century: empathy, fellow-feeling, recognition of the self in the other and of the other in oneself. This psychic wreck is a utopian figure, bedraggled and beleaguered like every utopian image today.

Let me try to squeeze one more drop from Woody Allen's film. The utopia buried in Leonard Zelig is that of humanity, of the *Humanitäts-ideal* of the German Enlightenment and of the problematic German-Jewish dialogue. To be sure, critics of the dialogue are right on several counts. From the late eighteenth century (after Lessing and Kant) through 1933 and beyond, it was largely a Jewish monologue; non-Jewish German participation was always weak. Renunciation, moreover, was nearly always the Jewish, not the German task. Finally, the actual historical framework of Jewish German self-surrender was not transhistorical but narrowly national; Jewishness was to be given up, and often was given up, not for humanness but for Germanness, resulting in many cases in the sad figure of the Jewish German nationalist.

Such criticisms cannot be ignored or even momentarily shelved. But once again, they are not the final word. For example, several wings of the German-Jewish dialogue, small and weak as they may have been, were not circumscribed by the sharp limits outlined by the dialogue's later critics. One of these was the leftist, antinationalist wing, with figures from Karl Marx through Rosa Luxemburg and Paul Levi standing among its representatives, speaking not only of Jewish but of universal self-surrender, of a common renunciation of states and gods, and thereby of an affirmation of common or collective self-realization. But the Marxists are neither the sole nor the most interesting representatives. The ethical, libertarian current from Heinrich Heine, a forerunner, through Gustav Landauer and Erich Mühsam is more interesting because it is more complex, more sunk in ambiguities. They aimed at a path between Zionism on one side and assimilation on the other; they amounted to noble fragments and strands rather than a movement. Politically, they failed.

Among the leftist German-Jewish émigré intellectuals we find some of the finest as well as some of the saddest expressions of this type of Jew. And my point is that it *is* a Jewish type; it is a way of being a Jew in the modern world. But what distinguishes this way of being a Jew is that its representatives embraced and sustained central ideals of the German Enlightenment: the importance of *Bildung*, as George L. Mosse has vividly shown, the primacy of culture over politics and economics, the importance of friendship, dialogue, and tolerance. These German Jews or Jewish Germans helped to preserve the sparks of the "other Germany," Mosse notes, and in doing so they stood, in relation to the religious and nationalist Jews, as the other Jews. Consider, for example, the following words from Ernst Toller, who as a youth in Germany had passed through the unlit tunnel of Jewish self-hatred:

Is blood to be the only test? Does nothing else matter at all? I was born and brought up in Germany; I breathed the air of Germany and its spirit had molded mine; as a German writer I had helped to preserve the purity of the German language. How much of me was German, how much Jewish? I could not have said. All over Europe an infatuated nationalism and ridiculous pride was raging—must I too participate in the madness of this epoch. . . ? The words "I am proud to be a German" or "I am proud to be a Jew" sounded ineffably stupid to me. As well say, "I am proud to have brown eyes. . . ." Pride and love are not the same thing, and if I were asked where I belonged I should answer that a Jewish mother had borne me, that Germany had nourished me, Europe had formed me, my home was the earth, and the world my fatherland.[1]

These lines were written nearly a decade before the Holocaust, which Ernst Toller did not live to witness. He took his life in 1939. But I would not accept the claim that the Holocaust refutes Toller's words or renders them un-Jewish. They are Jewish, that is, German-Jewish or Jewish-German words primarily in their ambiguity, in their insistence on multiple definitions of self, and in their humane and desperate cosmopolitanism. In the same spirit are the words of another leftist German-Jewish émigré intellectual, Albert Einstein, who in 1948 rejoiced in the founding of Israel but noted that "my awareness of the essential nature of Judaism resists the idea of a Jewish state with borders, an army, and a measure of temporal power no matter how modest. I am afraid of the inner damage Judaism will sustain—especially from the development of a narrow nationalism within our own ranks."[2]

In their reckonings with the dialectic of universal (human) and particular (Jewish, German, émigré), the Tollers, Einsteins, and their scattered kindred spirits recognized that self-surrender cuts several ways; that just as the consistent assimilationists repressed their Jewish particularity, the more Jewish Jews who opted for the synagogue or for Jewish statehood repressed some of their universal humanity. Here, however, a familiar voice enters; it speaks in annoyed tones, saying, your left-wing German-Jewish intellectuals, after all, have no monopoly on cosmopolitanism. This is true, but for Jews and non-Jews alike, it is not a simple truth but a *verité à faire*, a historical truth, to be made, shared, and lived.

In the 1930s, 1940s, and after, the German émigré intellectuals, Jews and non-Jews, leftists and others, had their dramatic encounter with America, which has become the subject of a growing body of memoirs and analyses, including Anthony Heilbut's excellent *Exiled in Paradise* (1983). Among the numerous chapters of this story which await their interpreter, one is the specific encounter between German-Jewish émigré intellectuals on the left and their approximate counterparts among some mostly younger Americans. The encounter took place around Columbia University, the New School for Social Research, and the Smaller Institute for Social Research. I refer to the Americans involved as approximate counterparts not merely because of differences in age but because the ethnic heritage of most of the Americans—for example, Daniel Bell, Alvin Gouldner, and Seymour Lipset—was not German but East European. The class background, too, differed, with the Marcuses, Horkheimers, and Neumanns having come from commercial bourgeois families, whereas the Americans who had contact with them generally came from poorer, artisanal circumstances.

Perhaps there are some among us who could elucidate the inner thoughts of the participants in this intriguing gathering of displaced persons. Did the upwardly mobile Americans, fresh from the New York City Jewish ghettos, envy even as they resented the nonchalantly assimilated bearing of the Hegelian-Marxist *yekke* refugees from Hitler? And did the Frankfurt émigrés admire even as they were made uneasy by the apparently more Jewish-American Jews whose parents had likely fled from a czarist pogrom? Did they both ask themselves: I came here to find *this*?

While awaiting the history or the historical novel of this Jewish-German-American story, let me note that it is not only a thing of the past. It is part of a legacy with some contemporary merits. The Jewish-German leftist émigré idea meandered through the larger histories of the New Left movements in both West Germany and America in the 1960s, and it has cropped up more clearly and consciously among the group of Americans and Germans gathered around the leftist journal of Germanistik, *New German Critique*. In its pages one can find among other things lively discussion and reconstruction of the question of Germans and Jews, *yekkes* and *Ostjuden*, cosmopolitanism and nationalism. All these little chapters are, of course, part of a history of defeat. Alternatively, I would rather speak of the history of a small seed, which as always needs more nurturance than it can find. In the Tricentennial commemoration, we are likely to pay homage merely to two historic nationalisms, the American and the German, which, as nationalisms, have contributed little to the blossoming of a humane community. We would do better to join and encourage the Margarete Susmans, Ernst Tollers, and Leonard Zeligs, pushing with them beyond the narrow and devastating limits of religion, nation, and blood.

Notes

1. Ernst Toller, *I Was a German*, trans. Edward Crankshaw (New York: Morrow, 1934), 285–86.
2. Frederic Grunfeld, *Prophets Without Honor: A Background to Freud, Kafka, Einstein and Their World* (New York: Holt, Rinehart, Winston, 1979), 183.

20.
Critical Theory in the United States: Reflections on Four Decades of Reception

ANDREW ARATO

THE CRITICAL THEORY OF THE FRANKFURT SCHOOL in the United States has had an uneasy existence from the start. To a great extent a theory of American society as the most advanced version of modern capitalism, critical theory has never been in the full sense a theory for Americans. The intellectual traditions drawn upon, the scholarly problems addressed, and the political possibilities dreamed of by the founders around Max Horkheimer belonged to the Old World, even if the mass culture that reminded them of fascism was a product of the new. Even Herbert Marcuse, who in his late work reflected primarily upon the experience of American New Left movement, did not use a theoretical medium that could be understood by this potential audience or even by most of its intellectuals. And Jürgen Habermas, who has integrated into his theory some important results of American sociology, linguistic philosophy, and developmental psychology, is not usually understood on this side of the ocean for his deeper intellectual and political intentions.

In social theory at least, radical thinking in the United States is paradoxically dependent on European sources yet rarely capable of doing them full justice. The reason seems to me above all the inability to develop critical traditions of our own capable of a genuinely mature dialogue with French, German, and other traditions. There is, however, some hope that after forty years of experience with critical theory, autonomous paths of serious critical thought, enriched by this experience but growing beyond it, are finally developing around some journals and universities. It is safe (even if tautological) to say that if these possibilities manage to survive and develop, our future reception of European and in particular German thought will be deeper, more critical, creative, and interesting.

The four decades of reception of critical theory in the United States occurred in five phases: (1) simultaneous presence and non-reception in the social sciences of the 1940s, (2) a political reception *manque* in the 1960s, (3) reception in the history of ideas that began in the early 1970s and is still continuing, (4) a series of denunciations also beginning in the 1970s, and finally (5) a theoretical reception beginning in the mid-1970s, which is in the spirit of critical theory but tends to go beyond the original boundaries. I will comment briefly on the first four of these phases and then concentrate on the fifth, which in my own—to be sure, biased—opinion is the most significant, at least potentially.

1. When the members of the Frankfurt Institut für Sozialforschung came to the United States in 1934 and later,[1] they initially continued their efforts in a direction that has been called an interdisciplinary social science.[2] But this direction should perhaps be more properly characterized as working out the social scientific implications of a historical materialist functionalism in the epoch of the transition from liberal to organized capitalism. The members of the institute—now renamed the International Institute for Social Research and affiliated with Columbia University—were radical Marxists deeply disturbed by the collapse of "revolutionary subjectivity" that represented the subjective, that is, political and cultural, side of the same transition. They investigated the overall process on the levels of culture (high to mass culture), politics (liberal to authoritarian state), personality (the decline of the individual), law (general to particular laws), and of course economics (from laissez-faire to monopoly and state capitalism).[3] We can safely say, however, that the relevant efforts of Theodor W. Adorno, Leo Löwenthal, Herbert Marcuse, Max Horkheimer, Erich Fromm, Franz Neumann, Otto Kirchheimer, and Friedrich Pollock along with his coworkers, Kurt Mandelbaum and Gerhard Meyer, had little effect on the American context despite the institute's superficial involvement in the life of Columbia University. The same was even more true of the programmatic statements concerning the project of critical theory produced by Horkheimer and Marcuse in the mid- and late 1930s and especially the negative philosophy of history developed in the 1940s by Adorno and Horkheimer in works such as the "End of Reason," *Minima Moralia, Dialektik der Aufklärung*, and *Eclipse of Reason*. Nevertheless, in this later period the willingness of Adorno, Horkheimer, and

Löwenthal to participate in empirical research projects such as the one that led to the famous *Authoritarian Personality* implied a reception that cut two ways. On the one hand, some of the Frankfurt theorists turned, however temporarily, into social scientists in the American mold; on the other hand, some of their concerns could now be entertained by American and German-American researchers, albeit in a watered-down form. Yet in the social science world of the 1950s little trace of even this tame interaction with critical theory survived. An almost official functionalism that was more complex than the Marxism of the critical theory of the 1930s but was also deeply apologetic of American society did not tolerate any significant presence of the thought characteristic of the Frankfurt school. (The same was true for analytic philosophy and New Criticism.) It was primarily as teachers that the members of the group that stayed in America (Löwenthal, Neumann, Kirchheimer, and Marcus) continued to exercise a certain underground influence, though each continued to produce significant works even in the darkest time of American politics.

2. It is often supposed that Herbert Marcuse's works exerted major political influence in the late 1960s. For a few people, of course, *Reason and Revolution, Eros and Civilization* (both belatedly read), and *One Dimensional Man* worked like bombshells. Here were a series of critical works that fully penetrated the appearances of a conformist, manipulated society seemingly dominated by a "happy consciousness" and without a real opposition. One might also imagine that a major lesson of Marcuse's works was that one could criticize American society from a Marxian point of view which made no concessions to any other existing mode of domination—in particular to that of the Soviet Union—not even the usual Trotskyist ones. And yet even those few New Leftists who have read Marcuse's *Soviet Marxism*—a book whose critique of Soviet society was inconsistent—turned out on the whole to be speechless (as was Marcuse himself) when the bulk of the political movement turned in authoritarian and dogmatic Marxist directions. As Paul Breines once noted in a remarkable essay, the reception of Marcuse was not only limited to a very few people but was also extremely superficial.[4] It was also nonpolitical. The 1968–69 attacks on the magazine of the Maoist Stalinist Progressive Labor party ("The Professor Contemplates His Navel" and "Marcuse: Cop out or Cop") were not only not answered by any significant tendency in the movement, but Bernadine Dohrn, then secretary of Students for a Democratic Society (SDS), publicly insulted Marcuse at a dinner hosted by the magazine *Liberation*. Not only did Marcuse's libertarianism become

increasingly uncomfortable for a movement that sought its models among authoritarian states, but an audience entirely unschooled in German Idealism, Weber, Freud, and neo-Marxism, however sympathetic to him at first, simply could not understand his writings. Marcusianism, at least in the United States, always remained the affair of very small groups of people.

3. Beginning in the early 1970s a series of books, essays, and translations began to correct the problem of the missing context of reception. The works of Paul Breines, Dick Howard and Karl Klare, Frederic Jameson, Russell Jacoby, Trent Schroyer, William Leiss, Andrew Arato and Eike Gebhardt, Susan Buck-Morss, Mark Poster, Richard Wolin, Richard Bernstein, and above all Martin Jay, and the translation of a short but significant book by Albrecht Wellmer,[5] along with scores of essays in *Telos* and *New German Critique*, have managed to reconstruct not only the theories of the Frankfurt school but also their intellectual and political background on a level that clearly rivals the best works of this type in Germany and Italy and surpasses these in France and England.[6] A large number of new translations of Adorno, Benjamin, Horkheimer, Marcuse's earlier writings, and Habermas as well as the publication of Marcuse's last works could not be received with far more intelligence, if only by an almost exclusively academic community. In fact, in the absence of a movement comparable to that of the 1960s the weight of the new reception became primarily academic and backward-looking. This literature explored neither the possibilities nor the limitations of using theories based on the Frankfurt model, an attitude completely at variance with the method of critical appropriation worked out by members of the Frankfurt school. Even in the case of Habermas, who most emphatically works with contemporary problems, the reception typified by Thomas McCarthy's excellent and reliable work has been above all a reconstructive one.[7] Critical theory's reception within the context of philosophy and the history of ideas could not establish even indirect links with potential social actors (unlike in Germany) and threatened only established academic positions.

4. The stakes involved in academic life were apparently high enough to motivate some rather blind counterattacks. Whether from the point of view of already established positions such as that of Alasdair McIntyre, that of bitter outsiders such as Zoltan Tar, or that of Marxists seeking to denounce the academy altogether, as Phil Slater, works were written whose sole purpose was to dismiss and denounce.[8] For different reasons, similar motifs, if toned down, appear in the Trotskyist-inspired

work of Perry Anderson, as well as in the third, weakest, and most polemical volume of Leszek Kolakowski's *Main Currents of Marxism*.[9]
Habermas in particular has been the object of the least knowledgeable attacks, by Göran Therborn, Quentin Skinner, and most recently
Stanley Aronowitz. Paradoxically, the most academic and at the same
time the most political of critical theorists since 1940, he is especially
feared as a competitor in both of these camps.

5. In my personal opinion the weight of polemical reception is for
the moment more than adequately outbalanced by the positive reception from the point of view of the history of ideas. Nevertheless, a
positive reception that is confined to this level remains vulnerable to a
transcendent critique (Adorno) that claims a contemporary irrelevance
of critical theory. Only an immanently critical reception, an effort
capable of both criticizing the tradition and rescuing its valuable insights for a new critical theory of society has a chance of going beyond
the existing debate. In West Germany, Jürgen Habermas, Albrecht
Wellmer, Claus Offe, and others have already contributed much to
such an effort, and the continued reception and transmission of their
works remains crucial. But the reception of even a truly contemporary
theory is no substitute for independent theoretical work. In the mid-
1970s and later, two journals, *Telos* and *New German Critique*, earned
international attention as the best American efforts in such theoretical directions. To be sure, these journals have participated heavily in
Marcusianism, in the preservation and transmission of the works of
German critical theorists in the form of translations and scholarly re-
constructions. To a much smaller extent they have even published
some works of transcendent criticisms of critical theory—though almost never denunciations. But most important, they have explicitly
committed themselves to the critical continuation of the tradition.
Special attention to art and mass culture, fascism theory, and the problem of anti-Semitism has brought *New German Critique* especially
close to at least part of the *Ideenwelt* of the original *Zeitschrift für
Sozialforschung* and its immediate aftermath. Although a certain apologetic tendency toward the German Democratic Republic, long since
outgrown, tended initially to deflect the journal from its critical tasks,
the use of Habermas's conception of *Kritische Öffentlichkeit* later
pointed on the normative level in a direction challenging all contemporary forms of authoritarianism and injustice. On the analytical level,
the journal has been somewhat held back by its primarily literary and
German stress, which is perhaps unavoidable but nevertheless inter-
feres with the development of theory in the sense of the Frankfurt

school. Not similarly confined, *Telos* has long labored under a history of ideas heritage that involved the reception of a full spectrum of Western Marxist thought (Georg Lukács, Karl Korsch, Antonio Gramsci, Maurice Merleau-Ponty, and Jean Paul Sartre), Italian phenomenological Marxism, French post-Marxist thought, and East European Praxis philosophy, apart from critical theory, which was always the model and the main heritage. In the end this variety of intellectual backgrounds, along with a great freedom in the choice of topics (ranging from economics and politics to art and philosophy) did have a liberating effect on the journal, which in recent years began to produce its own original forms of theoretical analysis. Several political factors contributed to this outcome: (1) the exhaustion of the New Left in a context that seemed to refurbish concepts of critical theory pertaining to the integration of the opposition in advanced industrial societies, (2) the emergence of a post-Marxist dissidence in several East European countries in the mid-1970s, and (3) the rise of new types of social movements in several Western countries. Characteristically, focusing on one or another of these factors led to particular emphases on different phases of the Frankfurt tradition. No one, it seems, wanted to return to the world of 1930s materialist functionalism. Under the slogan of "artificial negativity," which implies a society so totally administered as to be able to plan its opposition, the fully pessimistic and resigned philosophy of the late Adorno has been revived by a small group around the editor, Paul Piccone. Another group (Paul Breines, Joel Kovel, Seyla Benhabib, and others) has sought to refocus the search for the revolutionary subject that began with *Eros and Civilization* and was continued by Marcuse into the 1970s around some of the new social movements, most recently the peace movement. Finally, a democratic theory derived from Habermas and related to some of the efforts of Neumann and Kirchheimer has been used by a third group to divest critical theory of its excessive utopianism (Joel Whitebook) and as a common framework to thematize the efforts of contemporary social movements both East and West to reconstruct "civil society" (Jean Cohen, José Casanova, Dick Howard, and Andrew Arato).

The affinity of the third group to nonfundamentalist elements of the German Green movement did not prevent a serious conflict with several like-minded West German colleagues. This conflict has received a caricatural expression in the journal *Links*, which published an article accusing *Telos* of neoconservativism. In fact, the conflict also took place within *Telos*. At issue was the evaluation of the peace movement, to which the "Adornoian" and "Habermasian" groups of *Telos*, each true to its segment of the tradition, refused to give unambiguous support. In this context the influence of the critique of "totalitarianism" worked out by French (Cornelius Castoriadis, Claude Lefort, and the journal *Esprit*) and East European (Jacek Kuron, Ivan Szelenyi, George Markus, Ferenc Feher, Viktor Zazlavsky, Adam Michnik, Jadwiga Staniszkis, and others) writers should not be underestimated. *Telos* has become the first medium in the tradition of critical theory to develop a full-fledged critique of Soviet societies, concentrating on social and economic structure, political culture and conditions of legitimation, social movements, political policy, and military posture. This many-sided critique, surpassing in an important respect the development of critical theory in its homeland that has for a long time had Soviet society as its veritable "blind spot," [10] blocked the way to a naive understanding of Soviet politics characteristic of most German leftists.

Although *Telos* never apologized for American foreign or armament policies, the critique of authoritarian state socialism and the Soviet empire has not yet been balanced by similar innovative work on late capitalism and American imperialism. In this respect our German critics have been right, even if some steps have already been taken toward the study of social movements in the West. Only a full development of theoretical insights gained over the last few years in the direction of our own societies can legitimate the continuation of the enterprise. [11] In an epoch in which the decomposition of the intellectual substance of classical liberal, conservative, and even socialist perspectives seems extremely rapid there is much need for a new critical theory of society that draws upon a rich tradition with reflection but without traditionalism. The production of such a theory or theories is up to us.

Notes

1. Martin Jay, *The Dialectical Imagination: A History of the Frankfurt School and the Institute of Social Research* (Boston: Little, Brown, 1973).

2. Helmut Dubiel, *Wissenschaftsorganisation und politische Erfahrung: Studien zur frühen Kritischen Theorie* (Frankfurt: Suhrkamp, 1978).

3. See the now reprinted *Zeitschrift für Sozialforschung* (Munich, 1980).

4. Paul Breines, *Critical Interruptions* (New York: Herder and Herder, 1970).

5. Ibid.; Dick Howard and Karl Klare, *The Unknown Dimension: European Marxism since Lenin* (New York: Basic Books, 1972); Frederic Jameson, *Marxism and Form: Twentieth Century Dialectical Theories of Literature* (Princeton: Princeton University Press, 1971); Russell Jacoby, *Social Amnesia: A Critique of Conformist Psychology from Adler to Laing* (Boston: Beacon Press, 1975); see also Jacoby, *Dialectic of Defeat: Con-*

tours of Western Marxism (Cambridge: Cambridge University Press, 1981); Trent Schroyer, *Critique of Domination: The Origins and Development of Critical Theory* (New York: Braziller, 1973); William Leiss, *The Domination of Nature* (Boston: Beacon Press, 1974); Andrew Arato and Eike Gebhardt, *The Essential Frankfurt School Reader* (New York: Urizen Books, 1978); Susan Buck-Morss, *The Origin of Negative Dialectics* (New York: Free Press, 1977); Mark Poster, *Critical Theory of the Family* (New York: Seabury Press, 1980); Richard Wolin, *Walter Benjamin: An Aesthetic of Redemption* (New York: Columbia University Press, 1980); Richard Bernstein, *The Restructuring of Social and Political Theory* (Philadelphia: University of Pennsylvania Press, 1978); Jay, *Dialectical Imagination*; Albrecht Wellmer, *Critical Theory of Society* (New York: Herder and Herder, 1971).

6. The best work in England is by David Held, *Introduction to Critical Theory* (London: Hutchinson, 1980); Held has studied in Boston with Thomas McCarthy.

7. Thomas McCarthy, *The Critical Theory of Jürgen Habermas* (Cambridge, Mass.: MIT Press, 1978).

8. Alasdair McIntyre, *Marcuse: An Exposition and a Polemic* (New York: Viking Press, 1970); Zoltan Tar, *The Frankfurt School: The Critical Theories of Max Horkheimer and Theodor W. Adorno* (New York: Wiley, 1977); Phil Slater, *Origin and Significance of the Frankfurt School: A Marxist Perspective* (London: Routledge & Kegan Paul, 1977). Slater is English, but he typifies one reception common among orthodox Marxists here as well.

9. Perry Anderson, *Considerations of Western Marxism* (London: NLB, 1976); Leszek Kolakowski, *Main Currents of Marxism: Its Rise, Growth and Dissolution* (Oxford: Clarendon Press, 1978). Both Kolakowski's and Anderson's books are extremely influential here, though of course they are not directly part of the American reception.

10. See Jürgen Habermas, "A Reply to My Critics," in David Held and J. B. Thompson, eds., *Habermas: Critical Debates* (Cambridge, Mass.: MIT Press, 1982), 281. This volume accomplishes much by way of the "critical appropriation" of Habermas's work.

11. The special issue on French socialism (Spring 1983), edited by Jean Cohen, and projected issues on contemporary forms of conservatism, civil society, and imperialism are further steps in this direction.

21.
Research on the Intellectual Migration to the United States After 1933: Still in Need of an Assessment

JOHN M. SPALEK

I WOULD LIKE TO BEGIN with two seemingly contradictory statements. First, during the last few years West German newspapers and journals have commented about the so-called "boom" in exile studies, suggesting that too many publications are crowding the field, or that most of the work has been accomplished, or that it has become a fad, or perhaps all three.[1] Second, however, American scholars have been noting the lack of studies on the migration of German talent to the United States. Most frequently called for are studies of certain professions not yet researched or inadequately treated and integrative studies of the post-1933 migration. David Hollinger, in his recent perceptive review of *The Muses Flee Hitler* (1983),[2] notes with surprise that fifteen years after the appearance of Donald Fleming and Bernard Bailyn's *The Intellectual Migration* (1968), no integrative assessment of this migration to the United States has yet been written.

There is in reality no contradiction between the statements. They represent two different points of view and address themselves to two different aspects of the post-1933 migration. A relatively large number of publications concentrating on German literature and politics in exile, written mainly in German, are seen by some German critics as an abundance of studies on the emigration.

The comment by American scholars about the need for studies of specific areas as well as for integrative works addresses itself not to German literature and politics in exile (that is a German topic) but to the intellectual migration as represented by the arts and the social and natural sciences, in other words, the artistic and academic migration to the United States.

The call for integrative studies of the emigration, though pertinent and to the point, will not be easily accomplished, considering the magnitude and diversity of the intellectual migration to the United States, involving some thirty professions, ranging from acting to theology. Before an integrative study can be attempted with any promise of success, a series of professions, as yet unresearched or barely touched, will have to be investigated (for instance, economics, history, political science, law, medicine, music, psychology, and sinology).

The preceding comments indicate that I am dividing the results of scholarship, for the sake of this presentation, into two parts: (1) research concerned with German writing and politics in exile, of interest mainly—though not exclusively—to German scholars; and (2) research on the academic, that is, scientific, professional, and artistic emigration, of interest mainly—though again not exclusively—to U.S. scholars. Although this distinction will hold up by and large, it is worth noting that the more recent general and introductory studies on the subject of German literature in exile—a "German" topic—have been done by scholars at American universities: Egbert Krispyn (University of Georgia), Manfred Durzak (Indiana University), Alexander Stephan (UCLA), Michael Winkler (Rice University), Helmut Pfanner (University of New Hampshire), and Joseph Strelka (State University of New York at Albany). In addition, most of the approximately eighteen volumes containing papers from conferences also deal mainly with literature in exile and are the result of meetings at American universities and other institutions: Universities of Kentucky, Wisconsin, Alabama, South Carolina (three times), California at Riverside (two times), Rice, Washington, and the Smithsonian Institution (two times).

Although the study of German politics in exile has also been carried out at American universities (Lewis J. Edinger, Peter Gay, H. Stuart Hughes), by far the largest number of studies on the political emigration, including individual personalities, has been done, as might be expected, by German and Austrian scholars. In particular, two collaborative projects between American and German scholars have been done: *International Biographical Dictionary of Central European Emigrés, 1933–1945*, edited by Werner Röder and Herbert A. Strauss, and the yearbook *Exilforschung*, edited by Thomas Koebner, Wulf Koepke, and Joachim Radkau.[3]

In this essay, I will assess the work accomplished to this time and will conclude with suggestions about areas that still need to be researched.

I shall proceed by dividing the literature into categories. There are, as far as I have been able to estimate, about 350 book-length independent publications by single or several authors, dissertations, encyclopedias, catalogs of exhibits, and indexes,[4] not including studies of the exile years of individual authors, artists, and scientists (another several dozen works at least). The same ought to hold true for articles in journals, which I am only marginally taking into account.

Of the 350 titles, there are approximately 50 reference works, such as encyclopedias (the most comprehensive being that by Werner Röder and Herbert A. Strauss), bibliographies, finding guides to archives (John M. Spalek, Adrienne Ash, Sandra Hawrylchak, Max Kreutzberger, W. Siegel) and to certain library holdings, as well as a variety of comprehensive and specialized indexes to periodicals (Lieselotte Maas, Harro Kieser, and Brita Eckert and several volumes published by Georg Heintz and the Aufbau-Verlag). Some of these works unavoidably repeat information. Four major projects are still in progress: the third volume of the Röder and Strauss *International Biographical Dictionary*; the second volume of the *Guide to Archival Materials* by Spalek and Hawrylchak; the forthcoming encyclopedia on the émigrés in the film industry by Straszek; and the ongoing series of bibliographical tools published by the Deutsche Bibliothek in Frankfurt.

Among the roughly 350 works mentioned, there are about 40 anthologies of texts: poetry (*Welch Wort in die Kälte gerufen*, edited by Heinz Seydel), drama (*Stücke gegen den Faschismus*, edited by Karl Heinz Schmidt), essays (Ernst Loewy's compendium *Exil: Literarische und politische Texte*), autobiographical texts (Egon Schwarz and Matthias Wegner's *Verbannung*), miscellaneous texts (Walter Zadek's *Sie flohen vor dem Hakenkreuz*), and several anthologies consisting of interviews with former émigrés, such as *Auszug des Geistes* by Radio Bremen, *Um uns die Fremde*, edited by Sender Freies Berlin, and *Die Zerstörung einer Zukunft*, edited by Mathias Greffrath. If we keep a running count, we can say that approximately 30 percent of the 350 works are reference works and anthologies.

The third category is comprised of studies, starting with the 1930s, about rescue operations and problems of immigration. Approximately twenty titles fit into this category. Most of these studies are of earlier date, and a comprehensive examination is still in order that would place the rescue effort against the background of the late 1930s, the end of the depression, would account for the idealism and altruism that inspired this effort, and would also integrate the work of the rescue organizations with that of foundations. (The foundations, such as the Rockefeller Foundation, led the way toward establishing contacts between German and American scientists through postdoctoral fellowships after World War I.)

By far the largest category of works on the emigration deals with the subject of German literature and writing in exile. As can be expected, practically all of these works are in German. Of the approximately 350 works, at least 110 deal with literature in a broad sense of the term, including drama and theater. This preponderance of studies of writing in exile seems understandable from the point of view of postwar Germany. Nearly two thousand professionally active journalists, critics, dramatists, screenwriters, novelists, poets, and others who earned their living by the pen, at least before emigration, were in exile. Additionally, the writer in exile is regarded as the exile per se. The quality that gives him this representative status is the tool of his trade: his native language, which he cannot abandon without simultaneously surrendering his identity with the culture he represents. The problem of identity does not affect a mathematician, an architect, or a musician the same way. Their tools and means of communication are much more easily understood and do not require the labor of translation. Thus we justifiably speak of literature in exile but we do not speak in the same sense of mathematics in exile.

As the number of works indicates, a great deal has been accomplished in the fifteen years since exile research began in earnest. There are now available introductions to German literature in exile, each with a different emphasis (Egbert Krispyn, Alexander Stephan, Manfred Durzak, Hans-Albert Walter), studies treating different aspects such as the novel or the drama or lyric poetry in exile, and studies focusing on literature and culture of exiles in different countries, such as Sweden, Holland, Czechoslovakia, Switzerland, the United States, and Soviet Russia. Many primary works have been reprinted or published for the first time (for example, the reprint series of the Gerstenberg Verlag, edited by Werner Berthold and Hans-Albert Walter); several authors (besides such obvious ones as Thomas and Heinrich Mann, Bertolt Brecht, Hermann Broch, Robert Musil, and Alfred Döblin) have appeared on the market in collected editions: Lion Feuchtwanger, Kurt Tucholsky, Oskar Maria Graf, Joseph Roth, Ernst Toller, Franz C. Weiskopf, Ernst Weiss, Anna Seghers; and, even more important, much of the German literature written in exile after 1933 is accessible in paperback form (Luchterhand, Hanser, Fischer, Rowohlt, Deutscher Taschenbuch Verlag).

Nevertheless, it can be argued that much primary literature still needs to be published or republished before German writing in exile is fully integrated into the history of German literature of the twentieth century.

I would like to illustrate the treatment of German exile literature in literary history by a personal comment. In a paper at our first U.S. conference on exile literature in 1971 at the University of Kentucky, I was reporting that almost no history of German literature published after 1945 contained a chapter on literature in exile and that although dissertations and theses were being written on authors who went into exile, their work was not seen and not examined from the point of view of their exile experience. It can be said that by 1983, in a relatively short time, research on German literature in exile has borne fruit.

Here are some examples. One-half of the tenth volume of the *Geschichte der deutschen Literatur*, published in East Germany, is devoted to exile. The recent *Handbuch des deutschen Dramas*, edited by Walter Hinck (1980), and the *Handbuch des deutschen Romans*, edited by Helmut Koopmann (1983), both have chapters on the exile period. The popular sixteen-volume Reclam series on German literature, edited by Otto F. Best and Hans-Jürgen Schmitt, has one volume devoted to the literature from the 1920s to the 1940s, and "Exil-Literatur" is one of the words on the title page. Volume 6 of the *Propyläen Geschichte der Literatur* has a chapter on German exile literature.

The integration of German literature in exile into the history of German literature does, however, present the problem of how to integrate writing in exile into the mainstream of literary history and at the same time stress that between 1933 and 1945 there were two German literatures, of which the most important part was being produced outside of Germany. As far as the short history of exile research is concerned, fifteen years ago the stress was on the assumption that literature written outside of Nazi Germany had to be radically different from that written within Nazi Germany. And it goes without saying that there are major differences: Thomas Mann's Joseph story (based on the Old Testament) could not have been written in Germany and neither could have Anna Segher's novel *Transit*. Numerous novels exposing the dictatorship in Germany, whether directly or symbolically, could have been written and published only in exile; formal developments in lyric poetry (Nelly Sachs, Rose Auslaender, Bertolt Brecht, Else Lasker-Schüler) went on in exile; the same can be said about the novels of Hermann Broch, Alfred Döblin, and Hans Henny Jahnn.[5] In addition, German literature was enriched by new themes reflecting the experiences in different countries as well as by a new look at German traditions and thought.

While keeping in mind the differences, there has recently been a noticeable tendency to stress the continuity of German literature in the twentieth century, the common background and frame of reference of all authors, whether émigrés or not. (This idea of continuity became apparent in the papers and discussions at the eleventh U.S. conference on German literature in exile in 1982 in Houston.) One formulation of the questions asked within the framework of continuity was: What happened to literary and intellectual traditions both in and outside of Germany after 1933? Questions were raised that no one would have thought of asking fifteen years ago.

Klaus Schöffling, in the postscript to his recent anthology of exile writings, *Dort, wo man Bücher verbrennt*, expresses the need for integrating exile literature into the mainstream. He concedes that many former exiled authors are in print but feels that they have been placed into a respectable ghetto.[6] In other words, the problem remains how to achieve integration without forgetting that the major part of German literature after 1933 was being written and debated outside of Germany's borders.

A second major problem of research on German exile literature seems obvious yet apparently is very difficult to solve. It is contained in the question: What is exile literature? It is an aesthetic, literary question and has to do with the literary expression of the writer's experience, that is, to what extent the exile experience affected the writer's means of expression, his language, and his style. So far there have been several short attempts to offer such description,[7] although a basic study of what constitutes exile literature is still lacking. Most of the studies thus far have emphasized history, political content, biography, and the psychology of the exile.

To say that German exile literature is politically different from that written in the Third Reich will not suffice, although that is the answer that has been given fairly consistently by Marxist critics, who tend to define exile literature as antifascist literature and in turn restrict the term "antifascist" to Marxist-oriented writings.

The fifth category, and the most important after literature in exile, is politics in exile. The studies in this group include the histories and activities of German and Austrian political parties in exile: Kommunistische Partei Deutschlands (KPD), Sozialdemokratische Partei

Deutschlands (SPD), Sozialistische Arbeiter-Partei (SAP), Deutsche Freiheitspartei (DFP), the group Neu Beginnen, the Volksfront movement, and the movement Freies Deutschland. These studies usually concentrate on the activities of a party in a particular country, especially the KPD and the SPD. These studies (books as well as numerous articles) accompany the equally numerous number of autobiographies, a large portion of which were written by political figures (Willy Brandt, Heinrich Brüning, Arnold Brecht, Julius Deutsch, Tony Sender, Kurt Schuschnigg, Friedrich Stampfer, Ernst Karl Winter). Even autobiographies not written by persons involved directly in political life, such as those of artists and scientists, are permeated with the political events and experiences that changed their lives.

There is not as yet an integrative study of the German political emigration as a whole that would address itself to such questions as the cooperation—or lack of it—between the various political parties in exile; the failure of a German government in exile to materialize; the effect of the activities of political émigrés in the United States; a thorough analysis of the debate among the émigrés about the future of Germany; and the role of émigrés as advisers to various sections of the U.S. government during World War II and in the years after 1945.

The studies on the German-language press in exile—foremost among them those by Hans-Albert Walter, followed by Benjamin Link, Sigrid Schneider, Hanno Hardt, Gertraude Dotzauer—attest to the interest in the subject and the extent of its coverage by exile research. This interest may have been aided significantly by the availability of reprints of the exile press, especially by Hans Peter Kraus, himself an émigré, now Kraus-Thompson Ltd.

In view of the relatively large number of studies on the exile press, a question seems in order: Could we be overevaluating the importance of the press in exile, especially the role of many short-lived, limited-circulation publications?

Research on the academic and artistic emigration to the United States has produced, in chronological order, the following works: *The Cultural Migration*, edited by William Rex Crawford (1953); *Die deutsche akademische Emigration nach den Vereinigten Staaten 1933–1941* by Helge Pross (1955); volume 10 (1965) of the *Jahrbuch für Amerikastudien*; Laura Fermi's *The Illustrious Immigrants* (1968); *The Intellectual Migration*, edited by Donald Fleming and Bernard Bailyn (1969); *The Sea Change* by H. Stuart Hughes (1975); *The Legacy of the German Refugee Intellectuals*, edited by Robert Boyers (1969–70); *The Muses Flee Hitler*, edited by Jarrell C. Jackmann (1983); John Russell Taylor's *Strangers in Paradise* (1983); Anthony Heilbut's *Exiles in Paradise* (1983); as well as individual articles in several journals with general overviews of a single profession or studies devoted to individual personalities. Finally, three more studies should be added in this context: Martin Jay's *The Dialectical Imagination: A History of the Frankfurt School and the Institute of Social Research, 1923–1950* (1973); Martin B. Dubermann's *Black Mountain: An Exploration in Community* (1972); and David Nachmansohn's *German-Jewish Pioneers in Science, 1900–1933: Highlights in Atomic Physics, Chemistry and Biochemistry* (1979).

In assessing these studies, we should note that their number (discounting earlier ones dealing with the rescue of science and learning) is still limited, especially when compared to the studies on German exile literature and politics. With the exception of the books by Helge Pross and several articles, they are written in English; they are typically composed of contributions by several scholars, underlining our inability to do cross-disciplinary studies; and they contain a large proportion of contributions by the émigrés themselves, including those published in German. Specifically, of the four volumes edited by William Crawford, Fleming and Bailyn, Robert Boyers, and Jarrell Jackmann and Clara Borden that consist of contributions by multiple authors, the émigrés have contributed heavily; of the five contributions in Crawford, four are by German émigrés (Neumann, Köhler, Panofsky, and Tillich); of the fourteen contributions in Fleming and Bailyn's volume, six are also by émigrés; of the nineteen contributions in Robert Boyers's volume, at least six are by former émigrés; of the nineteen articles in *The Muses Flee Hitler*, three are by first-generation émigrés. Finally, among the articles about the intellectual migration, a noticeable number are by the émigrés as well. A survey of the contents of these works indicates that they tend to concentrate on certain favored areas and selected figures that seem to be turning into focal areas of research, a kind of a "canon" of representative topics. In addition, the treatment of selected individuals tends to predominate over more comprehensive discussions of professions, groups, institutions, or trends. I believe that it is not too early to suggest that such a narrowing of focus is premature and does not do justice to the range and depth of talent of this migration.

Among the most frequent topics are the Institute for Social Research, physics, psychoanalysis, Gestalt psychology, Wiener Kreis, mathematics, and social science. To a lesser degree we find treatments of the Bauhaus, art history, and film. One or two articles are devoted to music, musicology, chemistry, classical philology, and literary criticism.

Individual émigrés receiving the greatest attention are Albert Einstein, Franz Neumann, Hannah Arendt, Max Horkheimer, Theodor W. Adorno, Heinz Hartmann, Erik Erikson, Paul Tillich, Mies van der Rohe, Paul Lazarsfeld, Ludwig Wittgenstein, and Karl Mannheim.

I would now like to indicate what, in my opinion, still needs to be done. By and large unresearched are still such professions as law, medicine, economics, history, psychology, music, and art. Less comprehensive areas include museum curators, publishers, and Oriental studies.

In the case of law and legal studies, we are dealing with such names as (in alphabetical order): Eberhard Bruck, Albert Ehrenzweig, Hans Kelsen, Friedrich Kessler, Stephan Kuttner, Karl Loewenstein, Alfred C. Oppler, Ernst Rabel, Max Rheinstein, Rudolph Schlesinger, and George Wunderlich. Besides specializing in topics such as Roman law and canon law, a number of legal scholars typically emphasized such areas as conflict of laws and comparative law. An interesting area of investigation would be their role, as advisers to the U.S. government, in the formulation of Japan's postwar legal system (Oppler, Steiner), their involvement in the postwar negotiations with Germany on such issues as rearmament (Riesenfeld), and Hans Kelsen's role in the formulation of the Austrian constitution after 1945.

In the case of medicine—numerically perhaps the largest area next to psychology—we have Erwin Chargaff, Rudolf Höber, Paul Kimmelstiel, Otto Krayer, Otto Loewi, Hans Popper, Leopold Lichtwitz, David Scherf, Henry Sigerist, and Siegfried Thannhauser. Due to its diversity, the medical field is especially difficult to assess. Some members of the medical profession are almost entirely in research and might be classified and treated under such headings as biochemistry. There are also overlappings with clinical psychology. The 1936 *List of Displaced German Scholars*, published in London, classifies the medical profession under such headings as bacteriology, biochemistry, dermatology, gynecology, internal medicine, neurology, pathology, physiology, radiology, and surgery.

In assessing the medical profession, a series of questions will have to be asked that have also been asked in works investigating the immigration of physicists and mathematicians. What were the contacts between the professions before 1933? What was the state of U.S. medicine at that time, particularly its research facilities? How difficult was it for the émigré M.D. to get established at a university or hospital or in practice?

In the field of economics—my third suggestion—there are essentially two groupings. The Austrian economists represent a classical conception of economics with the market as the basic regulating force; they are Gottfried Haberler, Friedrich August von Hayek, Fritz Machlup, Ludwig von Mises, Oskar Morgenstern, J. A. Schumpeter, Gerhard Tintner, and Henry Wallich.

The second grouping, to some extent members of the "Kieler Schule," German reform economics of the 1920s, is represented by members of the economics faculty (also the Institute for World Affairs) of the New School for Social Research, which was always the strongest department at the New School: Adolf Lowe, Gerhard Colm, Emil Lederer, Fritz Lehmann, Hans Staudinger, Frieda Wunderlich, and others. In addition, there are such names as Julius Hirsch, Karl Brandt, and Carl Landauer, as well as the former Menscheviks Jacob Marschak and Alexander Gerschenkron. A study of German reform economics that favored long-range planning and distrusted the regulatory ability of the market alone is in progress by Claus-Dieter Krohn from Hamburg, to whom I am indebted for some of this information.

Although the field of Gestalt psychology has been treated in different contexts, a substantive study that would do justice to this numerically largest profession to leave Germany and Austria (about four hundred psychoanalysts and clinical and experimental psychologists) is in order.

The field of history also needs assessment; it is represented by such names as Hans Baron, Dietrich Gerhard, Felix Gilbert, Wolfgang Hallgarten, Hajo Holborn, Ernst Kantorowicz, Hans Kohn, Alfred Vagts, and Veit Valentin.

Substantial work is also needed on the impact of émigré musicians, ranging from the famous conductors (Bruno Walter, Erich Leinsdorf, William Steinberg), composers (Arnold Schoenberg, Paul Hindemith), and singers, such as Lotte Lehmann, to teachers, voice coaches, members of symphonies and chamber groups, and, of course, musicologists. The tradition of chamber music, which, as a recent article in the *New York Times* stated, is here to stay, goes back mainly to the émigrés' activity and influence, such as Fritz Stiedry and the Busch Quartet, the Budapest Quartet, and the Kolisch Quartet.[8] Another example would be the performance on authentic instruments, which owes a great deal to Curt Sachs and Emanuel Winternitz. Still another example is the Haydn Renaissance, which must be attributed to Karl Geiringer and his student and author of the multivolume Haydn-biography, H. C. Robbins Landon.

I see the same need for assessing the transfer of art and again on different levels. We know of the work of Hans Hoffmann, Josef and Anni Albers, George Grosz, Laszlo Moholy-Nagy, and Max Beckmann, but what about Benedikt F. Dolbin, Arthur Kaufmann, Max Oppenheimer, Josef Scharl, Walter Nussbaum, Eugene Spiro, and Gert Wollheim? Furthermore, what about the role of art dealers and exhibitors, such as Curt Valentin, Otto Kallir (Gallery St. Etienne), Frederick Mont, Walter Schatzki? And what about the role of American museums in the transfer of modern art from Europe? The return of certain portions of the émigrés' work to Europe, specifically to Germany, would be an interesting study of the art market.

Despite some work on film (J. R. Taylor and H. B. Moeller, besides studies of such figures as Billy Wilder, Otto Preminger, and Fritz Lang), there is room for a sound and well-researched study of this subject.

The short study by William M. Calder III on classical scholarship should be expanded and augmented by an assessment of Near and Far Eastern specialists who came to this country after 1930: Hans Guterbock, Albrecht Goetze, Benno Landsberger, Wolfram Eberhard, Ludwig Bachhofer, Ferdinand Lessing, and Otto Maenchen-Haelfen.

Of the institutions at which émigrés played a significant role, the Frankfurt Institute for Social Research has been receiving the greatest attention, and Martin B. Duberman has studied Black Mountain College. Other institutions that deserve scholarly attention are the Roosevelt University in Chicago, the Institute of Fine Arts and the Courant Institute, both at New York University, the Institute of Oriental Studies at the University of Chicago, the Graduate School of Design at Harvard University, and the Illinois Institute of Technology.

Last but not least is the University in Exile, that is, the Graduate Faculty of Social and Political Science, founded in the fall of 1933 by Alvin Johnson. I believe that the University in Exile has been short-changed by research at the expense of the Institute for Social Research, and although there are some studies under way now (Peter Rutkoff's history of the New School for Social Research with a section on the University in Exile, a historical study of the Graduate Faculty by Benita Luckmann, and the study by Claus-Dieter Krohn on the economists of the Graduate Faculty), more intensive as well as comprehensive work is still needed. The comment by H. Stuart Hughes that the preponderance of émigré scholars at the New School was of little significance, that is, that the achievements of the New School were those of individual scholars, not of a group as in the case of the Institute for Social Research, seems premature.[9] This value judgment is echoed by Lewis Coser in a recent lecture at Columbia University, though for different reasons. The Institute for Social Research was a small group, whereas the University in Exile was a graduate faculty with a series of specializations that gradually evolved into departments. Hence its activities were more diversified and the assessment is more difficult. The reform economists (Adolf Lowe, Gerhard Colm, and Hans Neisser) represent a common programmatic approach. There is also a definite continuity in philosophy, starting with Felix Kaufmann and continuing with Alfred Schutz and Aron Gurwitsch. The weekly faculty seminars and their role in shaping the faculty would also deserve a closer look.

In view of the diverse areas of activity that the intellectual migration represents, the attempt to do a single integrative study of all areas may be impossible, at least in the near future. Instead, several volumes that try to integrate related fields may be a more realistic approach and permit greater depth: the natural sciences (including medicine); the social sciences (including psychology); the arts: painting, film, music, and theater; literature and politics; and a volume on the academic community as a whole, that is, the universities and institutions that became new professional homes for the émigrés.

Notes

I am indebted for suggestions and ideas to my longtime associate Sandra H. Hawrylchak, my former associate Adrienne Ash, and Claus-Dieter Krohn (Hamburg) and Will Schaber (New York).

1. Since about 1972, a series of "Forschungsberichte" have been published that deal with the results and the methodology of exile research: Richard Albrecht, "Exil-Forschung. Eine Zwischenbilanz (I)," *Neue politische Literatur* 28 (April–June 1983): 174–201; Siegfried Mews, "Quo vadis? Zur Situation der amerikanischen Exilforschung anlässlich des Exilsymposiums in Riverside/Kalifornien im April 1981," *Arbeitskreis Heinrich Mann. Mitteilungsblatt*, Sonderheft Siegfried Sudhof (1981): 192–203; Hans-Albert Walter, "Schwierigkeiten beim Kurs auf die Realität," [and] Eike Middell, "Methodenfragen," [followed by] Hans-Albert Walter, "Erwiderung auf Eike Middell," *Sammlung* 5 (1983): 92–114; Wolfgang Frühwald and Wolfgang Schieder, eds., "Einleitung," in *Leben im Exil. Probleme der Integration deutscher Flüchtlinge im Ausland 1933–1945* (Hamburg: Hoffmann und Campe, 1981), 9–27; Eike Middell, "Exilliteraturforschung. Zur Methodologie einer literaturwissenschaftlichen Disziplin," *Weimarer Beiträge* 27, no. 4 (1981): 7–35; Alexander Stephan, "Einführung: Erforschung der Exilliteratur, Exilforschung, Faschismuskritik," in *Die deutsche Exilliteratur 1933–1945* (Munich: C. H. Beck, 1979), 7–18; Joseph Strelka, "Probleme der Erforschung der deutschsprachigen Exilliteratur seit 1933," *Colloquia Germanica*, no. 2 (1976–77): 140–53; Reinhard Bollmus, "Österreichs Unabhängigkeit im Widerstreit. Neuere Arbeiten über das politische Exil der Österreicher in Grossbritannien und der Sowjetunion 1938–1945," *Zeitgeschichte* 4 (1976): 56–75; Hans-Albert Walter, "Bemerkungen zu einigen Problemen bei der Erforschung der deutschen Exilliteratur," *Jahrbuch für In-*

ternationale Germanistik 6, no. 1 (1975): 86–108; Manfred Durzak, "Das Elend der Exilliteratur-Forschung," *Akzente* 21 (April 1974): 186–88; and Peter Laemmle, "Vorschläge für eine Revision der Exilforschung," *Akzente* 20 (December 1973): 509–19.

2. "An Intellectual Migration," *Science* 220 (June 24, 1983): 1370–71.

3. The complete title is *Biographisches Handbuch der deutschsprachigen Emigration nach 1933/International Biographical Directory of Central European Emigrés, 1933–1945*, Herbert A. Strauss and Werner Röder, eds., vol. 1: *Politik, Wirtschaft, Öffentliches Leben*, Werner Röder and Herbert A. Strauss, eds., in cooperation with Dieter Marc Schneider and Louise Forsyth (Munich: K. G. Saur, 1980); vol. 2: *The Arts, Sciences, and Literature* (1983); vol. 3: *Index* (1983). The yearbook is *Exilforschung: Ein Internationales Jahrbuch*, published by *Text und Kritik*, Munich since 1983.

4. The most extensive published bibliography of secondary literature is found in Alexander Stephan, *Die deutsche Exilliteratur 1933–1945: Eine Einführung* (Munich: C. H. Beck, 1979), 335–62. The most complete unpublished listing (card file) is maintained by the Deutsche Bibliothek, Frankfurt/Main, Section Exil-Literatur.

5. See Adrienne Ash, "Lyric Poetry in Exile," in John M. Spalek and Robert F. Bell, eds., *Exile: The Writer's Experience* (Chapel Hill: University of North Carolina Press, 1980), 1–23; Klaus Weissenberger, "Dissonanzen und neugestimmte Saiten," *Literaturwissenschaftliches Jahrbuch der Görres-Gesellschaft* n.s., 17 (1976): 321–42; Joseph P. Strelka, "The Novel in Exile: Types and Patterns," in Spalek and Bell, eds., *Exile*, 24–31.

6. *Stimmen der Betroffenen*, Suhrkamp Taschenbuch, 905 (Frankfurt: Suhrkamp, 1983), 484.

7. Werner Vordtriede, "Vorläufige Gedanken zu einer Typologie der Exilliteratur," *Akzente* 15 (1968): 556–75; Michael Hamburger, "Einige Bemerkungen zur Kategorie Exil-Literatur," *Literatur und Kritik*, no. 128 (September 1978): 481–85; Hilde Spiel, "Psychologie des Exils," *Die Neue Rundschau* 84 (October 1975): 424–39; John M. Spalek, "Literature in Exile: The Comparative Approach," in Wolfgang Elfe, James Hardin, and Günther Holst, eds., *Deutsches Exildrama und Exiltheater*, Akten des Exilliteratur-Symposiums der University of South Carolina 1976 (*Jahrbuch für Internationale Germanistik*, Reihe A, Kongressberichte 3, Bern: Peter Lang, 1977), 14–26; and Joseph Strelka, "Topoi der Exilliteratur," *Zeitschrift für deutsche Philologie* 100, no. 2 (1981): 219–32.

8. Allan Kozinn, "After the 'Boom': Chamber Music Is Here to Stay," *New York Times*, January 8, 1984, pp. 19, 22.

9. H. Stuart Hughes, "Social Theory in a New Context," in Jarrell C. Jackman and Carla M. Borden, eds., *The Muses Flee Hitler: Cultural Transfer and Adaptation, 1930–1945* (Washington, D.C.: Smithsonian Institution Press, 1983), 115.

PART VI:
A Special View

22.
Freud's America

PETER GAY

THE MIGRATION OF PSYCHOANALYSIS FROM EUROPE TO AMERICA
is familiar to us all. Its impact has been felt and amply demonstrated in
every large American city; it has been documented in several substantial studies. Nathan Hale has gracefully chronicled the early spread of
Freud's ideas in the United States—slight and slow—before America's
entry into World War I.[1] David Shakow and David Rapaport have given
a systematic, if economical, survey of the way that psychoanalysis has
come to pervade American society and psychiatry across the decades.[2]
And a small troop of writers—psychoanalysts and others—have
amassed an instructive literature recording the potent influence of refugee psychoanalysts after 1933. Popular periodicals catering to the educated market, like the *New Yorker*, have at once studied and
exemplified the fascinated interest—sometimes faddish, often wary—
that Freud's science continued to arouse in this country. It is a complicated story, as all histories of migrating ideas must be, but I think I can
summarize it without doing too much damage. In short, Freud's science migrated to the United States in two discontinuous waves, of
which the second made a significantly bigger splash than the first. The
first wave rolled over this country largely in consequence of Freud's
much-described visit of September 1909 to Clark University, at Worcester, Massachusetts. That visit left a lasting impression on the psychologist G. Stanley Hall, host of the conference. But it left its mark
also on the skeptic William James, who wrote to a friend late in September 1909: "Clark University, of which Stanley Hall is president,
had a little international congress the other day in honor of the twentieth year of its existence. I went there for one day in order to see what
Freud was like." James liked what he saw—within diagnostic limits: "I
confess that he made on me personally the impression of a man
obsessed with fixed ideas. I can make nothing in my own case with

his dream theories, and obviously 'Symbolism' is a most dangerous method." At the same time, James, generous and adventurous, wished Freud well: "I hope that Freud and his pupils will push their ideas to their utmost limits, so that we may learn what they are. They can't fail to throw light on human nature."[3]

James Jackson Putnam, possibly America's most distinguished neurologist, who also attended the Worcester conference, was ready to see the mind by that light. After the meetings were over Putnam, much taken with Freud, invited him, Carl Gustav Jung, and Sandor Ferenczi for three days to his camp in the Adirondacks to talk about psychoanalysis. The result was that Putnam enlisted in the Freudian ranks, developing a passionate partisanship that did much for psychoanalysis in this country at an early point in its public career. Freud's celebrated visit also secured for him a minor, though by no means inconsequential, burst of popularity among American Bohemian and avant-garde circles. Abraham Brill, Freud's first translator, recalled that in the winter of 1913 he spoke of psychoanalysis to a gathering in Mabel Dodge's salon in Greenwich Village. It was a notable affair. "The person who invited me to speak there," Brill remembered, "was a young man named Walter Lippmann, a recent Harvard graduate working with Lincoln Steffens. There I met radicals, littérateurs, artists, and philosophers."[4] These people, at least some of them, proved hospitable to Freud.

Then came the relative doldrums of the 1920s—relative, for even then, generally dismissive American psychologists toyed with parts of the Freudian dispensation and even, more or less unconsciously, absorbed some of it. Robert S. Woodworth, a noted dynamic psychologist, had described himself in 1917 as "very skeptical" of "the Freudian teaching." But in 1931, he could calmly conclude: "The atmosphere has cleared somewhat; both adherents and opponents have become more discriminating; and the Freudian psychology is now generally regarded, we may safely say, as an important contribution to our growing science."[5]

But two years after Woodworth's assessment Hitler came to power in Germany, and, by subverting psychoanalysis there, forced it to emigrate. "I could not imagine," Heinz Hartmann once said to me late in the 1960s in New York, "any psychoanalyst working with a picture of Hitler on the wall." And so, after 1933, they went—some to England, some to Argentina, a few to Palestine, most to the United States. "Hitler is my best friend," Walter Cook, chairman of the Institute of Fine Arts at New York University, used to say in the 1930s, "he shakes the tree and I collect the apples." The same could be said, even more emphatically, about psychoanalysts. The immigrants, impressively learned in their arcane discipline and eccentric enough to be continually interesting, entered American folklore through innumerable comedians' imitations and cartoons. They found it hard to adjust, especially in the beginning, but they were welcomed into American psychoanalytic institutes; they opened profitable private practices, achieved positions of power in the psychiatric profession, and even set the tone of debates within the psychoanalytic community. After all, Karen Horney, Erich Fromm, and, more recently, Heinz Kohut, all of them source and focus of fundamental dissensions on matters of technique and essential elements of metapsychology, were born and trained in Europe. It was sometimes as though the United States supplied only the forum for foreigners arguing over the Freudian legacy. Gradually, of course, the Americans joined in, and as the refugees grew old, Americans took over and began to work and quarrel on their own.

The second wave of immigrants, far more than the first, experienced the absorptive and exhausting qualities of American life. In the 1950s, the golden decade of psychoanalysis in the United States, excessive, often pathetic hopes clustered around Freud's therapy and swelled the ranks of psychoanalysts. In the leaner 1970s, excessive, often pathetic despair has scattered the public of American sufferers among a smorgasbord of mind cures, curtailed interest in psychoanalysis among medical students and psychiatrists, and generated predictions of its imminent demise.

The forecast is, I think, premature. But sardonically, Freud had foreseen much of this turmoil. He thought that America would embrace psychoanalysis—and so it has. He thought that America would ruin it—but here he was not quite on the mark. Freud's America is a strange and fascinating country. But it is essentially a country of the mind. And it is this country to which I will devote the rest of my remarks.

I propose to speak about Freud's America quite literally, about the country that Freud constructed, the fantasy that became, for him, a reality. His attitudes toward the United States are well known, but they conceal a paradox that has never received the exploration it deserves. It will tell us little about America perhaps, but much about Freud.

Freud's most widely quoted observations about American culture are pungent and almost uniformly derisive. Some of them, to be sure, were—and are—commonplaces among cultured Europeans, but Freud added some curious twists of his own. In July 1915, he wrote to

James J. Putnam: "Sexual morality, as society—and at its most extreme, American society—defines it, seems very despicable to me. I stand for a much freer sexual life."⁶ Although Freud immediately protested that he had made very little use of the moral space he was working to free up for modern society, it is certain that he saw himself as a reformer face to face with the embodiment of what needed most radically to be reformed: American culture, with its prudishness and hypocrisy. Freud did not confine himself to this one sally against America, but his letter to Putnam discloses his central perception, and it remained central all his life. Woodrow Wilson's moralistic politics and sanctimonious posture, which enraged him, gave him further material to feed his prejudices; it lured him into the most unfortunate, least characteristic, project of his life—his collaboration with William Bullitt in a psychobiography of Wilson. The book was a diatribe that violates every principle of benevolent neutrality and guarded abstinence that Freud had laid down for his profession and had scrupulously observed with everyone else. His share in *Thomas Woodrow Wilson: A Psychological Study* may have been fairly insignificant, but it is instructive that he should have lent his name to the venture at all.⁷ Clearly, he relished it. Moreover, it is symptomatic that he irrationally blamed America for ailments from which he had been suffering before he ever set foot on American soil. Thus he called his digestive troubles, picturesquely but without justification, his "American dyspepsia."⁸ He feared that Americans would crush psychoanalysis in an indiscriminate embrace and, as he put it, water it down.⁹ No wonder that near the end of his life, in March 1939, he could characterize the United States, in a letter to Arnold Zweig, as an "anti-Paradise." Many years earlier, he had summed up his distaste for that anti-Paradise in a memorable remark to Ernest Jones: "America is a mistake, a gigantic mistake, it is true, but none the less a mistake."¹⁰ He was not averse to making phrases, but this phrase came from the heart.

Among his anti-American crotchets, perhaps the most absurd charge was that his handwriting had deteriorated after his American visit. Jones, to whom he confided this complaint and others, sensibly characterizes Freud's cluster of prejudices as "obviously unfair," and he suggests, reasonably enough, that they call for some explanation.¹¹ They do, for Freud's tenacious anti-Americanism palpably contradicts a salient trait of his character: his superb capacity for absorbing evidence and changing his mind. For Freud could scarcely deny—and did not deny—that America had been very good to him and to his personal creation, psychoanalysis. When he was young, penniless, and engaged to be married, he contemplated, more than once, emigrating to the United States to practice medicine there. Still more significant, for the paradox I am uncovering, is that he had some highly agreeable experiences with Americans when he finally did come over. American informality seems to have shocked him a little, and American food seems to have presented him with a series of nasty surprises. But he repeatedly recorded, with astonished delight, that the Americans had proved both generous and open-minded. And he did not fail to draw invidious comparisons to his native habitat. In 1914, in his polemical account of the history of the psychoanalytic movement, he explicitly noted that it was "in the lecture-room of an American university" that he had his "first opportunity of speaking in public about psychoanalysis," and he characterized the occasion as "a momentous one" for his work.[12] Nor did he spare his European readers the reminder that "the introduction of psycho-analysis into North America was accompanied by very special marks of honour." With his customary candor, he acknowledged how unexpected the atmosphere at Clark University had been to him: "To our great surprise, we found the members of that small but highly esteemed University for the study of education and philosophy so unprejudiced that they were acquainted with all the literature of psychoanalysis and had given it a place in their lectures to students."[13] And he added, tempering appreciation with disparagement, "In prudish America it was possible, in academic circles at least, to discuss freely and scientifically everything that in ordinary life is regarded as objectionable." He did not ask himself—he, the perceptive, perpetually probing scientist of the mind who was always asking questions—how it was that prudish America could generate an atmosphere of such candor, even at Clark. It is an interesting question for Freud not to ask in 1914.

Nor did Freud ask it later. Yet his pleasure in his American venture remained vivid to him. In 1925, in his brief autobiographical essay, he remembered how admirable he had found both James J. Putnam and William James; and he remembered, too, the honorary doctorate from Clark University. Once again, in 1925 as in 1914, he gave every indication that, culinary and gastrointestinal disappointments apart, he had enjoyed himself enormously. "At that time," he wrote, "I was only fifty-three. I felt young and healthy, and my short visit to the new world encouraged my self-respect in every way. In Europe I felt as though I were despised; but over there I found myself received by the foremost men as an equal." Freud was no snob, but, being only human, he welcomed applause; his reception had evidently done him much good; it vastly boosted his self-esteem, as he freely admitted. It was a fantasy come true. "As I stepped on to the platform at Worcester to deliver my *Five Lectures on Psycho-Analysis*, it seemed like the realization of some incredible daydream: psychoanalysis was no longer a product of delusion; it had become a valuable part of reality." [14]

Such language suggests that if there was ever a pro-American European in the making, it was surely Sigmund Freud. After all, as he graciously put it in accepting his honorary degree, it was America that had given him through his associates "the first official recognition of our efforts." [15] America had proved far more receptive to Freud's scandalous ideas than the most sophisticated of European capitals. Freud had anxiously and long sought such recognition and receptivity in vain on his home ground; by comparison, American food or naiveté were trivial defects. And yet, as I have shown, Freud judged American culture with brusque contempt.

This, then, is the paradox. In his appraisal of America, Freud did not learn from his experience, stirring though that had been. He neglected the evidence he had cited in his reminiscences. His complaint to Putnam that American sexual morals were despicable, remained, in his mind, the decisive American reality. And this, as I have noted, was not like him. The history of Freud's thinking, from his earliest cases of hysteria around 1890 to his last book, begun nearly half a century later, is a history of a scientist's flexibility. His first patients made him revise his diagnoses and taught him to listen, not to his fond constructions but to the material before him. His clinical experience as much as his theoretical needs induced him drastically to rethink his theory of infantile seduction and his conceptions of the drives, the mental apparatus, and anxiety. If a listener like Freud refuses to listen for once, we have a contradiction on our hands, and a contradiction, as psychoanalysis has taught us, is the symptom of a conflict. To be sure—and Thomas Kuhn has built a career on this truth—scientists normally resist evidence running counter to their cherished theories and will construct the most elaborate epicycles to keep on thinking what they had thought all along. But Freud, as I continue to insist, did not usually take unreasoning pride in his assertions but recognized that such pride conceals a resistance. Freud's anti-Americanism, then, is a resistance of some sort, and, therefore, a clue to something important. As Ernest Jones shrewdly observes, it "actually had nothing to do with America itself." [16] But if not America, then what?

I suggest that Freud clung to his misreading of America because it formed part of a highly valued and highly charged self-perception; it was a self-perception to which he gave expression precisely in a letter to an American, the letter to Putnam from which I have already quoted. Freud perceived himself principally as a scientist, a highly trained and highly gifted voyeur lifting the veils covering some of mankind's best-kept secrets. But his was not a gentle, pacific voyeurism: in one arresting self-appraisal Freud called himself a conquistador. And one of the countries he wanted to conquer was the land of sexual hypocrisy. Conquistadors thirst for large and difficult territories on which to test their mettle, adversaries worthy of their finest efforts. Freud himself said more than once, and correctly, that he had always needed an enemy. In his capacity of cultural critic—specifically, of sexual reformer—he found that enemy in bourgeois sexual morality. And America was that enemy in its most concentrated form. I maintain, then, that Freud's stubborn misreading of America was an indispensable ingredient in a larger, if necessary, misreading of nineteenth-century bourgeois sexuality.

My assertion, I know, is risky, and I want to make clear what I am not saying. I am not charging Freud with some central failure of vision. He was, as I have already said, the most sensitive, most attentive of observers, alert to the slightest change in his patient's tone of voice or pattern of gestures. He missed very little, in his patients and in his world, and if there are some things he did not see and which we are in a better position to see now, four decades after his death, I know of no evidence suggesting that in his time others saw what he overlooked. His discoveries in human sexuality remain epoch-making. Nor am I associating myself with the popular canard that the validity of Freud's insights was confined to the narrow, highly restricted spectrum of his patients, the bored, wealthy, Jewish Viennese housewife. I am on record elsewhere that, in the first place, Freud's clientele was far more varied than this myth allows, and second, that the psychoanalytic vision Freud distilled from his patients, including that most privileged of his patients, himself, holds for cultures and ages to which Freud had no direct access.

But it remains certain that Freud's America—principal exhibit in his indictment of bourgeois morality—was something of a caricature. True, the United States was cursed with its Anthony Comstocks, who raided newspaper offices for salacious advertisements and prosecuted art dealers for displaying photographs of nudes. But it was blessed, at the same time, with humor magazines making sturdy fun of such censors. And they insinuated, almost as if they had read Freud, that Comstock's avid and indefatigable crusades revealed some rather unsavory sexual preoccupations in the reformer. American psychiatrists could readily testify that abysmal ignorance about human physiology and harrowing guilt over sexual appetites caused widespread mental suffering among the genteel. But this situation was duplicated in wicked Europe and had been under severe criticism in America long before World War I, even before Freud came to Clark University. Why did Freud not see this?

It is essential to classify Freud's opinions about the United States. They rank among his ventures into cultural criticism, a body of work different from his clinical and metapsychological writings. Freud, as we know, essayed such sweeping criticism on a number of occasions. When he did, he was of necessity less self-critical, less sure of his ground, than he could be in his professional papers.

Yet he ventured forth, with great zest, though not with invariably happy results. In an important paper of 1908, " 'Civilized' Sexual Morality and Modern Nervousness," Freud accepted the general view, as common among physicians as it was among pedagogues and editorial writers, that in the modern world, nervousness was sharply on the increase. He offered a characteristically original explanation—it was, he said, the excessive demands made by respectable bourgeois culture for sexual restraint that caused this nervous malaise. But he was far from original in taking for granted that it was typically modern and more and more threatening. How did he know? How could anyone know?

Freud's credulity is revealing; it should prepare us for what I have called Freud's misreading of middle-class sexuality in the nineteenth century. For that sexuality was, as my own research in the past few years has demonstrated, for all the widespread prudery and ignorance, far less harrowing and far more gratifying than we have been taught to suppose. Even physicians writing treatises presumably proving woman's inferior capacity for sexual excitement unwittingly showed the range and intensity of female erotic experience. When in the early 1860s, the young social scientist Lester Ward courted what he called, in his secret French diary, "the girl," he recorded the couple's slow advance into intimacy—from the tender kiss to the passionate embrace, to sleeping in the same bed, until at long last one night, some months before they were to be married, the two, he wrote, "entered paradise together."[17] Here was paradise—for two—in America, the anti-Paradise. There were, in the nineteenth century, thousands of such couples for whom sexual contentment meant the full satisfaction of both partners. If many women never consulted a gynecologist, that might betoken fear, ignorance, or resignation to their unhappy, passionless fate. But it also meant, for many, that they had no need to consult a gynecologist. What Freud and other nerve doctors saw were the casualties of their culture. Incomplete as the evidence now is, and must always remain, it seems clearer and clearer that these casualties did not represent the average bourgeois.

It is essential to visualize Freud's position in the mid- and late 1890s and the first decade of the twentieth century, when he developed his psychoanalytic theories. They are, of course, wholly enmeshed in the workings of sexuality, both in potentiality and performance. In 1896 he was forty, an ambitious scientist who had come close to fame and failed more than once. Now human sexuality was offering itself as a master key to much of human behavior. The Oedipus complex, infantile eroticism in general, the sexual etiology of the neuroses, the zones of eros, the repression of sexual wishes—all this cluster which, together, we call psychoanalysis, came together from about 1893 on and with increasing tempo and intensity after 1895. Freud's stake in sexuality was enormous. In the interview with Heinz Hartmann to which I have already referred, he said to me: "You don't suppose, do you, that Freud, a respectable Austrian physician, was *pleased* with the discovery of infantile sexuality?" I did not then have the wit, or the knowledge, to reply that I thought he was pleased, at least in part. His discoveries were also discoveries in his own sexuality. But its central role in human life was his claim to fame, indeed to immortality. He defended it that way, and defending it, he resorted to a mechanism known in his profession as splitting.

All small children are incurable dualists. They live in a world of unrelieved melodrama. There are no small joys; there is only bliss. There are no small setbacks; there is only disaster. When mother leaves, it is a permanent desertion; when she supplies food and affection, satisfaction is complete. The child's universe is filled with love and hate; even its emotion directed at a single person will undergo the rhythmic cycles of adoration and detestation: the mother whom the small boy wants dead in the morning he wants to marry in the afternoon. This splitting of experience into good and bad is not a defense mechanism; it is, rather, a primitive technique for making sense of a complex world by gathering its phenomena into two sharply defined baskets.

Shadings of gray are a later acquisition. As the ego develops its capacity to synthesize diverse experiences and to tolerate delay, it can put together, into a single person, the alternations of favors and pun-

ishments, positive and negative feelings. Children are, in an almost literal sense, crazy; they must be coaxed into sanity, into perceptions of
imperfection. Once they are, a late dinner is no longer a threat of starvation. Once it understands this, the child rises above melodrama to
recognize, and even value, the complexities of its experience and to
realize that its allies have some flaws and its adversaries some virtues;
it sees something to be said for several points of view.

This acquisition of the power of discrimination is not without cost.
The ego compels the drives to mute their violence and to moderate
their expression. But "everything," as Sigmund Freud said more than
once, "has to be paid for in one way or another."[18] The ability to modu-
late judgments in a mature way requires the sacrifice of some in-
stinctual gratifications, aggression as much as sexuality. Hence this
perception of complexity, this liberality, must be precarious. It is dizzying to be sane and to acknowledge reality for what it is, dizzying and
not wholly gratifying.

The urge to regress to a simpler, more categorical view of the
world is therefore always latent and often irresistible. In times of strain
or war, this regressive urge is particularly acute. Sigmund Freud was
at war with reigning values and the medical establishment at the same
time. Recent researchers have shown, sometimes with malicious in-
tent, that Freud was not wholly alone, that there were in his time sex-
ologists who had unrespectable things to say about the human body
and its passions. But Freud was the synthesizer of what some people
knew; and beyond that he added a great deal of material that he alone
knew—or understood. As he listened to his patients, the sexual origins
of their sufferings imposed themselves upon him. He learned to respect both the power and the vulnerability of the sexual drives. And his
private experience, notably his long and frustrating engagement, supplied him with added poignant evidence of how wounding sexual
abstention and how crippling obedience to contemporary standards
could be. His stake in sexuality, then, was high; his investment in it
was all he could afford. Late in the 1890s, he put most of his chips on
that one number.

I am not saying that he was wrong and lost. On the contrary, he
was right and won. But in the process of developing the crucial propositions of his science, he was bound to see the cultural situation too
starkly and too simply and to treat bourgeois society—his society—as
the enemy, at least in this one important respect. And human psychology exacts that an enemy gathers to himself all negative qualities and
sheds all positive qualities. This makes combat easier—in fact, makes
it possible at all.

There is no question that among all of Sigmund Freud's discoveries, the cluster of propositions around sexuality was by far the most scandalous. Nathan Hale has unearthed some contemporary reports on Freud's five lectures at Clark University and noted that on the theme of infantile sexuality, reporters were critical, incredulous, summary, or wholly silent. Freud, of course, was aware of this reaction. I am not suggesting that he imputed a conspiracy to the medical and journalistic professions, but he took their desperate gentility as one more bit of evidence that his theories must be correct: they were just shocking enough to be right.

Freud, in short, had a stake not merely in his sexual theories but also in his detractors. That is why, in his polemical writings, he made light of his supporters. And that, finally, is why he needed America as the model of the hypocritical culture that his theories, correctly interpreted, would forever subvert. The more obtuse, the more mendacious, the more powerful the enemy, the more radical his own work.

If the thesis I have here developed stands up, it raises a most intriguing point, on which I want to close. Freud, I have argued, did not do justice to nineteenth-century bourgeois sexual life. It was far less traumatic and far more cheerful and sensual than he had supposed. But this very misreading was a gratifying and essential impulse for him: it guided his researches, organized his hypotheses, strengthened his conclusions. And those researches were epoch-making; those hypotheses, well-founded; those conclusions, essentially right. Since Freud, we know immeasurably more about ourselves than we did before him. And so it would appear that his misreading proved immensely fertile. It must stand as one of the happiest mistakes in the history of science. If Freud did much for America, America did much for Freud—more than he knew.

Notes

1. Nathan Hale, *Freud and the Americans: The Beginnings of Psychoanalysis in the United States, 1876–1917* (New York: Oxford University Press, 1971).

2. David Shakow and David Rapaport, *The Influence of Freud on American Psychology.* Psychological Issues vol. 4, no. 1, Monogr. 13 (New York: International Universities Press, 1964).

3. Henry James, ed., *The Letters of William James*, 2 vols. (Boston: Atlantic Monthly Press, 1920), 2:327.

4. Abraham Arden Brill, "The Introduction and Development of Freud's Work in the United States," *American Journal of Sociology* 45 (1939): 322.

5. Shakow and Rapaport, *The Influence of Freud on American Psychology*, 69.

6. Nathan Hale, ed., *James Jackson Putnam and Psychoanalysis: Letters between Putnam and Sigmund Freud, Ernest Jones, William James, Sandor Ferenczi and Morton Prince, 1877 to 1917* (Cambridge, Mass.: Harvard University Press, 1971), 376.

7. William Bullitt and Sigmund Freud, *Thomas Woodrow Wilson: Twenty-Eighth President of the United States: A Psychological Study* (London: Weidenfeld and Nicolson, 1967).

8. Ernest Jones, *The Life and Work of Sigmund Freud*, vol. 2, *The Years of Maturity, 1901–1919* (New York: Basic Books, 1955), 65.

9. James Strachey and Anna Freud, eds., *The Standard Edition of the Complete Psychological Works of Sigmund Freud*, 24 vols. (London: Hogarth Press, 1953–74), 20:52.

10. Jones, *Life and Work of Freud*, 2:60.

11. Ibid., 59.

12. Strachey and Freud, eds., *Standard Edition*, 14:7.

13. Ibid., 31.

14. Ibid., 20:52.

15. Jones, *Life and Work of Freud*, 2:57.

16. Ibid., 59.

17. Lester Ward, French Diary, October 25, 1861, Lester Frank Ward Papers, John Hay Library, Brown University; see Peter Gay, *The Bourgeois Experience: Victoria to Freud*, vol. 1, *Education of the Senses* (New York: Oxford University Press, 1984), 129. See also vol. 2, *The Tender Passion* (New York: Oxford University Press, forthcoming 1986).

18. Strachey and Freud, eds., *Standard Edition*, 23:76.

PART VII:

Americanism and Mass Culture

23.
Mass Culture and Modernity: Notes Toward a Social History of Early American and German Cinema

ANTON KAES

WHAT I PROPOSE IN THE FOLLOWING PAGES is a shift of focus in the discussion of mass culture from the question of its aesthetic evaluation to that of its social function. Rather than positing a timeless opposition between "bad" mass culture and "good" canonized high culture, I want to examine the specific historical and social function of the emerging mass culture in the United States and Germany from the 1890s to the 1920s.[1] A comparison of the beginnings of mass culture in these two countries will have to address the following questions: What were the conditions under which mass culture could evolve in the United States and in Germany? What impact did it have on the social life of both countries in the historical context of modernization, mass consumption, and leisure? What were the American and German reactions to the emergence of cinema as the most powerful form and institution of mass culture? Such questions touch upon differences in the historical origins and functions of American and German mass culture—differences which today have virtually disappeared in what has become *one* indistinguishable global mass media culture. In tracing the roots of mass culture in both countries, I am thus not only concerned with an archaeology of the past but equally, in the words of Michel Foucault, with a "history of the present."[2]

From 1890 to 1920 more than 23 million immigrants from eastern Europe and southern Italy entered the United States, found work, and settled in the large industrial centers on the East Coast. Uprooted from a world of small-scale agriculture and handicraft, they were thrust into a social environment that threatened to destroy all of their traditional values and orientations. They found themselves confronted with a fragmented and mobile lifestyle based on consumption and the monetary exchange value of labor and were faced with the rapid disintegration of their previously close family, church, and communal ties. Moreover, they were overwhelmed by what may be called the "semiotization" of daily life in a big city: by the profusion of signs and messages in advertising, by the onslaught of novel and tempting images in illustrated papers and on billboards, and by the general sensory overload of a consumption-oriented environment. To survive the transition from the rural life of their homelands to the big city life in the New World, the immigrant workers had to be willing to cut loose their ties to the past and to be open to the processes of acculturation and modernization. A new culture sprang up to help displaced and bewildered immigrant workers make sense of their lives in the new environment. In particular, the mass circulation newspapers of William Randolph Hearst and Joseph Pulitzer presented themselves as champions of the immigrants and the industrial poor. The "yellow" journalism of Hearst's *Journal* and Pulitzer's *World* simplified the news in big headlines and with ample pictures to make them accessible even to those who could hardly read the language. Comic strips, with their use of basic English, were particularly effective in communicating problems of adjustment in a humorous way. Many of the comedians of the popular vaudeville theaters in the 1890s likewise translated the anxieties and fears of immigrant life in America into farce and mockery. They acted out the troubles that arose from misunderstanding the customs and codes of the American way of life and often took out their frustrations against the common enemies—slum landlords, judges, and cops— who were invariably outwitted by simple immigrants. The comedians brought the irreverent, often antiauthoritarian, and subversive spirit of the immigration vaudeville comedy with them to the early cinema. We well remember Mack Sennett's Keystone Cops comedies and such Charlie Chaplin classics as *The Immigrant* and *A Dog's Life*. These films challenged and inverted the ideological assumptions and social norms of the American way of life from the perspective of the outsider. In this critical and carnivalesque spirit early American cinema retained traces of old folk culture.[3]

Between 1895 and 1910 immigrant workers used the nickelodeon and film theater as a substitute community center and secularized church where families and friends gathered for laughter and diversion from the hardships of mechanical work and crowded tenement living. By 1909 New York City alone had more than 340 movie houses and nickelodeons, which were attended daily by a quarter of a million people and on Sundays by a half million. Russel Nye, in his book *The Unembarrassed Muse*, notes: "Five, ten and fifteen cent prices brought theatrical entertainment to audiences that neither vaudeville nor the popular stage had ever touched. Nickelodeons and cheap movie houses, located in the city's poorest and most congested districts, supplied exactly what the urban masses wanted."[4] It is no coincidence that many of the early film entrepreneurs and producers were immigrants who understood the cultural needs and desires of the immigrant working-class public. Carl Laemmle, for instance, one of the most innovative, aggressive, and powerful pioneers of the emerging film industry, was the son of a German estate agent. Harry Cohn was the son of a German immigrant tailor and Marcus Loew the son of an Austrian waiter. The films of the first two decades supplied images and representations that transmitted (and made comprehensible) the social totality of what it meant to be an American. The movies thus aided in the acculturation and Americanization process of large masses of immigrant workers: at the movies they found their personal experience, desires, fears, and frustrations visually represented and thereby objectified. By dramatizing the daily battles of the immigrant in the form of slapstick comedies and crude melodramas, movies resolved tensions, provided meanings, and channeled utopian as well as critical impulses; in short, they suggested and in fact constituted a certain way of perceiving and comprehending social reality. In so doing, early American mass culture fulfilled two functions: first, it used fiction and fantasy to compensate for deficiencies of meaning that were caused by the mechanical and dehumanizing process of industrial production; second, it absorbed and deflected critical tendencies in the working class.

As the incipient film industry tried to expand its markets and enlarge its audiences to include more of the prosperous middle class, film soon lost its specific character as an anarchic, carnivalesque folk entertainment directly related to the cultural needs of the immigrant working class. D. W. Griffith regarded movies primarily as an instrument for the moral and political education of the masses. "The increase of knowledge," Griffith wrote in 1913, "the shattering of old superstitions, the sense of beauty have all gone forward with the progress of the screen. Our heroes are always democratic. The ordinary virtues of American life triumph. No Toryism. No Socialism."[5] Earlier cinema, he argued, was merely titillating mass entertainment and lacked the necessary social and ethical content. Here we can already observe a shift in the social function of film from an unrefined and populist expression of working-class culture to a subtle instrument of social guidance and control. Between 1910 and 1913 most of the film production companies moved to Hollywood, then a suburb of Los Angeles, where they built gigantic studios and back lots in a climate that allowed filming all year long. As films gained in length—two or three hours were not uncommon—the production costs also grew dramatically. The pressure to ensure production profit resulted in the development of the star system. (Charlie Chaplin or Douglas Fairbanks, for example, could demand up to one million dollars per film.) It led as well to advertising on a grand scale. Making movies now required a huge capital investment, which increasingly involved large Wall Street banks and corporations and began the irreversible entanglement of American big business with mass culture. By 1915 the film industry had become big business and the word "Hollywood" soon came to mean the commercial entertainment industry in general.

When comparing the debates about the emergence of mass culture in the United States with those in Germany, one notices some striking differences. The form and function of American mass culture responded to and was shaped by the cultural needs of the huge immigrant working class. Although film was introduced in Berlin in the same year (1895) as in New York, there was no comparable large public to cater to in Germany and therefore no economic incentive for expansion. For the first fifteen years the German nickelodeons and cheap movie houses were mainly sanctuaries for the illiterate, poor, and unemployed. Only after 1910 were some attempts made to introduce feature-length narrative films (instead of the customary one-reel slapstick scenes). In contrast to the American cinema, which at that time had already established an industry directed at the entertainment needs of the urban masses, the German cinema maintained a predominantly literary emphasis. Most of the early German feature films were based on nineteenth-century novels and stage plays or on scripts written by renowned writers such as Hugo von Hofmannsthal.[6] The strong links between the German cinema and the established institution of theater also were reflected in its players: most German film actors at that time came from the legitimate stage, which may explain the specifically unnaturalistic and fundamentally uncinematic acting style that later was an important element of the Expressionist cinema. The literarization of the German cinema between 1910 and 1920 did not win many friends either among the working-class public who went to

the movies for distraction and entertainment and not for a literary education, or among the intellectuals who criticized and deplored the de-
basement of "high" art translated into the unrefined language of film.
Moreover, early German cinema's dependence on the novel and theater impeded the development of a truly cinematic narrative syntax,
which by 1914 had elsewhere reached a high level of sophistication in
such pioneering films as D. W. Griffith's *Birth of a Nation*. The German cinema was less interested in narratives than in atmosphere and
neo-Romantic imagery. As early as 1913, Stellan Rye's production of
the *Student of Prague* introduced the theme of psychological horror
and obsession in a supernatural setting—a theme that later became
the hallmark of German Expressionist avant-garde film in the 1920s.
Clearly these openly experimental films with their motifs of paranoia,
loss of identity, and narcissism were not likely to attract a mass audience. The German public seemed to prefer slapstick comedies, melodrama, and action films, mainly titles imported from France, Italy, and
above all from the United States. The outbreak of World War I, however, brought a sudden end to the importing of all foreign films and cut
Germany off from the international market. To respond to the pressures of the increased demand for domestic films, the government
ordered the merger of all German production companies as well as exhibition and distribution firms into one single conglomerate. Univer-
sum Film Aktiengesellschaft (UFA) was subsidized to produce and
distribute German propaganda films as psychological weapons against
the enemy. At the end of the war in November 1918, UFA was sold to
corporations including Krupp, Deutsche Bank, and I. G. Farben and
transformed into a private company. The concentration of most, if not
all, of the talent and resources in one company made UFA the largest
single studio in Europe before World War II, and for a brief time in the
1920s it competed successfully with American cinema in foreign markets. It is ironic (and not much different from the situation of the New
German Cinema) that the German avant-garde film of the 1920s, for
which UFA became rightly famous, found more critical acclaim in the
United States than in Germany. *The Cabinet of Dr. Caligari*, for instance, visually probably the most daring film of 1920, was shown with
great success in New York a year after it was released in Berlin, where
it stirred only mild interest. Using *Caligari* as an example of an artistic
film that could not and would not be produced by Hollywood, American film critics polemicized against the entire American entertainment industry, which, as one American critic put it in 1921, made
films for "a group of defective adults at the nine-year old level."[7]

Facing page. The stereotypical "brutal German" in American film. Negative clichés of Germans and German-Americans have existed since the turn of the century, but the entry of the United States into the First World War in 1917 made the image of the German as "the Hun" common fare for theatergoers. The stereotype of the sadistic German in uniform who tortures and rapes women essentially originated about this time in films such as D. W. Griffith's anti-German *Hearts of the World* (1918), which portrays the brutal occupation of a peaceful French village by German troops. Top: a scene from Griffith's film in which a German soldier tortures the young heroine (Lillian Gish).

While similar stereotypes were also employed during the Second World War, there was at times a marked differentiation between Germans and Nazis. While Germans, usually the "common people," might be portrayed in a more positive light, the cold and brutal Nazi clearly represented the embodiment of evil. In this scene from *Hitler's Children* (bottom), a box-office hit of 1943 about young people who were to form the breeding stock of the new master race, both groups appear next to one another. The young heroine, an American, is brutally arrested by SS soldiers during a church service.

Films of the postwar era made even sharper distinctions between Germans and Nazis, especially the Nazi in the role of the military officer, spy or scientist. The Nazi has found a permanent place among typical villains of the American film alongside of the Communist and the Oriental. (Museum of Modern Art; courtesy of RKO General)

This critical notion of mass culture was quite different from that held in Germany after the war. German avant-garde writers and intellectuals at that time understood American mass culture in its original sense as a modern folk culture that grew out of the needs of large urban masses. Up to the mid-1920s this image generated a powerful appeal in Germany, where the Berlin avant-garde saw American mass culture as a vehicle for the radical modernization and democratization of both German culture and life. It stood not only for Charlie Chaplin and the movies, for jazz, the Charleston, boxing, and spectator sports; it represented above all modernity and the ideal of living in the present.

No other country embraced modernity more feverishly than did Germany after the war. "America was a good idea," a German intellectual remarked retrospectively in 1930,

it was the land of the future. It was home in its century. We were too young to know it for ourselves; nevertheless we loved it. Long enough had the glorious discipline of technology appeared only in the form of tanks, mines, shell-gas, for the purpose of the annihilation of man. In America it was at the service of human life. The sympathy expressed for elevators, radio towers, and jazz demonstrated this. It was like a creed. It was the way to beat the sword into a plowshare. It was against cavalry, it was for horsepower.[8]

All Quiet on the Western Front (1930), Hollywood's successful film version of Erich Maria Remarque's novel, is unique among American war films for its positive portrayal of a German soldier. He stands as a symbol of the soldiers on both sides in the senseless struggle of the First World War. The photo above shows the hero, Paul Bäumer, who is killed shortly before the end of the war. (Museum of Modern Art, New York/Courtesy of Universal Pictures)

This infatuation with America implied a rejection of the recent German military past and a disillusionment with the old European humanist values that had proved to be powerless against the misuse of technology for the purposes of war. After the collapse of the old political order with the military defeat and the demise of the Kaiser's authoritarian rule, all traditional aristocratic notions of culture inherent in the old political system were called into question. The German avant-garde used early American mass culture as a model that could undermine and subvert all false pretensions of traditional elite culture. In a 1923 article ironically entitled "Book Review," Hans Siemsen boldly admits that instead of reviewing some books as he was supposed to, he would rather review new popular jazz records with titles like "California, Here I Come," Negro spirituals, and American folk songs.[9] He called jazz "the undignified expression of a new untragic sense of life filled with the youthful energies of America." In an earlier article he alluded to the populist-critical impulse of early American mass culture, expressing the wish that all politicians and professors be forced to dance jazz in public: "How nicely they would be robbed of their dignity! How human, pleasant and comical they would look!. . . . Had only the Emperor danced jazz—all that happened would never have occurred. But he would have never learned it. To be Emperor of Germany is easier than to dance jazz." [10] Siemsen dismissed as irrelevant the question whether jazz was to be considered art. Jazz was simply part of living in the present, an expression of the tempo and rhythm of the urban lifestyle. American jazz signified being up to date and culturally modern.

For the Berlin avant-garde in the immediate postwar years, American mass culture offered a substitute revolution. After the failure of the political revolution in 1919 and the subsequent ebbing of the revolutionary spirit, the literary avant-garde virtually withdrew from active political involvement and shifted their interest to a reformulation of the status and social function of culture. They hoped that a radical modernization of German culture and lifestyle would provide an energy and dynamism that might transform life in Germany so that even traditionally calcified institutions such as literature and the theater could be revolutionized. American mass culture was seen as the vehicle to mobilize Germany for modernity. Of course, the political and social changes brought about by war and inflation had already severely shaken the foundations of nineteenth-century German culture with its orientation on Goethe and Schiller. Both the Dadaist deconstruction of the idea of art as an institution and the political instrumentalization of art as a weapon in class struggle in the proletarian-revolutionary literature after the war had also helped to weaken the resistance against the influx of American mass culture.

"How boring Germany is," wrote Bertolt Brecht in a short diary entry dated June 18, 1920. After finding fault with all classes of German society—peasants, middle class, and intellectuals—he concludes by saying: "Remains America." [11] For Brecht, as for other avant-garde writers of the early 1920s, America was the only modern, progressive alternative to the semifeudal lifestyle of Germany. America—more than Russia—was consistently represented as the *New* World, the alternative, the Other. The relationship between Germany and America was understood as a historically momentous encounter between two radically different cultures, two ways of perceiving and interpreting the world, a battle between two divergent cultural languages and systems of signs. The fascination with an alternative and thoroughly modern cultural language is evident in much of the literature of the Weimar Republic. For instance, in Brecht's early play *In the Jungle of the Cities* (1923) a priest is shown sitting alone at a side table in a bar, spelling out loud the various beverages on the list: "Cherry-Flip, Cherry-Brandy, Gin-Fizz, Whisky-Sour, Golden Slipper, Manhattan Cocktail, Curaçao extra sec, Orange, Maraschino, Cusinier, and the special drink of this bar: egg-nog. This drink alone consists of raw egg, sugar, cognac, Jamaican rum and milk."[12] This brief excursion into the world of American drinks, which has no motive in the dramatic action, illustrates the linguistic lure and magic of the American consumption-oriented lifestyle. Images of this modern lifestyle proliferated in the Weimar Republic and influenced fashion, manners, beauty, taste, sexual mores, leisure, and entertainment. American movies in particular celebrated the ideals of consumption and magnified the promises of material abundance. They created the images and fantasies about the New World that were crucial in shaping the German assessment of modernity.

American mass culture had a worldwide appeal. It implicitly undermined the ethnic-cultural concept of the nation-state and was seen by German intellectuals as an antidote to the belligerent patriotism of World War I. The popularity of Charlie Chaplin transcended national boundaries and virtually transformed many different nations into one big simultaneous audience united in common enjoyment of Chaplin's comedy. American mass culture was regarded in Germany as truly democratic and egalitarian. In an essay in 1926 on the democratization of culture, the art critic Adolf Behne argued that the European idea of culture was dictatorial whereas American civilization was "built upon the hearts and minds of the masses."[13] He suggested destroying the elitist principle of art and turning from "luxury production" to "utilitarian production." He preferred film over literature because "the film is from its hour of birth democratic."[14] Film began as "mass art" and hence could not exist as an "individualistic work of art." German masses (according to Behne) flocked to see the films of Charlie Chaplin because his films were in tune with the needs and desires of masses everywhere.

By the middle of the 1920s, a new mass audience had developed in Germany. It consisted mainly of white-collar workers: secretaries, clerks, and salesmen who lived in the big cities and had an assured income, fixed working hours, and much leisure time at their disposal. Berlin as the largest industrial and high-technology center in Germany had the highest share of Germany's white-collar workers (with 31 percent of its labor force). In the words of Siegfried Kracauer, the white-collar workers constituted "the masses whose existence in Berlin and other big cities increasingly takes on a unified tendency. Uniform occupational and collective contracts determine the style of existence." [15] In the process there evolved a "homogeneous metropolitan public which, from bank director to sales clerk, from film diva to secretary, has one mentality." [16] Kracauer sees Berlin as "the city of the most explicit white-collar culture today, that is to say a culture which is made by white-collar workers for white-collar workers and accepted as culture by the majority of white-collar workers." [17] Kracauer is obviously ironic about this culture, which aims mainly to distract. Mass culture for the white-collar working class nonetheless increasingly fulfilled a sociopsychological role: it offered imaginary escape routes from the tedium of a clerical job that often consisted of routine mechanical tasks with little or no responsibility and satisfaction. Mass culture provided thrills and the excitement lacking in the humdrum and boredom of one's daily life; it filled the void created by alienating and meaningless work. The declining status and importance of the individual clerical worker were compensated for by increased attention to leisure and entertainment needs. Gigantic cinemas were built in the 1920s, both in the United States and Germany, to attract the new middle-class public. The architecture of these pleasure palaces with their luxurious interiors, bombastic lobbies, and extravagantly decorated walls and ceilings signified a world apart from "real life." The films shown also reflected the change in the moviegoing public. The dominant thematics no longer were the adaptation and survival problems of immigrants and blue-collar workers in an industrial society, but rather the perplexities (real and imagined) of middle-class life. Matters of marital fidelity and romance were played in endless variations in melodramatic or ironic keys, frequently removed from the present and placed in historical or exotic settings. More and more of these openly escapist films were directly imported from Hollywood.

The increased influx of American films after the mid-1920s can be attributed to the effects of the American Dawes Plan of 1923, which was designed to help Germany repay its war debts. A clause in the plan that stipulated the curtailment of all German exports had disastrous consequences for the German film industry. Numerous independent film companies went bankrupt, and German film production decreased sharply. Hollywood took advantage of the opportunity to pour more films into Germany, buy up theaters, and even set up distribution outlets in Germany. When UFA was close to collapse in 1925, the American studios Paramount and Metro-Goldwyn-Mayer came to the rescue and lent money in exchange for collaborative rights to UFA studios, theaters, and personnel. Many UFA film directors and artists, among them Ernst Lubitsch, F. W. Murnau, Berthold Viertel, Conrad Veidt, and Greta Garbo, to name only the most famous, took on temporary assignments in Hollywood. Some would stay; others returned to Germany only to go back a few years later when Hitler came to power.[18]

The increasingly obvious and seemingly irreversible domination of Hollywood over German film and mass culture did not go unnoticed among German intellectuals and may account for the growing criticism of the so-called "cultural Americanism" after the mid-1920s. Herbert Ihering, an influential theater critic and one of the most ardent proponents of mass culture and cultural modernity, wrote in 1926: "The number of people who watch movies and do not read books is in the millions. They are all subjugated by the American taste, they become standardized and uniform. . . . The American film is the new world militarism. It marches on. It is more dangerous than the Prussian military. It does not devour individuals but whole countries."[19] There was widespread fear not only among conservative critics such as Adolf Halfeld, Oswald Spengler, and others, but also among left avant-garde intellectuals such as Lion Feuchtwanger and Bertolt Brecht that the ongoing Americanization of Germany would result in the loss of its cultural identity—that it would be devoured, as Ihering put it, by American mass culture.

By the mid-1920s, with the beginning of a five-year period of relative political and economic stabilization, a noticeable shift in the image of America took place. It no longer connoted the mass culture of jazz, sports, and cinema (as in the early Weimar years); rather, it generally became associated with technology and industrial rationalization. Americanism in the economic sphere meant efficiency, discipline, and control. A bitter disillusionment set in among German avant-garde writers and intellectuals. They had idealistically championed America and mass culture as symbols of social, political, and cultural modernity with a progressive potential for the democratization and modernization of culture. Instead they now had to concede that the dynamics of the capitalist market had led to a film production that was based on standardization, concentration, and cost-effective uniformity. Siegfried Kracauer, one of many German intellectuals who had argued for mass culture as a logical extension of mass democracy and technological progress, criticized cultural Americanism in 1929 as a fad designed

Marlene the legend. Despite the efforts of director Josef von Sternberg in the early 1930s to turn the Berlin actress Marlene Dietrich into an international Hollywood star, she is still part of the American public's image of the Germans. As a mixture of the androgynous vamp and the "new woman" of the twenties, she embodied a new kind of character that, even after 1933, was seen as typical of Germany during the Weimar period. This photo was taken from the film *Morocco*, directed by Sternberg in 1930. (E. R. Richee, Courtesy of the Museum of Modern Art, New York)

to distract the "homeless" white-collar masses with entertainment instead of enlightening them about their exploited status.[20] The function of middle-class mass culture as a powerful instrument of social control was well recognized by the end of the 1920s. It came as no surprise to intellectuals such as Kracauer and—later in the same tradition—Theodor W. Adorno and Max Horkheimer that Hitler and his Propaganda Ministry were able to misuse mass culture for a grand-scale manipulation of the masses.

The changing attitudes of the German intellectuals of the 1920s toward American mass culture captured an ambivalence that has characterized debates about its social functions to the present day. On the one hand, the fictional world of mass culture is able to offer critical, often carnivalesque perspectives and utopian alternatives to our necessarily constrained social and emotional lives; on the other, it functions as an all-encompassing and often cynical apparatus for the social control and manipulation of legitimate desires. Even though we may no longer believe in mass culture as the prime mover for the democratization of life in Germany or the United States, it seems to me that the debate about its historical functions is far from over.[21]

Notes

1. The following recent American publications provide the larger discursive context in which my paper can be situated: Daniel J. Czitrom, *Media and the American Mind: From Morse to McLuhan* (Chapel Hill: University of North Carolina Press, 1982); Stuart Ewen and Elizabeth Ewen, *Channels of Desire: Mass Images and the Shaping of American Consciousness* (New York: McGraw-Hill, 1982); Lary May, *Screening Out the Past: The Birth of Mass Culture and the Motion Picture Industry* (New York: Oxford University Press, 1980); Gerald Mast, ed., *The Movies in Our Midst: Documents in the Cultural History of Film in America* (Chicago: University of Chicago Press, 1982); Judith Mayne, "Immigrants and Spectators," *Wide Angle* 5, no. 2 (1982): 32–40; Robert Sklar, *Movie-Made America: A Social History of American Movies* (New York: Random House, 1975); Robert C. Toll, *The Entertainment Machine: American Show Business in the Twentieth Century* (New York: Oxford University Press, 1982). There are no comparable studies on the social history of early mass culture in Germany. This essay can only try to map out, from a comparative (American-German) perspective, some of the areas such a history would have to cover.

2. See Foucault's description of his "project" in *Discipline and Punish: The Birth of the Prison*, trans. Alan Sheridan (New York: Random House, 1977), 30–31: "I would like to write the history of this prison. . . . Why? Simply because I am interested in the past? No, if one means by that writing a history of the past in terms of the present. Yes, if one means writing a history of the present."

3. The art historian Erwin Panofsky considered film originally to be "a product of genuine folk art" ("Style and Medium in the Motion Pictures," in Gerald Mast and Marshall Cohen, eds., *Film Theory and Criticism: Introductory Readings* [New York: Oxford University Press, 1979], 243).

4. Russel Nye, *The Unembarrassed Muse: The Popular Arts in America* (New York: Dial Press, 1970), 364.

5. Quoted in May, *Screening Out the Past*, 61.

6. For further details on the interaction between literature and film in Germany, see my *Kino-Debatte. Texte zum Verhältnis von Literatur und Film* (Tübingen: Max Niemeyer, 1978).

7. Alfred B. Kuttner, "The Foreign 'Invasion,'" *Exceptional Photoplays*, Bulletin 10 (November 1921). *Exceptional Photoplays* was an independent critical film review without motion picture advertising. For a brief account of the American reception of this film see Michael Budd, "The Cabinet of Dr. Caligari: Conditions of Reception," *Cinetracts* 3 (Winter 1981): 41–49.

8. Hans A. Joachim, "Romane aus Amerika," *Die neue Rundschau* 41 (September 1930): 397–98. See also the extensive debate about cultural "Amerikanismus" in my *Weimarer Republik. Manifeste und Dokumente zur deutschen Literatur 1918–1933* (Stuttgart: J. B. Metzler, 1983), 265–86.

9. Hans Siemsen, "Bücher-Besprechung," *Die Weltbühne* 21 (June 1923): 858.

10. Hans Siemsen, "Jazz-Band," *Die Weltbühne* 10 (March 1921): 287.

11. Bertolt Brecht, *Gesammelte Werke*, 20 vols. (Frankfurt/Main: Suhrkamp, 1967), 20:10.

12. Ibid., 1:181.

13. Adolf Behne, "Die Stellung des Publikums zur modernen deutschen Literatur," in Kaes, *Kino-Debatte*, 161. See also William Fox's description of cinema as a democratic institution in 1912 (cited in May, *Screening Out the Past*, 152–53): "Movies breathe the spirit in which the country was founded, freedom and equality. In the motion picture theaters there are no separations of classes. . . . In the movies the rich rub elbows with the poor and that's the way it should be. The motion picture is a distinctly American institution."

14. Ibid., 161.

15. Siegfried Kracauer, *Die Angestellten. Aus dem neuesten Deutschland* (Frankfurt/Main: Suhrkamp, 1974), 65.

16. Siegfried Kracauer, "Kult der Zerstreuung. Über die Berliner Lichtspielhäuser," in Kaes, *Weimarer Republik*, 249.

17. Kracauer, *Die Angestellten*, 15.

18. See exhibition catalog, Ernst Schürmann, ed., *German Film Directors in Hollywood: Film Emigration from Germany and Austria* (San Francisco: Goethe Institute, 1978).

19. Herbert Ihering, "UFA und Buster Keaton," in Rolf Badenhausen, ed., *Von Reinhardt bis Brecht: Eine Auswahl der Theaterkritiken von 1909–1932* [von Herbert Ihering] 3 vols. (East Berlin: Aufbau, 1961), 2:509.

20. Kracauer, *Die Angestellten*, 100.

21. See the special issue of *New German Critique*, no. 29 (Spring–Summer 1983), titled "Mass Culture in Imperial Germany, 1871–1918," esp. the essays by Jochen Schulte-Sasse, "Toward a 'Culture' for the Masses," and Miriam Hansen, "Early Silent Cinema: Whose Public Sphere?"; see also Thomas Elsaesser, "Film History and Visual Pleasure: Weimar Cinema," in Patricia Mellencamp and Philip Rosen, eds., *Cinema Histories, Cinema Practices* (Los Angeles: American Film Institute, 1984), 47–84.

24.

The Rise and Fall
of Americanism in Germany

FRANK TROMMLER

IN THINKING OF HISTORICAL DEVELOPMENTS that moved America and Europe closer together in the twentieth century, it may be helpful to start with some quotations that attest to the distance to be overcome. Georges Clemenceau's presumptuous and notorious putdown of America is not unique: "America? That is the development from barbarity to decadence without the detour through culture." Without ever setting foot on their shores, Heinrich Heine said of Americans: "Worldly utility is their true religion and money is their God, their one all-powerful God." In his *Fröhliche Wissenschaft* Nietzsche even draws the unwitting Indians into his assessment that an "Indian-like wildness, characteristic of Indian blood, lies in the American way of striving for gold." [1]

The distance was indeed large, and the eagerness to espouse it in innumerable proclamations, reflections, and publications is so strikingly obvious that one is tempted to conclude that Americans and Europeans usually were more interested in defining their differences than their common bonds. Obviously the interest for each other is not necessarily synonymous with an expression of kinship. Both the term "Americanization," which was widely used at the turn of the century, and the parallel term "Americanism," which was propagated in an almost ideological manner in the 1920s, contained a strong element of ambiguity, tilting more toward the negative than the positive. Although the United States was seen as the model for social and industrial modernization, the connotation was often critical, alarmist, and even hostile. As early as 1901 the British critic W. I. Stead made it clear in his comprehensive survey *The Americanization of the World or the Trend of the Twentieth Century* that Americanism or Americanization were considered synonymous with modernization, invoking the fear of being confronted with soulless rationalization, mass society, and mass culture. He made it equally clear that the definition of Americanism remained vague and was more or less determined by the different views on modern life.

Stead's conclusions were confirmed thirty years later by the Dutch historian and secretary of the World Council of Churches, Visser't Hooft, who stated that the America myth cultivated in Europe was a psychological reality of far greater importance to the Europeans than the truth about America. For Europe, Visser't Hooft wrote in 1931, "will be more influenced by its own picture of America than by America itself." He arrived at the following distinction, which gives the gist of most definitions of Americanization: "There are then two different European reactions to America; they come from two different types of mind: on the one hand the technical and economic, represented by employers and employed alike who study American methods and who advocate rationalization, and on the other hand the cultural, represented by those who would resist Americanization because they see in it an attack upon the elements of European life which they value most. . . . The tragic paradox of European-American relations is that the nearer we get together in superficial ways, the further we seem to get away from each other in the deeper things in life."[2] The distinction between economic and cultural Americanization is fundamental. Although it lost some of its weight after World War II it remained valid for many contemporaries.

Overlooking the enormous array of European assessments of America and Americanism, one is struck by the similarities of the criticism. Again and again the authors strike out against the ugly face which modernization has revealed in America. Although most innovative in the areas of economics and industrial organization, Americanization is seen as a phenomenon of cultural alienation which should be avoided. In other words, what Europeans reject in modernization is labeled "American." Europe seems to need America and Americanism as a scapegoat for its difficulty in coping with the alienating effects of modernization and keeping a clearly circumscribed image of itself.

Less has been written about the mirroring of this phenomenon almost in kind in the United States. In his book *America and the Image of Europe* (1976), Daniel Boorstin summarized the history of the American self-perception: "We stand for everything that Europe is *not*." Boorstin then shows how this self-perception was shattered in the twentieth century, especially by the Great Depression and America's involvement in the wars. Boorstin calls it the "fall of the American Adam," who had to—but did not want to—come to grips with the fact that he shares the ills that have overcome Europe. "The consequence of these and other facts," Boorstin concludes, "has not been to make us abandon our familiar way of thinking—our traditional tendency to see the United States of America at the one end of the antithesis and an image of all possible evils at the other. It has led us rather to fill the framework with a new content. Whereas formerly we were a Non-Europe, now we have become a kind of non-communism. If throughout most of our history Europe was a handy mirror in which to see what we were not, and hence to help us discover what we were, now communism does us the same service."[3] Even though the statement originated in the 1950s, Boorstin has a valid point. He gives important arguments for the assessment that there is a strong correspondence between the European concept of Americanism and the realization of the Americans that they lost their uniqueness in the twentieth century. This interrelation is complex. Despite all talk about the Western alliance, it still plays an influential role in the relations between the two continents.

In the case of Germany, the major trends in the perception of the United States in our century have followed this pattern, but they were, as we know, affected by certain complications. The two world wars and subsequent recovery periods have resulted in extreme reactions toward America and Americanism, both pro and con. Although a major study of the long-term developments in Germany does not yet exist, some general thoughts and suggestions might be helpful, particularly in light of the perceived new antagonism between Europe and the United States.

Despite the enormous exodus of Germans to the New World until the beginning of this century, knowledge of and interest in America were negligible in German political and social thinking. As German imperialism was strongly nourished by an overcompensated provincialism, the isolation of the country in World War I did not help to provide a clearer view of the emerging world power on the other side of the Atlantic. On the contrary, a strong ideological justification for the war effort derived from the concept of the fight against the mass democracies and decadent civilization of the "West." And America, although only a thin silhouette on the western horizon behind France and Britain, came to represent a part of it. When the United States entered the war in 1917, German politicians and writers felt compelled to reassure the world—at least their world—that America was a nation without culture—at least without the German concept of culture.

This verdict, deeply ingrained in the German self-perception of a *Kulturnation*, retained its weight long after World War I. Klaus Schwabe has shown how the anti-Americanism of the war years was maintained by the political Right in Germany, in particular in the years after the end of inflation in 1923, when the Weimar Republic began to stabilize economically as well as politically.[4] Since modernization exemplified by industrial rationalization and political democratization was seen as an official trait of the Weimar Republic, fighting Americanization and fighting the new republic often were one and the same.

When the chaotic postwar years ended and the topic of a peaceful modernization moved onto center stage after 1924, the term "Americanism" was especially played up by two segments of society, engineers and businessmen on the one hand, and journalists and intellectuals on the other. The first group experienced a peak of public attention in the second half of the 1920s. The studies and travelogues of German visitors carried the message that the American economic miracle, *Wirtschaftswunder*, could and should be a model for the economic recovery of Germany. The term appeared in the title of an influential book by a professor of the University of Cologne and later a member of the German Ministry of Economics, Julius Hirsch. In his book *Das amerikanische Wirtschaftswunder* (1926), Hirsch analyzed the challenge the United States presented to the world. Of course, he tried to show that American prosperity was not a miracle but built on a new form of industrial organization that should be adopted.

The coining of the term *Wirtschaftswunder* and its application by Germans in referring to the United States in the 1920s is telling in view of the later use of the word for the German economic recovery after World War II. It points to continuities in perceptions and to concrete continuities in the economic sphere that did not dissolve in the 1930s and 1940s. Many visions of a unified economic policy that were formulated in the 1920s and began to exert influence shortly before the American depression hit in 1929 retained their power to inspire for a long time. The take-off of the German economy after 1933 was likened to the American example. "Strangely enough," an American historian observed, "many of the defenders as well as the critics of Americanism found hope in the Hitler movement. Insofar as Americanism had been an inspiration, it was the spirit of initiative, its dynamism, its will to the future which was emulated. Democracy *per se* carried little appeal except as it reflected a sense of comradeship, of solidarity in meeting national problems, and for many Germans these were also reflected in the Nazi movement."[5] These were strange bedfellows, one could add, but less strange considering the speed with which the German leaders of business and industry recaptured their sense of dynamic expansion after the unconditional surrender of 1945, not to mention the spirit of hard work with which the West German society reestablished the perception of well-earned success in the 1950s and 1960s.

Having mentioned Julius Hirsch's endorsement of Americanism, to which one could add the emulation of Henry Ford as its prophet by many contemporaries, one should also turn to his antipode in the Weimar Republic, Adolf Halfeld, whose book *Amerika und der Amerikanismus* (1927) became the rallying text for the anti-Americanism of large segments of the cultural elite. Its chapter titles express the

America, symbol of the modern age, as portrayed on the jacket of one of the numerous travelogues printed in the 1920s. New York's skyscrapers and the great transcontinental trains were common symbols underlying the German's image of America. This image, a mixture of optimism, repulsion, and European self-criticism, also served as an impetus to progress after both wars. As America's greatness rose to mythical proportions in European eyes, the vulnerability of this image grew correspondingly. (Garden Court Collection)

orientation toward the existing clichés and prejudices: "The Business State," "Chains of the Spirit," "The Omnipotence of the Idea of Success," and the like. The book carried a note that it was "das Gegenstück zu Henry Ford"[6] ("the answer to Henry Ford"), and its cover bore the inscription: "The culture of Europe, in particular of Germany, developed by tradition, is threatened by America with its concentration on materialism and the mechanization of life. Rationalization on the American example is trump, regardless of whether it kills the human in mankind."[7] Halfeld's concerns were shared by many contemporaries who saw in the rise of "dollar imperialism" a confirmation of the decline not just of Germany but of the old European culture in general. Oswald Spengler's prophecy seemed to come true, and even writers such as Hermann Hesse who acknowledged the importance of American mass culture, especially jazz and film, as the expression of the present time did not hide their fear and dismay. "Would Europe become like this?" Hesse asks in *Steppenwolf.* "Was it already on its way?"

America redefines itself as a "Land of Limited Opportunities." This cover of *Der Spiegel* from 1979 summarizes, from a European perspective, the abandonment of the American myth by America itself during and after the period of the Vietnam War and Watergate. The traditional European criticism of America remained part of this perspective, which in the last twenty years has at times been expressed very harshly—that America, created as a source of hope for mankind, has betrayed that heritage and will have to bear the consequences. (*Der Spiegel*)

In view of the strong objections which so many writers put forward against America and Americanism, a well-informed observer has remarked: "One of the most puzzling aspects of the Weimar period is the predominance of virulently anti-American literature in the midst of a strong current of 'Americanization' in Germany!"[8] An explanation might be that the book-producing intelligentsia did not represent German society and in particular its businessmen, engineers, and workers. But one should, I think, go a step further in the explanation and expand on the problem most intellectuals considered crucial for their work and existence: how to cope with the accelerating modernization process. This problem was a vital issue in a country that had lost the war and had to restructure itself on a much smaller and poorer base. Since Germany was then forced to modernize on a much grander scale, the objections were all the more vigorous. And since Germany had placed so much weight on cultural principles in the confrontations of the war, the frustration about the apparent economic dominance of the West was especially evident in presumptuous claims in the cultural sphere.

The reciprocity between economic dependence and cultural resentments is obvious. It was shared by large segments of the middle classes that had been impoverished by war and inflation. Modernization, of course, had been going on long before the war. But it had been embedded in an ideology of national pride and, after the outbreak of war, in a new feeling of a *Schicksalsgemeinschaft*, a community of fate. Now the middle classes were confronted not only with Germany's defeat but also with the crude, unveiled rationalization process and the secularization of the political institutions. While they cherished the values of a preindustrial society and a corresponding political system, they learned to blame America for the evils that were an inevitable price of economic recovery.

It follows that the success of the Nazis resulted not least of all from their ability to tap these ambivalent sentiments. They promised prosperity and work for all without the alienating effects of modernization. They succeeded in conjuring up the veil of a national community that seemed to give protection from the cold winds that blew in the capitalism of the West. That the Nazis did not immediately enter into a propaganda confrontation with America, although they enjoyed— rather did not enjoy—a mostly bad press in that country, seems astounding. But they were well aware of the advantages which Roosevelt's New Deal offered to their propaganda if they sold the American recovery from the depression as a venture of national and social concentration under a strong leadership similar to their own.[9] Nonetheless the ambivalence toward America always remained visible. When Hitler declared war on the United States in 1941, his minister, Joseph Goebbels, immediately requested a set of propaganda materials which he hoped to sell to the German public. Characteristically, these materials were mainly cultural. Goebbels demanded "the production of printed materials which are directed at the German intelligentsia and show in an objective manner that the USA has practically no culture of its own. Rather, it should be pointed out that the cultural products of the United States are essentially the products of European achievements. In this context the American film should be scrutinized. In addition, very popular reading materials should be distributed which are directed at the German public in general and the German youth in particular. These materials should show that the uncritical acceptance of certain American standards, for example, jazz music, means a loss of culture."[10] Again, cultural anti-Americanism was propagated to distract the public from the harsh economic realities of a war with the United States. Like many events of World War II, it followed the pattern of World War I.

It is not surprising that the Americans made a special effort in their reeducation attempts after 1945 to break the institutional base of the educational class system in Germany, in which the concept of cultural superiority had become a political tool of the bourgeoisie. And it is not surprising that the Americans did not succeed in their democratization of the German school system but did succeed in reforming the crucial institutions of mass communication, the radio and the press. Many documents of the postwar period show a strong German resistance concerning the issue of education and cultural institutions. And not without reason: although the Germans had lost their say in political and economic matters, culture was, as the Allies stressed in their proclamations, an area of limited responsibilities. Whatever was left of public resistance against the wishes of the occupation forces emerged in this area, and conservative groups and the churches soon gained much influence. Of course, the bulwark of resistance lay in the part of Germany where Americans especially like to be stationed: in Bavaria.

It would be misleading, however, to assess the second postwar period as just a repetition of previous constellations. This time the American involvement in European and particularly German affairs was much more comprehensive and the political dominance almost absolute. With the onset of the Cold War between the United States and the Soviet Union, a new political identification process was set in motion, which pointed beyond national borders and pitted the so-called West, including the western part of Germany, against the so-called East, including the eastern part of Germany. This process found a ready audience in West Germany, where Hitler's policy of confrontation with the Soviet Union suddenly seemed to receive some justification. The Germans in the western occupation zones were only too eager to join in this identification with the West because they had to cover up so much of their inhuman dealings with the East in World War II. Adenauer's declarations concerning the German commitment to the West sounded as if there had never been a battle against the decadence of the West. Only in East Germany did part of the anti-Western rhetoric survive, fostered by the formulas of Russian condemnation of Western decadence and American imperialism.

In a few years the main objections to the American predominance were dropped and public life in West Germany adjusted visibly to a pro-American attitude. This turnaround was so impressive that observers started to ask whether the American reeducation had failed, as many critics had concluded. Many sections of literature, theater, the visual arts, and popular culture were redirected toward the American cultural scene, which attested to a genuine interest of writers and intellectuals, not to mention scientists and academics, much beyond the America-orientation of politicians and businessmen. Was this turnaround just a result of the Cold War? Or was it even a late result of the reeducation endeavor of the Americans and to a lesser degree of the other Western occupation forces?

These and related questions have received surprisingly little attention. Much has been written about the various steps that led to the political integration of the newly founded Federal Republic into the Western Alliance, but the postwar cultural adjustment to the West both of the cultural elite and the population at large is still to be studied. Why, for instance, did Ernest Hemingway achieve such a high status and why was he imitated over and over again as the most "contemporary" writer? Why were Thornton Wilder's plays and books so successful in Germany despite serious literary shortcomings? Was it just the clever translation of his play *The Skin of Our Teeth* with a German title that captured the core of German thinking after 1945: *Wir sind noch einmal davongekommen?*

The answers to these questions will have to reflect America's presentation of itself in the works of these and such other writers as Thomas Wolfe, William Faulkner, and Eugene O'Neill as different from the one that caused the stormy debates about Americanism as the synonym for modernization in the 1920s. American writers of the 1930s and 1940s showed a new view of life, which had been noticed in Europe as the perspective of the so-called lost generation but had not shaped the image of the United States. Whatever nasty and flattering statements Bertolt Brecht and his friend Lion Feuchtwanger had made about America in the 1920s were closely tied to the optimistic America myth of those years. Now, after the depression years, the Spanish civil war, and many other earth-shattering events in which America was involved, the "fall of the American Adam," as Boorstin calls it, manifested itself in American literature and culture and drew enormous attention in Europe, most notably among the existentialist mandarins of Paris.[11] The European intellectuals were struck by the tragic dimension of this literature. It was, by no means, a literature of tragedy. Rather, it was a literature that tried to reassure the integrity of the individual against all odds and failures. It built upon an identification process in a time of severe personal loss and insecurity. Although it embraced much of the idea of individual freedom, it was by no means an expression of the official self-adulation of Western values, let alone the emulation of America as the guardian against communism, as Senator Joseph McCarthy formulated it.

Even more influential in shaping cultural perspectives after 1945 was the American popular culture, which had never ceased to captivate broad masses of the Germans, in particular the young generation, as even Goebbels had to admit. In the 1950s and 1960s it succeeded in what Brecht had hoped for in the 1920s, namely to become a challenge to the traditional German perceptions of *Kultur* as a kind of church service without prayers. The young generation came to idolize American popular culture, symbolized by James Dean, Elvis Presley, and Marlon Brando, as one in which modernization and alienation were being given full and—most important—creative attention. This phenomenon, which took the shape of a generational opposition against the prevailing tradition in culture and everyday life, was also built on an aesthetics of identification.

In short, the approach to American culture had drastically changed in comparison with the 1920s from the polarizing model of what many considered the future to be to the paragon of an almost existential identification. Germany was by no means unique in this development, but it seemed to be particularly susceptible to it. And no wonder: the country had not only lost the war but also, after the excesses of Nazi rule, a viable image of itself. Writers and intellectuals—some of them former prisoners of war in the United States—and younger people were particularly aware of this sad heritage of the Third Reich. They learned to find a new sense of themselves through the mirror of the American experience. The draw of this experience was so strong that it affected the German population at large.

There can be no doubt that today the pendulum has swung back. A decade and many anti-Vietnam-War demonstrations later, the young generation came to formulate its emancipation in a distancing process from the United States while the older generation became the defender of America. It is indeed a strong reversal of the preceding constellation. One can safely conclude that the intensity with which the new antagonistic spirit finds expression is intimately related to the intensity with which a previous generation had identified with American models. And it is in keeping with the tradition that the new sense of national or European identification emerges in a distancing process toward America, not Russia. We can see the repetition of a familiar pattern. It will be interesting to watch how far the pendulum will continue to swing before it returns.

Notes

1. Wolfgang Wagner, "The Europeans' Image of America," in Karl Kaiser and Hans-Peter Schwarz, eds., *America and Western Europe* (Lexington, Mass.: D. C. Heath, 1977), 24.

2. William T. Spoerri, *The Old World and the New: A Synopsis of Current European Views on American Civilization* (Zurich: Max Niehans, 1936), 231–32.

3. Daniel J. Boorstin, *America and the Image of Europe: Reflections on American Thought* (Gloucester, Mass.: Peter Smith, 1976), 37–38.

4. Klaus Schwabe, "Anti-Americanism within the German Right, 1917–1933," *Jahrbuch für Amerikastudien* 21 (1976): 89–107.

5. Earl R. Beck, *Germany Rediscovers America* (Tallahassee: Florida State University Press, 1968), 255.

6. Ibid., 30.

7. Ibid., 161.

8. Ibid., x.

9. Hans-Jürgen Schröder, *Deutschland und die Vereinigten Staaten 1933–1939. Wirtschaft und Politik in der Entwicklung des deutsch-amerikanischen Gegensatzes* (Wiesbaden: Franz Steiner, 1970), 93–119.

10. Willi A. Boelcke, ed., *Wollt Ihr den totalen Krieg? Die geheimen Goebbels-Konferenzen 1939–1943* (Munich: Deutscher Taschenbuch Verlag, 1969), 259–60.

11. Manfred Henningsen, *Der Fall Amerika. Zur Sozial- und Bewusstseinsgeschichte einer Verdrängung. Das Amerika der Europäer* (Munich: List, 1974), 53–75.

Contributors

ANDREW ARATO is Associate Professor of Sociology in the Graduate Faculty of the New School for Social Research in New York. He is on the editorial boards of *Telos* and *Praxis International* and is currently working on the theory of democracy, the sociology of nationalism, and an analysis of East European societies. He is coauthor of *The Young Lukács and the Origins of Western Marxism* (1979) and coeditor of *The Essential Frankfurt School Reader* (1978).

PAUL BREINES is Associate Professor at Boston College where he teaches modern European intellectual history. He is coauthor with Andrew Arato of *The Young Lukács and the Origins of Western Marxism* (1979) and various articles dealing with leftist ideas and intellectuals in Europe. He is presently working on a book on images of violent Jews in recent popular fiction in America.

REINHARD R. DOERRIES is Professor of Modern History at the University of Hamburg. His publications in the fields of German, Irish, and American history include *Washington-Berlin 1908/1917* (1975), presently being revised for publication in the Supplementary Volumes Series of *The Papers of Woodrow Wilson* (edited by Arthur S. Link) and *Iren und Deutsche in der neuen Welt* (1984).

PETER GAY is Durfee Professor of History at Yale University. Among his numerous books on European intellectual history and political philosophy since the Enlightenment are *Weimar Culture* (1968), *Style in History* (1974), *Art and Act* (1976), and *Freud, Jews and Other Germans* (1978). He has recently published the first volume of *The Bourgeois Experience: Victoria to Freud* (1984).

WOLFRAM F. HANRIEDER is Professor of Political Science at the University of California, Santa Barbara. He has published extensively in the area of West German foreign policy and transatlantic relations. He is the author of *West German Foreign Policy, 1949–1963* (1967) and *The Stable Crisis: Two Decades of German Foreign Policy* (1970). His most recent books are *Fragmente der Macht:*

Die Aussenpolitik der Bundesrepublik (1981) and *Economic Issues and the Atlantic Community* (ed., 1982).

ANTHONY HEILBUT received his Ph.D. in English from Harvard University. He has taught at New York University and Hunter College. He is the author of *Exiled in Paradise: German Refugee Artists and Intellectuals in America from the 1930s to the Present* (1983; paperback, 1984). He is also the author of *The Gospel Sound: Good News and Bad Times* (1975) and numerous magazine articles and reviews.

JOST HERMAND is Vilas Research Professor of German at the University of Wisconsin, Madison. Among his books on modern German literature and culture are *Deutsche Kunst und Kultur von der Gründerzeit bis zum Expressionismus* (5 vols. with Richard Hamann, 1959–75), *Interpretive Synthesis: The Task of Literary Scholarship* (1975), *Die Kultur der Weimarer Republik* (with Frank Trommler, 1978), *Orte. Irgendwo. Formen utopischen Denkens* (1981). He is currently writing a cultural history of the Federal Republic of Germany.

DETLEF JUNKER is Professor of History at the University of Heidelberg. In addition to articles on American history, German history, and the theory of history, he is the author of *Der unteilbare Weltmarkt. Das ökonomische Interesse in der Aussenpolitik der USA 1933–1941* (1975) and *Franklin D. Roosevelt. Macht und Vision: Präsident in Krisenzeiten* (1979).

ANTON KAES is Associate Professor of German and Comparative Literature at the University of California, Berkeley. He has written on drama and film in Germany and the United States and is the author of *Expressionismus in Amerika* (1975), as well as the editor of *Kino-Debatte: Literatur und Film 1909–1929* (1978). His comprehensive edition *Weimarer Republik: Manifeste und Dokumente zur deutschen Literatur 1918–1933* appeared in 1983.

VICTOR LANGE, John N. Woodhull Professor of Modern Languages Emeritus at Princeton, is the author of numerous studies in German-American cultural relations and in German and comparative literature. He has written extensively on Goethe and eighteenth-century intellectual history. His most recent book is *The Classical Age of German Literature* (1982).

CHARLES S. MAIER is Professor of History at Harvard University. Among his publications on twentieth-century European political and economic history and recent United States diplomacy are *Recasting Bourgeois Europe: Stabilization in France, Germany and Italy in the Decade after World War I* (1975) and *The Origins of the Cold War and Contemporary Europe* (1978). He is currently working on a study of the United States and European reconstruction after World War II.

JOSEPH MCVEIGH is Assistant Professor of German at Smith College in Northampton, Massachusetts. He is the author of *Kontinuität und Vergangenheitsbewältigung in der österreichischen Nachkriegsliteratur* (1986) and essays on modern German and Austrian literature.

ARNOLD A. OFFNER is Professor of History at Boston University, where he teaches twentieth-century United States political and diplomatic history and the history of international relations. His major works include *American Appeasement: United States Foreign Policy and Germany, 1933–1938* (1969) and *The Origins of the Second World War: American Foreign Policy and World Politics, 1917–1941* (1975). At present he is writing a book on Truman and American foreign policy after 1945.

LA VERN J. RIPPLEY is Professor of German at Saint Olaf College in Northfield, Minnesota. He has published extensively on the culture and history of the German-Americans. He is the author of *The German-Americans* (1976, 1983) and *Research Possibilities in the German-American Field* (with Heinz Kloss, 1980). Other publications include *Of German Ways* (1970), *Excursions through America by Nicholaus Mohr* (1973), and *Russian-German Settlements in the United States* (1974).

HENRY J. SCHMIDT is Professor of German at Ohio State University and editor of the *German Quarterly*. He has published several books on Georg Büchner (1969, 1970, 1971, 1977) and essays on German literature and drama since the eighteenth century. He has recently initiated new ventures in the historiography of German-American cultural history.

HANS-JÜRGEN SCHRÖDER is Professor of History at the University of Giessen. His research focuses on contemporary German history and American foreign policy. He is the author of *Deutschland und die Vereinigten Staaten 1933–1939* (1970) and has coedited *Politische und ökonomische Stabilisierung Westdeutschlands 1945–1949* (with Claus Scharf, 1977), *Die Deutschlandpolitik Grossbritanniens und die Britische Zone* (with Claus Scharf, 1979), *Der Berliner Kongress von 1878* (with Ralph Melville, 1982), and *Die Deutschlandpolitik Frankreichs und die Französische Zone 1945–1949* (with Claus Scharf, 1983). He is currently working on a survey of economic aspects in German foreign policy since World War I.

KLAUS SCHWABE is Professor of History at the Technische Hochschule, Aachen. He has worked extensively on American-European relations in the twentieth century and the history of historiography. He has published *Wissenschaft und Kriegsmoral* (1969), *Woodrow Wilson* (1971), *Deutsche Revolution und Wilson-Frieden* (1971), *Der amerikanische Isolationismus im 20. Jahrhundert* (1975), and coauthored *Die USA und Deutschland 1918–1975* (1978).

THEO SOMMER is the editor-in-chief of the Hamburg weekly *Die Zeit*. He has published widely on national and international issues. Among his books are *Deutschland und Japan zwischen den Mächten 1935–1940* (1962), and *Reise in ein fernes Land* (with Marion Dönhoff, Rudolf Walter Leonhardt, 1964). His most recent work is *Blick zurück in die Zukunft. Betrachtungen zur Zeit 1973–1983* (1984).

KURT SONTHEIMER is Professor of Political Science at the Geschwister-Scholl-Institut of the University of Munich. Among his numerous publications on political and intellectual developments in modern Germany are *Antidemokratisches Denken in der Weimarer Republik* (1961), *Thomas Mann und die Deutschen* (1962), *Grundzüge des politischen Systems der Bundesrepublik Deutschland* (8th ed., 1979), *Das Elend unserer Intellektuellen* (1976), and *Zeitenwende? Die Bundesrepublik zwischen alter und alternativer Politik* (1983).

JOHN M. SPALEK is Professor of German at the State University of New York at Albany and has been instrumental in establishing a bio-bibliographical documentation of German intellectual migration to the United States after 1933. He is the author of numerous works on German literature in exile, among them *Ernst Toller and His Critics: A Bibliography* (1968), *Lion Feuchtwanger* (1972), *Guide to the Archival Materials of the German-Speaking Emigration to the United States after 1933* (ed., 1978), and *Deutsche Exilliteratur seit 1933*, vol. 1: *Kalifornien* (coed., 1976).

FRITZ STERN is Seth Low Professor of History at Columbia University in New York, where he has also served as Provost. Among his many publications on modern European—particularly German—history and culture and on contemporary foreign politics are *The Politics of Cultural Despair* (1961), *The Failure of Illiberalism: Essays on the Political Culture of Modern Germany* (1972), and

Gold and Iron: Bismarck, Bleichroeder and the Building of the German Empire (1977).

HERBERT A. STRAUSS has published widely on the history of Jewish immigration to the United States from Nazi Germany. After underground life in Berlin in 1942–43, he escaped to Switzerland and came to the United States in 1946. Professor of History at the City College of New York, he temporarily returned to Berlin in 1982 as Founding Director of the Zentrum für Antisemitismusforschung at the Technische Universität. He is the coeditor (with Werner Röder) of *International Biographical Directory of Central European Emigrés, 1933–1945* (1980–83), and *Jewish Immigrants of the Nazi Period in the USA* (1978).

CHRISTINE M. TOTTEN is Professor of German at Clarion University of Pennsylvania and has written extensively on the image of Germans in the United States. She is the author of *Deutschland—Soll und Haben. Amerikas Deutschlandbild* (1964), *Das deutsche Bildungswesen* (1978), and *Roots in the Rhineland: America's German Heritage in 300 Years of Immigration* (1983).

FRANK TROMMLER is Professor of German at the University of Pennsylvania in Philadelphia. He has written on modern German literary, cultural, and social history. Among his works are *Roman und Wirklichkeit* (1966), *Sozialistische Literatur in Deutschland* (1976), *Die Kultur der Weimarer Republik* (with Jost Hermand, 1978), *Jahrhundertwende* (ed., 1982), and *Der Mythos Jugend "Mit uns zieht die neue Zeit"* (coed., 1985).

GERHARD L. WEINBERG is William Rand Kenan, Jr., Professor of History at the University of North Carolina, Chapel Hill. Among his numerous publications on the history of Germany and its relations with the United States and the Soviet Union between the world wars are *Guide to Captured German Documents* (1952), *Germany and the Soviet Union, 1939–1941* (1954, 1972), *Hitlers zweites Buch* (1961), *The Foreign Policy of Hitler's Germany: Diplomatic Revolution in Europe, 1933–1936* (1970), *The Foreign Policy of Hitler's Germany: Starting World War II, 1937–1939* (1980), and *World in the Balance: Behind the Scenes of World War II* (1981).

Index